Economic Crisis and Economic Thought

T0362151

The ongoing economic crisis has revealed fundamental problems both in our economic system and the discipline which analyses it. This book presents a series of contrasting but complementary approaches in economic theory in order to offer a critical toolkit for examining the modern capitalist economy. The global economic crisis may have changed the world in which we live, but not the fundamental tenets of the discipline.

This book is a critical assessment of the relation between economic theory and economic crises: how intellectual thinking impacts on real economic events and vice versa. It aims at challenging the conventional way in which economics is taught in universities and later adopted by public officials in the policymaking process. The contributions, all written by distinguished academics and researchers, offer a heterodox perspective on economic thinking and analysis. Each chapter is inspired by alternative theoretical approaches which have been mostly side-lined from current academic teaching programmes. A major suggestion of the book is that the recent economic crisis can be better understood by recovering such theoretical analyses and turning them into a useful framework for economic policymaking.

Economic Crisis and Economic Thought is intended as a companion to economics students at the Master's and PhD level, in order for them to confront issues related to the labour market, the financial sector, macroeconomics, industrial economics, etc. with an alternative and complementary perspective. It challenges the way in which economic theory is currently taught and offered via alternatives for the future.

Tommaso Gabellini is a PhD Student at the Institute for Innovation and Public Purpose, UCL, UK. He holds a Master's in Economics from the University of Pisa and Sant'Anna School of Advanced Studies, Italy. His main areas of interest are the role of State investment banks in developed countries, the monetary and financial economics of contemporary market economies, and institutional economics.

Simone Gasperin is a PhD Student at the Institute for Innovation and Public Purpose, UCL, UK. He holds a Master's in Economics from the University of Pisa and Sant'Anna School of Advanced Studies, Italy. His main areas of interest are the role of the State in the economy (in particular through State-owned enterprises), the economics of the European Monetary Union, and Italian economic history.

Alessio Moneta is Associate Professor of Economics at the Institute of Economics of Sant'Anna School of Advanced Studies, Italy. He holds a PhD in Economics from the same school. His main areas of scientific interest are macro-econometrics, consumer demand, and methodology of economics, with a focus on causal inference and model validation.

Routledge Studies in the History of Economics

For more information about this series, please visit www.routledge.com/series/SE0341

Economic Crisis and Economic Thought

Alternative Theoretical Perspectives on the Economic Crisis

Edited by Tommaso Gabellini, Simone Gasperin and Alessio Moneta

Routledge
Taylor & Francis Group

LONDON AND NEW YORK

First published 2019 by Routledge

2 Park Square, Milton Park, Abingdon, Oxfordshire OX14 4RN
52 Vanderbilt Avenue, New York, NY 10017

Routledge is an imprint of the Taylor & Francis Group, an informa business

First issued in paperback 2020

British Library Cataloguing-in-Publication Data
A catalogue record for this book is available from the British Library

Library of Congress Cataloging-in-Publication Data
Names: Gabellini, Tommaso, 1990- editor. | Gasperin, Simone,
    1990- editor. | Moneta, Alessio, editor.
Title: Economic crisis and economic thought : alternative
    theoretical perspectives on the economic crisis / [edited by]
    Tommaso Gabellini, Simone Gasperin and Alessio Moneta.
Description: Abingdon, Oxon ; New York, NY : Routledge, 2019. |
    Includes bibliographical references and index.
Identifiers: LCCN 2018044607 (print) | LCCN 2018046887
    (ebook) | ISBN 9781315619958 (eBook) | ISBN
    9781138665378 (hardback : alk. paper)
Subjects: LCSH: Economics. | Business cycles. | Financial crises.
Classification: LCC HB71 (ebook) | LCC HB71 .E236 2019
    (print) | DDC 338.5/42—dc23
LC record available at https://lccn.loc.gov/2018044607

ISBN: 978-1-138-66537-8 (hbk)
ISBN: 978-0-367-66202-8 (pbk)

Typeset in Bembo
by Swales & Willis Ltd, Exeter, Devon, UK

Contents

Figures

Tables

Contributors

Riccardo Bellofiore is Professor at the Department of Economics at the University of Bergamo, Italy.

Emiliano Brancaccio is Associate Professor of Economic Policy at the Department of Law Economics Management and Quantitative Methods at the University of Sannio, Italy.

Andrea Califano is a PhD candidate in Economics at the University School for Advanced Studies, IUSS Pavia and Sant'Anna School of Advanced Studies, Pisa joint doctoral programme, Italy.

Sergio Cesaratto is Professor of Political Economy at the Department of Economics and Statistics, University of Siena, Italy.

Guglielmo Forges Davanzati is Professor of Political Economy at the Department of History, Society and Human Sciences, University of Salento, Italy.

Tommaso Gabellini is a PhD candidate in Innovation Theory and Public Policy at the Institute of Innovation and Public Purpose, University College London, UK.

Simone Gasperin is a PhD candidate in Innovation Theory and Public Policy at the Institute of Innovation and Public Purpose, University College London, UK.

Matteo Lucchese is a researcher at Istat in Rome and he has been a contract professor of Economics of Innovation at the University of Urbino, Italy.

Alessio Moneta is Associate Professor of Economics at the Institute of Economics, Sant'Anna School of Advanced Studies, Pisa, Italy.

Leopoldo Nascia is a Researcher at the Italian National Institute of Statistics (ISTAT), Rome, Italy.

Marco Veronese Passarella is a Lecturer of Economics, based in the Economics Division of the University of Leeds, UK.

Fabio Petri is Professor of Political Economy at the Department of Economics and Statistics, University of Siena, Italy.

Mario Pianta is a Professor of Economic Policy at the University of Roma Tre, Department of Law, and at the University of Urbino "Carlo Bo", School of Economics, Department of Economics, Society and Politics, Italy.

Tommaso Redolfi Riva is a Researcher at the Department of Economics at the University of Bergamo, Italy.

Robert Skidelsky is Professor of Political Economy at University of Warwick, UK.

Domenico Suppa is Professor of Political Economy at the Distance Learning University "Giustino Fortunato", Benevento, Italy.

Anna Maria Grazia Variato is Associate Professor at the Department of Economics at the University of Bergamo, Italy.

Alessandro Vercelli is Professor of Economics at the Department of Economics and Statistics, University of Siena, Italy and Visiting Professor at the School of Oriental and African Studies (SOAS), University of London, UK.

Foreword

The introduction to this important collection of essays, edited by young 'alternative' economists, starts with a striking inversion of Plato's image of the cave. Plato's cave is the world of appearances, of shadows. Beyond the appearance lies the reality, the truth. Like all social sciences, economics has set itself the task of escaping from the shadows into the sunlight. Reality for economists typically consists of the logical relationships which lie behind the apparent formlessness of the experienced world. Economists have seen themselves as the philosopher kings, faced by the hostility of those unwillingly dragged from the cave of myopia.

Not so, argue Gabellini and Gasperin. It is the mainstream economists who are imprisoned in the shadows of their own theoretical reasonings. They view reality through the distorting lens of formal models – distorted, because to make the models work mathematically requires simplistic axioms and unreal assumptions. As Tony Lawson of Cambridge University rightly says 'claims widely recognised as unrealistic are a feature of all mathematical deductivist endeavour in modern economics' (*Reorienting Economics*, Routledge, 2003). It is the remoteness of mainstream economic theory from the real world, coupled with the claim of its practitioners to be philosopher kings of that world, which explains what the editors call the 'vicious relationship' between economic theory and economic crisis.

A crucial example of this disjunction between theory and reality, and its baleful consequences for policy, was the claim of pre-Keynesian economics that unemployment was voluntary. This implied that policies to reduce unemployment should be based on increasing workers' incentives to work. Keynes showed that at all times, but especially in the downward phase of the business cycle, most unemployment is the involuntary consequence of deficient aggregate demand. The policy required to 'conquer unemployment' was, therefore, to ensure enough total demand to employ all those who wanted to work.

This common-sense of the matter did not require any formal modelling of the incentives facing individual workers in the labour market. In fact, it was hostile to it, because persisting involuntary unemployment is inconsistent with the standard assumptions of micro-economic theory.

The existence of involuntary unemployment was an application of Keynes's major epistemological insight: the prevalence of uncertainty. We have no certain knowledge of future events and, in many cases, not even probabilistic knowledge. The existence of uncertainty led Keynes to argue that the portion of current earnings withheld from consumption need not be applied to investment in new capital goods, i.e. that Say's Law did not hold. This is because in face of uncertainty it is perfectly rational not to create assets but to hoard them. So, if investment is left entirely to the private sector, 'enterprise will falter and die'. Whereas the mainstream denied any positive value to public investment, Keynes gave government the task of maintaining a sufficient volume of investment to offset the private sector's 'liquidity preference'.

Since the 1970s, these and other efforts to escape from the cave have been blocked. The reason given is that they escape formal modelling and therefore lie 'outside' economics. And it is true that it is very hard to 'model' such phenomena as 'momentum trading' (herd behaviour) in financial markets. As a consequence, mainstream economics, as Gabellini and Gasperin note, was unable to deal adequately with the causes and consequences of the economic collapse of 2007–8.

Specifically, it was unable to explain the role played by modern finance or give an adequate account of the transmission mechanism between money and inflation. In the mainstream view, banks are simply intermediaries allocating savings to different types of investment. On this assumption, 'finance' could not have been an independent cause of the trouble which hit the real economy in 2008: in fact, it was not necessary to 'model' finance at all. Neither has standard theory been able to explain the failure of central banks to hit their inflation targets since 2008, despite their pumping an unprecedentedly large quantity of money into the economy. In summary (see Introduction): 'the prevailing methodological approaches in economic theory and analysis, although logically coherent and intelligently perfected, present some severe limitations when it comes to understanding the *capitalist economy*, let alone the fundamental differences among national *economies*'.

Two questions arise: why is so much economics trapped in the cave? And how can it escape from it?

The first raises the important, but very difficult, question of the relationship between ideas and power. Is it simply the case that mainstream economics is the ideology of the powerful (in contemporary life the financially powerful), its methodology designed to make invisible the location of power in the modern capitalist economy? Certainly there are grounds for arguing this (as indeed Gramsci did), but the persistence of a certain kind of economic discourse through time suggests that the discipline has acquired a continuity which is independent of shifts in the power structure. For example, the marginalist revolution occurred before finance became dominant in the capitalist economy.

The second question points to the need for alternatives. Gabellini and Gasperin are surely right to say that economics students should learn to keep a 'critical distance' from what they are being taught. The best way to secure this is to expose them not just to the history of economic thought (which exhibits more variety than can be captured by any textbook) but to other sets of facts and styles of thinking, such as are to be found in economic history and sociology. In short, what needs to be recaptured is the sense of economics as a moral science, concerned with the social organisation, purpose, and ends of economic activity, as well as with the most efficient means of conducting it. Only when economists have reached this higher plateau of wisdom will they be fit to be philosopher kings.

Robert Skidelsky

Introduction

Escaping from the economics cave

Tommaso Gabellini and Simone Gasperin

'Suppose nature brought this state of affairs to an end,' I said. 'Think what their release from their chains and the cure for their ignorance would be like. When one of them was untied, and compelled suddenly to stand up, turn his head, start walking, and look towards the light, he'd find all these things painful. Because of the glare he'd be unable to see the things whose shadows he used to see before. What do you suppose he'd say if he was told that what he used to see before was of no importance, whereas now his eyesight was better, since he was closer to what is, and looking at things which more truly are? Suppose further that each of the passing objects was pointed out to him, and that he was asked what it was, and compelled to answer. Don't you think he'd be confused? Wouldn't he believe the things he saw before to be more true than what was being pointed out to him now?'

(Plato, *The Republic*, Book VII, p. 221.
Ed. G. R. F. Ferrari (2000) Cambridge University Press)

1. A Janus-faced crisis

Nobody apart from Mr Barnard of Monty Python's Argument Clinic would dispute that, over the past ten years, the Western world has lived through a severe economic crisis, unlike others since the Great Depression in the 1930s. Nonetheless, much more disagreement remains over the true causes of the crisis, its frantic development and its supposed end. An increasing number of commentators, let alone the general public, have started to question the role, if not the responsibility, of the so-called economic "experts". Even Queen Elizabeth II of the United Kingdom has notoriously blamed the community of economists for failing to predict the financial crisis of 2007 and its dramatic consequences. In many cases, prominent economists and economic policymakers have been forced to provide justifications and excuses for their astonishing analytical oversight. The recent crisis has manifested itself as a Janus-faced one: we have experienced a serious and almost unprecedented economic crisis but also a severe crisis in economic thinking. The purpose of this book is precisely to address this vicious relationship between economic theory and economic crisis.

During the 1930s, John Maynard Keynes suggested that the economic crisis and its dreadful consequences represented moral "diseases" to which economists should find a technical solution "by a right analysis of the problem".[1] The "Keynesian revolution" provided the theoretical arsenal to solve what was later labelled by Joan Robinson[2] as the "first crisis in economic theory", which arose from the incapacity of previous conventional theory to "account for the *level* of employment". The "second crisis of economic theory", emerging in the early 1970s, was supposed to represent the inability to "account for the *content* of employment", namely distributional issues and the allocation of government spending. Today, several economic questions seem largely unanswered by conventional economic theory. What is the real role of finance in a modern capitalist economy? Why does expansionary monetary policy not lead to higher inflation? How is it possible for many economies to be "statistically" close to full employment but showing at the same time no sign of inflationary pressures? Those and other questions could then be related to an all-embracing one. Are we living through a *third* crisis in economic theory?

2. Plato against the economists

Our starting point is a tribute to the ancient roots of what Alfred Marshall – in his *Principles of Economics* (1890) – began to name as "economics". Before that, the preferred reference to that infant social science was "political economy", which became an established field of study after David Ricardo's *On the Principles of Political Economy and Taxation*, published in 1817. Even more remarkably, Adam Smith, the founding father of modern economics, would have not called himself a "political economist", but rather a "moral philosopher".

Our collection of chapters on the double-faced crisis will therefore commence by referring to an illustrious philosophical text, from which we have derived a symbolic interpretation of recent developments in economics. We refer to the narrative provided by the "allegory of the cave", illustrated by Plato in his Socratic dialogue *Republic* (Πολιτεία). Plato's *Republic* is generally known for being a classic work in political philosophy, composed at the beginning of the fourth century BC. Nevertheless, the famous allegory contained in its seventh book represents an excursus which might appear out of topic. In fact, the "myth of the cave" is of particular importance for the field of gnoseology, the philosophy of knowledge and cognition, from the greek words *gnosis* ("knowledge", γνῶσις) and *logos* ("discourse", λόγος). We have to specify though, that we do not intend to borrow Plato's theory of knowledge for our interpretative purposes. As such, we are not adopting the categories of phenomena and ideas, with the distinction between opinions resulting from the perception of the world (δόξα) and true knowledge of the intellect (ἐπιστήμη), to our interpretation of the current economic debate. Instead, we aim to establish a much simpler analogy, based on the narrative of the myth and detached from its original philosophical apparatus.

It might be recalled that, at the beginning of the story, Socrates invites Glaucon to picture a situation in which some people have been imprisoned and chained in a cave. They have all lived there ever since they were born. Those inhabitants can observe each other but they are forced to give their backs to a wall behind them, which hides the existence of other people walking past and carrying simulacra over their heads. Further away there is a fire whose light projects the shadows of those objects on the surface of the cave's wall, which the prisoners face. They cannot see anything but the shadows of those "puppets" on display. Hearing the fuss made by the people behind the wall, they believe the shadows to be the ultimate source of those noises. At this point Socrates explains that the shadows are the only real and intelligible beings for those prisoners, because they have never had any different sensorial experience. Therefore, they cannot perceive that those simulacra are simply a misrepresentation of the reality beyond the wall, namely the carriers of the aforementioned objects. It is further supposed that one prisoner is freed and he can finally look at things as they really are. Nevertheless, as Socrates suggests, he would not be able to convince their inmates of the reality he has experienced, upon his return to the inner cave. His intention of freeing them would encounter fierce resistance: the unreleased prisoners would rather kill him for daring to drag them out of the cave.

Moving back to the events of recent decades, our new allegoric suggestion is that most economists have been living in a Plato's cave from which only few unheard voices have escaped. Contrary to their intentions and misunderstanding the nature of their science, economists have created a world of shadows which they believed to represent reality. Conventional economic models have literally represented the misleading shadows of Plato's cave. Their abstract formalism facilitates the creation of a distorted view of the real world. This is further reinforced by several unrealistic and dogmatic assumptions on which mathematical models are built upon and from which controversial policy recommendations are formulated. However, the global financial crisis of 2007–8, which has been affecting the real economy ever since, has at least created the conditions for the liberation from the cave and its misguided representation of reality. The wall between the prisoners in the cave and those carrying the objects at its mouth seems to have fallen. Nevertheless, most economists seem to be lost in the darkness of the cave, ignoring what is meanwhile occurring outside it.

3. Shadow economic theory versus real economic phenomena

> People who don't like dynamic stochastic general equilibrium (DSGE) models are dilettantes. By this we mean they aren't serious about policy analysis.

This is the first sentence of a recent working paper by Christiano et al. (2017, p. 1)[3] which has been written by some of the world's most distinguished macroeconomists. It is paradigmatic in its defence of the prevalent way in which economic models have been elaborated since the late 1970s. It testifies the rather impressive state of isolation of those academics: shielded in their physical and ideological ivory towers, in most cases their thought and work have not been affected by the traumatic external conditions which we have lived through. The macroeconomics of the "Great Moderation" is still considered to be the dominant vulgate, although it provides little if no coherent explanation for the "Great Recession" and for what has been recently defined as "Secular Stagnation".[4] One has the impression that the only purpose of this paper is to advocate the usefulness and superiority of a theoretical product: the so-called dynamic stochastic general equilibrium models (DSGE) which have dominated macroeconomic policy analysis for several decades. In fact, the authors conclude with the following overconfident statement: "We do know that DSGE models will remain central to how macroeconomists think about aggregate phenomena and policy. There is simply no credible alternative to policy analysis in a world of competing economic forces".

What those renowned authors seem to neglect is the simple fact that "policy analysis" eventually depends on the theoretical perspective and on the methodology that the social scientist adopts. They are far from being neutral, as the Italian economist Paolo Sylos Labini remarked in his essay on social classes:[5]

> The physicist studies atoms, but he is not himself an atom. The microbiologist studies microbes, but he is not himself a microbe. The economist, not differently from the sociologist, studies the society to which he belongs: he is not an external object of study, in the particular sense that is valid for the natural scientist. As a consequence, the scholar of social sciences, in his intellectual – and political – activity is necessarily conditioned from the education that he has received, from his family background, from his preferences regarding the evolution of the society in which he lives – in one word: from his *ideology*.

In the specific context we are dealing with, the possibility of obtaining certain results, as opposed to others, arises from the pivotal role played by the initial assumptions that underlie theoretical and econometric models. Perhaps the most notable of them is the existence of at least one equilibrium price which clears the markets of goods and services. In a world in which prices convey all the necessary information needed to decide the amount of production and consumption, economic crises are logically impossible events. Markets are believed to be efficient in allocating resources among agents and between different time periods. The worst that can happen is that reaching the equilibrium between supply and demand, provided that this static notion is of any use in an inherently dynamic world, might take longer than expected. However, there are certain conditions that must be satisfied in order for this conclusion to be verified, not only at the microeconomic level but also in aggregate terms. Leaving aside – for a moment – the debate on whether more realistic assumptions would bring more reliable conclusions, it is interesting to remember that the most "dangerous" critique[6] to the Walrasian micro-funded macroeconomic models was implicitly asserted by a theoretical conclusion reached within the very same neoclassical school. We are referring to the Sonnenschein-Mantel-Debreu theorem, whose main result on the non-existence of a unique and stable equilibrium at the aggregate level carries some serious consequences for the coherence of DSGE macroeconomic models.[7]

A similar criticism can be moved against the interpretation of unemployment. In conventional labour economics, the unemployment rate is said to be "frictional", meaning that its value is negligible and ultimately resulting from individual decisions. In fact, most of today's models deny the possibility of involuntary unemployment by showing that agents rationally choose the amount of work and leisure according to a combination of the real interest rate and the prevalent real wage. As in the case of the goods market, these particular prices are then considered as the key variables which equilibrate the supply of and demand for labour. Voluntary unemployment will appear either when the level of real wages is above its market-clearing value or when the real interest rate is such that agents prefer to intertemporarily substitute work with leisure. For a given marginal productivity of labour, determined by technological factors, the supply of labour will exceed the demand for labour requested by firms. At the aggregate level, the dominant explanation of unemployment is provided by one of many definitions of the natural rate of unemployment embedded in the structure of real wages and associated with the equilibrium of the labour market.[8] This concept has been subsequently embedded in the Phillips curve framework, and it has justified the existence of a non-accelerating inflation rate of unemployment. In a nutshell, most of macroeconomic models developed today by central banks and international organisations are based on the assumption that there exists a certain rate of unemployment which is considered to be structural. Nothing apart from implementing policies of labour market liberalisation or waiting for a long run adjustment of the economy, can change this particular variable. Very little emphasis, if none, is put on the role of aggregate demand and to the economic effects that adopting different productive techniques can induce to the structure of the labour market. For instance, the heated policy debate on Industry 4.0 and the so-called "platform" or "gig economy" is fundamentally snubbed by the majority of economists. As a result, there is no established academic research agenda that is currently investigating those crucial developments in contemporary capitalism.

Another distinctive reason which hindered the predictive power of standard models is the mistreatment, or even the complete absence, of the financial sector. Finance is nowadays treated as a distinct branch from economics. The former deals with problems such as portfolio optimisation and risk management, adopting a pure microeconomic perspective. A political economy approach to monetary and financial issues cannot be found in most contemporary textbooks. Banks and other monetary financial institutions are analysed as neutral intermediaries of funds which have essentially no role in affecting the distribution of monetary resources. According to the standard view, the main purpose of financial markets is to efficiently transfer the property rights of capital stocks among businesses. This process is made possible by the allocative power of equilibrium prices emerging from the interaction between utility-maximising agents. Such equilibrium prices should reflect the fundamentals of the economy upon which financial analysts, investors and other market operators are supposed to base their expectations. The tools that economists use to understand whether this is the case are the statistical and econometric extrapolations of present values of financial securities from past prices of assets and liabilities. This type of empirical investigation relies on some other assumptions, the most frequently used being the "Efficiency Market Hypothesis" put forward by Eugene Fama in 1970.[9] According to the weak version of this hypothesis, financial markets are efficient because past data cannot be used to predict the future price of shares. This implies that securities are always traded at an equilibrium price, so that in the long run it is not possible for an economic agent to realise a capital gain by picking an undervalued share to then sell it at a higher price. Even if the hypothesis is confirmed by empirical studies that show how the evolution of a security's price over time follows a random walk, most finance theorists would acknowledge that financial markets are indeed quite imperfect. However, those same scholars admitting such unspoken truth would not dare to support the view that "theory should start from a consideration of the historical reality of markets, rather than assumptions about how they might work".[10] The contemporary approach to finance is thus very far from the institutional approach to financial relationships that was developed by scholars such as Allyn Young, Alvin Hansen, Edward Shaw, Karl Polanyi, Michal Kalecki and Hyman Minsky. In Italy, a similar but distinct approach could be found in Augusto Graziani's work on the monetary circuit, according to which financial relationships are not just about flows of money from one agent to another; but they are instead social relationships framed into an institutional context.

Another central tenet of standard economic theory is the interpretation of banks as money dealers between surplus and deficit units. Monetary and financial intermediaries' only function is to transfer deposits from economic units who possess excess savings to those lacking them. In line with this view, investment is determined by savings, which are deemed to be the same as credit instead of simply originating from the difference between income and expenditure. The way in which credit is channelled from banks to productive uses is formalised by the "money multiplier" view, according to which deposits are lent to borrowers. At the macro level, the effect of a change in the money supply is described by the quantity theory of money, originally formulated by David Hume in 1752 in his essay *On Money*.[11] The simple equation relating the amount of currency, the velocity of circulation, the price level and real output was then re-discovered by monetarist economists, who read it as a causal relationship running from the growth in money supply to the change in the price level. In the words of Milton Friedman: "inflation is always and everywhere a monetary phenomenon in the sense that it is and can be produced only by a more rapid increase in the quantity of money than in output",[12] the first being controlled by the central bank. This shows the main reason why one of the central policy prescriptions of the so-called "Chicago School" was for central banks to remain independent from governments. In this way, the stability of prices can be preserved by autonomous and purely technocratic monetary authorities that would impose restrictions on the growth rate of the monetary base. However, the very same institutions that monetarist economists wanted to exclude from the task of guaranteeing financial stability have come to recognise that monetarism itself has never been seriously applied. As an example, the power of endogenous creation of money possessed by commercial banks, despite being notably theorised by Knut Wicksell in the 19th century, has also been exposed recently by the Bank of England.[13]

Table 0.1 elaborates on the paper by Cristiano et al. (2017),[14] where they present the conventional wisdom on certain economic topics, matched by an alternative vision, therefore attempting to demonstrate the existence of a true dialectic within the discipline. However, what they suggest to be the alternative theories appear to be as slight deviations from the mainstream, neglecting the contribution of other theoretical perspectives whose very recognition would profoundly challenge the validity of the conventional wisdom itself. Table 0.1 is only an impressionistic sketch, but we believe it functions to represent how economic analysis can be highly susceptible to the investigator's point of view, mostly based on his or her cultural, sociological and contextual background.

4. Economic models as modern simulacra

The Polish economist Michał Kalecki is once said to have stated: "economics consists of theoretical laws which nobody has verified and of empirical laws which nobody can explain".[15] Although this statement might appear somewhat "nihilistic", it contains some elements of truth, which have possibly increased in recent years. Our interpretation of Kalecki's quip is that the prevailing methodological approaches in economic theory and analysis, although logically coherent and intelligently perfected, present some severe limitations when it comes to understanding the *capitalist economy*, let alone the fundamental differences among national *economies*.

The dismaying state of current economic thinking should not merely be attributed to the flawed assumptions of what is normally called "neoclassical economics". The problem of the "economics prisoners" is not limited to their misleading representations of reality. In Plato's cave, not even the carriers of simulacra can be ascribed as the "real" phenomenal world. Out of the allegory, we would argue that there is something profoundly worrying with the methodological abuse of models, be they mathematical simulations or econometric techniques, because their intrinsic nature produces simplified and decontextualised representations of the real economic world.

Despite being criticised by many influential economists such as Paul Romer, the former Chief Economist at the World Bank,[16] extreme mathematical

Table 0.1 Authors' elaboration on Christiano et al. (2017)[17]

	Conventional wisdom	On the other hand . . .
Exchange rate depreciation	Exports are expected to increase as domestic goods become relatively cheaper than foreign goods. Potential adverse effects on financial balances might appear depending on the proportion of foreign debt relative to domestic debt.	Exports are mostly driven by foreign demand and by "technological" competitiveness. The dynamic of exports depends more on the quality of goods than on their price. Exchange rate depreciation might have the immediate effect of increasing the value of imports, without a significant effect on the volume of exports.
Financial regulation	There is a trade-off between the frequency of financial crises and the amount of credit.	Financial crises have negative and long-lasting effects that may be prevented by tighter financial regulation. The amount of credit depends mainly on the demand for it.
Government spending	Increases in government spending stimulate demand but pose solvency problems, distort the intergenerational distribution of wealth and debt, and crowd-out private investment through an increase in the interest rate.	Government investment is a decisive component of aggregate demand because of fiscal multipliers being higher than unity. Investment can be relatively insensitive to a change in nominal interest rate. Evidence on the so-called "Ricardian equivalence" is controversial and not conclusive. No intergenerational problems arise if the central bank guarantees the solvency of the Treasury.
Unemployment benefits	Unemployment benefits can be introduced or raised at the cost of higher unemployment.	Unemployment benefits and other "automatic stabilisers" dampen the fall in aggregate demand during recessions.
Wage flexibility	Falling wages increase the demand for labour and help the economy to reach a full-employment equilibrium.	Flexible wages facilitate the fall in aggregate demand during recessions and create a dangerous vicious spiral of more unemployment and lower wages.

formalisation of economic "laws" continues to dominate the economic research agenda, even among certain critical schools of thought (i.e. Post-Keynesian, neo-Schumpeterian, etc.). In his *The General Theory of Employment, Interest and Money*,[18] John Maynard Keynes, who himself read Mathematics at Cambridge, famously expressed his scepticism towards the abuse of a still embryonic mathematical "formalisation":

> Too large a proportion of recent "mathematical" economics are merely concoctions, as imprecise as the initial assumptions they rest on, which allow the author to lose sight of the complexities and interdependencies of the real world in a maze of pretentious and unhelpful symbols.[19]

Indeed, this represents a further level of criticism to the discipline: the over-indulgence of mathematical models in elaborating theory, with very little attention to institutional, political and sociological concerns. Nevertheless, the intelligent wit of Keynes was not confined to economic theory. He was also challenging a certain approach to the analysis of economic data:[20] "When statistics do not make sense, I find it generally wiser to prefer sense to statistics". Keynes was sceptical on the use of early econometric models on the grounds that the knowledge content of economics – being a moral science – was profoundly affected by values, motives, expectations and uncertainty. "What place is left for expectations and the state of confidence relating to the future? What place is allowed for non-numerical factors such as inventions, politics, labour troubles, wars, earthquakes, financial crisis?" he was asking. In short: the social, historical and human complexity of the process of economic development is forcefully sacrificed through such a reductionist approach. His serious criticism of econometric techniques was voiced against the pioneering work of the Dutch economist Jan Tinbergen,[21] but its validity holds true even more now that econometrics has increased its sophistication, becoming the only "scientific" method of empirical research in economics and other social sciences too.

An intelligent use of statistics and economic history has therefore been side-lined by the overshadowing recourse to increasingly sophisticated econometric techniques, which are nonetheless rather simplistic and trivial in their assumptions and results. This has not always been the case. In his *History of Economic Analysis*, Joseph Schumpeter was clearly defending the case for performing economic analysis on a more solid historical foundation:

> First, the subject matter of economics is essentially a unique process in historic time. Nobody can hope to understand the economic phenomena of any, including the present, epoch who has not an adequate command of historical facts and an adequate amount of historical sense or of what may be described as historical experience. Second, the historical report cannot be purely economic but must inevitably reflect also "institutional" facts that are not purely economic: therefore it affords the best method

for understanding how economic and non-economic facts are related to one another and how the various social sciences should be related to one another. Third, it is, I believe, the fact that most of the fundamental errors currently committed in economic analysis are due to lack of historical experience more often than to any other shortcoming of the economist's equipment.[22]

However, given the current state of affairs within economics, it is highly unlikely for a scholar who performed historical and comparative case studies to receive an adequate recognition of his or her work from the academic community of economists. This is particularly evident in the attribution of what is commonly referred to as the "Nobel Prize in Economics", despite it being simply an award sponsored by the central bank of Sweden. With only minor exceptions, since the late 1980s, the "Sveriges Riksbank's Prize in Economic Sciences" has generally been awarded to economists belonging to the dominant neoclassical school of thought, for works with a high degree of formal abstraction and mathematical formulation. At the same time, towering intellectual figures such as Albert O. Hirschman, Piero Sraffa, Joan Robinson, Pierangelo Garegnani, Nicholas Kaldor, Luigi Pasinetti, John Kenneth Galbraith, Charles P. Kindleberger, Alfred D. Chandler, Robert Triffin and many others have been systematically excluded from this recognition, thus delegitimising not only their work but also their methodological approaches to the study of economics.

5. The old is dying, but . . .

In his *Prison Notebooks*,[23] the Italian Marxist political philosopher Antonio Gramsci famously lamented:

> The crisis consists precisely in the fact that the old is dying and the new cannot be born; in this interregnum a great variety of morbid symptoms appear.

Has something "new" been born out of the recent economic crisis? So far, it is very difficult to say. Nonetheless, it has to be noted that, after 2008, several students of economics have been engaged in organising reading groups, seminars, conferences and lectures. They have demanded a more dialectic and interdisciplinary teaching, a request that was followed by the elaboration of alternative economics curricula, such as the one conceived and proposed by the Institute for New Economic Thinking.[24]

This volume is based upon a series of seminars organised between 2014 and 2015, whose original title was *Critical Economics in Times of Crisis*.[25] At that time, two of the authors[26] were postgraduate students in economics at the University of Pisa and Scuola Superiore Sant'Anna. Their ambition was to organise a series of lectures that would be both critical and complementary to what they were taught in their official curriculum. The purpose of the initiative was to open a debate within the economics department, among students and professors. The results have been quite satisfactory: the series of seminars has been replicated every single year since then, reaching its third edition. With different underlying themes, these new series of seminars have continued to attract an increasing number of students and scholars who are interested in critically debating unsettled issues in economics. Finally, the initiative – the series of seminars and the book – is fundamentally an Italian enterprise, given the nationality of the authors and the context in which it has taken place. Yet, the purpose and content are not secondary elements. The Italian tradition in economics was a well-respected one in the past century, with towering intellectual figures the likes of Franco Modigliani, Paolo Sylos Labini, Augusto Graziani, Piero Sraffa, Pierangelo Garegnani, Luigi Pasinetti and others. Italian economics faculties were also famous for being centres of knowledge-learning and *loci* of vibrant discussions around the most compelling issues in economic theory and policy. That richness has nowadays been lost in favour of standardised curricula, dominated by Anglo-American thought, topics and methodologies. This volume, accessible also to the English-speaking community, would also wish to be a useful testimony of a diminished but living relevance of the Italian "school" of political economy.

It has been mentioned earlier that the original title of the series of seminars contained two words: "Critical" and "Crisis". They share the same etymological origin in the term κρίνω, an ancient Greek verb which signifies "to separate" but also "to judge". We have deliberately played this little semantic game by implying that it is rather arduous to draw absolute statements on the real world without first maintaining a critical distance from the dominant vulgate. The economic crisis has given us the opportunity and motivation to reflect on the dominant *Weltanschauung* of recent decades. At the same time, a critical understanding of the world should help us make more sense out of it. The two processes, we insist, should go together, and they might also help us to investigate why the economic crisis and the crisis in the economics discipline have not sparked an intellectual revolution, similar to the "Keynesian revolution" in the aftermath of the Great Depression. "The Return of the Master"[27] has lasted too little. Ten years after the financial crisis, both the "Master" and the economies of many Western countries seem to have fallen once again into a state of lethargy or "secular stagnation".

This volume is intended as a companion for students of economics at the postgraduate level.[28] It is aimed at providing a basis for reflecting upon methodological and epistemological issues within the discipline. As well as presenting a comprehensive overview of different schools of thought, it seeks to stimulate a participated debate on the role and nature of theory for a better understanding of real-world economic phenomena, "outside the cave". Moreover, it aims to challenge the concept of "empirical research", nowadays reduced to abstract and limited econometric testing, with little space for presenting, discussing and interpreting "stylised view of the facts", as Nicholas Kaldor suggested.[29]

6. Our economics menu

The first part of the book deals with methodology in economics. Alessio Moneta initiates the discussion by identifying a few tensions that affect economic methodology. In particular, he delves into the dilemma between theory-guided and data-driven approaches to learn about causal relationships in economics. Emiliano Brancaccio and Domenico Suppa show that, by exchanging exogenous variables with endogenous ones, the logical relations of standard models are reversed. This is particularly useful in explaining the differences between identities and causal relationships.

The second part of the book offers an overview on alternative economic theories, which are approached through the lens of the history of economic thought. The section is inaugurated by the chapter of Riccardo Bellofiore and Tommaso Redolfi Riva, who focus on the reception of Karl Marx's ideas in Italy. The chapter underlines the context-determined nature of theoretical debates that universal abstraction sometimes impoverishes and trivialises. In his contribution, Fabio Petri explains the current relevance of an almost forgotten theoretical framework which was first elaborated by Piero Sraffa in 1960,[30] animating an important debate which became known as the "Cambridge capital controversy". The approach of Sraffa and his theoretical predecessors (i.e. classical economists such as Ricardo and Marx) is also the main inspiration of Sergio Cesaratto's chapter, which explains the central tenets of the Modern Classical Theory and contraposes it to the Marginalist approach. In the following chapter, Marco Veronese Passarella elaborates Marx's reproduction schemes with the purpose of understanding the recent financial crisis from a different theoretical perspective. Guglielmo Forges Davanzati discusses Nicholas Kaldor's theory of the labour market, challenging the controversial neoclassical assumption of a negative relationship between high wages and faster economic growth. Alessandro Vercelli's chapter analyses the historical evolution of economic thought – and the continuous debate between different schools – on the understanding of financial crashes. The chapter elaborated by Anna Maria Grazia Variato assesses the contribution of Hyman P. Minsky, who studied the financial and monetary system of advanced capitalist economies and produced a theory of financial instability which gives fundamental insights into understanding the global financial crisis of 2007–8.

The final part of the book is dedicated to economic analysis and policymaking. Andrea Califano, Tommaso Gabellini and Simone Gasperin provide an empirical assessment of the technological and productive performance of a selected group of EU member States since the beginning of the 1990s. Their suggestion is that there is no such a thing as a homogeneous "European model" of science and technology. National differences among countries appear to be substantial and persistent through time, contradicting the theoretical prediction that economic and financial integration naturally leads to a process of convergence in productivity and living standards. Finally, Mario Pianta, Matteo Lucchese and Leopolodo Nascia have presented a detailed assessment of the recent industrial policies that have been implemented within the EU – by its institutions and member

States – arguing that they have been ineffective, if not detrimental. Some policy alternatives are suggested to "reshape" the European economies.

7. Looking for the light at the end of the . . . cave

Eventually, any general debate on economic theory and policy has to confront the concluding suggestion put forward by Keynes in his *General Theory*: that "the world is ruled by little else" than by the "ideas of economists and political philosophers".[31] Even if one disagrees with Keynes, arguing that theoretical elaborations are most of the time *ex-post* rationalisations for decisions that are taken independently from the surrounding intellectual atmosphere, a serious problem with the "ideas" of economists persists. Its influence on the army of technocrats and high-level civil servants should not be underestimated. Our suggestion is that economics, rightly vilified for its usefulness before and after the crisis, should humbly look back to its origins of being a moral and political philosophy. A modern form of political economy can flourish and offer some sensible answers to the compelling questions that the changing world economy raises only if nurtured by the richness that history, philosophy, sociology and psychology can provide to both economic theory and analysis.

It is not a case perhaps that Keynes himself was so influenced by the interactions with towering intellectual figures in Cambridge, such as Bertrand Russell and Ludwig Wittgenstein.[32] The modern Hamlet would admonish the economist Horatio about the fact that "there are more things in heaven and earth than are dreamt of" in his *economics*. On the contrary, the rigid departmentalisation and hyper-specialisation of economics has created real "monsters", in Goya's sense. Books are not anymore considered as the utmost achievement of scientific knowledge. Economists have become part of a very closed and self-referential sect of priests that communicate through the arid, convoluted and abstract language of academic papers that very few individuals apart from them read, quote and discuss. Indeed, the economic and political discourse has not been transformed by the journal article with the most elegant model or the most sophisticated econometric analysis. What has really fuelled the debate about, say, globalisation, inequality and innovation has been the publication of relevant, richly documented and insightful books[33] that have addressed those problems from an historical and empirically valid point of view.

In conclusion, having supported the relevance of a sounder philosophical approach to the study of the capitalist economy, having mentioned Wittgenstein and having thus argued in favour of treatises, we would like to introduce the book with a quote from Wittgenstein's *Tractatus Logico-Philosophicus*. We believe that instead of dealing with pointless sophisticated techniques and the fetishisation of economic theories into abstract models, economists should stick to the object of their investigation: the real and constantly changing economic world in which every human being lives as a "political animal".[34]

Die Welt ist alles, was der Fall ist.[35]

Notes

1 Keynes, J. M. (1936). *The General Theory of Employment, Interest and Money*, chapter 24, p. 260 in (ed.) Skidelsky, R. (2015). *The Essential Keynes*. Harmondsworth, UK: Penguin Classics. See p. 97 for a presentation of Keynes's approach on economic theory and policy, as illustrated by the editor.

2 Robinson, J. (1972). "The Second Crisis of Economic Theory". *The American Economic Review*, 62(1/2), 1–10.

3 Christiano, L. J., Eichenbaum, M. S. and Trabandt, M. (2017). "On DSGE Models", http://faculty.wcas.northwestern.edu/~yona/research/DSGE.pdf. The published version on the *Journal of Economic Perspectives* (32(3) – Summer 2018) does not present the strong statement of the original working paper, which prompted a significant amount of (mostly negative) reactions within the economics academic community.

4 Summers, L. (2014). "U.S. Economic Prospects: Secular Stagnation, Hysteresis, and the Zero Lower Bound". *Business Economics*, 49, pp. 65–73.

5 Sylos Labini, P. (1974). *Saggio sulle classi sociali*. Laterza, Italy: Bari. Authors' translation from Italian, p. 3, italics added.

6 Hahn, F. (1975). "Revival of Political Economy: The Wrong Issues and the Wrong Argument". *The Economic Record*, 51(135), 360–364.

7 Kirman, A. (1992). "Whom or What Does the Representative Individual Represent?" *The Journal of Economic Perspectives*, 6(2), 117–136.

8 Milton Friedman defined the natural rate of unemployment as "the level that would be ground out by the Walrasian system of general equilibrium equations provided there is embedded in them the actual structural characteristics of the labor and commodity markets, including market imperfections, stochastic variability in demands and supplies, the cost of gathering information about job vacancies and labor availabilities, the costs of mobility and so on". Friedman, M. (1968). "The Role of Monetary Policy", *American Economic Review*, March.

9 Fama, E. (1970). "Efficient Capital Markets: A Review of Theory and Empirical Work", *The Journal of Finance*, 25(2), 383–417.

10 Toporowski, J. (2000). *The End of Finance. Capital Market Inflation, Financial Derivatives and Pension Fund Capitalism*. Oxford, UK: Routledge, p. 2.

11 Hume, D. (1985 [1752]). *Political Discourses*. 1777, 11th edition reprinted as part of *Essays: Moral, Political, and Literary*, ed. Eugene F. Miller. Indianapolis, IN: Liberty Classics.

12 Friedman, M. (1970). *The Counter-Revolution in Monetary Theory: First Wincott Memorial Lecture, Delivered at the Senate House, University of London, 16 September, 1970* (Vol. 33). Institute of Economic Affairs.

13 McLeay, M., Radia, A., and Thomas, R. (2014). "Money Creation in the Modern Economy". *Bank of England Quarterly Bulletin*, 2014 Q1.

14 Christiano et al. (2017). "On DSGE Models".

15 Quoted by Joseph Steindl in (ed.) Maxine Berg (1989) *Political Economy in the Twentieth Century*. Oxford, UK: Philip Allan.

16 Romer, P. M. (2015). "Mathiness in the Theory of Economic Growth". *American Economic Review*, 105(5), 89–93.

17 Christiano et al. (2017). "On DSGE Models".

18 Keynes (1936, chapter 21).

19 Keynes (1936, p. 298).

20 Letter to E. Rothbarth, 21 January 1940, quoted in Skidelsky, R. (2000). *John Maynard Keynes: A Biography*, Vol. 3. Basingstoke, UK: Macmillan, 70.

21 Keynes's reflections on Tinbergen's econometric approach are found in the correspondence with R. Tayler and R. F. Harrod in 1938. See pp. 275–281 in (ed.) Skidelsky, R. (2015). *The Essential Keynes*. Harmondsworth, UK: Penguin Classics.

22 Schumpeter, Joseph (1954). *History of Economic Analysis*. New York: Oxford University Press, chapter 2, 10–11.

23 Gramsci, A. (1996 [1930]). *Prison Notebooks*. Volume II. New York: Columbia University Press, 32–33.

24 Details of the INET proposals are available from www.ineteconomics.org/education/curricula-modules/economics-curriculum-committee.

25 For further information about the initiative, as well as for the materials and videos of the seminars, see https://criticalseminars.wordpress.com/.

26 Simone Gasperin and Tommaso Gabellini.

27 Skidelsky, R. (2009). *Keynes: The Return of the Master*. Harmondsworth, UK: Penguin.

28 Another example of how traditional economic theory can be studied in comparative terms with alternative approaches is found in Brancaccio, E. and Califano, A. (2018). *Anti-Blanchard Macroeconomics: A Comparative Approach*. Cheltenham, UK: Edward Elgar.

29 Kaldor, N. (1961). "Capital Accumulation and Economic Growth". In Lutz, F.A. and Hague, D. C. (eds) *The Theory of Capital*. Basingstoke, UK: Palgrave.

30 Sraffa, P. (1960). *Produzione di merci a mezzo di merci*. Turin, Italy: Einaudi.

31 Keynes (1936, chapter 24).

32 Piero Sraffa was also part of the intellectual environment in Cambridge at that time, being particularly close to Wittgenstein. The latter is said to have profited immensely from Sraffa, notably when he challenged the Austrian philosopher to account for the way Italian people gesticulate into his philosophy of language.

33 Among the others, here we refer for instance to Joseph Stiglitz's *Globalization and Its Discontents* (2002, Harmondsworh, UK: Penguin), to Thomas Piketty's *Capital in the Twenty-First Century* (2013, London: Verso) and to Mariana Mazzucato's *The Entrepreneurial State* (2013, London: Anthem).

34 From Aristotle's definition of the man as a "political animal" (ζῷον πολιτικόν) in his *Politics* (Τὰ πολιτικὰ).

35 From Proposition 1.1 "The world is the totality of facts, not of things". In Wittgenstein, L. (1961 [1922]). *Tractatus Logico-Philosophicus*. Oxford, UK: Routledge, 5.

Part I

Alternative methodologies

1 Critical dilemmas in the methodology of economics facing the crisis

Alessio Moneta

1. Introduction

The aim of this chapter is to provide a personal assessment of the status of economics in the face of the current economic crisis, from the point of view of the *methodology of economics*. Many scholars have observed that the status of economics, and in particular that of *macroeconomics*, is far from being in a good shape. For example, Joseph Stiglitz has recently written that:

> No one would, or at least should, say that macroeconomics has done well in recent years. The standard models not only didn't predict the Great Recession, they also said it couldn't happen—bubbles don't exist in well-functioning economies of the kind assumed in the standard model. Not surprisingly, even after the bubble broke, the models didn't predict the full consequences, and they haven't provided good guidance to policymakers in responding to the crisis.
>
> (Stiglitz, 2015)

Here I shall point out some *dilemmas* in the methodology of economics. A dilemma is a problematic situation in which there are offered two possible solutions, neither of which seems satisfactory. The methodology of economics is "the study of how economics functions, how it could function, and how it should function".[1] In the study of the *functioning* of economics, it is very likely you would come across some *impasses*, which probably have always existed in the discipline but which have become particularly evident and critical after the economic crisis. I call these problematic situations 'dilemmas'; but this term should not be taken too literally: in most cases the duality of the (failed) solutions is only *prima facie*. However, this term may help in framing the different problems and their connections.

The first dilemma concerns the problem of causal inference, i.e. the problem of uncovering causal-effect relationships that can in turn be useful for predicting, explaining and intervening in the economy. The two 'horns' of the dilemma are here the *data-driven* and the *theory-driven* approaches. The second problematic situation is the fact that economic phenomena are usually explained through (mathematically) formalised models. Here there are two possible approaches: the first aims at searching for pragmatic relevance. In other words, scholars who take this route want models to be able to give precise, simple and *useful* answers to economic-relevant questions, rather than to mirror the complex economic reality. This is typically done through *abstraction* and *idealisation* of the reality. The alternative route is to aim at developing explanatory models which are true and verified, but at the cost of facing the problem of replicating a complex and seemingly unstructured reality, neglecting pragmatic relevance. The third dilemma concerns the problem of falsification of economic-theoretical hypotheses: should we develop methods that attempt to severely falsify them or should we renounce this task given the fact that economic-theoretical hypotheses cannot be easily confronted with the data? The fourth dilemma concerns the alternative view of economics as a scientific and moral discipline.

Beside the note of caution about 'dilemmas' that may contain more than two 'horns', I should also add that the four dilemmas presented here may not exhaust all the difficulties one might encounter in studying how economics functions. But this simplification may be useful to illustrate the difficulties the methodology of economics should address. Moreover, in the rest of the chapter, for reasons of space, I will devote much more effort to explaining the first dilemma (see section 2) than the other three, which will only briefly be introduced in section 3 and shown how they are intertwined with the first.

2. The dilemma of causality

2.1 Theory-driven vs. data-driven approaches

Questions about cause-effect relationships are pervasive in economics, but they come in many different forms. We may ask for the cause of the great recession, where 'recession' is an event or an historically defined set of events. We may enquire about the effect of conventional and unconventional monetary policy on macroeconomic variables in a particular country, monetary area or even in general in the market economy. We may pose retrospective (e.g. what was the effect of austerity policy?) or prospective (e.g. what would be the effect of Italy exiting the Euro area?) causal questions. Another important issue is measurement. Sometimes it is crucial to attach numbers to causal influences. What is the size of the government spending multiplier (the ratio between change in national income to the change in government spending that causes it) in a particular country, in a particular period?[2]

We should note that questions about causality are important in any scientific discipline, but in economics they assume a particular relevance because economics is a *political discipline*: it attempts to provide reliable knowledge on which to ground policy. Policy is about intervening in the (social and physical) reality to influence or control some output. Causal knowledge is, among other things, knowledge of connections that permit intervention and control.

Thus, it is no wonder that policy discussions in economics are also discussions about what causes what.

Questions about causality in economics concern events (or types of events) of quite a different nature, can be framed in many different manners, and are addressed in the literature using diverse methods. Nevertheless, they share a common problem, which I call here the 'causality dilemma'.[3] Indeed, to settle these questions, one needs to substantiate some sorts of causal claims, and in economic research there seem to be two radically different traditional ways to justify cause-effect relationships. One way is to let (economic) theory guide us in our attempts to infer causal relationships from observations. The other way is not to let theory guide us and to rely instead on statistical methods jointly with rules of inference and restrictions which allow us to estimate causal relationships from data.

The first horn

If we let theory guide us, we build theoretical models on the basis of our theoretical knowledge and background knowledge in general. But in economics theoretical or background knowledge is often uncertain or contentious. At least there is no consensus on the assumptions upon which theoretical models are built. It is easy to build models with conflicting policy implications by (sometimes slightly) modifying the initial conditions.

Consider, for example, the question about monetary policy: which instruments are controlled by the monetary policymaker, and how is their modification transmitted to real economic activities? This is, undoubtedly, one of the most discussed issues in macroeconomics: the way it is framed and addressed is at the basis of the different schools of thought in economics. An answer is crucial for the solution to the current economic crisis, but the issue goes back to at least David Hume's essay 'Of Money' (1985 [1752]), which, as pointed out by Hoover (2001), is framed in explicit causal terms. (Incidentally, David Hume is also the most prominent figure in the modern philosophical analysis of causality.) But let us consider here the way the issue of monetary policy was framed by mainstream economists in the 1950s and 1960s. The most used approach was, at that time, the so called 'Cowles Commission' econometric approach. Essential to this approach was a clear distinction between exogenous and endogenous variables. The variables controlled by the monetary policymaker were assumed to be exogenous, while the variables representing final outcomes of the policy were taken as endogenous. As illustrated by Favero (2001, p. 103), the Cowles Commission approach starts by specifying a theoretical model, which is usually a *large-scale* macroeconometric model, i.e. consisting of a large number of variables and equations describing the economic system. The model is then identified by imposing a number of *a priori* restrictions that ascribe exogeneity status to a number of variables. It is also essential in this approach that the error terms entered into the behavioural equations of the model follow a definite probability distribution, so that the model can be analysed by standard statistical tools (Hoover, 2012). Further steps are estimation of the relevant parameters (through standard regression models) and simulation of the effects of policy interventions.

The consensus in mainstream economics around the Cowles Commission approach broke down in the mid-1970s for various reasons, one of which (perhaps the most relevant) was the lack of trust on the theoretical assumptions used in this approach. Particularly popular were the critiques of Lucas (1976) and Sims (1980). Lucas attacks the identification framework proposed by the Cowles Commission by pointing out that the large-scale macroeconometric models built within this scheme do not take into account the forward-looking behaviour of rational economic agents. More specifically, these models are not micro-founded, they do not consider the 'deep parameters' of the economic systems, which should be related only to the preferences of individual economic agents and the technological structure of the economy. Thus, Lucas argues, the structural coefficients that are identified in the Cowles Commission approach cannot be stable, because they are inevitably mixtures of deep and expectational parameters, which are unstable, because they strategically interact with policy interventions. Lucas adds also the interesting point that a theoretical causal structure that may describe and explain well the functioning of an economic system may not be suited to guide a policy intervention, because it automatically breaks down once it is applied, since the economic agents may adapt their behaviour to the new policy.

Sims's (1980) critique runs parallel to that of Lucas, but it is more targeted to the general idea of deciding *a priori*, on the basis of economic theory or institutional knowledge, that a set of variables is exogenous. He deems such restrictions to be "incredible". This criticism triggered the development of approaches to causal inference belonging to the second horn of the dilemma: the data-driven approach.

The strand of macroeconomic research that took seriously and incorporated literally the Lucas critique was the intertemporal optimisation-Real Business Cycle approach by Kydland and Prescott (1982), which forms the skeleton of the well-known Dynamic Stochastic General Equilibrium (DSGE) models. For the purpose of monetary policy analysis, in the early 2000s, DSGE models became very popular to address quantitative policy questions (Christiano et al., 2010). But after the 2008 crisis, they have been object of a heated debate. DSGE models are indeed the *standard models* mentioned in Stiglitz's quote at the beginning of this chapter.

Stiglitz (2017) argues further that the current dissatisfaction with DSGE models lies in their failure to provide insights into the deep downturns that have occurred repeatedly and into what should be done in response. An important point (for the purposes of this chapter) raised by Stiglitz is that the DSGE models move from the *wrong* micro-foundations: they are based on "a simplified version of the competitive equilibrium model – just as that model was being discredited by advances in behavioural economics, game theory, and the economics of information" (Stiglitz, 2017). In their paper, Christiano et al.

(2018) respond to this and other critiques moved by Stiglitz and many other scholars. It is not now in the scope of this chapter to enter into this debate. But it is worth noting that a line of defence by Christiano et al. is that "all models – including those advocated by Stiglitz – are inconsistent with some aspects of micro evidence" (Christiano et al., 2018).

My argument here is that when we let theory guide us in causal inference, our causal claims will always be "incredible" because our theoretical knowledge in a complex setting is doomed to be uncertain. This may suggest examining the opposite approach: let us move away from the data. Before rushing to the other horn of the dilemma, I would like to add two important notes of caution. The fact that all theoretical models are, to some respect, "false", in the sense that they all misrepresent, to some extent, some pieces of evidence, does not imply that they all should be treated as equal from an epistemological point of view.[4] For example, one may discriminate between different 'false' (in this sense) models on the basis of the ability or not to represent the target structure (causal mechanisms) of interest, where the target of interest may differ among modellers. Or, one may claim that a model misrepresents the evidence less worse than another and therefore it should be preferred. Second, it is important to ask and investigate, building upon the current econometric literature, what are the reliable criteria that allow us to say that one model represents a particular evidence better than another model. Both points will be discussed in section 4.

The second horn

Let us now focus on the second horn of the dilemma: we do not let theory guide us. Of course, our theoretical background knowledge cannot be cancelled and is at least implicit in any choice of variables and even in the most innocuous assumption of the most strenuous empiricist. But, given a choice of variables and set of assumptions not directly related to the causal mechanism one is interested in uncovering, theoretical knowledge can be 'bracketed' and forced to play a minimal role when inferring causal relationships from data. A consolidated tradition in econometrics follows this path, although it is not always explicit on dubbing the inferred claims as 'causal'. In such a short text, I cannot provide a comprehensive review of the diverse econometric techniques that were developed in tune with this general view: for example, Granger-causality, Vector Autoregressive (VAR) models, instrumental variables, difference in differences, Rubin causal models.

Instead, let us consider again the question of the instruments and the transmission mechanism of monetary policy. We mentioned earlier Sims's (1980) criticism of the *a priori* restrictions used in the Cowles Commission approach to attribute the status of exogeneity to a set of variables, in order to achieve identification and estimation of the causal effects of policy. Sims proposed instead to consider a model consisting of a limited number of time series variables that have to be considered, at least in a first step, all equally endogenous. Thus each variable at time t is made dependent on lagged values (up to a certain number of lags) of all the other variables, omitting the possible influence of contemporaneous variables. This is called a vector autoregressive (VAR) model. In the VAR approach questions about monetary policy are addressed with an important switch in the focus of interest. The question is not so much (or, at least, is not directly): 'What is the optimal response of the monetary authority to movements in the macroeconomic variables to achieve given targets for the same variables? Rather it is: 'Which combination of error terms better captures the shock to monetary policy?' and also: 'What are the effects of a monetary policy shock on the macroeconomic variables of interest?' As argued by Christiano et al. (1999), addressing these latter questions, besides being interesting per se and eschewing the Lucas critique, can be very useful in collecting stylised facts that allow the researcher to evaluate theoretical models.

Identifying causal relationships posed in the VAR framework, however, in spite of their relative simplicity, turns out to be hard without further restrictions or assumptions. Indeed, the estimation of the 'structural impulse response functions', which describe the dynamic causal effects of an independent (and economically interpretable) innovation related to one (or more) variable(s), requires a specific and unique 'rotation' (i.e. a linear transformation) of the estimated coefficients and error terms of the reduced-form model (in which all the terms on the right-hand side of each equation are predetermined). Finding the right rotation requires in turn restrictions or assumptions about the possible causal relations linking the variables and the shocks. The so-called 'structural VAR' literature deals precisely with this issue. Sims's original strategy was to assume a recursive causal structure among the contemporaneous values of the modelled variables ('Choleski identification scheme'), studying the sensitivity of the results under all the possible causal orders. Other scholars (see e.g. Bernanke, 1986) have proposed to incorporate at this stage restrictions directly derived from economic theory. Recently, more sophisticated identification schemes have emerged, based on assumptions that are independent of economic theory and are linked only to general conditions about restrictions that causal structures impose on probability distributions (see e.g. Swanson and Granger, 1997; Demiralp and Hoover, 2003; Moneta et al., 2013; Capasso and Moneta, 2016).

The identification of the structural impulse response functions can be eschewed if one restricts the analysis to the reduced-form VAR model. This is done, for example, in the Granger-causality framework which aims to test whether a variable provides an information-theoretic contribution to another variable in terms of 'incremental predictability', given the values of all the other variables (Granger, 1980).

In general, any data-driven approach has to face two daunting epistemological problems. One is the *problem of induction*, which goes back to David Hume (1739), that we cannot guarantee that our conclusions are true of the sample. In other words, although we observe a sample of individuals or a sample of realisations of some variables, and we can easily estimate statistical associations, we do not observe the causal relationships, which always require some leap from the observations. But suppose we obtain some evidence that makes us believe that there exists a causal relationship for the observed individuals. Without an understanding of the underlying mechanisms, it is difficult to generalise to the entire population or to other populations and settings. We call this second issue the *problem of external validity*.

2.2 Debates in the history of economic thought

This dilemma has been touched on in several disputes that we find in the history of economic thought (see also Reiss, 2013). John Stuart Mill, in his seminal essay on methodology of economics ('On the Definition of Political Economy; and of the Method of Investigation Proper to It'), first published in 1836, favoured the 'theory-driven' approach. The economic system, Mill argued, is too complex a setting to permit a data-driven approach. Indeed, the presence of many interacting variables confounds any link between variables that we observe and measure, so that the inference from data to causal claims is not feasible. Mill was not concerned with the difficulties of the theory-driven approach because he maintained that our theoretical knowledge about the economy is well grounded in our capacity for introspection that all the humans share. Early critics of John Stuart Mill pointed out that his theoretical knowledge about economic behaviour was not well rounded and was reduced to the concept of *homo oeconomicus*, a term that was coined just for that occasion (Persky, 1995).

Another episode in the history of economic thought, which can be read as a dispute between a theory-driven and a data-driven approach, is the so-called *Methodenstreit*. This controversy took place in the 1880s between the Austrian school, represented by Carl Menger, and the German historical school, led by Gustav von Schmoller. Menger and his followers defended a deductive and axiomatic view of economics, which was seen as not amenable to statistical analysis. Schmoller distrusted theories not derived from historical evidence and argued for a development of economics grounded on the collection of statistical and historical material.

There are probably many other controversies in the history of economic thought reflecting this dilemma. I would like now to mention some debates strictly linked to econometrics. Indeed, econometric approaches can also be theory-driven or data-driven. This may sound a bit paradoxical, because econometrics is the discipline which is based on data analysis. Nevertheless, there are two opposing views on how to consider data analysis. In rough terms, one view considers econometric analysis as a tool to measure causal relationships which are dictated by economic theory. The opposite approach sees econometric analysis as a tool for uncovering interesting (possibly, but not exclusively, causal) links from the data.

For example, Tjalling Koopmans, from the Cowles Commission, had a debate in the late 1940s with Rutledge Vining, from the NBER, which is referred to as the "Measurement without theory debate" (Hammond, 2005).

Koopmans sided with the theory-driven approach, while Vining defended an 'a-theoretical' approach to econometrics. Similar debates can be found in the 1980s between Christopher Sims (data-driven side), who developed the VAR models, and Thomas Cooley who, jointly with Stephen LeRoy, criticised the "a-theoretical macroeconomics" (Cooley and LeRoy, 1985). More recently, the 'data-driven' approach has been defended by the *Mostly Harmless Econometrics* school of Angrist and Pischke (2008). This approach has been criticised by Deaton (2010) for being not guided by "an understanding of underlying mechanisms".

Considering the regularity and frequency with which this kind of debate is occurring in the history of economic analysis, one might think that a solution comes from the integration of both sources of knowledge (theory and evidence), which includes both a problematisation of the empirical knowledge (e.g. accepting its partial theory-ladenness) and a strengthening of theoretical knowledge by making explicit the sensitivity of theoretical hypotheses to changes in the empirical conditions. I shall argue that such an integration is indeed useful, but reaching such an integration turns out in practice to be difficult.

2.3 Possible integration

Some routes to address the dilemma of causality are based on the rejection of the idea that *there are no alternatives* to the two (seemingly uncomfortable) possibilities. Doing so, one denies the existence of such a dilemma. For example, one may argue that the problem is ill-posed because both data-driven approaches and theory-driven approaches are based on some background knowledge. There are many types of knowledge: for instance derived from economic theory, derived from statistical theory, grounded on observation of institutional mechanisms, on repeated evidence, etc. It is indeed extremely difficult to draw a line between the different types of knowledge, and it may be misleading to dub a portion of it as 'theory' and another portion as 'data'. Although this argument raises interesting points, it is also difficult to deny that the sources of knowledge in the so-called theory-driven approach are different in many important respects to the sources of knowledge used in the data-driven approach.

Another possible argument against the no-alternatives claim is the one in favour of an integration of the 'theory-driven' and 'data-driven' positions. To go back to the question of monetary policy in macroeconometrics, an example of the strand of research that attempted to integrate the two approaches has been the so-called LSE approach[5] (see Favero, 2001, chapter 5). The LSE approach shares with the Cowles Commission approach the idea that, in order to evaluate the effect of a monetary policy, one has to identify and estimate a structural model of the economy: it is not sufficient to work with reduced-form equations. In the Cowles Commission tradition, however, the researcher starts from economic theory, which suggests a structural form, from which he or she derives a set of reduced-form equations that can be directly estimated. In the

LSE approach, on the other hand, the reduced form is specified through a rigorous and severe series of tests of restrictions on the statistical model. Since the statistical model at the beginning of the procedure is formalised in very general (and not very informative) terms and later reduced through sequential testing, this approach is also referred to as "general-to-specific modelling" (Campos et al., 2005). Among the various specifications there is also the classification of variables into endogenous and exogenous, as in the Cowles Commission tradition. However, in this approach, the specified model is considered a congruent representation of the data-generating process only if the null hypothesis of the absence of symptoms of misspecifications (e.g. non-normality of residuals, autocorrelation, heteroscedasticity, non-stability of parameters) is not rejected. In this approach, policy analysis like the evaluation of a monetary policy intervention is possible only if the condition of *superexogeneity* is satisfied, which requires that changes in the distribution of the exogenous variables do not affect the structural parameters of the model. Empirical testing of these conditions may be difficult, but this approach is able to provide scientific rigour to model specification (Favero, 2001).

Generally speaking, integrating approaches driven by economic-theoretical or substantive knowledge with approaches guided by statistical knowledge is desirable for causal inference. Indeed, pure statistical inference is grounded on data observations, but faces major difficulties in distinguishing between statistical and causal dependence. On the other hand, pure economic theory or substantial knowledge posits clear mechanisms but needs always to be validated *vis-à-vis* the data. From a certain point of view the two approaches seem complementary. However, more research is needed to understand both the difference between the two sources of knowledge and the plurality of evidence upon which causal inference can be built. As pointed out by Moneta and Russo (2014), there is an important point of contact between statistical and economic-theoretic knowledge: both are based on the construction of models. This should suggest that integration is possible and desirable, but also that it may be difficult to find a general and strict procedure that delivers it. It is to be found more on a case by case basis, considering the specific problem at hand. This is why econometrics may often be seen as more of an 'art' than a science.

3. More dilemmas

The theory- vs. data-driven conundrum is connected with other difficulties that the practical economist may encounter in his or her research, which are of deep methodological nature. Although in this brief text I shall not analyse each of them at length, here I mention the most relevant one.

3.1 Idealisation vs. description

When mentioning possible problems of a pure theory-guided approach, I was mentioning the fact that economic-theoretical models seem to misrepresent many aspects of the reality, which is in tune with the common aphorism that *all models are wrong.* They actually often do that to better focus on the aspects of reality they aim to represent. But the fact that models present simplified and often idealised accounts of the phenomenon creates a puzzle that Julian Reiss has called "the explanation paradox" (Reiss, 2012, 2013). In short Reiss argues that three inconsistent hypotheses about economic models are widely held: (i) economic models are false, (ii) economic models are nevertheless explanatory, and (iii) only true accounts explain. In the same writings Reiss discusses three solutions of the paradox that are found in the literature on economic methodology. A first route to get out of this impasse, Reiss argues, is to challenge the idea that economic models are false. Models represent specific target systems of interest. For example, the real business cycle (RBC) model by Kydland and Prescott (1982) aims at representing (well or accurately or not well at all) the mechanism by which shocks to productivity affect fluctuations in output. In doing so they isolate some aspects of the reality and abstract or idealise away other (disturbing) factors. This claim has been recently defended by Mäki (2011). This is also one of the core ideas of scientific realism, a tradition that in the philosophy of economics goes back to Mill (1836). Reiss argues against this view that, due to the peculiar nature of assumptions made in economics, the model result is specific to the situation that is being modelled (Reiss, 2013, p. 131). The model result is derived from the model assumption. But it is not obvious from inspecting the model that one particular subset of assumptions is driving the results rather than another (Cartwright, 2007, chapter 15).[6] We know some assumptions to be false under any empirical situation. For example, in the RBC model, it is assumed that individuals are identical and live infinitely. It is not straightforward to assess how the results of the importance of a productivity shock in driving macroeconomic fluctuations are dependent or independent of this particular assumption.

A second route to solve the paradox, Reiss argues, is to deny that economic models are per se explanatory. Some methodologists defend the view that models are "conceptual explorations" (Hausman, 1992) (which, however, necessitate theoretical hypotheses to be confronted with real phenomena) or heuristics for constructing modal hypotheses (Alexandrova, 2008; Grüne-Yanoff, 2009). This view may indeed account for several models proposed by the economic community. But it cuts off what a large part of the profession sees as one of the main task of the economist: explaining economic phenomena showing and describing (quantitatively) its structure, so that it can be used for policy analysis (see e.g. Stock and Watson, 2001).

The third route, which Reiss critically discusses, defends the claim: explanation does not require truth. If a model is credible, because, for example, of its power of unifying phenomena of different kinds, then one may argue that it is explanatory. The claim of models as "credible world", i.e. as artefacts in which it is possible to develop counterfactual reasoning and which resemble aspects of the real word without faithfully mirroring it, has been sustained by Sugden (2000, 2011). The view of explanation as unifying power has been proposed by Kitcher (1981). There are two problems with this approach, as argued by

Reiss (2013, pp. 135–140). The first is that credibility (even if shared within the community of professional economists) of an account of an economic phenomenon per se is not sufficient to make it explanatory. For example, credibility (without a truth claim) may be affected by ideological preferences, etc. Second, the accounts of economic phenomena typically presented in (especially mainstream) economics are not genuinely unifying. As argued by Reiss, often the unification is purely linguistic: for example, the concepts of 'utility' and 'equilibrium' are used in many different settings, but refer to many different things. Thus we do not have different phenomena subsumed under the same concept, as in a genuine unifying explanation.

Reiss (2012, p. 141) concludes that "the paradox of economic modelling is genuine . . . previous attempts to resolve it have failed" and there are not "many likely avenues for future attempts". I argue that because of this conundrum, which looms in the practice of economic research (even if economists often reject one of the three theses making up the paradox or simply ignore it), economists often find themselves in a sort of dilemma. Because of the difficulty of providing an account of economic phenomena that are at the same time empirical, reliable ('true') and causal (structural),[7] economists are often ahead of a dilemma. Should one push idealised representations of economic structures, which have the advantage of being causal and therefore easily exploitable for policy analysis, or should one focus on rendering reliable and accurate descriptions of the economic reality? Idealised models are causal but risk being empirically unreliable. Descriptive models are empirically reliable but tend to be silent about causality. But this also raises the question of how to assess whether a model is empirically reliable or descriptively adequate.

3.2 Testing models

Testing economic models or theories, assessing their empirical reliability, discriminating between different accounts of the same phenomena, are tasks normally ascribed to econometrics. However, as Spanos (1995) points out, econometrics has not performed particularly well in weeding out invalid theories. Discussing in detail why this is the case is a complicated and subtle issue, in part overlapping with the discussion about the limits of the falsificationist programme in science and economics (see Caldwell, 1982; Backhouse, 2012). Given the limited space of this chapter, I am here, surely a bit schematically, just pointing out some related issues and a further 'dilemma':

1   Testing or confirming theoretical hypotheses is part of inductive reasoning, which is by definition uncertain and fallible. The idea of applying probability theory and statistics to such an inference is to control the error inevitably associated with it. Haavelmo, in his classic monograph, "The Probability Approach in Econometrics" made the point of confronting economic theory with data on the basis of the Neyman-Pearson theory of testing statistical hypothesis (Haavelmo, 1944, p. iv). It is worth noticing

that Jerzy Neyman preferred in this contest the term "inductive behaviour" rather than "inductive reasoning": the point is not to attach a probability to the truth of a particular hypothesis, rather to the error associated with taking a specific action (e.g. publishing a result, undertaking a policy intervention, etc.) (Neyman, 1957; Mayo and Spanos, 2006).

2   The process of falsification belongs to deductive inference (Popper, 1959). However, as pointed out for example by Sawyer et al. (1997), economic hypotheses are tested against data jointly with a set of auxiliary hypotheses, so that strict falsificationism is rarely applicable in economics.

3   Several econometricians and philosophers of science (see Mayo and Spanos, 2006, 2010) have pointed out that both in a context of confirmation and in a context of falsification it is fundamental that the tests to be faced by theoretical hypothesis fulfil some criterion of severity. For example, Karl Popper insisted that a certain empirical evidence can be accepted as supporting a theoretical hypothesis only if the related observations or experiments "are severe tests of the theory" (Popper, 1994). Mayo and Spanos (2010, p. 329) propose the following meta-statistical principle to assess whether, given data X, a hypothesis H passes a test T with severity. The necessary condition for severity is that (i) X agrees with H, and (ii) if H were false, with very low probability test T would have produced a result that accords with H better than or as well as X does.

Confronting economic-theoretic models with data may yield the following dilemma. A way to say that a model has passed some tests of reliability is to say that it replicates some stylised facts or certain statistical properties (for example, moments of distribution of macro-variables). However, this hardly passes the threshold of a "severe test" (Spanos, 1989). An alternative route would be to replicate causal structures. After all, an economic-theoretic model isolates possible causal structures of the economy that can be matched with causal structures derived from the data. For example, a macroeconomic model such as a DSGE or agent-based model can generate impulse response functions that can be confronted with impulse response functions estimated directly from the data, through a VAR model (Del Negro et al., 2006; Guerini and Moneta, 2017). The problem here is that causal structures have difficulties being inferred directly from the data (as pointed out earlier in section 2), so that both routes (replicating statistical stylised facts and replicating causal structures) have hurdles.

3.3 But what kind of science is economics?

The last dilemma is about two views of economics: one sees economics mainly as a moral discipline; another sees economics a scientific discipline as many others. For example, Milton Friedman, in his Nobel prize lecture, claims that there is no difference, in terms of methods of inquiry and reliability of knowledge, between economics and, say, physics or biology (Friedman, 1977).

Friedman is also known to have claimed that there is a clear division between normative and positive economics (Friedman, 1953).

John Stuart Mill (1836) also defended the view of a separation between normative and value-free economics. But he also defended the view that economic theories can hardly be confronted with the data because of the presence of disturbing factors. John Maynard Keynes seemed also to believe in the untestable nature of economic theories. This is connected to his view as economics "essentially as a moral science not a natural science" (Keynes, 1971) (see also Pesaran and Smith, 1985; Davis, 1991).

Without entering this debate, let me point out that the two horns of this dilemma (moral vs. natural science) correspond to two different views of causality in economics. The claim of economics as a moral science is often in tune with an interpretation of causal relationships in economics as structures among social entities which cannot be easily measured or straightforwardly confronted with data. Causal structures are historically evolving and are better understood (as opposed to explained) through historical methods that shed light on the underlying human motives and powers (or through introspection, as Mill suggested).

The claim of economics as standard scientific enterprise, on the other hand, is often associated with a view of causality as a relationship between random variables where the cause makes a difference to the probability of its effect. In this context, the link with data, which are interpreted as the realisation of a stochastic generating mechanism, is straightforward, with all the difficulties highlighted earlier in section 2.1. Many economists and many approaches have attempted to integrate both views, with difficulties similar to the ones pointed out in section 2.3.

4. Concluding remarks

In this short chapter, I have pointed out some dilemmas or open questions in economic methodology that may hinder the development of the discipline. My aim here was not to propose solutions to these issues but to make them explicit and to show how they are intertwined with philosophical issues about causality in economics. I would like to conclude with two notes of caution about two popular positions among economists and methodologists of economics: pluralism in economics and evidence-based economics.

Since the status of economics is plagued by the open issues presented here, one may see as desirable a pluralist position in which different views about economics, different methods and approaches are seen as acceptable and compatible. While different levels of analysis and openness to many types of evidence in economics, as in many other disciplines, are indeed desirable and probably necessary (Mitchell, 2003), one should be careful in distinguishing between different types of pluralism. Ontological pluralism (referring to the plurality of entities existing in reality), for example, should not be confused with epistemological (referring to a plurality of possible explanations of the reality) or methodological (possibility of different methods to analyse the reality) plural-ism (Dow, 2012). Indeed, not all types of pluralism should be seen as desirable and are not implied by the open position towards the different 'dilemmas' in the methodology of economics.

The position of a more 'evidence-based' economics, in the spirit of a more 'evidence-based policy' and 'evidence-based medicine' should also be seen as a sound attempt to integrate the theory-driven and data-driven horn and therefore as desirable. I see, however, a potential limitation to consider as unique benchmark evidence data collected in a randomised control trial, as many proponents of the evidence-based economics movement seem to suggest (see Reiss, 2013, chapter 11), since causal claims, as suggested by Moneta and Russo (2014) can be sustained by a plurality of evidence and indicators.

Acknowledgments

This chapter was first presented in the series of seminars *Critical Economics in Times of Crisis* in November 2014 at Sant'Anna School of Advanced Studies, Pisa, Italy. I would like to thank Tommaso Gabellini and Simone Gasperin for comments on that presentation. I retain responsibility for any errors.

Notes

1 See the description of Methodology of Economics Research Area by U. Mäki and N. E. Aydinonat in https://eaepe.org/?page=research_areas&side=a_methodology_of_economics.
2 For a discussion of different causal questions, see Hoover (2001, pp. 1–2).
3 The term and the framing of the problem is inspired by Julian Reiss's critical discussion of evidence-based policy in Reiss (2013, p. 206).
4 The famous sentence attributed to the statistician George Box "all models are wrong, but some are useful" has points of contact with this argument.
5 This is called after the "London School of Economics" perspective on econometric modelling proposed by Denis Sargan in the 1960s and led later by David Hendry (Hendry, 1995; Spanos, 2014).
6 For this matter, robustness analysis is a useful and powerful tool.
7 Note that this difficulty is not only linked to the paradox presented by Reiss but also to the theory- vs. data-driven dilemma described in Section 2.1.

References

Alexandrova, A. (2008). Making models count. *Philosophy of Science* 75(3), 383–404.
Angrist, J. D. and J.-S. Pischke (2008). *Mostly Harmless Econometrics: An Empiricist's Companion*. Princeton, NJ: Princeton University Press.
Backhouse, R. E. (2012). The rise and fall of Popper and Lakatos in economics. In U. Mäki (ed.), *Philosophy of Economics*. Amsterdam: North Holland.
Bernanke, B. S. (1986). Alternative explanations of the money-income correlation. Carnegie-Rochester Conference Series on Public Policy, 25, pp. 49–99. Oxford, UK: Elsevier.

Caldwell, B. (1982). *Beyond Positivism*. Oxford, UK: Routledge.

Campos, J., N. R. Ericsson, and D. Hendry (2005). General-to-specific modeling: An overview and selected bibliography. *Board of Governors of the Federal Reserve System International Finance Discussion Papers*. https://econpapers.repec.org/paper/fipfedgif/838.htm.

Capasso, M. and A. Moneta (2016). *Macroeconomic Responses to an Independent Monetary Policy Shock: A (More) Agnostic Identification Procedure*. Technical report, Laboratory of Economics and Management (LEM), Sant'Anna School of Advanced Studies, Pisa, Italy.

Cartwright, N. (2007). *Hunting Causes and Using Them: Approaches in Philosophy and Economics*. Cambridge, UK: Cambridge University Press.

Christiano, L. J., M. Eichenbaum, and C. L. Evans (1999). Monetary policy shocks: What have we learned and to what end? *Handbook of Macroeconomics* 1, pp. 65–148.

Christiano, L. J., M. S. Eichenbaum, and M. Trabandt (2018). On DSGE models. *Journal of Economic Perspectives*, 32(3), 113–140.

Christiano, L. J., M. Trabandt, and K. Walentin (2010). *DSGE Models for Monetary Policy Analysis*. National Bureau of Economic Research.

Cooley, T. F. and S. F. LeRoy (1985). Atheoretical macroeconometrics: A critique. *Journal of Monetary Economics*, 16(3), 283–308.

Davis, J. (1991). Keynes's view of economics as a moral science. In B. Bateman and J. Davis (eds.), *Keynes and Philosophy*. Cheltenham, UK: Edward Elgar.

Deaton, A. (2010). Instruments, randomization, and learning about development. *Journal of Economic Literature*, 48(2), 424–455.

Del Negro, M., F. Schorfheide, et al. (2006). How good is what you've got? DGSE-VAR as a toolkit for evaluating DSGE models. *Economic Review-Federal Reserve Bank of Atlanta*, 91(2), article 21.

Demiralp, S. and K. D. Hoover (2003). Searching for the causal structure of a vector autoregression. *Oxford Bulletin of Economics and Statistics*, 65(s1), 745–767.

Dow, S. C. (2012). Methodological pluralism and pluralism of method. In *Foundations for New Economic Thinking*, pp. 129–139. Dordrecht, the Netherlands: Springer.

Favero, C. (2001). *Applied Macroeconometrics*. Oxford, UK: Oxford University Press.

Friedman, M. (1953). *The Methodology of Positive Economics*. Chicago, IL: University of Chicago Press.

Friedman, M. (1977). Nobel lecture: Inflation and unemployment. *Journal of Political Economy*, 85(3), 451–472.

Granger, C. W. (1980). Testing for causality: A personal viewpoint. *Journal of Economic Dynamics and Control*, 2, 329–352.

Grüne-Yanoff, T. (2009). Learning from minimal economic models. *Erkenntnis*, 70(1), 81–99.

Guerini, M. and A. Moneta (2017). A method for agent-based models validation. *Journal of Economic Dynamics and Control*, 82, 125–141.

Haavelmo, T. (1944). The probability approach in econometrics. *Econometrica: Journal of the Econometric Society*, iii–115.

Hammond, J. D. (2005). *Theory and Measurement: Causality Issues in Milton Friedman's Monetary Economics*. Cambridge, UK: Cambridge University Press.

Hausman, D. M. (1992). *The Inexact and Separate Science of Economics*. Cambridge, UK: Cambridge University Press.

Hendry, D. F. (1995). *Dynamic Econometrics*. Oxford, UK: Oxford University Press on Demand.

Hoover, K. D. (2001). *Causality in Macroeconomics*. Cambridge, UK: Cambridge University Press.

Hoover, K. D. (2012). Economic theory and causal inference. In U. Mäki (ed.), *Philosophy of Economics*. Amsterdam: North Holland.

Hume, D. (1739). *A Treatise of Human Nature*. Harmondsworth, UK: Penguin.

Hume, D. (1985 [1752]). Political Discourses. 1777, 11th edition reprinted as part of *Essays: Moral, Political, and Literary* ed. Eugene F. Miller. Indianapolis, IN: Liberty Classics.

Keynes, J. M. (1971). *The Collected Writings of John Maynard Keynes: The General Theory and After: pt. 2, Defence and Development*, Volume 14. Basingstoke, K: Macmillan.

Kitcher, P. (1981). Explanatory unification. *Philosophy of Science*, 48(4), 507–531.

Kydland, F. E. and E. C. Prescott (1982). Time to build and aggregate fluctuations. *Econometrica*, 50(6), 1345–1370.

Lucas, R. E. (1976). *Econometric Policy Evaluation: A Critique*. In Carnegie-Rochester conference series on public policy, Volume 1, pp. 19–46. Oxford, UK: Elsevier.

Mäki, U. (2011). Models and the locus of their truth. *Synthese*, 180(1), 47–63.

Mayo, D. G. and A. Spanos (2006). Severe testing as a basic concept in a Neyman–Pearson philosophy of induction. *The British Journal for the Philosophy of Science*, 57(2), 323–357.

Mayo, D. G. and A. Spanos (2010). *Error and Inference: Recent Exchanges on Experimental Reasoning, Reliability, and the Objectivity and Rationality of Science*. Cambridge, UK: Cambridge University Press.

Mill, J. S. (1836). *On the Definition of Political Economy and of the Method of Investigation Proper to It*. Reprinted in *Essays on Some Unsettled Questions of Political Economy* (1844), 3rd ed. London: Longmans Green & Co., 1877, pp. 120–164.

Mitchell, S. D. (2003). *Biological Complexity and Integrative Pluralism*. Cambridge, UK: Cambridge University Press.

Moneta, A., D. Entner, P. O. Hoyer, and A. Coad (2013). Causal inference by inde-pen-dent component analysis: Theory and applications. *Oxford Bulletin of Economics and Statistics*, 75(5), 705–730.

Moneta, A. and F. Russo (2014). Causal models and evidential pluralism in economet-rics. *Journal of Economic Methodology*, 21(1), 54–76.

Neyman, J. (1957). Inductive behavior as a basic concept of philosophy of science. *Revue de l'Institut International de Statistique*, 25(1–3), 7–22.

Persky, J. (1995). Retrospectives: The ethology of homo economicus. *The Journal of Economic Perspectives*, 9(2), 221–231.

Pesaran, H. and R. Smith (1985). Keynes on econometrics. In T. Lawson and H. Pesaran (eds), *Keynes' Economics. Methodological Issues*. Oxford, UK: Routledge.

Popper, K. (1959). *The Logic of Scientific Discovery*. London: Hutchinson.

Popper, K. (1994). *The Myth of the Framework: In Defence of Science and Rationality*. Oxford, UK: Routledge.

Reiss, J. (2012). The explanation paradox. *Journal of Economic Methodology*, 19(1), 43–62.

Reiss, J. (2013). *Philosophy of Economics. A Contemporary Introduction*. New York: Routledge.

Sawyer, K. R., C. Beed, and H. Sankey (1997). Underdetermination in economics: The Duhem-Quine thesis. *Economics & Philosophy*, 13(1), 1–23.

Sims, C. A. (1980). Macroeconomics and reality. *Econometrica*, 48, 1–48.

Spanos, A. (1989). Early empirical findings on the consumption function, stylized facts or fiction: A retrospective view. *Oxford Economic Papers*, 41(1), 150–169.

Spanos, A. (1995). On theory testing in econometrics: Modeling with nonexperimental data. *Journal of Econometrics*, 67(1), 189–226.

Spanos, A. (2014). Reflections on the LSE tradition in econometrics: A student's perspective. *Œconomia. History, Methodology, Philosophy* 4(3), 343–380.

Stiglitz, J. E. (2015). Reconstructing macroeconomic theory to manage economic policy. In E. Laurent and J. Le Cacheux (eds), *Fruitful Economics: Papers in Honour of and by Jean-Paul Fitoussi*, pp. 20–56. Basingstoke, UK: Palgrave Macmillan.

Stiglitz, J. E. (2017). *Where Modern Macroeconomics Went Wrong*. National Bureau of Economic Research.

Stock, J. H. and M. W. Watson (2001). Vector autoregressions. *Journal of Economic Perspectives*, 15(4), 101–115.

Sugden, R. (2000). Credible worlds: The status of theoretical models in economics. *Journal of Economic Methodology*, 7(1), 1–31.

Sugden, R. (2011). Explanations in search of observations. *Biology & Philosophy*, 26(5), 717–736.

Swanson, N. R. and C. W. Granger (1997). Impulse response functions based on a causal approach to residual orthogonalization in vector autoregressions. *Journal of the American Statistical Association*, 92(437), 357–367.

2 "Anti-Blanchard"

A comparative technique for macroeconomics

Emiliano Brancaccio and Domenico Suppa

1. Signals of crisis in the 'core' of contemporary macroeconomics

Since the beginning of the "great recession" in 2008 (IMF 2012), growing doubts have characterized the field of economic theory. A question that arises is whether the current crisis will lead to another revolution in economists' ideas regarding the working of a capitalist market economy and the role of economic policy. Some scholars suggest that the so-called "mainstream" approach to macroeconomics already addresses the typical failures of a market economy as the causes of instability and recession. Economists should therefore be able to correct forecast errors and suggest solutions to the crisis by drawing on existing studies in the predominant literature (Tabellini 2009). According to this view, it is not necessary to disrupt what Olivier Blanchard calls the "core" of mainstream macroeconomic theory, and hence there is no need to rewrite the textbooks on which that core is based (Blanchard 2000; Blanchard et al. 2010; see also Taylor 2000).

The key propositions of the core of mainstream macroeconomics can be summarized in the following statements. First, it is assumed that in a market economy free of imperfections, rigidities and asymmetries, all macroeconomic variables would be anchored to a Pareto-efficient, full employment "natural" equilibrium determined by the "fundamentals" of the economy: tastes, technological development, the existing workforce and the capital stock available. It is also stated, however, that in the real world the natural equilibrium may be far from full employment and related Pareto-efficiency because of asymmetries and imperfections that can be due to several causes, including the market power of large companies and labor unions. Second, by provoking a drop in demand, a crisis can, in the short run, cause temporary deviations of production, employment and real wages from their respective natural levels. Nevertheless, in the long run, market forces should be able to spontaneously bring the economy back to its natural equilibrium. More specifically, unemployment above its natural rate should trigger a decline in wages and prices to support aggregate demand, production and employment recovery. Market forces alone, however, may fail to bring the economy back to equilibrium sufficiently quickly. In this sense, while mainstream economists tend to consider fiscal policy detrimental to private investments, they emphasize the capacity of monetary policy to boost demand and speed return to the natural equilibrium after a crisis. Third, in any case, the main role of economic policy is not the management of aggregate demand aimed at stabilizing the economy around its natural equilibrium. Rather, the most important goal of economic policy should be the elimination, through so-called "structural reforms", of all the obstacles and rigidities that may prevent the working of free market forces and may keep the natural equilibrium far away from a Pareto-efficient full employment of labor and other productive resources.

Whereas it is not possible to consider the mainstream as a monolithic paradigm, the basic framework just described represents well its nucleus and is widely supported by economists. However, this framework appears to overlook some problems that have recently emerged within the debate about the economic crisis. One of these difficulties concerns the relevance of the mainstream distinction between short-run fluctuations and long-run natural equilibrium. This distinction seems to be contradicted, for example, by the fact that the multiplier effects of an increase in public spending – especially public investment – seem to last much longer than expected, with positive implications for debt/GDP dynamics (IMF 2012, 2014). The same distinction comes into conflict with the contributions of some celebrated mainstream economists and major international institutions who suggest that growing income inequalities can have depressive effects on aggregate demand and production in the long run (Fitoussi and Stiglitz 2009; IMF-ILO 2010). The fact that this interpretation has been adopted by influential mainstream economists calls into question the heuristic self-sufficiency of the prevailing macroeconomic theory, given that it rules out long-term causal relations between income distribution and aggregate demand and production.

These and several other problems seem to indicate some cracks in the core of the dominant approach and a weakening of the general consensus surrounding it. This is one reason why it may be time to revive the debate between the nucleus of mainstream approach and other paradigms.

2. Rediscovering a comparative approach to economic theory and policy

It is well known that several rigorous research programs are focused on the critique of the mainstream approach and the development of alternative paradigms in economic theory and policy (among many others, see Leontief 1977; Kurz and Salvadori 1995; Pasinetti 2007; see also Minsky 1986; Graziani 2003; Godley and Lavoie 2006; on the critique of the mainstream, see Brancaccio and Fontana 2011; Lucarelli and Lunghini 2012). However, there is little tangible sign of any exchange of views or debate among advocates of these respective views. Since the early 1990s we have observed an almost total breakdown in communication and debate between mainstream scholars and members of critical schools of economic thought. This separate development in water-tight compartments has not enhanced the quality of economic research but, on the contrary, seems to have impoverished and damaged it. Even a leading mainstream economist like Blanchard complained about the risk of "too much convergence" among economists with regard to the future development of research (Blanchard 2008). More recently, Blanchard welcomed the revival of alternative approaches such as those of Kaldor and Minsky as possible signs of a fruitful Lakatosian dispute in political economy (IMF Survey 2015).

Today, however, a renewed debate between schools of economic thought is impeded by the unprecedented preponderance of mainstream scholars in the academies. In some departments, especially among the younger generations, there seems to be no mention, and perhaps even no awareness, of the existence of a plurality of voices in the field of economic analysis. This situation, of course, was not born by chance. At least in part it reflects the current balance of powers in society (Skidelsky 2010), which generate a prevailing demand for a main-stream narrative of the dynamics of capitalism and even of its crises. Alongside this, however, there is also a problem of communication among scholars. Years of undisputed dominance by orthodox thinking led to a drying up of critical language and of the ability to make complex comparisons among paradigms.

There are some reasons to think, then, that a relaunch of the debate among economists could be encouraged by a return to a simple method of comparing alternative theories, which was widely adopted during the 20th century (see, for example, Hahn and Matthews 1964). This method consists of a compara-tive approach based on the use of just one system of equations for all the theo-ries examined. The transition from one theory to another takes place through modification of the functional forms of equations and reversal of the positions of exogenous and endogenous variables, which also implies a reversal in the logical relations between them. The initial system of equations thus acts as a sort of *stereogram*: very different conclusions will be reached in terms of economic analysis and policy in relation to the viewpoint from which they are examined. While this method of comparison does not, of course, make it possible to examine the entire range of epistemological differences among the approaches compared, it presents the unquestionable advantage of immediacy by showing that apparently marginal changes in hypotheses can lead to completely different deductions. This is hardly surprising, as the choice of the exogenous variables, on which this method is based, is considered crucial by many for the correct specification of an economic theory (Dobb 1973; Garegnani 1990; Kurz and Salvadori 2002). This comparative method can be applied at various levels and in different areas of economic analysis. For example, in the field of pure theory it allows us to prove, even within one-sector models of growth and distribu-tion, that attempts to consider the classical theory of prices as merely a special case of neoclassical theory are marred by mistakes and misunderstandings and that actually they are radically alternative approaches (Brancaccio 2010).

3. "Anti-Blanchard": a comparative approach in the sphere of teaching

A fruitful use of the comparative method can also be made in the sphere of teaching by applying it to Blanchard's well-known version of the mainstream AS-AD macroeconomic model (Blanchard 2000; Blanchard et al. 2010). It is possible to show how some basic differences between mainstream and alternative approaches to economic theory and policy can be summarized in the mere choice of the endogenous and exogenous variables and modification of functional forms of equations in the AS-AD model. The choice of exogenous variables and functional forms of the same system of equations allows us to skip from Blanchard's macroeconomic model to a reversed version of it, which has been defined "Anti-Blanchard" (Amighini et al. 2012; Brancaccio and Califano 2018; see also Brancaccio and Saraceno 2017). This technique, as we shall see, allows us to highlight and criticize the hypotheses from which the prevailing macroeconomic theory derives some of its fundamental policy prescriptions.

Here we shall analyze only one example of the controversy over the hypotheses and related policy prescriptions of macroeconomic models. We shall apply the comparative method to see why the mainstream approach states that, at least in principle, an economic crisis could be solved by spontaneous market forces through monetary wage and price deflation, while the alternative paradigm suggests that the same forces may not work in the right way and in some cases could even drag the economic system into a debt deflation crisis. For this purpose, we summarize the AS-AD model in the following two equations:

$$AS : P = \frac{(1+m)}{A} P_{t-1} \left[1 - a \left(1 - \frac{Y}{AL} \right) + z \right]$$

$$AD : Y = bE + c \left(\frac{M}{P} \right)$$

where P represents the price level, m is a mark-up coefficient, A denotes labor productivity, L is the total workforce given by the sum of employed and unemployed workers, Y represents the real GDP, z could be interpreted as a "rate of conflict" of workers, E represents the autonomous components of aggregate expenditure, M is the money supply, b is the multiplier of autonomous expenditure, c is the multiplier of monetary policy, and a represents the sensitivity of wage claims to the unemployment rate given by $(1 - Y/AL)$. The AD equation describes a typical macroeconomic equilibrium in which production depends on autonomous expenditure and its multiplier, and the expenditure is also influenced by the real quantity of money. The AS equation derives from the price equation $P = (1 + m)W/A$, where the bargained monetary wage W is assumed to be an increasing function of the parameter of conflict and a decreasing function of the unemployment rate: $W = P_{t-1} [1 - a(1 - Y/AL) + z]$.

This price equation is a relevant feature of Blanchard's model, which has an impact on the determination not only of absolute prices but also relative prices and income distribution. This prerogative might be interpreted as a potential departure from the neoclassical conception of relative prices founded on utility and scarcity and a possible theoretical bridge for a fruitful dialogue with those alternative schools of thought which determine relative prices on the basis of costs. Finally, P_{t-1} represents the expected price level under the simplest assumption of static expectations.

In Blanchard's version of the AS–AD model, the terms m, a, z, b, c are all assumed to be greater than zero. The only unknowns are Y and P; the other terms are exogenous, being either parameters or variables chosen by policy-makers. The term $c > 0$ incorporates an inverse relationship between the price level and aggregate expenditure: deflation, in other words, should provoke an increase in demand. The assumption of both z and m as exogenous variables can be interpreted in the sense that there is no interaction between the rate of conflict of workers and the mark-up and related distribution of aggregate income. In this model, monetary wages and prices are stabilized and expecta-tions are realized ($P_t = P_{t-1}$) when real wages demanded by workers are equal to real wages that firms determine by means of mark-up: $W/P_t = [1 - a(1 - Y/AL) + z]$ and $W/P_t = A/(1 + m)$, then $A/(1 + m) = 1 - a(1 - Y/AL) + z$. Under given assumptions of functional forms, in this case the system admits a unique "natural" equilibrium:

$$Y_n = \frac{A\left[A + (a - z - 1)(1 + m)\right]}{a(1 + m)}L$$

$$P_n = \frac{acM(1 + m)}{A\left[A + (a - z - 1)(1 + m)\right]L - abE(1 + m)}$$

We may thus observe that the "natural" level of production Y_n is determined solely by A, z, m, a, L and is not influenced by aggregate expenditure E and money supply M, which only contribute to fix the price level P_n. One of the implications of this model is that if an economic crisis occurs, a market econ-omy should be able to emerge spontaneously, without the help of expansion-ary fiscal and monetary policies, to support aggregate demand. To illustrate, we can assume that a sudden change in the "animal spirits" of entrepreneurs reduces the autonomous expenditure E. According to Blanchard's version of the AS–AD model, market forces will push down the monetary wage and the price level to the point where aggregate demand will return to a level cor-responding to natural production. The reduction in E, therefore, will cause a change in the equilibrium level of P without affecting natural production and other real variables in any way. Blanchard admits that the adjustment process can be slow and bumpy, but he seems to believe that the natural equilibrium, in the last instance, is stable (Blanchard 2000).

Let us now apply the comparative method. The conclusions of Blanchard's AS-AD model radically change if we assume, for example, that there is no clear relationship between prices and aggregate demand, a hypothesis that can be summarized in the assertion that $c = 0$ and that m, instead of being exogenous, can be influenced by the rate of conflict z. In this "Anti-Blanchard" case, for any given P_{t-1} the equilibrium corresponds to:

$$Y = bE$$

$$1 + m = \frac{A}{1 - a\left(1 - \dfrac{bE}{AL}\right) + z}$$

As we can see, in this case the level of production Y depends exclusively on the multiplier and on the autonomous expenditure. In addition, the mark-up m and thus the distribution of income are determined endogenously and are dependent on the parameter of conflict of workers z. Finally, it can be noted that in this different theoretical structure the level of current prices P can be determined only in light of the level of the previous period. In the equilibrium, the production level and the mark-up m have been determined. Although extremely simplified and indicative of only one of several possible outcomes, this alternative system refers to a type of solution very different from the typical "natural" equilibrium of mainstream macroeconomics. Rather, we could call it a "conflicting" type of equilibrium, in which the level of income is based on the Keynesian principle of effective demand, and its distribution is influenced by the state of power relationships between social classes (Amighini et al. 2012; Brancaccio and Califano 2018). In this different scenario, it should be noted that a sudden collapse in the autonomous expenditure E implies a fall in the equilibrium level of output Y. Then, the fall of Y causes an increase in the unemployment rate $(1 - Y/AL)$ and an associated decline in the wages demanded by workers $W/P = [1 - a(1 - Y/AL) + z]$, which in this case will result in an increase in the mark-up m and related income distribution. The crisis, therefore, changes the equilibrium level and distribution of aggregate income, and it will not in any way be overcome by means of a price deflation.

Once again, the comparative approach helps us to understand that some formal changes in the AS-AD standard model, only seemingly minor, can lead to a reversal of results from the point of view of economic analysis and of its political implications.

4. Further comparisons between alternative paradigms: monetary policy rules

The comparative approach to economic analysis can also be successfully used in other contexts, such as the descriptive analysis of monetary policy. For example, it is possible to reverse the so-called "Taylor rule" (Taylor 1993) or other traditional monetary policy rules to suggest a different interpretation of the actual behavior of monetary authorities. According to this alternative view, central bankers are no longer considered to be managers of nominal income, inflation or real GDP to keep them near their "natural" equilibrium levels; rather, their actual behavior is interpreted as a regulation of a social conflict between solvent and potentially insolvent economic units which influence, among other things, the processes of capital centralization (Brancaccio and Fontana 2013, 2016).

The Taylor rule equation is embedded in a conceptual framework that appears to have won acceptance since the late 1990s and can be encapsulated in the following assertions (Taylor 2000). First, the economy tends in the long run towards a "natural" equilibrium that can be correctly described by the condition of proportional growth of the neoclassical model of Solow (1956) or one of its many variants, such as those based on Cass-Koopmans dynamic optimization models. However, due to imperfections and asymmetries that cause prices to become temporarily rigid, a trade-off emerges in the short run that can give rise to fluctuations of the system around the natural equilibrium. The scale of fluctuations depends, among other things, on the monetary policy decisions of the central banker. These decisions can be interpreted in terms of monetary policy "rules", according to which the nominal interest rate constitutes the policy tool, and the stabilization of real GDP and inflation near their equilibrium levels represents the goal of the central banker. The last of these propositions precisely describes the Taylor rule equation. These assertions represent the kernel of current mainstream macroeconomic thinking and can be summarized in the following system of equations.

The model describes an economic system closed to foreign trade. The actors taken into consideration are workers, firms and their owners regarded as a whole, and the central bank. Regarding technology, the simplified case in which a single good is produced by means of labor and the good itself is considered. Where not specified, the period of reference is t. K is the quantity of the good available as capital and therefore for use as a means of production, L the quantity of homogeneous labor employed and Y the physical quantity of the good produced. Therefore, the production function can be defined as $Y = F (K, L)$. The rate of capital depreciation is assumed to be equal to one, which means that the means of production are exhausted within the space of a single period. It is also assumed that the production function has constant returns to scale. By positing $\alpha = 1/L$ and defining $k = K/L$, the quantity of product per unit of labor employed is: $y = f(k)$, where $y = f(k) = Y/L$. It is assumed that this function is continuous and differentiable and that the following conditions are met: $f(0) = 0, f'(k) > 0, f''(k) < 0$. It is assumed that the income produced is shared entirely between profit-earners and wage-earners. Using W to denote the monetary wage, r the own rate of interest on capital and P the monetary price of the only good produced, it follows that $PY = WL + (1 + r)PK$. Dividing the whole by PL, then:

(1) $\quad f(k) = \dfrac{W}{P} + (1+r)k$

Second, it is assumed that labor and capital are remunerated in proportion to their respective marginal productivity. This can be expressed as follows in per capita terms:

(2) $\quad f'(k) = 1 + r$

The final element to be considered is the equation of equilibrium between produced income and expenditure, all of which are expressed in physical terms: $Y = C + I + Z$. The term $C = (1 - s)Y$ indicates consumption as a function of income Y and the propensity to save s. The term $I = (1 + g)K$ indicates investment, which corresponds to the replenishment and growth of capital at the rate of accumulation g. Finally, Z represents real autonomous expenditure that does not generate productive capacity (for example, autonomous private consumption). The model also assumes that the income produced and saved is transformed entirely into investment. The equilibrium of production and expenditure is therefore given by $sY = (1 + g)K + Z$. This is divided once again by L to express the whole in per capita terms. In equilibrium of proportional growth $g = g_n$, where g_n is the growth rate of the workforce. By defining $z = Z/Y$, then it is:

(3) $\quad sf(k) = (1 + g_n)k + z$

The system of equations (1), (2) and (3) concisely describes the well-known neoclassical model of growth developed by Solow (1956). Given the customary hypotheses regarding production technology, it is shown that the economy tends towards the equilibrium of proportional growth. The exogenous variables required to determine this equilibrium are z, s and g_n. Regarding the endogenous variables, equation (3) determines k, while r and W/P are obtained from (2) and (1), respectively. Moreover, for every given period of time t, it is also possible to determine the equilibrium levels of the absolute magnitudes. Given the growth rate of the workforce, if the hypothetical initial endowment of labor L_0 is known, then the current endowment of labor L can also be determined. Once L is known, with k and $f(k)$ being already determined, the levels of K and Y will also be determined. In accordance with a tradition well established in neoclassical economics, the values corresponding to the equilibrium of proportional growth will be defined from now on as values of "natural" equilibrium and therefore marked with an asterisk (r^*, Y^*, ...).

Once the equilibrium of the growth model has been determined, it is necessary to examine the possible temporary deviations from it. To this end, g_d

is used to represent the percentage deviation of current production Y from the natural level Y^* deriving from Solow's equilibrium: $g_d = (Y_{t+1} - Y_t^*)/Y_t^*$. Assuming that $u = Y/Y^*$ and taking into account that $Y^* = Kf(k)/k$, the term g_d can always be related to the rate of accumulation g on the basis of the following relation: $1 + g_d = u(1 + g)$. It is now possible to introduce the so-called Taylor rule equation, according to which the central banker sets the nominal interest rate i on the basis of the divergence of current inflation π from a specific target rate π^T, and on the basis of the percentage deviation g_d of current production from its level of natural equilibrium. One typical formulation of the rule is the following:

$$i - \pi = r^* + \theta\left(\pi - \pi^T\right) + \lambda g_d$$

The term r^* represents the natural real interest rate derived from the equilibrium of proportional growth. The Taylor rule equation shows that if inflation rises above the target and production above its natural level, the central bank will tend to set a nominal interest rate that must, net of inflation, be higher than the natural interest rate. The opposite course of action is taken if the opposite conditions prevail. A central bank can stabilize the economy by raising the nominal interest rate more than one-for-one in response to a higher level of inflation. If, instead, current inflation coincides with the target $(\pi = \pi^T)$ and current production Y with the natural level Y^* (for which $g_d = 0$), the nominal interest rate net of inflation must coincide with the natural interest rate. The Taylor rule equation can then be re-written as follows:

(4) $$i = \left(r^* - \theta\pi^T\right) + \left(1 + \theta\right)\pi + \lambda g_d$$

In accordance with Taylor's assertions, two particular versions of the *IS*-type equation and Phillips equation are introduced into the model. The *IS*-type of equation describes an inverse relation between the nominal interest rate i minus the current rate of inflation π, and the deviation g_d of current production from its natural level:

(5) $$g_d = g_0 - \beta\left(i - \pi\right)$$

The Phillips curve defines a direct relation between the deviation of production from its natural level and the rate of variation of inflation $\Delta\pi$:

(6) $$\Delta\pi = \phi g_d$$

It is possible at this point to complete the solution of the system. Given the target rate of inflation, and assuming that the current rate of inflation was determined at the end of the previous period, (4) and (5) simultaneously determine the nominal interest rate i and the deviation g_d of production from its natural level. Finally, once g_d is known, (6) determines the rate of variation of inflation $\Delta\pi$.

The system of equations (1) to (6) thus constitutes a typical mainstream macroeconomic model, which highlights the logical dependency of the Taylor rule equation on the typical equilibrium solution of proportional growth derived from Solow's neoclassical model. It is possible, however, to formulate an equation similar to (4) within a theoretical context alternative to the mainstream model. The alternative model presented here has the following basic features. Starting with the equation of income produced: $PY = WL + (1 + r)PK$ and dividing the whole by PL, it follows that:

(1') $$f(k) = \frac{W}{P} + (1+r)k$$

Regarding technology, it is assumed here that there is only one production technique, which corresponds, in conditions of normal utilization of productive capacity, to $k = K/L$ and $f(k) = Y/L$. It therefore follows that:

(2') $$k = \overline{k}$$

It is now assumed that the exogenous rate of profit r represents "normal" distribution, which depends on a set of political and institutional factors and ultimately on the balance of power between different macroeconomic agents. For every given monetary wage W, equations (1') and (2') therefore make it possible to determine not only the normal level of the real wage but also the monetary price P corresponding to normal distribution. It is also assumed, however, that actual distribution may persistently deviate from its normal value. The reason is that changes in monetary wages and prices or in the use of productive capacity can determine continuous changes in the current rate of profit. The deviation of the current profit r_t from the normal rate r is represented by $\gamma = r_t/r$. Finally, it is assumed that workers save a share s_w of their income, and firms and their owners save a share s_f of theirs, with $s_f > s_w$. Given all these hypotheses, the macroeconomic equilibrium is defined as follows:

$$WL + (1+\gamma r)P_{t-1}K = (1 - s_w)WL + (1 - s_f)(1+\gamma r)P_{t-1}K + (1 + g)PK + PZ$$

By dividing the whole by PY, defining the total amount of the rate of inflation as $(P/P_{t-1}) = (1 + \pi)$ and rearranging the terms, the condition of macroeconomic equilibrium is:

(3') $$1+\gamma r = \frac{(1+\pi)}{s_f}\left[1 + g + z\frac{f(k)}{k} - s_w\frac{W/P}{k}\right]$$

At this point, it may be worth considering the problem of solvency. For the sake of simplicity, it is assumed that at the end of the current period firms must repay to banks the loans obtained in the previous period for investment. At the end of each period, firms are solvent (on average) if their incomes and the loans they obtain are greater than or equal to their expenditures, repayments of previous loans and net acquisitions of assets:

$$WL + (1+\gamma r)P_{t-1}K + FL \geq (1 - s_f)(1+\gamma r)P_{t-1}K +$$
$$(1+g)PK + (1+i)FL_{t-1} + WL + NA$$

where FL represents the loans obtained and NA is the net acquisition of assets by firms in the current period. If it is assumed that in the aggregate $NA = 0$ and that the owners of firms do not finance consumption by means of debts, then the amount of loans in each period corresponds to:

$$FL = (1+g)PK + \lambda(1+i)FL_{t-1}$$
$$FL_{t-1} = (1+g)P_{t-1}K_{t-1} + \lambda_{t-1}(1+i)FL_{t-2}$$

The term λ represents the degree of "financial instability" in Minsky's sense and indicates to what extent firms draw on refinancing. This parameter does not simply reflect the behavior of firms. Rather, it depends on the orientation of the institutions that regulate the financial system. When $\lambda = 0$ firms can be considered "hedge" borrowers because they pay back all maturing loans and relative interests at the end of each period. When $\lambda \leq 1/(1 + i)$ firms can be defined as "speculative" borrowers because instead of refunding all the debt, they demand and obtain a renewal of the loan on part of the capital borrowed. When $1/(1 + i) \leq \lambda \leq 1$ firms are "ultra-speculative" or "Ponzi" borrowers because they rely on a renewal of the loan, not only on capital but also on interest due. Following the literature on the "financial instability hypothesis", it is assumed that after a period of "financial tranquility" public authorities tend to loosen their controls over the financial system and economic agents move from hedge to speculative positions. To examine the effects of this change, the degree of financial instability of the previous period is set at $\lambda_{t-1} = 0$. On the basis of these definitions and hypotheses, the average solvency condition of firms becomes:

$$(1-\lambda)(1+i) \leq s_f(1+\gamma r)$$

By substituting (3′) in the solvency condition, remembering (1′), considering πg and πr negligible, and imposing the symbol of strict equality, it follows that:

$$(4') \qquad i = \left(\frac{1}{1-\lambda}\right)\left[1 + s_w(1+r) + \left(1 + (z - s_w)\frac{f(k)}{k}\right)\pi + g\right] - 1$$

The alternative scheme described by equations (1′) to (4′) is complete at this point. There is in fact no space left for a re-visitation of equations (5) and (6) of the mainstream model because the alternative approach presented here denies the existence of deterministic causal relations between interest rates and aggregate demand, and between aggregate demand and variations in inflation. The solution of the alternative system is thus as follows: given k, W and r, (1′) and (2′) determine P and therefore W/P too; with P known and P_{t-1} given from the previous period, π will also be determined; given g from the autonomous decisions of firms, and assuming that z is also given, (3′) determines γ and then the current rate of profit γr capable of ensuring macroeconomic equilibrium; finally, (4′) determines the rate of monetary interest compatible with the average solvency condition of firms.

Remembering that it is always possible to relate the deviation g_d of current production from its normal level to the rate of capital accumulation g, it is not difficult to note a formal similarity between equation (4′) and equation (4), representing the Taylor rule. It is, however, important to clarify that the meaning of (4′) changes radically in this context with respect to the original equation. Taylor sees the optimal rule described by (4) as indicating the intention of the central banker to calibrate interest rates in relation to the objective of ensuring the stability of inflation around the target rate and the convergence of income towards its natural rate equilibrium. Within the alternative approach, (4′) instead assigns to the central bank the very different task of adjusting interest rates in relation to the average conditions of the solvency of firms. In other words, (4′) can be seen as a sort of "solvency rule" for the monetary authorities. By following this rule, the central banker assumes the role of "regulator" of a social conflict of production and distribution between firms that are capable of accumulating profits much higher than interest rates, and hence that are abundantly solvent, and firms that tend to make losses and hence become insolvent. The higher the interest rates set by monetary policy with respect to that deriving from (4′), the greater the number of firms at risk of insolvency and the greater the probability of a tendency towards bankruptcies, takeovers and hence the "centralization" of capital in the sense of Marx (1976 [1867]). The solvency rule then reveals a link between monetary policy and the conflicting and hierarchical relationships among firms, which does not find a place in the standard model (Brancaccio and Fontana 2013, 2016).

For a textbook description of the comparison between the Taylor rule and the solvency rule, see also the "Anti-Blanchard" (Brancaccio and Califano 2018).

5. Which paradigm fits better with the data? Some empirical tests

The comparative approach described thus far raises an important issue: once the existence of different paradigms of economic theory and policy is admitted, which of them can be considered more consistent with the reality of contemporary capitalism? Which general view better responds to facts? Here we have no intention of dealing with complex problems of scientific research methodology; neither do we intend to analyze the characteristics of such problems in the field of economic science. We here simply observe that the comparative approach described in these pages helps to create a framework that allows two conflicting theories to be put under the same test of empirical verification, and in this way may provide some element to clarify which part of the theory is relatively less resistant to this test. The empirical test, in this case, would be used to choose between different causal relations implied in different paradigms and related selections of exogenous variables and functional forms. Of course, the study of the nexus between causal theoretical relations and empirical analysis raises complex epistemological questions (see, for example, Moneta et al. 2011). This is one of the reasons that it is not possible to choose between different causal relationships implied in different theoretical paradigms only on the basis of empirical testing. This does not allow us to overlook, however, the fact that some empirical analyses seem to contradict the causal relations suggested by mainstream macroeconomics and to support an interpretation of economic reality more consistent with the choice of exogenous variables and functional forms proposed by critical approaches to economic theory.

A well-known example, in this sense, comes from the empirical literature on the relationship between Employment Protection Legislation (EPL) and the unemployment rate. Data indicate that the statistical correlation between the two variables turns out to be zero or even negative: a decrease in EPL is not related at all to reductions in unemployment. This evidence emerges from various studies (see, for example, OECD 1999, 2004; Boeri and Van Ours 2008). Even Blanchard clearly acknowledged that these two magnitudes are broadly uncorrelated in the empirical literature (Blanchard 2006). Moreover, it is interesting to note that some econometric analyses of panel data with fixed effects, able to take into account the heterogeneity between countries, estimate a significant inverse linear relationship between the unemployment rate and EPL (Suppa 2018).Without claiming to give explanatory value to teaching tools, it may be worth noting that this evidence is in line with the alternative "Anti-Blanchard" macroeconomic model described earlier rather than the standard one.

A further example comes from monetary analysis. It can be observed that empirical tests give support to the argument that central banks determine interest rates as a function of nominal income growth but deny that interest rates have a direct impact on aggregate spending and nominal income, and thus on real GDP and inflation. These findings are consistent with the overall pattern in which the so-called "solvency rule" is inscribed, although they seem to contradict equations (5) and (6) of the standard model from which the Taylor rule and all conventional monetary policy rules have their origins (Brancaccio et al. 2015).

The choice between paradigms is the result of complex interactions among epistemology, history, theory and statistics. Empirical analysis can never be considered as a definitive test. However, it is interesting to note that empirical tests seem to raise further doubts about the heuristic relevance of mainstream macroeconomics and therefore increase the urgency of stimulating a renewed comparison between alternative approaches to economic theory and policy.

References

Amighini, A., Brancaccio, E., Giavazzi, F., and Messori, M. (2012). A New Textbook Approach to Macroeconomics: A Debate. *Rivista di Politica Economica*, luglio-settembre, VII–IX, pp. 101–129.

Blanchard, O.J. (2000). *Macroeconomics*, 2nd ed. Harlow, UK: Pearson Education Company.

Blanchard, O.J. (2006). European Unemployment: The Evolution of Facts and Ideas. NBER Working Paper No. 11750. November 2005.

Blanchard, O.J. (2008). The State of Macro. *NBER* Working Paper No. 14259.

Blanchard, O.J., Amighini, A., and Giavazzi, F. (2010). *Macroeconomics: A European Perspective*. Harlow, UK: Pearson Education Limited.

Boeri, T., and van Ours, J. (2008). *The Economics of Imperfect Labor Markets*. Princeton, NJ: Princeton University Press.

Brancaccio, E. (2010). On the Impossibility of Reducing the Surplus Approach to a Neo-Classical Special Case. A Criticism of Hahn in a Solowian Context. *Review of Political Economy*, 22(3), pp. 405–418.

Brancaccio, E., and Califano, A. (2018). *Anti-Blanchard Macroeconomics. A Comparative Approach*. Cheltenham, UK: Edward Elgar..

Brancaccio, E., and Fontana, G. (eds.) (2011). *The Global Economic Crisis. New Perspectives on the Critique of Economic Theory and Policy*. London and New York: Routledge.

Brancaccio, E., and Fontana, G. (2013). Solvency Rule versus Taylor Rule: An Alternative Interpretation of the Relation between Monetary Policy and the Economic Crisis. *Cambridge Journal of Economics*, 37(1), pp. 17–33.

Brancaccio, E., and Fontana, G. (2016). "Solvency Rule" and Capital Centralisation in a Monetary Union. *Cambridge Journal of Economics*, 40(4), pp. 1055–1075.

Brancaccio, E., Fontana, G., Lopreite, M., and Realfonzo, R. (2015). Monetary Policy Rules and Directions of Causality: A Test for the Euro Area. *Journal of Post Keynesian Economics*, 38(4), pp. 509–531.

Brancaccio, E., and Saraceno, F. (2017). Evolutions and Contradictions in Mainstream Macroeconomics: The Case of Olivier Blanchard. *Review of Political Economy*, 29(3), pp. 345–359.

Dobb, M. (1973). *Theories of Value and Distribution since Adam Smith*. Cambridge, UK: Cambridge University Press.

Fitoussi, J.P., and Stiglitz, J. (2009). *The Ways Out of the Crisis and the Building of a More Cohesive World*. The Shadow GN, Chair's Summary, LUISS Guido Carli, Rome, May 6–7, 2009.

Garegnani, P. (1990). Classical versus marginalist analysis. In Bharadwaj, K. and Schefold, B. (eds) *Essays on Piero Sraffa*. London: Routledge.

Godley, W., and Lavoie, M. (2006). *Monetary Economics: An Integrated Approach to Credit, Money, Income, Production and Wealth*. Basingstoke, UK: Palgrave Macmillan.

Graziani, A. (2003). *The Monetary Theory of Production*. Cambridge, UK: Cambridge University Press.

Hahn F., and Matthews R.C.O. (1964). The Theory of Economic Growth: A Survey. *Economic Journal*, 74, pp. 779–902.

IMF Survey (2015). Interview with Olivier Blanchard: Looking Forward, Looking Back. *IMF Survey Magazine: IMF Research*, August 31.

International Monetary Fund (2012). *World Economic Outlook, October.* Washington, DC: IMF.

International Monetary Fund (2014). *World Economic Outlook, October.* Washington, DC: IMF.

International Monetary Fund and International Labour Organization (2010). The Challenges of Growth, Employment and Social Cohesion. Joint ILO-IMF conference in cooperation with the office of the Prime Minister of Norway, Olso, 13 September 2010.

Kurz, H.D., and Salvadori, N. (1995). *Theory of Production: A Long-Period Analysis.* Cambridge, UK: Cambridge University Press.

Kurz, H.D., and Salvadori, N. (2002). "Classical" vs. "Neo-Classical" Theories of Value and Distribution and the Long-Period Method. In Hahn, F. and Petri, F. (eds) *General Equilibrium. Problems and Prospects.* London: Routledge.

Leontief, W. (1977). *Future of the World Economy: A United Nations Study.* New York: Oxford University Press.

Lucarelli, S., and Lunghini, G. (2012). *The Resistible Rise of Mainstream Economics.* Bergamo, Italy: Bergamo University Press and Sestante.

Marx, K. (1976 [1867]). *Capital*, vol. I. Harmondsworth, UK: Penguin.

Minsky, H.P. (1986). *Stabilizing an Unstable Economy.* New Haven, CT: Yale University Press.

Moneta, A., Chlaß, N., Entner, D., and Hoyer, P. (2011). Causal Search in Structural Vector Autoregressive Models. *Journal of Machine Learning Research: Workshop and Conference Proceedings*, 12, pp. 95–118.

OECD (1999). *Employment Outlook.* Paris: OECD.

OECD (2004). *Employment Outlook.* Paris: OECD.

Pasinetti, L. (2007). *Keynes and the Cambridge Keynesians. A "Revolution in Economics" to be Accomplished.* Cambridge, UK: Cambridge University Press.

Skidelsky, R. (2010). The Crisis of Capitalism: Keynes Versus Marx. *Indian Journal of Industrial Relations*, 45(3), pp. 321–335.

Solow, R.M. (1956). A Contribution to the Theory of Economic Growth. *The Quarterly Journal of Economics*, 70(1), pp. 65–94.

Suppa, D. (2018). Appendix 1. Labour Flexibility and Unemployment. In Brancaccio, E., and Califano, A. (eds.) *Anti Blanchard Macroeconomics. A Comparative Approach.* Cheltenham, UK: Edward Elgar.

Tabellini, G. (2009). Il mondo torna a correre. L'Italia non si fermi. In *Il Sole 24 Ore*, Lezioni per il futuro.

Taylor, J.B. (1993). Discretion versus policy rules in practice. Amsterdam: North Holland, Carnegie-Rochester Conference Series on Public Policy, 39, pp. 195–214.

Taylor, J.B. (2000). Teaching Macroeconomics at the Principles Level. *American Economic Review*, 90(2), pp. 90–94.

Part II

Alternative theories

3 The originality of the Italian debate on Marx

Riccardo Bellofiore and Tommaso Redolfi Riva

In this chapter we will focus our attention on some key moments of the Italian debate on Marx. We shall concentrate mainly on the discussion among economists after 1960, the year when *Production of Commodities by Means of Commodities* was published.[1] Our perspective does not have an antiquarian intention: Italian debate on Marx is not a theoretical relic that can only be used to shed light on a concluded political and historical stage. On the contrary, Italian debate on Marx is still alive and represents an on-going laboratory to find original elaborations of problems regarding our present ones. What follows can be seen as a "backwards reading" in Sraffa's sense. We will read past debates from a contemporary perspective, i.e. from what we think are the relevant open issues today.

1. Value and the falling rate of profit: Croce and Gramsci

It is useful to begin with two important authors and with their contributions written between the end of the 19th and the first half of the 20th centuries: Benedetto Croce and Antonio Gramsci. In both cases we shall focus on how these interpreters look at the theory of value and at the falling rate of profit.

What is interesting is Croce's mostly positive appreciation of the theory of value. His idea is that Marx's "sociological" approach has to be set alongside, and not against, the pure economics of marginalism. The fundamental point of Marxian value theory is its "elliptical comparison" between a "working society" in which the whole value produced is allotted to the workers, and the "capitalist society" where there is a deduction from workers' income explaining the presence of a surplus value. On the other hand, Croce is very critical of the Marxian theory of the falling rate of profit, because for him technical progress determines an increase in the rate of profit due to the devaluation of the prices of the elements of constant capital, which is complemented by the devaluation of variable capital.[2]

Gramsci denies the possibility of an integration of a general theory of economics with the critique of political economy. Gramsci rather insists on the macro-social, and not individualistic, nature of the Marxian approach. Marx makes use of the Ricardian concept of "determined market": a determined relation of social forces in a determined structure of the productive apparatus, this relationship being guaranteed (that is, rendered permanent) by a determined political, moral and juridical superstructure. About the falling rate of profit, Gramsci criticises the interpretation in terms of collapse theory. The stress is on the notion of the "tendential" character of the law, which Gramsci sees as historically determined in its development. According to Gramsci, it should be re-read against the background of Taylorism and Fordism understood as "progressive" attempts to overcome the effects of the increase of constant capital.[3]

2. Traditional Marxism: Dobb, Sweezy and Meek

From the 1940s onwards, the *koinè* in the interpretation of Marxian economic theory was the one later labelled as "traditional Marxism". The most important exponents were Maurice Dobb, Paul Marlor Sweezy and, later, Ronald Meek. The starting point for traditional Marxism is that "abstract labour" has to be understood as a mental generalisation; the theory of value is an equilibrium approach; the transformation from (exchange) values to prices (of production) is the transition from a first to a second approximation of relative exchange ratios.

On this background, *Capital* Volume I has to do with the first approximation about the macro-class distribution of the objectification of labour in capitalism. This discourse is developed at a high level of abstraction and abstracts from the differences in the value composition among the different competing capitals. At this initial layer of the argument, the division of the new value produced between (gross) profits and wages is shown to be the result of workers' "exploitation". The problem arises of whether *Capital* Volume 3 – the second approximation, characterised by a lower level of abstraction and a higher level of concreteness – confirms that thesis or not.

Maurice Dobb,[4] commenting on Sraffa's book, declares that *Production of Commodities* is in absolute agreement with this Marx. The substance of the theoretical argument is supported and the conclusions are confirmed in an updated contemporary version contrasting the neoclassical counter-revolution. Prices of production are related to the "objective" conditions of production, while the division between profits and wages manifests the antagonistic relationship between labour and capital.

3. Abstract labour as a "real abstraction": Lucio Colletti

In the Italian debate on Marx of the late 1960s and 1970s, an important role was played by some philosophers. The most influential among them was Lucio Colletti, especially in his writings between 1968 and 1970, when he departed from Galvano Della Volpe and developed a criticism of traditional Marxism. According to Colletti,[5] abstract labour cannot be reduced to a mental generalisation of the researcher. The "abstraction" is real and actual: it takes place daily in the circulation of commodities.

The theory of value is at the same time a theory of alienation and a theory of fetishism: as Colletti soon discovered, this meant that it is also based on dialectical contradiction, as in Hegel. It expresses the expropriation of the subjectivity within a topsy-turvy, inverted reality. Value, social unity becoming an object, leads to the paradox of the social bond as a self-positing relationship that posits itself independently of the individuals to whom it ought to relate and mediate – it is a relationship that becomes a thing, which, posited outside individuals, dominates them like God, though it is their own estranged social power.

Behind the relative exchange value there is a real *absolute* or *intrinsic* value, existing in the related things themselves – namely, a *hypostatisation of 'value'*. Answering the criticism by Myrdal and Joan Robinson, Colletti wrote that:

> Marx, *horribile dictu*, accepts the argument that value is a metaphysical entity, and merely confines himself to noting that it is the thing, i.e. the commodity itself or value, that is the scholastic entity . . . These contradictions are innate in the subject-matter, not in its verbal expression. This society based on capital and commodities is therefore the metaphysics, the fetishim, the "mystical world" – even more so than Hegel's *Logic* itself.[6]

That's why the value dimension fully exhibits the reality of capital already in *Capital* Volume I. For Colletti, Marx's value theory has to account not only for equilibrium but also for disequilibrium. If it is not a first approximation, what about prices? Famously Colletti concluded that Sraffa opened the door to that "revisionism" that made a bonfire of Marx's work.

4. Value and prices of production: Pierangelo Garegnani, Marco Lippi and Fernando Vianello

In the following we shall not give a chronological account of the subsequent Italian debate in the 1970s. We will rather look at it backwards, to provide a better understanding of the key conceptual turning points.

Let us begin with Pierangelo Garegnani. From an analytical point of view, Marx's political economy is seen as a direct revision and prolongation of Ricardo's theory: the rate of profit is defined as the (value of) social product minus the (value of) necessary consumption. The social relations of production are identified with the distribution between wages and profits. The problem that Ricardian-Marxian tradition has to solve is the determination of the rate of profit in a non-circular way, as in Smith. Marx's attempt was internal to the tradition of value as "contained labour": it failed because of the insufficiencies of the analytical and theoretical means available at the time. Though without any reference to the labour theory of value, Sraffa's paramount result is located exactly in this "core" of economic theory: the correct simultaneous determination of the prices of production, given either the subsistence wage or the outcome of distributive conflict, and given the objective/physical setting of the economic system. According to Garegnani, this analytical progress leaves untouched the other parts of Marx's economic theory, in particular his accumulation theory.[7] Two points, building a bridge with Keynes and radicalising the Neokeynesian-Cambridge tradition, are particularly interesting here: a) the circumstance that Sraffa's quantities are "given" is justified through effective demand which fixes the output; and b) the capacity utilisation rate has always to be considered as variable, which means that an increase in the rate of accumulation does not have to imply a necessary fall in workers' real wages. A perspective even more Ricardian than Garegnani's one is that developed by Pasinetti. A first moment in his argument is devoted to constructing a pure economic theory: as it happens in his structural dynamics, built-up from a model where labour is assumed to be the only factor of production. It follows a second moment in which he gives account of the specifications determined by the institutional context.

Marco Lippi's contribution to the debate has been dramatic.[8] His thesis is that Marx's labour theory of value is linked to a meta-historical, "naturalistic" dimension in which labour is the only "real" social cost. Value represents the form assumed by this cost in capitalism. According to Lippi, in Marx's theory of value there is a logical primacy of the laws of general production relative to the laws ruling with the market and capital. The "physiological" determination of labour effort gives way to an objective (and not a psychological) cost. This is what dominates Marx's theory of value, both as an attempt to determine the prices of production starting from labour-values and as the basis of the identity between the sum of values and the sum of prices (Marx's conservation principle of living and dead labour). Lippi deems that Marx's conclusions cannot be confirmed after Sraffa. It is true that in Sraffa the fetishistic nature of capitalist reality is even more pronounced than in *Capital*, but Marxian economic theory has no place anymore for a labour theory of value.

The contribution of Lippi can be placed side by side with the contributions of other young Sraffians that had expressed their ideas in some seminars, later published in a volume edited by Paolo Sylos Labini between the late 1960s and the early 1970s.[9] Among these young Sraffians it is important to remind ourselves of the arguments of Luca Meldolesi and Fernando Vianello. In his introduction to a collection of essays by Ludwig von Bortkiewitz, Meldolesi maintains that the labour theory of value is not necessary to defend Marx's notion of exploitation.[10] It is enough to show that "behind" gross profits there is a surplus labour – that is, a positive balance resulting from the amount of labour needed to produce the net product less the amount of labour needed to produce the wage-goods. Gross profit is seen as a "minus-wage", as a "deduction" from the situation in which the whole value of the net product is going to pay workers. This is an argument that, according to the testimony of Claudio Napoleoni, seems to correspond with Sraffa's ideas as expressed in a private conversation. The condition of possibility of a positive rate of profit is the existence of a positive surplus labour.

Fernando Vianello's point of view is even more interesting, particularly as it is stated in his 1970–73 writings.[11] He agrees with Colletti: commodities are values, i.e. nothing but contained labour. Nevertheless it is not necessary that the concept of value is prolonged into the concept of exchange-value (prices proportional to the labour contained in the commodities which have been sold on the market[12]) as a relative exchange-ratio coming before the price of production (prices that includes an equal rate of profit). Abstract labour is independent of exchange ratios and distribution. Given that for the economy as a whole "values" express qualitatively nothing but the labour contained in them, quantitatively the price rule cannot but reallocate among producers the objectification of living labour, i.e. the new value added in the period. In this way, Vianello breaks away not only from sequentialism but also from dualism, which was at the time the dominant position in the Marxist price theory. He was then able to maintain a fundamental link with the labour theory of value as the origin of (new) value, even if he criticised the traditional Marxist original argument seeing the labour theory of value as a macro theory of distribution between capital and labour.

5. Value and the social relations of production: Claudio Napoleoni

Claudio Napoleoni's position was intimately connected to Colletti in the early 1970s. Before going into that, a few words about his previous intellectual itinerary are in order.[13] In the 1950s, before the publication of Sraffa's masterpiece, Napoleoni advocated the complementarity of the neoclassical theory of value with the classicals and Marx. While the neoclassicals stress the role of scarcity and efficiency, the classicals and Marx insist on the moment of labour as negativity. According to the thought developed by Napoleoni in these years, the transformation problem does not express a logical contradiction between values and prices, but rather reflects a contradiction in the reality itself. In the 1960s, Napoleoni introduced, about 15 years before Steedman's *Marx after Sraffa*, the idea that labour-values are redundant in the determination of prices of production.

Napoleoni complained that the origin of (gross) profits remained unexplained in *Production of Commodities*. The generation of a surplus by the given methods of production (the given "productive configuration", in Napoleoni's terminology) could be explained thanks to the reference to the dynamic process of the generalisation of innovations. Since, in the "pure" logic of capital distributive conflicts are arbitrary, and hence the net product going to workers should be assumed to be zero, the surplus expresses nothing but a productivity of capital (in a non-neoclassical meaning). In capitalism exploitation comes from the permanence of rent: a permanence which is however necessary in order to prevent the breakdown of the system due to the insufficiency of (consumption) demand. The political outlook was that of a "proletarian management of capital" without the capitalists.

Napoleoni was the target of harsh attacks from some young Sraffians, in particular between 1970 and 1971, after the publication of the first edition of his book *Smith Ricardo Marx,* where these last conclusions were spelled out. Paradoxically, in the same years, after a profound self-criticism due to a deep re-reading of Marx after the publication of previously unpublished materials (*Grundrisse* and *Results of the Direct Production Process*), Napoleoni changed his mind and counter-attacked. Together with Colletti, he proposed a reconstruction of the Marxian labour theory of value as a (philosophic and economic) critical science of the capitalist totality. Without the labour theory of value, he now argued, it is impossible to maintain that profits (and not only rents) come from the exploitation of wage workers.[14]

Napoleoni's counter-attack was targeted at Luca Meldolesi and Fernando Vianello. The criticism against Meldolesi can be reduced to the idea that out of the labour theory of value (that is, the twin theses that the commodity product is originated by nothing else than labour and that the wage contains nothing else than necessary labour) there is no justification for bringing back surplus value to surplus-labour. Napoleoni's criticism against Vianello is even more noteworthy for our discourse. Vianello, as we have seen, wanted to preserve a strong association with Marx's concept of value. The objection against Vianello is that exchange-value is an essential mediation that cannot be cut. If this link is broken, Marx's qualitative analysis (value) is separated from quantitative analysis (price). The single commodities, being nothing else than values as long as they are produced for circulation, have to exchange one against the other, so they have to relate to each other as exchange-value: this is where the transformation problem emerges. In the early 1970s Napoleoni recognised it to be one of the "open" issues in Marxian theory (together with crisis theory, beyond collapse theory; and the nature of a communist society, beyond planning), without providing a convincing answer.

This train of thought, however, led Napoleoni into several different and interesting lines of research in 1971–1975, as proved by the archival materials in Turin: a tentative new "research programme" which would soon be abandoned. It is interesting to remind ourselves of at least two particular lines of research. The first is about the "form of value": the value content needs to be expressed in money as the universal equivalent. Napoleoni remains here on the grounds of qualitative intuition, even if he anticipates an important topic that will be at the heart of some new approaches to Marxian economic theory after 1980. At the same time we may see here a possible bridge to Graziani's theory of monetary circuit. The connection between (surplus-)value theory and the monetary circuit has been explored by some of his pupils since the end of the 1970s, by which time Napoleoni had already abandoned this research programme.

The second line of research is the idea that labour is "abstracted", not only in universal (final) circulation but also (and before that) in the "capital relation" going on between capital and wage workers. Hence Napoleoni's conclusion that abstract labour is wage labour producing commodities to be sold against money in generalised exchange. "Wage labour" is, on the one hand, the labour-power which is bought and sold on the labour market by the workers; and it is also, on the other hand, the living labour spent in immediate production by those same workers, reduced to nothing but "time's carcass" (Marx 2010). Though Napoleoni did not explicitly develop the implications, they are clear. Abstract labour is a process, not a state. Capitalists expect that the potential (capacity to) work attached to the workers they have hired is actualised as "labour in motion". Within production, workers' activity is not only concrete but is also abstract: "in becoming". And firms manipulate the material/technical side of production so that it corresponds to the formal/social relation: the same activity is form-determined. Even though they are still "immediately private labour", the collective workers organised by capitalist firms materialise their efforts in an (objectified) contained labour which is already "mediately social" by the expected exchange among things. These commodities are ideal money, subject to the "mortal leap" (cf. Marx 2010 [1859]) of their metamorphosis in real money, which is the incarnation of the only immediately social labour. And the ex post socialisation, the final validation of commodities against money as the universal equivalent, needs to be ante-validated by money as capital.

We will come back to this. At present, suffice it to say that this conceptual journey of the valorisation as value in process – that we have reconstructed from Napoleoni's early 1970s insights – resembles, once again, the monetary circuit as money in motion. It is full of uncertainties and conflicts, and probably is the reason why in these years Napoleoni states that the theory of value pertains not only to the equilibrium dimension but also to the disequilibrium; moreover, it is one with the theory of crisis.

6. Logic and history in *Capital*: Cesare Luporini

We introduced the role of Lucio Colletti in the discussion among economists. Another important input for some of the ensuing debate came from other Italian philosophers. The first to consider is Cesare Luporini.[15] During the 1960s, he began a dialogue with Althusser and his school. The emphasis was on the concept of "structure", which was employed to underline the "systematic" aspects of Marxian presentation in *Capital* as well as to attack the "invertebrate historicism" plaguing a large part of Italian approaches to Marx. Very soon, Luporini developed his "systematic" reading of Marx's value theory with a reference to the commodity and the form determination (rather than structure) in a Hegelian fashion.

Luporini saw in Marx a particular notion of "historicity" in the form of motion of capital as opposed to a too generic historicity that lies before and out of the system. In *Capital* he recognised two moments: the historical-genetic and the formal-genetic. The former moment is the presupposition of the theoretical construction: the empirical moment that has to be included in (and shaped) by the formal-genetic moment. It is only from this latter moment that it is possible to understand the distinctive historicity of capital. The historical concreteness that lies before, and out of, the systematic model is only a "rhapsody" that can be appreciated only when structured by means of a system able to assign "order and influence" to the different categories.

This interpretative perspective leads Luporini towards a logical reconstruction of the conceptual development in *Capital*. The priority of the formal-genetic moment can never be taken as a complete separation. This is confirmed when the historical-genetic moment "breaks into" the formal-genetic: as in the transition from the universal equivalent to the money-form; or in primitive accumulation grounding the separation between worker and the means of production. However, the "commodity" opening Marx's argument is not an empirical assumption; neither is it the commodity as it initially appeared in history: it is a specific conceptual form from which the whole systematic presentation begins. The scientific character of Marx's critique of political economy lies in the detection of a non-empirical (formal) access to the empirical.

The link between these two different levels – development of the forms; empirical processuality – depends on the fact that the empirical moment is the presupposition of the development of the forms, but the empirical moment is understood in its own dynamic only by means of the system. Engels proposed an alternative between a historical and a logical method, but this is a false opposition. Marx's method of presentation is a synthesis of logic and history which is able to produce theoretically the form of motion of capital, a logic which is historically specific and which has to be presupposed for every empirical historiography of capitalisms.

7. The method of presentation in *Capital*: Lorenzo Calabi and Alessandro Mazzone

Like Luporini a logical reading of the method of presentation in *Capital* is also put forward by Lorenzo Calabi.[16] His criticism is initially oriented to Engels' "historicist" misunderstanding of Marx's method in the transformation of values into prices of production: a confusion replicated by traditional Marxists like Meek. In his "historical" approach to the transformation problem, Engels argued that the law of value is only valid in a simple commodity production society, where workers own their means of production. In capitalism, where there is a separation of subjective and objective conditions of production, the law of value is substituted by the law of the prices of production. According to Calabi, instead, Marx deals from the outset of his presentation not with a simple commodity society but with capital.

Furthermore, Calabi is interested to show what he defines as the "irremediable dichotomy between political economy and its critique".[17] According to Calabi, Marx's critique of political economy cannot be coupled with the surplus approach: surplus is too generic a category to reveal the mode in which it is produced, since it lacks any determination of form. Marx was interested in the unique form in which surplus is produced and appropriated under capital.

Within a logical reading of the critique of political economy Alessandro Mazzone develops the role of ideology, outside the poor metaphor of structure and superstructure.[18] Within his reading of *Capital* the categories of political economy refer to objective manifestation of the system itself and are not just a subjective organisation of economic data. The task of a Marxian theory of ideology is to understand the formal structure of bourgeois consciousness like an objective moment of the system of capital. Bourgeois political economy cannot be reduced to illusion or false consciousness. It is necessary to recognise it and its shortcomings as a necessary and objective part of social capitalistic reproduction.

8. Value and the transformation as a pseudo-problem: Rodolfo Banfi

An original interpretation of the Marxian theory of value and of the transformation problem can be found in the contributions by Rodolfo Banfi. According to Banfi, in order to understand the transformation it is necessary to understand what distinguishes the Marxian theory of value from the classical theory of value.[19] Banfi develops a philosophically informed reading of *Capital* through the prism of the *Theories of Surplus-value* and the *Notes on Adolf Wagner*. In this latter work Marx writes that neither value nor exchange value are the subject of his presentation: the subject is the commodity. The theoretical development of the categories of use value, exchange value and value has to begin from the specific social structure in which the products of labour assume the form of commodity. From there we can see a triple separation going on: a) between production and consumption; b) between exchange value and use value;[20] and c) between value (social labour) and exchange value (as its own phenomenal form of manifestation). These separations are peculiar to the society where the effective contribution to total social labour of the single and separated unity of production can be assessed only *a posteriori*, in circulation as the system of exchanges of "things" among private producers.

Banfi proposes to understand the first three chapters of Marx's *Capital* as a "phenomenology" of exchange value: an investigation of how value presents itself on the market, in the use value of another commodity. The difference between value and exchange value has not been grasped by Marxists, and this confusion led to a misunderstanding about the role of the use value in the critique of political economy. If the labour privately spent within productive units is only mediately social, the condition for it to eventually become social rests in the "embodiment" in a use value of which there should be some (qualitatively and quantitatively determined) "social need". The occurence of this fact cannot be ascertained before the final commodity exchange.

Within the traditional approach to the "transformation", the phenomenology of the exchange value (the dialectical development of the genesis of the forms allowing value to exist) was erased, and the phenomenal forms of the manifestation of value were identified with value itself. From this outlook, to deduce a system of prices of production in the way Marx himself explored in *Capital* Volume 3 is an impossible task. Such a deduction is based on a relationship between the private expenditure of labour and value which contemplates only the immediate production process. It excludes by definition the possibility of the (partial or total) non-realisation of private expended labour in competition. If that happens, the product of labour will not (partially or totally) assume the form of value. The transformation problem is not, like Sweezy maintained, a secondary problem. It is a pseudo-problem, if Marx's theory of value is taken seriously.

9. Value and social need: Guido Carandini and Sandra Caliccia

A similar perspective is what we see at work in Guido Carandini. This author is extremely clear: it is necessary to argue with Marx against Marx.[21] In this article, and in his book published in 1971, he stresses the unique capitalist form of the allocation of labour in the different productive sectors.[22] There is no immediate correspondence between the commodities produced and "social need": this latter must be equipped with buying power. This can be stated in another way: there is no immediate relationship between the quantity of labour actually spent in commodity production within a particular branch of production, or even the quantity of labour spent according to the technical average, and the quantity of labour-time necessary to produce according to the social need. The Marxian concept of social need plays a crucial role in the definition of "socially necessary labour", which now has a double determination: on the one hand, labour with an average productivity; on the other, labour needed to satisfy a determined demand on the market.

On this view, the effective "magnitude" of value of a commodity is known only *after* the final exchange. Once again, as in Banfi, the transformation's procedure, as developed by Marx in chapter IX of *Capital* Volume 3, is incompatible with the theory of value of *Capital* Volume 1. The former presupposes that the magnitudes of values are known *ex ante*; the latter denies it. If the question is asked "what is the meaning of the theory of value, if it cannot provide the determination of prices of the commodities on the market", Carandini would answer that the law of value operates at an abstract social level not at the concrete level of individual exchanges. The law represents, at a level underlying prices, the social norm that rules the division of the whole social labour time.

Another relevant book on the same theoretical agenda is the one published by Sandra Caliccia.[23] She too reads the concept of "socially necessary labour time" going beyond the technical definition, in immediate production. The demand definition – where the socially necessary labour time depends on the social need equipped with buying power – looks at the condition of the realisation of immediately private labour into social labour. Caliccia argues that the line Dmitriev-Bortkiewicz-Sraffa, fails to acknowledge the *differentia specifica* of Marx's theory of value, read along the lines of Ricardo. Marx himself remains a Ricardian in chapter IX of *Capital* Volume 3.

10. Between Ricardo and Keynes: Giorgio Lunghini, Alessandro Roncaglia and Marcello Messori

Giorgio Lunghini, in an intervention in a debate at the Italian Society of the Economist "on the short and long period", presented an original reading which also dealt with the connection between production and circulation.[24] Marx was located between Ricardo and Keynes's *The General Theory*. Keynes was seen as one political (not vulgar) economist after Ricardo. Like the classicals his analysis is scientific but confined in the "superficial" moment of circulation. In the same years another enlightening interpretation was developed by Alessandro Roncaglia in his book *Sraffa and the Theory of Prices*.[25] For Roncaglia, the theoretical core of *Production of Commodities* gives a "snapshot" of the economic system – a picture taken "after the harvest" and before the actual exchange on the market. This account of Sraffa's theory is confirmed by the Sraffa Papers at the Wren Library, Cambridge, UK. It can be prolonged to claim a complementarity between Sraffa and Marx escaping the sterile diatribe about the continuity/discontinuity between the two authors. On this outlook, Sraffa examines the skeleton of the economic system, i.e. the relationship between prices and given methods of production. He confines his theoretical scheme to the phenomenal level, and this leaves open the possibility of an inquiry going deeper into the fundamental characteristics – we could even say, into the analysis of the "constitution" – of that system. This, of course, shifts the terrain of the discussion on Marx and Sraffa out of the petrified orthodoxies in both camps.

Although paradoxical, we can classify the contribution of Marcello Messori in a not too distinct line of reasoning: a pupil of Napoleoni in the early 1970s, who then worked with Graziani on the monetary circuit. In a 1979 book, Messori was very critical of Sraffa.[26] Accepting the Marxian labour theory of value and defending the idea of the essentiality of the exchange value, he rewrote the invariance condition for the transformation. Instead of the identity between the sum of values and the sum of prices, he proposed the equality between the net product measured in terms of "values" (value of labour-power + surplus value) and the net product measured in "prices" (wages and gross profits). The amount of living labour crystallised as direct (or present) labour – that is, the expression in money of the labour objectified during the period – is unchanging to the modification in the price rule. The paradox lies in the fact that Messori's normalisation fits well within a non-dualistic perspective like the one proposed by Vianello. In fact, the new invariance condition transforms Vianello's qualitative assumption into a quantitative determination, though this latter has yet to be theoretically grounded.

Messori, for some years, pursued a quantitative definition of exploitation before the final exchange on the commodity market. He wanted to avoid the reduction of (gross) profit to a simple "deduction" from the value of the net product, realised *ex post* on the market.[27] Like Napoleoni, he would admit his own failure. He attributed it to the fact that money, contrary to what Marx thought, is not essentially a commodity, but rather a sign.

11. Value and the monetary circuit: Augusto Graziani

The writings of Augusto Graziani between the end of the 1970s and the beginning of the 1980s play a crucial role in our survey. He implicitly adopted a Marxian stance, for example in 1982 when he cherished a subterranean Marxist stream in the monetary heterodoxy Wicksell-Schumpeter-Keynes – that is, the older circuit theory of money.[28] The reference was to the cycle of money capital in Volume 2, and to interest bearing capital in Volume 3. Later on, in 1983, he published in *l'Unità* an article whose title was very explicit: "Let's rehabilitate Marx's theory of value".[29] In the same year, Graziani wrote two papers on Marx's theory of money.[30]

To place Marx within a monetary circuit perspective implies a new look at the Marxian labour theory of value, reread as a macro-social and macro-monetary theory about capitalist production and reproduction. It also implies a reorientation of the monetary circuit approach: to put Marx within the circuit requires including the circuit in Marx. The macro-agents of Graziani's circuit are the two main social classes: on the one hand, capital, as "financial" capital (or monetary capital: the banking system) and as "industrial" capital (the totality of productive firms); and on the other, wage labour. The capitalist process is a monetary sequence opened by bank credit as sign–money: firms need finance from banks to buy labour-power and activate production. The money recovered by firms at the closure of the circuit could be less than the money capital advanced, as a consequence of hoarding: a bridge to Keynes, since the presence of a demand for money as a store of value is recognised as a possible origin of the crisis. The final finance that firms get back at the end of the circuit cannot be higher than the initial finance (unless reserves are disinvested). For Graziani, the production of abstract wealth (*Geld*, or money) could, however, exceed the capital advanced in circulation (Münze, or currency). The reason is that surplus value – that is, the value of all the commodities which are not made available to workers – encompasses the value of the new means of production, which are capital as long as their private ownership promises future positive returns (systemically, through the exploitation of living bearers of labour power).

According to Graziani, neither the Walrasian and nor the Sraffian schemes of price determination deal with "valorisation", properly speaking – that is, with the macro-social process of the extraction of new value (and surplus-value) from workers by capital. The object of inquiry of general economic equilibrium or of the surplus approach is, in Marxian terms, the determination of individual prices in competition. Valorisation concerns the social relation between capital as a whole versus the working class; in contrast, price determination has to do with the relative position of the many capitals when they compete to allocate the new value extracted from workers, to obtain an equal rate of profit. In a closed and macro setting, the vertically integrated firm sector has only one external purchase to do: to buy labour-power so that capitalist production gets going.

The circumstance that money as capital is a sign – hence, that it is valueless in itself – does not create any problems, at least in Graziani's interpretation.

Initial finance is regulated by the wage bill at the subsistence level. The value of the bank credit advanced to firms is then the labour required to produce the real wage of the working class. The production process yields a potential money output, whose value corresponds to the total labour contained in the commodities, estimated at expected prices. If firms' expectations are met, ideal money translates into real money, and all the labour spent in production is confirmed as social in circulation. The reasoning could be redefined in terms of expected magnitudes, distinguishing the value and the price of labour-power. Graziani, contrary to Messori (and Napoleoni), is not compelled to bear the weight of a microeconomic foundation of his reasoning. Furthermore, in Graziani, there is a distinction (that is, a logical priority) between the buying and selling of the labour-power on the labour market and the final exchange of the commodity in the general market.

12. Crisis theory: Claudio Napoleoni and Mariano D'Antonio

In those same years, Mariano D'Antonio was writing some contributions on Kalecki that integrated accumulation and crisis within the discourse on value and exploitation.[31] To understand this new theoretical level, let us take a preliminary look at the dialogue that Napoleoni engaged in with Sweezy on crisis theory in 1970.[32]

Napoleoni accepted Sweezy's taxonomy of crisis theories where the tendential fall of the rate of profit is opposed to realisation crisis, and is in its turn dichotomised in a disproportionality approach versus an underconsumptionist approach. Napoleoni thought that the theory of the falling rate of profit does not hold water, since the counter-tendencies (rise in the rate of surplus value, devaluation of commodities, etc.) may prevail over the tendency (rise in the composition of capital). He opted for the realisation crisis, arguing that it happens thanks to the interaction between underconsumption and the occurrence of disproportions. However, he recognised in this synthesis a theory of the "originary" collapse of capitalism due to the fact that in capitalism there is a divorce of the economic circular process from a "natural" orientation to consumption. None of these crisis theories crucially depends on the labour theory of value.

In his Turin courses on Economic Policy of the early 1970s Napoleoni, as should be expected, gave a solid Marxian twist to his reading of crisis theory.[33] The theory of the falling rate of profit is now intimately connected to value theory: it is, in fact, transformed in a meta-theory of the crisis which incorporates in itself all the others. The law is dialectically confirmed when the counter-tendencies prevail over the tendency. The traditional formulation worked quite well in anticipating the Long Depression, i.e. the profitability crisis at the end of the 19th century. When – thanks to the technological and organisational innovations of Fordism and Taylorism – the increase in the rate of surplus value more than offset the rise in the value composition of capital, the tendency to lower the rate of profits was turned into a crisis because of too much (potential) profit: the realisation crisis, like in the Great Crash of the 1930s. The latter "big" crisis was overcome thanks to a massive devaluation/destruction of capital (variable, but above all constant). This was not only caused by the crisis itself but also by the Second World War. After the war, a positive influence on profits came from the huge injection of effective demand by governments: the Keynesian public expenditure, which Kalecki defined as domestic exports.

The tendency to a structural crisis was not cancelled, however. The reason was that Keynesianism favoured production as such, rather than production for surplus value, giving way to a relative expansion of the non-productive over the productive area. There is a convergence here between Napoleoni and Paul Mattick, though Napoleoni believed with Baran and Sweezy that waste and unproductive consumption could avoid a profitability crisis for a while. The price to be paid to maintain growth was a continuous pressure to increase the exploitation of productive workers, something that became socially unbearable and opened the way to a new form of profitability crisis due to an insufficiency of surplus value. It was a direct social crisis within the same "capital relation": not just wage conflicts but the struggle on the extraction of living labour in immediate production. The result was the Great Stagflation.

Let us see the interpretation of Kalecki by D'Antonio, on the background of the debate between Tugan Baranovski and Luxemburg.[34] The starting point is the schemes of reproduction, with wages entirely spent on consumption. In the early 1930s, Kalecki showed that the level of profits depends on capitalist autonomous expenditure for investment and consumption. Given the degree of monopoly, which registers the state of class struggle and gives us the share of profits in income, it is possible to define the level of income: from there we may obtain the level of employment. Such a perspective, while anticipating some aspects of Keynes's principle of effective demand (but within a class perspective), seems compatible with Marx's labour theory of value. Even more so is Kalecki's 1943 prophetic paper on the long-term unsustainability of permanent full employment in capitalism. This compatibility is confirmed by the convergence of the 1943 article with Napoleoni's (and D'Antonio's) interpretation of the crisis of the early 1970s.

13. The renewal of the debate in the 1990s

Italian debate on Marx vanishes, *de facto*, after 1983. That year was the 100th anniversary of Marx's death and of the birth of Keynes and Schumpeter, so many were the conferences and the publications on the matter: actually, it is probably true that the death of the debate must be anticipated. Paradoxically, the 1980s marked the beginning of new macro-monetary readings of Marx and also of interesting developments on capitalist dynamics. In Italy, however, the legend grew that the labour theory of value had to be rejected because it was universally recognised as false, and that the theory of crisis was also nothing but an obsolete collapse theory. The impact was huge. The macro-monetary approaches elsewhere were poorer than Graziani's. In them "macro" just means "aggregate". Moreover, the discussion on the theory of crisis did not confront the unitary interpretation developed by Napoleoni in the 1970s.

In the new approaches, the identity between labour and value is read as the (monetary) equivalent of the new value and living labour (a point anticipated by Messori).[35] But this is assumed to be a "postulate" and not theoretically grounded. It is a kind of metaphysics, often justified through a Smithian – and definitely unMarxian – vision according to which labour is the only active factor in production. "Necessary labour" is redefined as the objectified labour "commanded" (bought) on the market by the money wage. It is also assumed that simple prices and production prices are alternative and not sequential, the price rules allotting the direct labour spent in the period (a point anticipated by Vianello). Through these assumptions, by definition, one arrives at the equality between surplus-value and (gross) profits.

Duménil's and Foley's "New Interpretation", formulated in the early 1980s, is the most convincing version of this view. It came to Italy only at the end of the 1980s. It was surveyed and included in Bellofiore's re-reading of Marx's monetary labour theory of value.[36] In the 1990s, Stefano Perri combined the New Interpretation with Pasinetti, following Andrea Salanti's lead: this author argued for the possibility to maintain a Marxian definition of the rate of exploitation (as surplus labour) with Sraffian prices of production.[37] Roberto Marchionatti, another of Napoleoni's pupils, objected that the reference to labour in Salanti was not theoretically essential.[38] Salanti replied that discussions like these are inconclusive, since the Marxian notion of exploitation belongs to metaphysics.

In the early 1990s, Dario Preti – a non-academic researcher – presented some novel ideas about Marx and Sraffa.[39] In a non-dogmatic reading, finding faults even in Marx, he reconstructed the transition from values to prices in a temporalist perspective.[40] Out of Italy, within an approach willing to show Marx was free of any inconsistency, temporalism was submitted by Andrew Kliman, Alan Freeman and Guglielmo Carchedi as the only valid interpretation, empirically confirmed. What is most interesting and unique in Preti was that he detected in Sraffa a "macro" labour-value foundation of the "micro" determination of prices. Preti's textual reference is to § 10 and § 12 of *Production of Commodities*, where the net product is accounted for in prices and set equal to 1 and, at the same time, the direct labour spent within the period is also set equal to 1. We find again Messori's identity of the surplus, measured in terms of values and prices, or the New Interpretation postulate. For this translation of Sraffa into the new approaches to Marx to be operative, we must assume as constant the parameter expressing the so-called MELT: the Monetary Expression of (socially necessary) Labour Time. The MELT allows for a confrontation between the net product at prices with expended labour time as values: without it, the two dimensions are incommensurable (a point raised by Carlo Benetti in the early 1970s).

Within this line of reasoning, which happily redefines the discussion about the (dis)continuity between Sraffa and Marx, we may quote also Giorgio Gattei and Giancarlo Gozzi, and in some sense Stefano Perri again, when they try to look at Sraffa as a labour-value Marxist.[41] The argument begins with Pasinetti again, maintaining that the labour value paradigm can be upheld in the case of a pure labour economy. Then the case is generalised to an economy with labour and capital, adopting the point of view of the net product typical of the New Interpretation. As background, the idea is that Sraffa agreed with a law about the conservation of direct labour (Preti).

These authors have used some of Bellofiore's writings on the Sraffa Papers. His position is in fact more prudent than theirs: unpublished manuscripts have to be used with caution against published material, which is open to different interpretations. It is a fact that Sraffa was very reticent: in general, but even more so on these subjects. Archives may generate surprises, which are useful for the questions they raise (for these reasons it is important that the Sraffa Papers are made available for researchers, with no restrictions, and possibly put online: a point on which Scott Carter rightly insists). Questions, however, are questions, not ready-made answers. The archival material at the Wren Library has disclosed the long and tortuous path leading to *Production of Commodities*: a solitary run by Sraffa, in a certain sense, just like the making of *Capital*.

Thanks to the Sraffa Papers, we now know that Marx played a crucial role in Sraffa's journey to his book. Sraffa worked on it from the end of 1927 onwards. Though he took note of Marx's metaphysics, Sraffa's first notes are along the lines of a "physicalism" that leads him to criticise the labour theory of value – those remarks may actually be referred to as analogous to Steedman's perspective. However, since 1940, when he re-read *Capital* Volume 1, his approach changed. In the early 1940s his research programme mutated into an original (and maybe idiosyncratic) renewal of the labour theory of value and of the theory of the tendency of the rate of profit to fall. In both cases, Bortkiewicz was a target of his criticism. In a few years he understood the impracticability of this perspective in its original (we may say "heroic") form. All this notwithstanding, Sraffa continued to stress the continuity of what he was writing with Marx and with his transformation procedure. What is more interesting, after its publication, Sraffa explicitly interpreted his book in terms of Marx's exploitation of labour and deciphered the profit and wage shares into surplus and necessary labour. The crucial points of the argument – the identity of new product at prices with direct labour; and the definition of necessary labour in terms of the objectified labour commanded on the market – are clearly akin to the New Interpretation.[42]

What is more remarkable, is that Sraffa is maybe the only interpreter who correctly saw how the origin of surplus value was deduced by Marx in *Capital* Volume 1. The "method of comparison" (an expression we borrow from Rubin) that Marx employed to explain the origin of surplus value was not carried out, like in Croce or Rubin, contrasting a supposedly not yet capitalist configuration (where the outputs and inputs are given, and the value of production is entirely going to workers) against a capitalist situation (which differs from the former only through a fall in wages, as it actually happens in *Production of Commodities*). In his 1940 Notes, Sraffa very clearly intended that Marx's "comparison" highlighted the prolongation of the working day relative to the situation in which living labour is equal to the necessary labour required to assure workers' reproduction. Living labour exceeds necessary labour, but (*contra* Croce) both are immanent concepts pertaining to the present mode of production. They express the *differentia specifica* of a society in which, for the first time in history, workers are "free" and "equal", so that exploitation takes the form of the forced labour of free subjects. Here is the ultimate ground of the identity of the net product in simple prices and production prices.

Looking from the perspective of capital as a whole, valorisation depends only on the capacity to extract from the living bearers of labour power more labour than is required to assure the reproduction of the working class.[43] The constitutive role of the "consumption" of the bodies (and minds) of the workers themselves, which is crucial also in our reading, has been at the heart of the reflection of another Italian philosopher, Massimiliano Tomba. A quantitative corollary of this argument must be stressed because it differs from most interpreters, including Sraffa. In the most abstract investigation about valorisation, what is relevant is not how much (commanded) labour is "exhibited" in the individual money wage, but how much (contained) labour is required to produce the wage goods. In this macro-foundation of price determination, "exchange-value" accounting is essential. Even if the individual pricing rule may be different, the macro-social "exchange" between capital and workers is perfectly captured in simple prices. That is why the notion of the "value of labour-power" has to be understood in both dimensions: contained labour versus commanded labour. In Volumes 1 and 3 it is the real wage basket of the working class: but first it is evaluated at simple prices and then at prices of production. Since capital composition is different among the different aggregates (value of the net product, value of labour power, value of means of production), the labour commanded by the wage bill diverges by the labour contained in the subsistence of the working class.[44] This duality of the concept of necessary labour and of the value of labour-power add to the obfuscation of capitalist reality at the superficial level of circulation.

This Sraffa-inspired line of thought gives us the possibility to develop a "discourse on Marx" in his own terms: not contradictory with, but surely independent from, the analytical framework of *Production of Commodities*. In this book, given the methods of production (the inputs and the outputs), the theoretical questions posed by Marx and Keynes are "frozen". At this point in the circuit, living labour has turned into dead labour, since it is already objectified: no surprise labour magnitudes are redundant. Effective demand, the interest rate, initial finance are fixed "elsewhere". We suspect that Sraffa very well knew this. We can – and probably should – look at his "still image" as a "film frame" and conceive of the movie as nothing but the temporal unfolding of the dialectics between tendency and counter-tendencies. In an open interpretation of the Marxian theory of crisis, like the one hinted at by Napoleoni, it is possible to see the unconscious working of Gramsci's suggestions about the tendential fall of the profit rate.

14. Conclusions

The originality of the Italian debate on Marx can be related to two particular aspects (today at the risk of extinction) of the Italian tradition in economic theory. On the one hand, there was a two-way avenue going from the history of economic thought to original analytical researches, and back. Among the benefits there were cross-fertilisation and immunity from sectarian closures. On the other hand, the theoretical discussions extended into economic policy debates: as a consequence, the sin of a void abstraction and formalism was also avoided. The plurality of economic theories in competition, rather than a methodological commitment to "pluralism", was practised. After what Spaventa called a "U-turn" in economic theory, however, the debate on Marx became barren, also because of its absence in international debate, with only a few exceptions.

Nonetheless, some insights from the 1970s and 1980s debates are a peculiarity of an Italian reading of the critique of political economy. Among them, a macro-social and macro-monetary theory of exploitation is the most original. At the same time, the researches in the Sraffa Archive put in question the too quick dismissal of Marx deduced by most from the propositions of *Production of Commodities*. Beyond the contrasts that separate the authors, which we have elaborated here, every contribution seems to find its own place as pieces of a puzzle which may have its own coherence.

Notes

1 Sraffa 1960.
2 Cf. Croce 1900.
3 Cf. Gramsci 1929–35.
4 Cf. Dobb 1967.
5 Cf. Colletti 1969a and 1969b.
6 Colletti 1969b, p. 280.
7 Cf. Garegnani 1981.
8 Cf. Lippi 1976.
9 Cf. Sylos Labini 1973.
10 Cf. Meldolesi 1971.
11 Cf.Vianello 1970, 1973.
12 In the English-speaking debate these prices have sometimes been called "simple" prices.
13 Cf. Bellofiore 1991.
14 Cf. Napoleoni 1972a, 1972b, 1972c, 1973.
15 Cf. Luporini 1966, 1972.
16 Cf. Calabi 1972.
17 Cf. Calabi 1973.

18 Cf. Mazzone 1976, 1981.
19 Cf. Banfi 1965, 1966.
20 When labour is immediately private the use value needs to be "realised" taking the form of value, thereby becoming an exchange value.
21 Cf. Carandini 1976.
22 Cf. Carandini 1971.
23 Cf. Caliccia 1973.
24 Cf. Lunghini 1977.
25 Cf. Roncaglia 1978.
26 Cf. Messori 1979.
27 Cf. Messori 1984. That reduction seems the common fate of the approaches insisting on the unity of production and circulation. Against the intentions, the risk is of making Marxian economic theory indistinguishable from a circulationalist (purely monetary or institutionalist) perspective, or from conflictualism. The more so if Napoleoni's question – "why value expresses nothing but labour?" – is not answered. What reamins is just a different philosophy.
28 Cf. Graziani 1982.
29 Cf. Graziani 1983.
30 Some of these writings are translated into English in Bellofiore 1997.
31 Cf. D'Antonio 1978.
32 Cf. Napoleoni 1970.
33 Cf. Bellofiore 2015. An interpretation of crisis theory indebted to Napoleoni is Bellofiore 2011. It is prolonged into an interpretation of the ascent and crisis of current capitalism in Bellofiore 2013.
34 Cf. D'Antonio 1978.
35 Some of what follows is detailed in Bellofiore 2007, 2012, 2014.
36 Cf. Bellofiore 1989.
37 Cf. Perri 1991, Salanti 1991, 1997.
38 Cf. Marchionatti 1993a, 1993b, 1995.
39 Cf. Preti 1996, 2014.
40 A precedent was the iterative solution (like in Anwar Shaikh), but the reference to time was logical not historical. In Italy, the iterative solution was proposed by Marcello Cini and by Laise, Pala and Valentino in the 1970s.
41 Cf. Gattei and Gozzi 2010; Perri 2010, 2014.
42 Cf. Bellofiore 2001, before most other commentators.
43 A very early commitment on this line of thought is in Bellofiore 1980. For a development, see Bellofiore and Finelli 1998; Bellofiore 2004.
44 It is interesting that before and after *Production of Commodities* Sraffa thought that Marx was "statistically" justified in discarding these divergences in his transformation: the standard commodity, however, was a way to make the calculation precise.

References

Banfi R. (1965), "Uno pseudo-problema: la teoria del valore-lavoro come base dei prezzi di equilibrio", *Critica marxista*, n. 3, pp. 135–158.

Banfi R. (1966), "Abbozzo di una ricerca attorno al valore d'uso nel pensiero di Marx", *Critica marxista*, n. 1, pp. 137–175.

Bellofiore R. (1980), "Lavoro, valore e prezzo di produzione", *Studi economici*, n. 35, pp. 57–87.

Bellofiore R. (1989), "A monetary labor theory of value", *Review of Radical Political Economics*, Vol. XXI, n. 1–2, pp. 1–26.

Bellofiore R. (1991), *La passione della ragione. Scienza economica e teoria critica in Claudio Napoleoni*, Milano, Unicopli.

Bellofiore R. (ed.) (1997), "Marxian theory: The Italian debate", *International Journal of Political Economy*, n. 27, pp. 97–118.

Bellofiore R. (2001), "Monetary analyses in Sraffa's writings: A comment on Panico", in Cozzi T, Marchionatti R. (eds), *Piero Sraffa's Political Economy: A Centenary Estimate*, London, pp. 362–376.

Bellofiore R. (2004), "Marx and the macro-economic foundation of microeconomics", in Bellofiore R. and Taylor N. (eds), *The Constitution of Capital: Essays on Volume One of Marx's Capital*, Basingstoke, UK, Palgrave Macmillan, pp. 170–210.

Bellofiore R. (2007), "Quelli del lavoro vivo", in Bellofiore R. (ed.), *Da Marx a Marx*, Roma, manifestolibri, pp. 198–251.

Bellofiore R. (2011), "Crisis theory and the Great Recession: A personal journey, from Marx to Minsky", *Research in Political Economy*, n. 27, pp. 81–120.

Bellofiore R. (2012), "The 'tiresome objector' and Old Moor: A renewal of the debate on Marx after Sraffa based on the unpublished material at the Wren Library", *Cambridge Journal of Economics*, n. 36, pp. 1385–1399.

Bellofiore R. (2013), "Two or three things I know about her. Europe in the Global Crisis, and heterodox economics", *Cambridge Journal of Economics*, vol. XXXVII, n. 3, pp. 497–512.

Bellofiore R. (2014), "The loneliness of the long distance thinker: Sraffa, Marx and the critique of economic theory", in Bellofiore R. and Carter S. (eds), *Towards a New Understanding of Sraffa. Insights from Archival Research*, Basingstoke, UK, Palgrave Macmillan.

Bellofiore R. (2015), "Claudio Napoleoni e il Capitale monopolistico di Baran e Sweezy", *Moneta e Credito*, n. 269, pp. 3–39.

Bellofiore R. and Finelli R. (1998), "Capital, labour and time: The Marxian monetary labour theory of value as a theory of exploitation", in Bellofiore R. (ed.), *Marxian Economics: A Reappraisal. Vol. I – Method, Value and Money*, New York, St. Martin's Press; Houndsmills, UK, Macmillan, pp. 48–74.

Calabi L. (1972), "In margine al 'problema della trasformazione'. Il metodo logico-storico in Smith e Marx", *Critica marxista*, n. 4, pp. 109–179.

Calabi L. (1973), "Teoria economica e critica dell'economia politica", in Vv. Aa. *Marxismo ed economia. Un dibattito di "Rinascita"*, Padova, Marsilio, pp. 37–53.

Caliccia S. (1973), *Lavoro valore e prezzo nella teoria di Marx*, Roma-Bari, Laterza.

Carandini G. (1971), *Lavoro e capitale nella teoria di Marx*, Padova, Marsilio.

Carandini G. (1976), "Teoria del valore di scambio e problema della 'trasformazione'. Marx contro Marx?", *Problemi del socialismo*, pp. 79–129.

Colletti L. (1969a), *From Rousseau to Lenin*, London, New Left Books.

Colletti L. (1969b), *Marxism and Hegel*, London, New Left Books.

Croce B. (1900), *Historical Materialism and the Economics of Karl Marx*, London and New York, Macmillan.

D'Antonio M. (1978), "Kalecki e il marxismo", *Studi storici*, n. 19/1, pp. 17–44.

Dobb M. (1967), "Marx's *Capital* and its place in economic thought", *Science & Society*, n. 31, 4, pp. 527–540.

Garegnani P. (1981), *Marx e gli economisti classici*, Torino, Einaudi.

Gattei G., Gozzi G. (2010), "Sraffa come classico: una congettura possibile?" *Il Pensiero economico italiano*, n. 2, pp. 75–88.

Gramsci A. (1929–35), *Selections from the Prison Notebooks*, New York, International Publishers.

Graziani A. (1982), "L'analisi e la struttura del capitalismo moderno", in *Storia del marxismo*, vol. 4, *Il Marxismo oggi*, Torino, Einaudi, pp. 704–741.

Graziani A. (1983), "Let's rehabilitate the theory of value", *International Journal of Political Economy*, n. 2, summer 1997, pp. 21–25.

Kalecki M. (1943), "Political aspects of full employment", *The Political Quarterly*, n. 14, pp. 322–330.

Lippi M. (1976), *Value and Naturalism in Marx*, London, New Left Book.

Lunghini G. (1977), *La crisi dell'economia politica e la teoria del valore*, Milano, Feltrinelli.

Luporini C. (1966), "Realtà e storicità: economia e dialettica nel marxismo", in Luporini C. (ed.), *Dialettica e materialismo*, Roma, Editori Riuniti, pp. 153–211.

Luporini C. (1972), "Marx secondo Marx", in Luporini C. (ed.), *Dialettica e materialismo*, Roma, Editori Riuniti, pp. 213–294.

Marchionatti R. (1993a), "Sulla significatività del saggio di plusvalore dopo Sraffa", *Economia politica*, n. 10, pp. 203–221.

Marchionatti R. (1993b), "Sull'assenza di 'presupposti non empirici' in Sraffa. Una nota", *Rivista Internazionale di Scienze Economiche e Commerciali*, n. 40, pp. 599–603.

Marchionatti R. (1995), "Sul significato dell'assenza di 'presupposti non empirici' in Sraffa. Una replica", *Rivista Internazionale di Scienze Economiche e Commerciali*, n. 41, pp. 89–95.

Marx K. (2010 [1859]), "A contribution to the critique of political economy", in K. Marx and Friedrik Engels, *Collected Works*, Vol. 29, Lawrence & Wishart ebook, 2010, p. 325, and K. Marx, *Capital. A Critique of Political Economy*, Volume I, Harmondsworth, UK, Penguin, 1982, p. 200.

Marx K. (1981), *Capital. A Critique of Political Economy*, Volume III, Harmondsworth, UK, Penguin.

Marx K. (1982), *Capital. A Critique of Political Economy*, Volume I, Harmondsworth, UK, Penguin.

Marx K. (2010), *The Poverty of Philosophy, Collected Works*, Volume 6, Lawrence & Wishart ebook, p. 127.

Mazzone A. (1976), "Il feticismo del capitale. Una struttura storico-formale", in Vv. Aa. *Problemi teorici del marxismo*, Roma, Editori Riuniti, pp. 105–164.

Mazzone A. (1981), *Questioni di teoria dell'ideologia*, Messina, La Libra.

Meldolesi L. (1971), Introduzione in L. V. Bortkiewicz (ed.), *La teoria economica di Marx e altri saggi su Böhm-Bawerk, Walras e Pareto*, Torino, Einaudi, pp. ix–lxxxv.

Messori M. (1979), *Sraffa e la critica dell'economia politica*, Milano, Franco Angeli.

Messori M. (1984), "The theory of value without commodity money? Preliminary considerations on Marx's analysis of money", *International Journal of Political Economy*, n. 27, pp. 51–96.

Napoleoni C. (1970), "Introduzione", in Colletti L. and Napoleoni C. (eds), *Il futuro del capitalismo crollo o sviluppo?* Roma-Bari, Laterza, pp. vii–lxx.

Napoleoni C. (1972a), "Interventi", in Istituto Gramsci, *Il marxismo italiano degli anni sessanta e la formazione teorico-politica delle nuove generazioni*, Roma, Editori Riuniti, pp. 184–193, 433–435.

Napoleoni C. (1972b), *Lezioni sul capitolo sesto inedito di Marx*, Torino, Boringhieri.

Napoleoni C. (1972c), "Quale funzione ha avuto la Rivista Trimestrale? *Rinascita*, n. 29, pp. 32–33.

Napoleoni C. (1973), *Smith Ricardo Marx*, 2nd ed., New York, Wiley and Sons.

Perri S. (1991), "La 'significatività' del saggio di plusvalore dopo Sraffa", *Rivista Internazionale di Scienze Economiche e Commerciali*, n. 38, pp. 573–584.

Perri S. (2010), "From 'the loaf bread' to 'commodity-fetishism': A 'new interpretation' of the Sraffa-Marx connection", *History of Economic Ideas*, n. 18, pp. 33–59.

Perri S. (2014), "The standard system and the tendency of the (maximum) rate of profit to fall. Marx and Sraffa: There and back", in Bellofiore R. and Carter S. (eds), *Toward a New Understanding of Sraffa. Insight from Archival Research*, Basingstoke, UK, Palgrave Macmillan.

Preti D. (1996), "L'ambigua inconsistenza della critica neoricardiana al valore-lavoro", in Guidi M. (ed.), Il terzo libro del 'Capitale' di K. Marx: 1894–1994, *Trimestre*, pp. 117–146.

Preti D. (2014), "On the Neoricardian criticism of irrelevance", in Bellofiore R. and Carter S. (eds), *Toward a New Understanding of Sraffa. Insight from Archival Research*, Basingstoke, UK, Palgrave Macmillan.

Roncaglia A. (1978), *Sraffa and the Theory of Prices*, New York, Wiley (1st It. ed. 1975).

Salanti A. (1991), "La teoria del valore dopo Sraffa: una nota", *Rivista Internazionale di Scienze Economiche e Commerciali*, n. 37, pp. 685–692.

Salanti A. (1997), "Plusvalore e sfruttamento: una nota", *Economia Politica*, n. 14, pp. 235–241.

Sraffa P. (1960), *Production of Commodities by Means of Commodities*. Cambridge, UK, Cambridge University Press.

Steedman I. (1977), *Marx after Sraffa*. London, New Left Books.

Sylos Labini P. (ed.) (1973), *Prezzi relativi e distribuzione del reddito*, Torino, Boringhieri.

Vianello F. (1970), *Valore, prezzi e distribuzione del reddito. Un riesame critico delle tesi di Ricardo e Marx*, Roma, Edizioni dell'Ateneo.

Vianello F. (1973), *Pluslavoro e profitto nell'analisi di Marx*, in P. Sylos Labini (ed.), *Prezzi relativi e distribuzione del reddito*, Torino, Boringhieri, pp. 75–117.

4 What capital theory can teach us[1]

Fabio Petri

1. The classical conflict-based view of wage determination

In 1953 Joan Robinson published an article criticizing the neoclassical treatment of capital as a single factor, arguing that the neoclassicals never clarify in what units capital is measured. This started a debate that took on renewed vigour after the publication in 1960 of Piero Sraffa's book *Production of Commodities by Means of Commodities*, in which Sraffa argued that a correct analysis of how normal prices and choice of technique depend on income distribution produces results that "cannot be reconciled with any notion of capital as a measurable quantity independent of distribution and prices". Subsequent contributions, in particular by Pierangelo Garegnani, argued that those results undermined the entire neoclassical approach to value and distribution; the neoclassicals denied it. The debate still continues, but nowadays generally it is not mentioned at all to economics students, who therefore cannot make up their minds as to its relevance. It is my task here to supply the minimal elements needed to understand why the results in capital theory at the centre of this debate are important.

Capital theory studies the effects of the presence of capital goods (produced means of production) on the determination of prices and income distribution; in particular, it studies what determines the rate of return on capital (rate of profits or rate of interest). Historically, this question has received two very different answers, connected with the two main approaches to income distribution, employment and growth that have dominated economic theory in succession: the classical or surplus approach of Adam Smith, David Ricardo and Karl Marx, and the neoclassical, or marginal, or supply-and-demand approach, which has dominated theory and textbooks since the end of the 19th century. In the 1950s and 1960s Piero Sraffa brought the surplus approach back to the attention of economists, arguing that it was in fact superior to the neoclassical approach, on the basis of new results precisely in the theory of capital. These results show that an apparent weakness of the surplus approach in the determination of the rate of profits is surmountable, while the neoclassical approach encounters insurmountable difficulties. A consistent minority of economists have been convinced by his arguments and have developed a non-neoclassical approach to value and distribution that combines the Keynesian role of effective demand with the views on income distribution of Marx, Ricardo and Adam Smith.

Adam Smith next to Marx may surprise you, because he is often presented as a precursor of the neoclassical view of competitive markets as very efficient, owing to his mention of an 'invisible hand'; in fact, it suffices to turn to the issue that most sharply distinguishes the classical from the neoclassical approach – what determines real wages – to see that Smith is clearly not neoclassical; indeed he sounds Marxist before Marx:

> The workmen desire to get as much, the masters [Smith's term for the employers, the capitalists] to give as little as possible. The former are disposed to combine in order to raise, the latter in order to lower the wages of labour.
>
> It is not, however, difficult to foresee which of the two parties must, upon all ordinary occasions, have the advantage in the dispute, and force the other into a compliance with their terms. The masters, being fewer in number, can combine much more easily . . . A landlord, a farmer, a master manufacturer, a merchant, though they did not employ a single workman, could generally live a year or two upon the stocks which they have already acquired. Many workmen could not subsist a week, few could subsist a month, and scarce any a year without employment. In the long-run the workman may be as necessary to his master as his master is to him; but the necessity is not so immediate . . .
>
> [The masters' combinations] are frequently resisted by a contrary defensive combination of the workmen; who sometimes too, without any provocation of this kind, combine of their own accord to raise the price of their labour . . . But whether their combinations be offensive or defensive, they are always abundantly heard of. In order to bring the point to a speedy decision, they have always recourse to the loudest clamour, and sometimes to the most shocking violence and outrage. They are desperate, and act with the folly and extravagance of desperate men, who must either starve, or frighten their masters into an immediate compliance with their demands. The masters upon these occasions are just as clamorous upon the other side, and never cease to call aloud for the assistance of the civil magistrate . . . The workmen, accordingly, very seldom derive any advantage from the violence of those tumultuous combinations, which, partly from the interposition of the civil magistrate, partly from the superior steadiness of the masters, partly from the necessity which the greater part of the workmen are under of submitting for the sake of present subsistence, generally end in nothing but the punishment or ruin of the ringleaders.
>
> (Smith, 1776, Bk. I, Ch. VIII, xi–xiii)

To say that Smith was Marxist before Marx is a paradoxical way to stress that Marx did not invent the general picture of capitalism he was proposing; he was simply inheriting and developing a much older approach, born with William

Petty, Cantillon and the Physiocrats. Marx makes the implications of this approach more explicit. These implications were perceived to be critical of the capitalist social structure much before Marx wrote, as made clear in 1831 by Richard Scrope, who accused the diffusion of Ricardian theory of being a *crime* because it sapped the foundations of the "principles of sympathy and common interest" fundamental for social peace:

> Surely the publication of opinions taken up hastily upon weak, narrow and imperfect evidence – opinions which, overthrowing as they did the fundamental principles of sympathy and common interest that knit society together, would not but be deeply injurious even if true – does amount to a crime . . . In their theory of rent, they have insisted that landlords can thrive only at the expense of the public at large, and especially of the capitalists; in their theory of profits, they have declared that capitalists can only improve their circumstances by depressing those of the labouring and numerous class . . . In one and all of their arguments they have studiously exhibited the interests of every class in society as necessarily at perpetual variance with every other class!
>
> (quoted in M. Blaug, 1958, pp.149–150)

Sraffa in his Cambridge lectures of 1928–30 quoted an analogous passage from H. C. Carey (1848):

> Mr. Ricardo's System is one of discords . . . its whole tends to the production of hostility among classes and nations . . . this book is the true manual of the demagogue, who seeks power by means of agrarianism, war, and plunder . . . The sooner they [the lessons which it teaches] shall come to be discarded the better will it be for the interests of landlord and tenant, manufacturer and mechanic and mankind at large.

Marx explained this violent rejection of Ricardo as ideological, due to the need to fight the rising labour movement. But what interests us now is that these condemnations of Ricardo confirm the picture emerging from Adam Smith's passage. In the surplus or classical approach, the distribution between wages and profits, of what is left of the social product after paying land rents and reconstituting used-up capital goods, is seen as determined by forces similar to those that determine the standard of living of serfs under feudalism. The reason why feudal lords are able to extract an income from their control of land is that peasants cannot subsist without access to land, and therefore the power to prohibit access to land gives the lord the power to pretend part of land's produce. The lower the subsistence of serfs, the more is left for the landlord. But a lower limit to reducing the serfs' subsistence is posed, first of all, by their need to eat (and to be protected from cold etc.) enough to be able to work and to reproduce, and, secondly, by their need for those consumptions in excess of strict physical subsistence that are deemed indispensable for social respect and self respect in the given society, and thus for preventing the explosion of popular insurrections. Capitalists, as Marx particularly stresses but Smith had already admitted, have a power over labourers analogous to the power of feudal lords over peasants, the power to exclude them from earning a living by refusing to employ them; because it is the capitalist class that owns the means of production and thus the firms and the control over the available jobs. But their power to compress wages finds a limit in the danger of explosions of protests, which may be accompanied by "the most shocking violence and outrage", if wages go below the level that custom has rendered the minimum deemed indispensable for a decent living. A persistent rise in real wages tends to change consumption habits and to make the new living standard as indispensable as the old one was: for example, being inserted in social life, even among the poorer sections of the working class, nowadays requires one not to stink; not so 150 years ago. Wage bargaining starts from the level that past wage levels have made customary, and its outcome depends on bargaining power. Relative to the time of Adam Smith, the elements influencing the relative bargaining power of the two opposed classes of capitalists and wage labourers have become more complex. Many more elements enter the picture, such as trade unions, the degree of unity of the working class, the enlargement of the right to vote, the greater role of state economic policies, the welfare state. The level of unemployment remains particularly important: unemployment is a necessity for capitalism to keep workers' demands in check (Kalecki 1943).

2. The neoclassical picture: capitalism as a fair and efficient cooperation of sacrifices

The picture of capitalism emerging from the marginal/neoclassical approach is very different; hence the importance of deciding which approach is correct. In order to understand how capital theory can help on this issue, we must be clear as to how the neoclassical approach determines income distribution. This approach conceives production as the cooperation of 'factors of production' and argues that if the free play of competition is not impeded, the economy tends toward the full employment of all factor supplies, with factors receiving rewards that reflect the contribution of each unit of each factor to social welfare. The idea is that the choices of firms and of consumers cause the demand for each factor to be a decreasing function of its *rental rate* (or simply *rental*, for brevity, that is the price of its services: the wage rate, in the case of labour; the rate of interest, in the case of capital). Then if the rental of a factor in excess supply decreases, the demand for it increases, and a tendency arises toward a full-employment equilibrium. (I will leave aside land supposing it is overabundant and hence free, because land rent is less important for the purpose of highlighting the differences between the classical and neoclassical approach.)

Let us briefly remember how the approach derives the decreasing demand for a factor, with reference to labour. Suppose an economy where there is only one product, corn, produced by two factors, labour L, and capital consisting of corn (seed) K. Land is overabundant and hence a free good. For simplicity, the supplies of labour and of capital are rigid. Capital is *circulating* capital, that is, used up in a single utilization. Production is performed by firms which, because of free entry and competitive elimination of less efficient producers, are price-takers and end up by all adopting the same technology, described by a production function C=f(K,L) where C is *net* corn product,[2] with well-defined and smoothly decreasing net marginal products.[3] This technology exhibits constant returns to scale at least at the level of the industry (which in this case coincides with the entire economy), because either there are constant returns to scale already at firm level, or at firm level returns to scale are first increasing and then decreasing, so there is an optimal firm dimension; in the latter case, the assumption of competition requires that this optimal dimension be small relative to total demand, and then variations in the *number* of identical, optimally sized firms ensures constant returns to scale for the entire industry. So we can treat the entire economy as a single giant firm with production function C=F(K,L) with constant returns to scale. Then marginal products depend only on factor *proportions*, and factor payments equal to marginal products exhaust the product (Euler's Theorem).

So for each given real wage (in terms of corn), all firms adopt the same L/K ratio, the one which renders the marginal product of labour equal to the real wage; this ratio increases if the real wage decreases. Assuming that the supply of capital is fully employed, the L/K ratio determines aggregate labour demand, and the labour demand curve is − with the wage in ordinate − the marginal product curve of labour in the economy as a whole, see Figure 4.1. The intersection with the vertical supply curve of labour determines a unique and stable equilibrium wage w_{eq}. Owing to our assumption that the supply of capital is fully employed, there is only one market on which equilibrium must be reached: the labour market, and if the real wage responds to excess demand, it

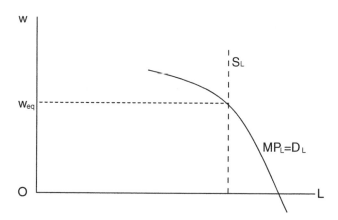

Figure 4.1 The labour demand curve D_L coincides with the labour marginal product curve MP_L.

tends toward the equilibrium level. (The product market is necessarily in equilibrium whatever the real wage, the moment it is assumed that all income goes to purchase the product, and that *only the employed factors have income to spend*.[4])

This construction is symmetrically applied to the demand for corn-capital, assuming labour is fully employed. The price of capital services, i.e. the net rental of capital, is the rate of interest. With labour fully employed (i.e. supply=demand), one derives the curve of the (net) marginal product of capital for the economy as a whole, and, with the rate of interest in ordinate, this curve is the demand-for-capital curve, again regularly decreasing and therefore ensuring the stability of the capital market. The assumption, when one studies the demand curve for a factor, that the other factor is fully employed, reflects what, according to this theory, will be the final result anyway, because the demand curve for a factor is decreasing for any given employment of the other factor. Therefore, the tendency toward equilibrium between supply and demand for a factor exists even when the other factor is not yet fully employed. So the simultaneous tendency toward full employment on either market sooner or later reaches full employment on at least one market and then also on the second market.[5] Competition and entry will anyway ensure that whatever earnings do not go to one factor will go to the other factor, because entrepreneurial pure profits tend to zero.

Behind both decreasing demand curves there is the fact that changes in relative factor rentals cause 'well-behaved' *factor substitution* in the choice of production methods by firms, where 'well-behaved' means in favour of the factor that becomes relatively cheaper and therefore conducive to stability. Factor substitution was perhaps not immediately evident in the derivation of the demand curve in Figure 4.1. In actual fact, when the real wage decreases, it is the rise in the optimal L/K ratio – that is, the convenience partly to substitute labour for capital in the production of any given output – that, when combined with a given K, allows us to conclude that the demand for labour increases; symmetrically, when capital becomes relatively cheaper, it is the convenience partly to substitute capital for labour in the production of any given output that reduces the optimal L/K, which, if L is given, allows us to conclude that the demand for capital increases.

Note that consumer choice was not needed to determine the equilibrium and to argue a tendency toward it in this simple economy. But consumer choice *among produced consumption goods* does have an important role in the approach (and this explains why so much space is devoted to it in teaching): it strengthens the approach[6] by supplying a reason, for decreasing demand curves for factors, *alternative* or *additional* to the mechanism of technological substitution among factors just illustrated. Let us assume our economy (still with labour and corn-capital the only factors) produces several consumption goods, and to make the role of consumer choice as clear as possible, let us assume fixed proportions between labour and capital in each industry, that is, no technical substitutability. Assume these fixed proportions differ as between industries. To determine the demand curve for labour let us assume, as before, that capital is fully employed. Suppose real wages decrease and the rate of interest rises;

this causes a relative cheapening of the goods produced with a high L/K ratio, and conversely a relative rise in price of the goods produced with a low L/K ratio. Then consumers, it is argued, will plausibly shift the composition of their consumption in favour of the goods that have become relatively cheaper, that is, the ones produced with higher L/K ratios.[7] This causes an expansion of the industries that use more labour relative to capital, and a contraction of the other ones. Since capital is fully employed, this entails the transfer of some units of capital from industries with a lower L/K ratio to industries with a higher L/K ratio. For example, some units of capital may have to leave an industry where each unit of capital is combined with 1 unit of labour and move to an industry where it is combined with 4 units of labour: each such transfer of a unit of capital raises the demand for labour by 3 units. The decrease in wages raises the *average* proportion L/K in the entire economy, by causing a relative expansion of the industries that use more labour per unit of capital. This mechanism too can be seen as a mechanism of factor *substitution*, in the 'production' of utility: a given utility level can be obtained with different combinations of strawberries and meat, and more strawberries and less meat mean the use of more labour and less capital. Since the change in overall L/K is indirectly caused by changes in consumer choices, this is called the *indirect* factor substitution mechanism, while the one based on changes of optimal production methods is called the technological or direct factor substitution mechanism.

We have illustrated the indirect factor substitution mechanism as an *alternative* basis of decreasing factor demand curves, operative even when the direct mechanism is paralyzed by the absence of technical substitutability; but of course the neoclassicals argue that generally both mechanisms are operative, and therefore a wage decrease raises labour demand both because consumers shift their demands in favour of 'labour-intensive' goods and because firms shift to using more labour and less capital per unit of output. The sum of the two effects allows arguing that factor demand curves are not only decreasing but also, in all likelihood, rather elastic, which gives credibility to two theses important for the plausibility of the approach: first, that a 'backward-bending' supply curve of labour does not cause instability because the demand curve is more elastic; second, that reaching equilibrium on the labour market does not require implausibly low real wages. We perceive here one reason why the neoclassical approach was found plausible: it seems to rest on an indubitable *factual foundation*, the existence of firms' choice among alternative production methods, and of consumer choice among different consumption baskets.

3. Differences between the two approaches

So far land was assumed to be a free good, but the derivation of decreasing factor demand curves can be applied also with more than two factors; given the employments of all factors but one, for the last factor the two substitution mechanisms allow the derivation of a decreasing demand curve, and then the market of that factor is, in all likelihood, stable, and in equilibrium the factor receives its full-employment marginal product.

Note then the symmetry: each factor receives its marginal product; the same law applies to all factors. Each unit of each factor receives its *contribution to production*, what society would lose if that unit withdrew from production. For capital, 'withdrawal' of a unit means that it is not reconstituted after being used up, because the owner prefers to consume the corresponding unit of corn instead of saving it again by allocating it to seed-corn. So what keeps capital existing, or increases it, is that its owners save, abstaining from consuming more. It becomes then possible to find a sacrifice behind each contribution: the wage rewards the sacrifice of unpleasant labour, the rate of interest rewards the sacrifice of abstinence from immediate consumption that makes it possible for society to enjoy the benefits of a positive stock of capital.

It becomes difficult, then, to argue that labour is exploited. Each labourer receives what she/he contributes to society, and each saver-capital owner too. Capitalism does not appear to be a society based on the extortion from labour of some of its product but instead a society of *co-operation* of sacrifices of factor owners (cooperation, because more capital raises the marginal product of labour, and vice-versa): the harmonious picture Richard Scrope was looking for.

The evaluation of unemployment too is very different from the classical/Marxian one. Labour unemployment results from a real wage higher than the equilibrium level; the cure must consist in lowering the real wage. If unemployment persists, the responsibility is with what prevents wages from decreasing: the power of trade unions, usually; or minimum-wage laws. So the workers whose support gives strength to trade unions, or to the political parties that passed the minimum-wage law, should ultimately blame themselves if unemployment persists.

The central analytical difference between the two approaches is the absence, in the classical approach, of the idea of factor substitution mechanisms, and therefore also of the idea of decreasing demand curves for labour or capital. This explains the different role of custom, social bonds, politics in the two approaches. In the neoclassical approach supply and demand, derived from consumer choices and firm choices, are capable of determining prices, quantities and income distribution on the basis of a very restricted set of institutions: essentially, competition and a general respect for contracts and for private property. In the classical approach, on the contrary, without a socio-political determination of the relative bargaining power of social classes (that has greatly fluctuated in the last two centuries) there would be no explanation for the level of wages. Custom and politics are *indispensable*; thus an Adam Smith or a Marx is also naturally a sociologist and a political scientist.

The two approaches are very different; the resulting pictures of capitalism are radically different. How does capital theory help in assessing which one is more solid?

4. Surmounting a weakness of the classical approach

As mentioned earlier in Section 1, Sraffa's advances in capital theory have shown that a weakness of the classical or surplus approach in the determination of the rate of profits, a weakness which was long believed to destroy the consistency of that approach, is in fact surmountable; while on the other hand, there are deficiencies in the marginalist/neoclassical treatment of capital that do not appear surmountable.

The classical weakness was an inability to arrive at a fully satisfactory determination of the *rate of profits*, the rate of return on the productive employment of capital. Classical authors knew that if income distribution between wages and profits changes, the normal relative prices of commodities change. Ricardo for example knew that if two commodities are both produced by a unit of labour, but the first is sold immediately after paying the wage, while the second must ripen for a further year before it is sold, then competition (that pushes prices to equal average costs) causes the normal, long-period price of the first to equal the wage, w, while the normal price of the second will be w(1+r) where r is the normal rate of profits. This is because the capital needed to advance the wage will need to earn the normal rate of return, or the commodity will not be produced; the normal relative price of this second commodity with respect to the first is (1+r), so it changes with r. Therefore there arises an apparent danger of a vicious circle. The given real wage and the given production methods adopted in the economy in a certain period make it possible to determine which goods, out of the total production of the economy in that period, go to the employed workers as wage goods, and which capital goods have been used to produce the total output. The vector of produced goods, minus the wage goods paid to workers, and minus the replacement of the used-up capital goods, yields the vector of surplus goods appropriated by the capitalists, whose value is total profits. The *rate of profits* is the ratio of the value of this vector to the value of the vector of capital goods employed. Since the two vectors have different compositions, this ratio depends on relative prices; but these depend on the rate of profits, so one cannot determine relative prices without knowing the rate of profits, and one cannot determine the rate of profits without knowing relative prices. To escape this vicious circle, Ricardo argued that the labour theory of value (relative prices equal to ratios of labours embodied[8] – determinable without needing to know the rate of profit!) was a sufficient approximation to actual normal relative prices; but it was a weak argument: in the example just given, the labour theory of value would indicate that the two commodities have the same price (both are produced by one unit of labour), which is false. Marx too relied, in ways I cannot specify now, on the labour theory of value. Subsequent anti-Marxist economists could accuse Ricardo's and Marx's entire approach of being wrong because it was based on an incorrect theory of normal relative prices.

Sraffa's equations that determine long-period prices have shown that this classical weakness was only apparent. It may help to start from the well-known Marshallian partial-equilibrium determination of the competitive long-period price of a commodity (produced good): free entry causes this price to tend to minimum average cost (inclusive of the normal rate of return on the capital employed that neoclassical economists identify with the rate of interest). But there is a deficiency in Marshall's argument. In order to determine the minimum average cost of a product, all input prices must be given; but this may be impossible before the price of the product is determined. Take steel. It is produced with the use, among other inputs, of machines made of steel. If we allow the price of steel to tend to minimum average cost, during this time an analogous tendency toward minimum average cost will operate for the machines that produce steel; so consistency requires that, in determining the minimum average cost of steel, the cost of these machines should be *their* minimum average cost. But this cannot be determined before we know the price of steel.

The solution is to determine *simultaneously* the minimum average cost of all produced commodities directly or indirectly entering the cost of steel, disaggregating the costs completely. Once one does it, one discovers that, if the real wage is given, the rate of profits is determined simultaneously with relative product prices. For simplicity, assume two goods only, corn and iron, produced by labour and by themselves (as *circulating* capital goods) in yearly production cycles. Assume, initially, that in both industries *technical coefficients* (efficient inputs needed per unit of output) are given. Land is free. Then price equal to minimum average cost implies two equations, where a_{ij} (i,j=1,2) is the given technical coefficient of input i in the production of good j, a_{Lj} is the given technical coefficient of labour in the production of good j, w is the wage rate (here assumed paid at the end of the production period, but one could also assume advanced wages), and r is the normal rate of return on capital (rate of profits, or rate of interest if one neglects risk):

$$p_1 = (1+r)(a_{11}p_1 + a_{21}p_2) + a_{L1}w \tag{1}$$

$$p_2 = (1+r)(a_{12}p_1 + a_{22}p_2) + a_{L2}w \tag{2}$$

The meaning of these equations is that to produce a unit of good 1, corn, the capitalist must anticipate capital at the beginning of the year to buy quantities a_{11} of good 1 and a_{21} of good 2, so the good's price must allow him or her to replace the used-up capital and must also yield him or her the normal rate of profits r on the capital employed (otherwise it would not be convenient to employ capital in that industry). The same holds for good 2, iron. The price of a good as input and as output is the same because we are determining *long-period* prices (Smith's natural prices), the persistent prices toward which competition and entry cause market prices to converge.

Once you write these Sraffian equations you see that the classical vicious circle is not there. Choose a numéraire, for example corn, $p_1=1$, and you have a system of two equations in three variables, the relative price of iron in terms of corn, the real wage in terms of corn, and the rate of profits. Take, with the classicals, the real wage in terms of corn as given, determined by the bargaining power of the opposed classes, w = a given amount of corn, and you are left with two equations in two variables: the rate of profits is determined simultaneously with relative prices, and without recourse to the defective labour theory of value. More than two goods introduce no additional theoretical difficulty because for each added commodity you add one more variable, the price of the commodity, and one more equation, the condition that this price must equal 'average cost' (inclusive of the normal rate of return on capital).

The theory can be extended to admit technical choice. The tool is the *envelope of wage curves*. For given technical coefficients, the above system of equations, once a numéraire is chosen, establishes a univocal connection between wage rate and rate of profits, a function w(r), often called *wage curve*. We could derive if from equations (1) and (2) but I prefer to do it for a simpler case, an example of so-called 'Austrian' technology, a simpler technology that will reappear in an example later. For each commodity, as long as among its inputs there are produced goods (capital goods), one can trace *their* inputs, and if these include produced goods one can go back to *their* inputs, and so on; if the technology is Austrian, in this backwards process from a good to its inputs one never finds the same commodity twice, and in a finite number of steps one finds only labour as an input (remember land is assumed to be free). Then the production of any commodity can be seen as being started by unassisted labour, which produces some circulating capital good which the next period, together with more labour, uses to produce another circulating capital good, which the subsequent period . . . (after as many more similar steps as necessary) finally produces the final commodity. An example is corn (good 1) produced by labour alone, and iron (good 2) produced by corn and labour; the production of iron can be seen as started by unassisted labour which produces a circulating capital good (corn), which the next period together with more labour produces iron. Let us determine the wage curve. Assume (to make the equations a bit less simple) that wages are *advanced* and that iron is the only consumption good (difficult to conceive? then reinterpret 'iron' to mean bread), hence the natural numéraire ($p_2=1$; w represents a quantity of iron, or of bread):

$$p_1 = (1+r)wa_{L1} \tag{3}$$

$$p_2 = 1 = (1+r)(p_1 a_{12}+wa_{L2}) \tag{4}$$

The second equation can be rewritten $1 = (1+r)[(1+r)wa_{L1}a_{12}+wa_{L2}]$, that implies:

$$w = \frac{1}{(1+r)^2 a_{L1}a_{12} + (1+r)a_{L2}} \tag{5}$$

This is the equation of the wage curve for this particular example; it shows that as r rises w decreases, and that (in this case) w remains positive for ever, tending only asymptotically to zero as r tends to infinity. The normal case, however, is not an 'Austrian' technology but one in which some commodities are directly or indirectly required as inputs in their own production and indeed in the production of *all* commodities; they are then called *basic* commodities. This is the case for both corn and iron in the corn–iron economy if corn needs iron as an input and iron needs corn as an input. When there is at least one basic commodity, then r cannot rise indefinitely, because at a certain point w becomes zero[9] and would become negative if r increased further; and economic meaningfulness requires that w does not become negative.

The study of the formal properties of the resulting system of equations is greatly aided by mathematical results on non-negative matrices, in particular by the *Perron-Frobenius theorem*, that I cannot explain here but whose relevance is briefly illustrated in the Appendix to this chapter. The Perron-Frobenius theorem shows that the wage curve associated with given technical coefficients is continuous, decreasing, and (as long as the economy is capable of producing a physical surplus if wages are zero, and technology is not 'Austrian') has positive intercepts on both axes. If one changes the production method of even only one industry, the wage curve changes.

Given the alternative production methods of each industry, having chosen a common numéraire, for each possible *technique* (that is, combination of production methods, one per industry) one can derive the corresponding wage curve w(r), and one can draw all these curves in the same diagram. Their North-East or 'outer' envelope indicates the maximum real wage obtainable for each rate of profits. We meet now a very important result. Assume the economy is using a certain technique, and that income distribution corresponds to point (r+,w+) on the wage curve of that technique, with associated vector of product prices **p**+ determined by the system of equations "price=average cost inclusive of normal r" (for the case of n commodities, equation (6) in Appendix) based on that technique's production methods. Assume also there is another wage curve corresponding to a different combination of the available methods (a different technique), which passes to the North-East of that point (that is, such that for the given w+ it determines a higher r). Then for at least one commodity

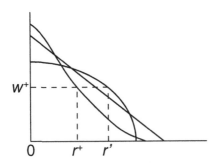

Figure 4.2 Three wage curves. If the economy is initially at (r+,w+), it will be pushed by cost minimization to change one, and then another, of the production methods until it reaches the outermost wage curve; if w is fixed at w+, the rate of profits will rise to r'.

entering the wage or its means of production, there is a production method belonging to the second technique but not to the first which, at the ruling prices and income distribution $(\mathbf{p}^+, r^+, w^+)$, allows production of that commodity at lesser cost and therefore allows extraprofits for the firm adopting it. Then firms in that industry will tend to adopt this method and thus the economy will change technique. But then entry will eliminate extraprofits in that industry, the economy will move to the more 'outside' wage curve, and r will rise if w stays fixed at w^+, or w will rise if r stays fixed at r^+. The repeated adoption of the cost-minimizing methods will bring the economy to the outer envelope of wage curves.

Thus even with technical choice, a given real wage determines relative prices and the rate of profits univocally; the wage curves allow us to see which technique is chosen.[10] The classical conflict-based approach to real wages *is* capable of determining relative long-period product prices and rate of profits.

5. Capital goods are different from lands

Neoclassical economists might still claim that their approach is superior, because it recognizes something that escaped classical economists: the fact that the indubitable existence of firms' choices among alternative production methods, and of consumers' choices among different consumption baskets, implies the factor substitution mechanisms from which the neoclassical approach derives its supply-and-demand-equilibrium determination of real wage and rate of profits (identified with the rate of interest[11]). However, unfortunately for the neoclassical approach, this claim founders on the impossibility to extend to economies with heterogeneous capital goods the picture illustrated earlier in Section 2 where capital was physically homogeneous.

The tendency toward equilibrium illustrated in Section 2 was based on the possibility to draw, for each factor, a supply curve and a decreasing demand curve. Let us pause and consider what these curves require. Besides the preferences of consumers, the supply curve requires a *given endowment* of the factor, on whose basis consumer choice can determine the supply of the factor to firms (in Section 2 this supply was assumed to be rigid[12]). The demand curve requires the determination of the general equilibrium for each given value of the rental of the first factor, and this, besides given preferences and given technological possibilities, requires (i) that the *other* factors be fully employed, and this again requires *given endowments, now of these other factors*,[13] and (ii) that when the first factor becomes cheaper, there be substitution (direct and/or indirect) in its favour so that the demand for the factor increases. Both requirements—given factor endowments, and 'well-behaved' substitution—have been shown to be untenable when capital is heterogeneous. Let us see why, starting with the first requirement.

One might think that each capital good could be treated in the same way as the different types of land: as a distinct factor with its given endowment. But the amounts in existence of capital goods differ from the amounts of the several types of land, in that most capital goods are continuously produced and used up in production, and their amounts can be quickly altered by differences between the flow of their production and the flow of their productive consumption by firms. The endowment (= the amount present in the economy) of a capital good will tend to adapt to the demand by firms and will stop changing quickly only when it has adjusted to the needs of firms, with the production of the capital good compensating its consumption by firms. *Any change in the demand for a capital good, be it due to change in production methods or in the outputs of industries that utilize that capital good, will quickly alter the amount of the capital good present in the economy, as its production and its normal inventories adjust to the changed demand.* Thus suppose in a nation there is labour immigration and one wants to determine the equilibrium corresponding to the increased labour supply. The trouble is that one does not know what the amounts will be of the several capital goods in the new equilibrium. The wage decrease caused by the increased labour supply prompts technical substitution inside firms and substitution in consumer choices. Both substitutions alter the demands for most capital goods, possibly drastically (the demand for some capital goods may even go to zero if they are required only by production methods that are no longer optimal). So after a short while the amounts in existence of most capital goods will have changed. Now, the time required for the change in wages to reach an equilibrium between supply and demand on the labour market is considerable. The change in labour demand in particular takes a considerable time to manifest itself: after a wage change, it takes time for product prices to change, for consumers to change their demands, for productive capacity in consumption goods industries to adjust so that prices go back to average costs, for the productive methods in all industries to adapt to the changed real wage. Clearly all these adjustments take months at least; and yet, the resulting new labour demand may still not be equal to labour supply, requiring further changes to the real wage and further adjustments taking more months. During this time the amounts in existence of most capital goods will change. So in order to determine the equilibrium corresponding to the changed labour supply, the endowments of the several capital goods cannot be considered *given*; they must be considered *variables endogenously determined by the equilibrium itself.*

6. Capital: the single factor of variable 'form', and long-period equilibria

Up to at least the 1930s *this was admitted* by marginalist/neoclassical economists, and *it was not viewed as a problem* because the several capital goods were conceived to be embodiments of a *single* factor 'capital', capable of changing 'form', that is, of embodying itself in different vectors of capital goods representing the same 'quantity of capital'; and it was the total 'quantity of capital', the endowment of this single factor 'capital', that was given. In this way the *composition* of capital, the endowments of the several capital goods, was left to be endogenously determined by the equilibrium, as required by time-consuming adjustments. The factor 'capital' was conceived as a quantity of exchange value 'embodied' at each moment in certain capital goods, but capable, by replacing the used-up capital goods with different capital goods of same value, of taking in time the 'form' best adapted to the amount of labour with which it was to cooperate. The idea was that, when certain capital goods are used up, the depreciation funds destined to repurchase them could also be used to pay for different capital goods; the factors that might reproduce the used-up capital goods would then be used to produce different capital goods whose value would be the same because they are produced by the same resources; the total value of capital will not change, but will be now 'embodied' in a different 'form' i.e. a different capital vector (see Petri 2004, p. 29). Thus in 1898 Knut Wicksell wrote that though "the forms of capital change, its total value remains unchanged, since, in place of the consumed capital goods, new ones of equivalent value enter successively".[14] Clearly, the general equilibrium based on this notion of capital, since it determined the 'form' of capital endogenously, aimed at determining the tendential result of time-consuming adjustments including changes in the composition of the vector of capital goods. General equilibrium then required that this composition reached an equilibrium, and this required the absence of reasons for wanting to alter it, that is, a *uniform rate of return* upon investing in any capital good. So this type of general equilibrium included the traditional condition of a uniform rate of return on the supply price of capital goods (equivalent to the classical condition of uniform rate of profit). Relative to taking the endowment of each capital good as given (a formalization these authors considered illegitimate for the reasons explained in Section 5), the additional degrees of freedom appearing in the general equilibrium equations owing to the treatment of the endowments of the several capital goods as variables, were eliminated by that condition, plus the condition of equilibrium between supply and demand for total 'capital'.[15] The prices determined by this kind of equilibrium were long-period prices, analogous to the classical natural prices, associated with a uniform rate of profits (rate of interest on supply price). Accordingly, this kind of general equilibrium can be called a *long-period* general equilibrium. Knut Wicksell's *Lectures* (1934) contain a clear formulation of such an equilibrium (a simplified version is contained in my 1978 article "The difference between long-period and short-period . . ." in *Australian Economic Papers*; space constraints prevent reproducing the model here). We will see later in Section 8 that contemporary general equilibrium theory is different.

There is a logical necessity behind the measurement of this factor 'capital' of variable 'form' as an amount of exchange value. All units of a factor tend to earn the same rental rate. Thus take two lands A and B of same quality; if land A earns, as *total* rent payments, twice as much as land B, this must mean that land A has a surface area twice the surface of B. Now consider two different capital goods A and B. Assume capital good A earns as net rental twice as much as capital good B. We want to see this as due to the productive contribution of a single factor 'capital' embodied in them; we must conclude that A contains twice as many units of 'capital' as B. But the net rental earned by a capital good is the interest on its value, and the rate of interest is uniform, so the value of

A is twice the value of B. Hence the 'quantity of capital' embodied in different capital goods is necessarily proportional to the value of those capital goods; hence 'quantity of capital' is necessarily *value* of capital. There is no other physical way to specify this quantity: weight or volume of capital goods have no univocal connection with productivity or earnings.[16]

Then the capital endowment of an economy is the value of the capital goods present in it, and traditional marginalist economists thought it legitimate to take this total value as given, as one of the data for the determination of equilibrium. But consider again the economy with labour immigration. When the wage rate starts to decrease, the composition of capital changes, and the neoclassical argument is that "in place of the consumed capital goods, new ones of equivalent value enter successively". But the composition of capital changes because demands change, causing changes in prices, so the revenues of firms will not generally allow setting aside the same depreciation funds as before. Furthermore, many capital goods are durable so they do not disappear quickly, but their value (like the value of land) can change very considerably if their prospective earnings change because of a change in income distribution. The value of capital goods at any given time will also depend on accidental transitional events such as a recession, a new invention that renders some existing plants obsolete, a stock exchange crash, prices not yet brought by competition to equal average costs, and so on. So the value of the capital goods existing in an economy does not have the *persistence* and *independence from the variables that the equilibrium should determine*, needed for legitimate inclusion among the data determining the equilibrium. One of the best marginalist economists, Knut Wicksell, was very honest on the issue. He wrote:

> But it would clearly be meaningless − if not altogether inconceivable − to maintain that the amount of capital is already fixed before equilibrium between production and consumption has been achieved. Whether expressed in terms of one or the other, a change in the relative exchange value of two commodities would give rise to a change in the value of capital.
>
> (1934, p. 202 of vol. 1)

A few lines later Wicksell admits that this implies an "indeterminateness" of the endowment of capital. But then, since there is no way to determine the given capital endowment, long-period general equilibria are indeterminable.

7. Reswitching

The problem explained in Section 6 prompted some neoclassical economists to propose a different, neo-Walrasian approach (see Section 8), which in recent decades has become the universally accepted one in general equilibrium theory. But up to at least the 1960s the general attitude was to disregard the problem and to consider it legitimate to treat capital as somehow a single factor, with a demand negatively elastic with respect to the rate of interest, because a lower rate of interest would cause substitution in its favour both in firms' choices and in consumer choices. A clear example of such a treatment of capital is Solow's 1956 growth model.

But in 1960 a result in Sraffa's book *Production of Commodities by Means of Commodities* showed that this notion of capital was indefensible. We can use a simpler example that reproduces his result, due to Paul Samuelson (1966). It is based on 'Austrian' technology, which because of the absence of basic commodities often permits simpler analyses. Consider an economy that produces two goods, champagne and whisky. Production is in periodic cycles. *Period* t goes from *date* t (moment t on the continuous time line) to *date* t+1, outputs of production processes carried out during period t are sold at date t+1, and wages of labour employed in period t are also paid at date t+1. Production of 1 unit of champagne requires the payment of 7 wages *two* periods before the sale of the product (i.e. if the product is sold at date t, which is the beginning of period t, the 7 units of labour were utilized during period t−3 and paid at date t−2). Production of 1 unit of whisky requires the payment of 2 wages three dates before, and of 6 wages one date before the date when the product is sold. Then long-period prices p_c of champagne and p_w of whisky must satisfy:

$$p_c = 7w(1+r)^2$$

$$p_w = 2w(1+r)^3 + 6w(1+r)$$

Put w=1, that is, choose labour as the numéraire, i.e. measure prices in *labour commanded* (how many units of labour one can 'command' i.e. purchase with the value of the good), then:

$$p_c = 7(1+r)^2 \tag{6}$$

$$p_w = 2(1+r)^3 + 6(1+r) \tag{7}$$

As r rises, both prices rise, so the *real* wage decreases in terms of both goods. Easily checked:

$p_c = p_w$ for r=50% and for r=100%

$p_w < p_c$ for 0.5<r<1

$p_c < p_w$ for 0<r<0.5 and for r>1

At r=0 it is $p_c < p_w$ because cost consists only of wages, and 1 unit of champagne requires the payment of 7 wages, against 8 for a unit of whisky. But the price difference decreases as r increases and is reversed as r becomes greater than 50%, because interest costs increase faster in the production of champagne than of whisky; however, as r increases further, compound interest causes a greater

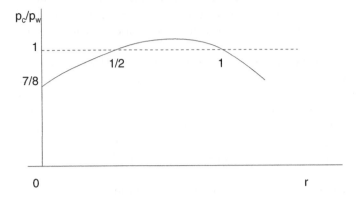

Figure 4.3 The relative price of champagne to whisky as a function of the rate of
profit (or rate of interest), in Samuelson's 1966 example.

increase in the cost of whisky, so the price of whisky starts approaching the
price of champagne and the ratio between the two prices is reversed again as
r becomes greater than 100%. This shows that the ratio between the normal
price of two commodities need not vary monotonically when the rate of profits (or rate of interest) rises.

When Sraffa produced the first example proving this result, he commented:

> The reversals in the direction of the movement of relative prices, in the
> face of unchanged methods of production, cannot be reconciled with
> *any* notion of capital as a measurable quantity independent of distribu-
> tion and prices.
>
> (1960, p. 38)

Indeed, if it were possible to ascertain independently of income distribution the
capital/labour proportion of the two production processes, as capital becomes
relatively more expensive the commodity with the higher K/L ratio should
always become more expensive relative to the other one. The price ratio p_c/p_w
should be a monotonic function of income distribution, as when the factors are
labour and land, or labour and corn-capital in the corn economy. The reversals
in the direction of the movement of relative prices mean that the K/L of the
two techniques is changing with distribution in spite of no physical change in
the methods utilized. This destroys the legitimacy of conceiving capital as a
single factor behaving analogously to labour or land.

This also affects technical choice. In the previous example, now interpret
p_c and p_w as the unit cost (in labour commanded) of producing the *same* good,
a consumption good (the sole one the economy produces), say a certain kind
of meat, with two different alternative techniques,[17] that, to continue with
the previous symbols, we may distinguish as 'C' and 'W'. Now the wage is

measured in meat; the maximum wage payable by each technique for a given r is the reciprocal of the labour-commanded price determined by equations (6) and (7). For each given r, the technique that competition imposes is the one that allows paying the higher wage, because the producers who adopt it can undersell the producers using the other technique since, at any common real wage, they have lower costs. Technique 'C' is the more convenient one, the cost-minimizing one, at r=0; it remains the more convenient one as r rises up to r=0.5, then the economy finds it convenient to switch to technique 'W', but it finds it convenient to *reswitch* to technique 'C' if r becomes greater than 1. This is the famous 'reswitching' result. So, with heterogeneous capital, the picture of the available techniques as arrangeable in order of decreasing capital-labour ratio, and of rises in the rate of interest (and decreases of the real wage) as always prompting changes toward using more labour and less capital, is impossible to sustain. The notion itself that it is possible to establish which one of two techniques uses more capital per unit of labour in some 'technological' sense is destroyed. Capital cannot be treated as similar to labour or land in the processes of technical choice.

8. Reverse capital deepening

Reswitching destroys the logical legitimacy of conceiving capital as a single factor of production. One of the effects is that it reinforces the conclusion that one cannot formulate a general equilibrium model in which there is a given endowment of this single factor capital. This can be seen as a *supply-side* criticism of neoclassical theory in its traditional versions, in that it destroys the way this theory determines one of its endowments. But reswitching also has *demand-side* critical implications: it undermines the assumption of decreasing demand curves for factors. In particular, it undermines the conception of aggregate investment as a decreasing function of the rate of interest. Once one gets rid of many confusions in the neoclassical theory of investment, which I cannot discuss here (see Petri 2004, ch. 7, and Petri 2015), it becomes clear that the real foundation of the mainstream view of investment as negatively inter-est elastic is the connection between investment and the neoclassical demand curve for capital. The argument runs as follows. One must distinguish two types of gross investment. First, replacement of used-up circulating capital (raw materials, component parts to be assembled into final products) for continuation of production in existing plants: the required circulating capital is conditioned by the machinery utilized and therefore generally no variability exists in technical coefficients unless the durable machinery is changed; so this part of investment allows nearly no variability in capital-labour proportions. Second, replacement of used-up durable capital (possibly with different durable capital), or as I put it for brevity, building of *new plants*: it is here that capital-labour normal proportions can be varied. Once the durable capital goods are chosen, technical coefficients are very rigid (some limited variability exists almost only in agriculture, where irrigation and fertilizers can be varied; but a car needs one engine and four tyres, and amounts of labour determined by how mechanized the factory is). In other words, technical choice can only be exercised when one invests in new plants; it is only in new plants that income distribution can determine the desired K/L ratio (see Petri 2004, section 4.3, and Petri 2017, for a better grasp of the reasoning). So imagine all durable capital in an economy lasts ten years and each year one-tenth of all plants is scrapped and one-tenth of the labour force is employed in new plants. It is in these new plants that firms are free to choose the K/L ratio. The neoclassical idea is that the interest rate determines the K/L ratio adopted in new plants. Once the full employment of labour is assumed, the denominator of this fraction is given. It is the fraction of the labour force 'freed' every year by the closing down of the oldest plants, one-tenth in our example; then the desired K/L ratio determines the K to be combined with labour in the new plants, that is investment. If the desired capital/labour ratio rises because the rate of interest decreases and prices adapt to the new income distribution, firms will want to combine more capital with labour in the new plants, so investment increases.

The capital demand curve is the K to be combined with the entire labour force once the rate of interest determines the optimal average K/L ratio, and it is decreasing because according to the neoclassicals the optimal K/L ratio is a decreasing function of the rate of interest. Investment is a decreasing function of the interest rate because it is a reduced-scale copy of the demand-for-capital curve, in that it reflects the application of the optimal K/L ratio, not to the entire labour force but only to the fraction of the labour force to be employed every period in new plants.[18]

There is more than one problem with this argument; here I illustrate the one evidenced by reswitching (another problem is pointed out in Petri 2015). The problem is that there is no guarantee that the demand curve for value capital (per unit of labour) is a decreasing function of the interest rate. To show it, we again refer to Samuelson's example, interpreted as applying to meat producible with the two alternative techniques 'C' and 'W'. Meat, the sole consumption good, is the numéraire. For each technique, we must assume the economy produces meat as net product; prices and industry dimensions are fully adjusted to income distribution and to the given technique; we must enquire which capital goods will be present in the economy per unit of labour, and with which value.

With technique 'C', if one unit of consumption good is produced every period then in each period the economy produces one unit of meat as net product and furthermore replaces the used-up capital goods; hence the following production processes go on simultaneously in each period:

- 7 units of unassisted labour produce as output a capital good that we can indicate as $c1$
- $c1$ alone, unassisted by labour, ripens into capital good $c2$
- $c2$ alone, unassisted by labour, ripens into one unit of consumption good.

Thus at the beginning of each period the economy's stock of capital consists of $c1$ and $c2$. The value of $c1$ is 7w; the value of $c2$ is 7w(1+r). Hence the value of capital is K_c=7w+7w(1+r) per unit of consumption good. Since a net output of 1 unit of consumption good implies the employment of 7 units of labour, the value of capital *per unit of labour* is K_c/7=w+w(1+r).

With technique 'W', each period the following production processes go on simultaneously:

- 2 units of unassisted labour produce as output a capital good that we can indicate as $w1$
- $w1$ unassisted by labour ripens into capital good $w2$
- $w2$ together with 6 units of labour produces capital good $w3$
- $w3$ unassisted by labour ripens into one unit of consumption good.

At the beginning of each period the economy's stock of capital consists of capital goods $w1$, $w2$ and $w3$. Their respective values are 2w; 2w(1+r); $2w(1+r)^2$+6w. The value of capital per unit of consumption good is K_w = $8w+2w[(1+r)+(1+r)^2]$, and per unit of labour it is K_w/8.

These values of capital are the normal 'demands' for capital per unit of labour implied by each technique. Let us calculate them at r=100%, where w is 1/28 for both techniques. It is K_c/7 = 3/28 = 3w, and K_w/8 = w+12w/8 = 5w/2, which is less than 3w. So as r *rises* from a little less to a little above 100%, technical choice is in favour of technique 'C', which implies a *higher*, and not a lower, value of capital per unit of labour: 'reverse capital deepening'. Thus a rise of r causes an increase of investment! This example, confirmed by many others, shows that there is no guarantee at all that as the rate of interest decreases, investment increases.[19] The mechanism on which the neoclassical approach relies to argue that investment tends to adjust to full-employment savings comes out to have been based on a false analogy between capital the value factor and factors measurable in 'technical' units such as labour or land.

This is very relevant, because the neoclassical tendency toward full employment requires that investment adjusts to full-employment savings, and the adjustment relies on the capacity of decreases in the rate of interest to raise investment if the latter is less than full-employment savings. The same supposed interest-elasticity of investment has been extremely important in the debates on Keynes, allowing the criticism based on the 'Keynes effect', namely, that reductions of the money wage do raise employment by causing a decrease of the price level, hence of the demand for money, hence of the rate of interest, with consequent increase of investment and hence of aggregate demand and of employment; therefore, full employment is not reached because money wages are not downward flexible. Reverse capital deepening undermines this criticism, strengthening the thesis that capitalist economies have no spontaneous tendency toward full labour employment.

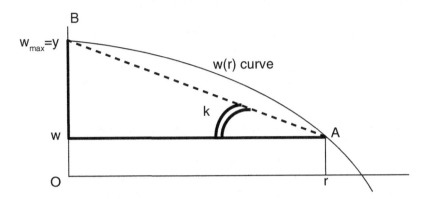

Figure 4.4 Derivation of k, the normal value of capital per unit of labour, from the wage curve. With a composite commodity with the same composition as the given net output as the numéraire, let y be net output per unit of labour; it is equal to w when r=0. From y=w+rk it follows that k=(y−w)/r, which is the absolute slope of segment AB from the point on the wage curve corresponding to the given r, to the vertical intercept y=w$_{max}$ of the wage curve.

The value of capital per unit of labour can also be determined graphically from wage curves, see Figure 4.4. Assume the net output is a quantity of a consumption good or basket of goods, which is the numéraire. Suppose the economy is on a wage curve at point (r, w(r)); the vertical intercept of the wage curve measures the net output per unit of labour, because if r=0 all net output goes to wages. Indicate this net output per unit of labour as y. When r>0, y is divided between one wage, and profits (or interest) at rate r over the value of capital per unit of labour, which we indicate as k; hence y=w+rk, that implies k=(y−w)/r. Now, y−w is the vertical distance from the vertical intercept of the wage curve to the given value of w; and r is the length of the segment in abscissa from the origin to the given value of r. Therefore k is the trigonometric tangent of the angle formed by the horizontal line through (r,w) and the segment connecting point (r,w) on that wage curve to its vertical intercept (Figure 4.4). If changes of r cause switches to another technique, y changes, and one finds the value of capital from the new wage curve (see Figure 4.5). If the technique does not change, but its w(r) curve is not linear, then k changes with r because of relative price changes.[20]

Then one can introduce technical choice, different wage curves crossing on the envelope of wage curves; then as r changes the value of capital will jump at each switch point from the value associated with one wage curve to the value associated with the other wage curve, and with reswitching the jump in the value of capital can be 'anti-neoclassical' (r rises and the switch is to a higher k), as at r$_2$ in Figure 4.5. This is *reverse capital deepening*. With many switch points on the envelope, one can have a behaviour of k as in Figure 4.6. Clearly, *even if* the supply of capital could somehow be determined, in no way could the curve in the right-hand diagram in Figure 4.6, with its several instances of reverse capital deepening (increases of r associated with increases of k), be viewed as a demand-for-capital curve determining a unique and stable intersection with the capital supply curve. More concretely, the neoclassicals argue that the supply of capital manifests itself as a succession of supplies of (gross) savings. In every period there will be a flow supply of gross savings, corresponding to resources *not* used to produce consumption goods which, if employed, allow producing capital goods for a value $K^\wedge$ (equal to the value of the savings), and there will be a certain portion $L^\wedge$ of the labour force that must be re-employed in new plants. Equilibrium requires that this supply of savings be absorbed by an amount of gross investment $I=K^\wedge$, which will happen if the rate of interest is such as to induce the adoption of an average capital-labour ratio $K^\wedge/L^\wedge$ in new plants, thus ensuring firms' demand for new capital goods for a value $K^\wedge$ that absorbs the flow of savings. The idea is that if investment is less than savings, the excess savings will cause the rate of interest to decrease, then firms will want a higher K/L ratio in new plants and $K^\wedge$ (gross investment) will rise. But reverse capital deepening shows that the K/L ratio need not be a decreasing function of the rate of interest; hence investment too cannot be considered a regularly decreasing function of the interest rate. So there is no reason to believe that the rate of interest can bring investment to adjust to full-employment savings.

Let us briefly indicate the implications of the above for the notion, fundamental in much applied neoclassical analyses, of a *decreasing demand curve for labour* and therefore of the need for real wages to decrease if labour employment is to increase. In a long-period framework, this curve is indeterminable because to determine the marginal product of a factor one needs given amounts (that is, for the neoclassicals, fully employed amounts) of other factors. So one needs to specify the endowment of capital, the single value factor, and, as argued, this endowment is indeterminable. In a Marshallian short-period framework where only the durable plants are given, the given plants mean that a gradually decreasing marginal product of labour has no plausibility because the given plants render the labour per unit of output generally rigid (see the substitution problem later). Furthermore, any increase in labour employment, entailing an increase in aggregate income and hence in savings, needs an increase in investment to be sustainable, and we have just criticized the adjustment of investment to savings as implausible. The implication is that employment depends on other things than the real wage – and then the obvious alternative is that it depends on aggregate demand and whatever determines it.

9. The shift to neo-Walrasian equilibria

Why so much insistence on the deficiencies of the neoclassical conception of capital-labour substitution, where capital is a single value factor, if anyway the endowment of such a factor is indeterminable and accordingly long-period

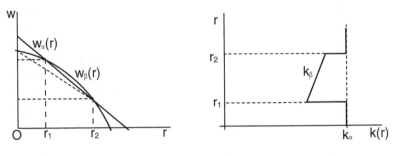

Figure 4.5 Reswitching as cause of reverse capital deepening. There are two techniques, α and β, with wage curves $w_\alpha(r)$ and $w_\beta(r)$ that cross twice. In the right-hand diagram of Figure 4.5, following usage, r (the 'price' of capital) is in ordinate and the value of capital k per unit of labour is in abscissa; for each level of r, k is determined as in Figure 4.4 by the wage curve on the outer envelope. As r changes, if the technique does not change, the value of capital changes as shown in Figure 4.4 and is constant for technique α whose wage curve is a straight line. At switchpoints, k is indeterminate because techniques are equally profitable so they can co-exist and can be used in variable proportions. The change in k when r increases from a little less to a little more than r_1 is downwards as neoclassicals expect, but at r_2 the opposite is the case. As r rises from a little less to a little more than r_2, k rises, as in Samuelson's example. So at r_2 there is reverse capital deepening. Figure 4.6 applies the same procedure to many wage curves.

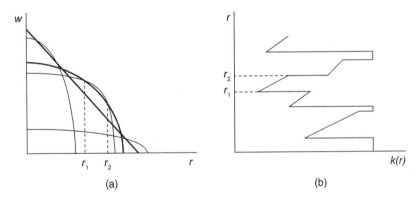

Figure 4.6 An example of possible behaviour of the value of capital per unit of labour as the technique changes with income distribution. The reader should be able to derive (b) from (a) following the procedure used in Figure 4.5.

equilibria cannot be determined? Because a continuing faith in traditional capital-labour substitution is the hidden reason for the support nowadays enjoyed by the contemporary versions of general equilibrium theory, where capital the single factor, a quantity of value, seems to be absent.

Nowadays general equilibrium theory, in order to avoid the problem with the endowment of value capital pointed out in Section 6, takes as given the endowment of *each* capital good[21] – precisely what was argued in Section 5 to be illegitimate. The resulting intertemporal or temporary equilibria are very-short-period equilibria, in that they do not give the composition of capital the time to change and adapt itself to the needs of firms. Equilibrium must be determined on the basis of whatever amounts of the several capital goods are available at the moment one considers. This creates three new problems (Garegnani 1990) that confirm the illegitimacy argued in Section 5.

Impermanence problem: since adjustments take time, the endowments of capital goods change during disequilibrium, and this changes the equilibrium too; so we do not know where disequilibria take the economy.[22] The unrealistic assumption of the auctioneer in the study of the stability of equilibrium is made precisely to prevent changes of the data of equilibrium, and therefore of the equilibrium itself, during disequilibrium adjustments. But to *assume* a problem away does not mean to surmount it. The actual path of economies cannot be the one based on instantaneous adjustments. But how large will be the distance between the actual path and the equilibrium path? The equilibrium path cannot tell us; and it cannot exclude an increasing divergence.

Price-change problem: since equilibrium relative prices cannot be assumed to be persistent (because the arbitrary initial endowments of capital goods will be generally quickly altered), one must allow agents to take into account, in their optimization, expectable price changes. But only two equally indefensible roads are available. First, intertemporal equilibria require the absurdity of complete futures markets (with yet-to-be-born consumers present at these markets!) or of perfect foresight (but how can future scientific discoveries, for example, be correctly predicted?). Second, temporary equilibria without perfect foresight (anyway nowadays abandoned) suffer from an *indefiniteness problem* because the single equilibrium as well as the path followed by a sequence of temporary equilibria come to depend upon arbitrary assumptions on unknowable initial expectations and on how these evolve over time.

Substitutability problem: there is nearly no substitutability among factors when capital goods are treated as distinct factors; different production methods generally require different capital goods, not the same goods in different proportions (see endnote 14). Thus the short-period demand for labour cannot but be nearly vertical, and the equilibrium real wage can easily be totally implausible, e.g. close to zero, and therefore very different from the real wage that will rule in the economy.

The implication is that the working of actual economies cannot be correctly described by these equilibria, since these: i) cannot even be *defined* without assumptions that grossly violate reality, like perfect foresight or complete futures markets; ii) would need instantaneous adjustments in order for the data determining them not to change significantly before the equilibrium is approached; and iii) can determine very unrealistic equilibrium values of capital goods' rentals and of the real wage.

Since actual economies certainly behave differently, these equilibria do not tell us how close or how similar the *actual* path followed by the real economy can be presumed to be to the equilibrium path. Older neoclassical equilibrium theorizing, based on persistent data, could argue that disequilibrium actions did not alter the equilibrium itself, and then they could argue that learning, error correction, repetition of transactions would ensure a gradual tendency toward equilibrium. With very-short-period general equilibria this way of reasoning becomes impossible, because the equilibrium itself is altered by disequilibrium actions (possibly *very* relevantly, since the actual economy will certainly behave very differently from the equilibrium prediction owing to the absence of perfect foresight and to the substitutability problem), and in directions the theory cannot predict because it only gives us the equilibrium path. So one does not know where disequilibria will take the economy. (Note that this criticism arises independently of reswitching and reverse capital deepening.)

And yet, as one must expect (otherwise the neoclassical approach would have to admit total failure), these equilibria are attributed explicative value, that is, are considered indicative of actual paths. This can only be due to a *prior* belief that the qualitative characteristics of the equilibrium path traced by intertemporal equilibria or sequences of temporary equilibria are similar to those traced by actual paths. This belief cannot be based on the theory of the equilibrium path itself, because the latter says nothing on the actual path; so it must be based on the following type of reasoning: *The traditional time-consuming marginalist disequilibrium adjustments in the labour and capital markets do exist and operate, and they maintain the economy close, on average, to the path traditionally traced by long-period neoclassical analyses, the path nowadays represented in simplified form by Solow-type growth models. Now, disaggregated intertemporal equilibrium paths are qualitatively similar to Solow paths: they too trace a full-employment path, with income distribution determined by marginal products. It becomes then possible to argue that intertemporal equilibria too indicate sufficiently correctly the qualitative trend of the economy.*

But then it is a continuing faith in traditional neoclassical adjustments based on capital-labour substitution where capital is the single value factor, and therefore a faith in the capacity of old neoclassical analyses based on long-period tendencies to indicate the trends of market economies, that allows modern general equilibrium theory not to be laughed at as totally unbelievable.[23] But such a faith is groundless, because of Sraffa's results that undermine that conception of capital-labour substitution.

In particular, the theory of intertemporal equilibria *defines* equilibrium as a situation of continuous *full* resource employment but supplies no reason why this assumption should correspond to how actual economies behave. In these equilibria, the equality between investment and full-employment savings is not justified by acceptable adjustments. The declared abandonment of the conception of capital as a single factor prevents openly using traditional arguments to justify the stability of the savings-investment market. But recourse to the auctioneer-guided tâtonnement is no help, both because it is ridiculous nonsense if conceived for intertemporal equilibria (because then it requires the existence, today, of all futures markets, with yet-to-be-born consumers present today to announce their future demands and supplies), and because, as explained in Petri (2017), even the tâtonnement actually assumes a (very criticizable) version of Say's Law. As to the alternative assumption of perfect foresight, it is both unjustified (how can one have learned all the needed information?) and logically impossible (how can one predict future advances in scientific knowledge, or new creative ideas, e.g. new fashions? A brain cannot predict what new thoughts it will elaborate in the future). As to temporary equilibria, everything depends on expectations, which might be anything. Again the impossibility of being able to rely on traditional adjustments renders the equality between investment and full-employment savings an unjustified assumption. Thus to the impermanence, substitutability and price-change problems one must add a fourth crucial problem of contemporary general equilibrium theory, and of the current mainstream macro models which claim it as their microfoundation, the absence of any justification for the assumed equality of investment and full-employment savings. To justify this equality, in the back of their minds, the advocates of these models most probably have the kind of reasoning described above in the italicized lines, but, as explained, it is indefensible, and in fact it is not openly argued.

10. Alternatives

In view of these comments, it can be concluded that capital theory shows the need to abandon the neoclassical approach and to search for an alternative theory, logically consistent and more capable of making sense of the empirical evidence. The modern classical-Keynesian approach mentioned in Section 1 seems to be precisely such a theory.[24]

For the determination of aggregate output and employment, this approach gives a central role to aggregate demand. This will appear obvious, once one becomes fully aware of an aspect of real economies seldom stressed in teaching. Firms do not utilize their durable capital goods 24 hours a day all days at maximum speed; they can easily increase production if demand increases and if extra labour is available (and nearly always it is). In most firms an increase of production flows by even a considerable percentage is no problem at all: it only requires extra hours and overtime labour or extra hirings. For this reason, aggregate production levels are highly flexible, not only downwards but also upwards. Given its flexibility, production adapts to demand. It is therefore aggregate demand (determined in turn by its autonomous components and by the Keynesian multiplier) that determines production and hence employment. (The recent reduction in production and employment in many European nations, owing to austerity policies imposed by the euro treaties, is as clear a proof of this fact as one can desire.) Growth is not supply-side determined; it is demand-constrained. The supply-side potential is almost never fully exploited.

An implication of the classical-Keynesian perspective is that unemployment is not so difficult to eliminate. It can be reduced by public policy that stimulates aggregate demand and with no need to reduce wages (if there are balance-of-payments problems, it is unclear that it must be wages that must be reduced). If governments do not do it, the reason is political: as Marx said, and Kalecki (1943) confirmed ("Political aspects of full employment", a beautiful short article), governments *want* some unemployment and will intervene to *increase* unemployment (Margaret Thatcher!) when they feel the working class is too strong.

Further reading on capital theory

The issues discussed in this chapter are complex; further reading is recommended. Petri (2016b) is a short historical introduction. Petri (2004) presents more extensively the arguments summarized in this chapter, insisting on the great difference between long-period analysis and neo-Walrasian models, so as to dispel the many confusions due to an imperfect grasp of this difference. Garegnani (1990) is very dense and deep, but is absolutely recommended. Harcourt (1972) is the most detailed survey so far of the Cambridge debates, but it was written before Garegnani's clarifications. Garegnani (2012) is his last assessment of the state of the debate, published posthumously (he died in 2011). Petri (2015) points out those other problems with the neoclassical theory of investment, alluded to but left unexplained in Section 8 of this chapter. Dvoskin and Petri (2017) confirm the argument advanced here in Section 9 and clarifies the relevance of the Marshallian short period. For more on long-period price analysis (and its extension to land rent, fixed capital, joint production) one can turn, in order of increasing complexity, to Mainwaring (1984), Pasinetti (1977) and then Kurz and Salvadori (1995).

Appendix

This appendix aims to give a taste of how results on non-negative matrices help in the theory of long-period prices, hoping to whet your appetite for more. Let us reformulate price equations (1) and (2), generalized to any number of commodities, via matrices. There are n commodities, produced using labour and themselves (as *circulating* capital goods) in production cycles all lasting one period. Given production methods, one per industry; no joint production. $\mathbf{A}$ is the matrix of technical coefficients of produced inputs, with a_{ij} input i per unit of output j; a_{Lj} is the technical coefficient of labour in the production of commodity j. With $\mathbf{p}$ the vector of commodity prices, the price equations are (capital inputs are bought at the beginning of the period, wages are paid at the end):

$$\mathbf{p} = (1+r)\mathbf{pA} + w\mathbf{a_L} \tag{8}$$

(Each *column* of $\mathbf{A}$ is a different industry; $\mathbf{p}$, $\mathbf{a_L}$ are row vectors.) Choose any numéraire, for example $p_1=1$, or $\Sigma_i p_i=1$. When $w=0$, equation (8) becomes $\mathbf{p}=(1+r)\mathbf{pA}$; define $\lambda=1/(1+r)$ and obtain $\mathbf{pA}=\lambda\mathbf{p}$. This is a *left-eigenvector problem*: λ is an eigenvalue of square matrix $\mathbf{A}$, and $\mathbf{p}$ is the associated left eigenvector. Let us assume that all commodities appearing in $\mathbf{A}$ are basic;[25] this means that $\mathbf{A}$ is *indecomposable*. Then the Perron-Frobenius theorem states that $\mathbf{A}$ has a non-repeated real eigenvalue λ^* which is dominant (that is, not smaller in modulus than any other eigenvalue) and to it and *only to it* are associated real non-negative, and in fact positive, right-eigenvector and left-eigenvector (for a compact proof, see e.g. Heal et al. 1974, p. 120). So an economically acceptable solution of $\lambda^*\mathbf{p}=\mathbf{pA}$ exists *and is unique*, and it determines the maximum rate of profits r^* via $\lambda^*=1/(1+r^*)$, and positive prices. This maximum rate of profits is positive, i.e. $\lambda^*<1$ as long as $(\mathbf{A},\mathbf{a_L})$ allows the production of a positive net product. Now note that, if wages are *advanced* and physically specified, we can add them to the technical coefficients and obtain matrix $\mathbf{C}$ as the matrix of needed inputs inclusive of needed wage advances; that is, if the real wage allows purchasing on average z_1 units of good 1, z_2 units of good 2, etc., then $w=\mathbf{pz}$ (with $\mathbf{z}$ a column vector), and $\mathbf{p}=(1+r)\mathbf{pA}+(1+r)\mathbf{pza_L}$. If now in industry j we replace each coefficient a_{ij} with $c_{ij}=a_{ij}+z_i a_{Lj}$ then $\mathbf{p}=(1+r)\mathbf{pC}$ where $\mathbf{C}=\mathbf{A}+\mathbf{za_L}$ determines the same $\mathbf{p}$ and r, and now this r is r^* but it is the *actual* rate of profits corresponding to the given advanced real wage. Also, a rise of the real wage will increase some coefficients of $\mathbf{C}$; the Perron-Frobenius theorem states that λ^* is an increasing function of each element of $\mathbf{C}$, so r decreases. The proof of an inverse relation between real wage and r for the case of w paid *post factum* is only a bit more complicated. Back to equation (8), choose labour as the numéraire, that is, $w=1$; now prices measure *labour commanded*, the price of good i indicates how many units of labour one can purchase (or 'command') with a unit of good i. Then equation (8) becomes $\mathbf{p}=(1+r)\mathbf{pA}+\mathbf{a_L}$, and replacing $\mathbf{p}$ on the right-hand side with $(1+r)\mathbf{pA}+\mathbf{a_L}$, you obtain $\mathbf{p}=\mathbf{a_L}+(1+r)[(1+r)\mathbf{pA}+\mathbf{a_L}]\mathbf{A}=\mathbf{a_L}[\mathbf{I}+(1+r)\mathbf{A}]+(1+r)^2\mathbf{pA}^2$; repeat the replacement of $\mathbf{p}$ on the right-hand side with $\mathbf{a_L}+(1+r)\mathbf{pA}$, and reiterating this replacement again and again you obtain:

$$\mathbf{p} = \mathbf{a_L}\,[\mathbf{I}+(1+r)\mathbf{A}+(1+r)^2\mathbf{A}^2+(1+r)^3\mathbf{A}^3+...] \tag{9}$$

The Perron-Frobenius theorem shows that for $r<r^*$ the expression in square brackets converges to a finite positive matrix, $[\mathbf{I}-(1+r)\mathbf{A}]^{-1}$. Reassured on this, let us note that apart from the first, all elements in the square brackets on the right-hand side of (9) increase as r increases; hence all elements of $\mathbf{p}$ are increasing functions of r, that is, all prices rise relative to the wage as r increases, which means that the purchasing power of the wage decreases in terms of *all* goods as r increases, that is, the real wage unambiguously decreases.

Perron-Frobenius theorem

Let **A** be a square non-negative indecomposable matrix. Then:

(i) **A** has a real eigenvalue $\lambda^* > 0$, not repeated, and dominant (that is, not smaller in modulus than any other eigenvalue), and to it and only to it is associated a real non-negative, and in fact positive, eigenvector[26] **x***; for each other eigenvalue λ of A, it is $\lambda^* \geq |\lambda|$, and $\lambda^* > |\lambda|$ if A is positive[27]

(ii) $(\rho I - A)^{-1} > 0$ (where ρ is a real scalar) if and only if $\rho > \lambda^*$

(iii) λ^* is an increasing function of each element a_{ij} of **A**

(iv) if s is the smallest, and S the greatest, of the sums of the elements of a row of **A**, then $s < \lambda^* < S$, unless s=S in which case $s = \lambda^* = S$; the same holds for the sums of column elements of **A**.

If **A** is decomposable the previous results are weakened as follows:

(i′) **A** has at least one non-negative real eigenvalue; to the highest non-negative real eigenvalue λ^* is associated a semi-positive[28] eigenvector; if λ is an eigenvalue of **A**, then it is $\lambda^* \geq |\lambda|$

(ii′) $(\rho I - A)^{-1} \geq 0$ if and only if $\rho > \lambda^*$

(iii′) λ^* is a non-decreasing function of each element a_{ij} of **A**.

For convenience I report here another often used result:

Let **A** be a square matrix. It is $(I - A)^{-1} = \sum_{t=0}^{\infty} A^t = \mathbf{I} + \mathbf{A} + \mathbf{A}^2 + \mathbf{A}^3 + \ldots$ if and only if $\lim_{t \to \infty} A^t = 0$, and it is $\lim_{t \to \infty} A^t = 0$ if and only if all eigenvalues of **A** are less than 1 in modulus. (This result holds for any square matrix. For non-negative matrices it connects to (ii) or (ii′) of the Perron-Frobenius theorem if ρ=1.)

Notes

1 Revised version of a lecture delivered to graduate students at Università di Pisa on March 27, 2015, as part of a series of lectures on perspectives in economic theory insufficiently covered in teaching programs, a praiseworthy initiative organized by Simone Gasperin and Tommaso Gabellini. The reader is warned that time constraints made a very dense exposition inevitable. I hope it remains understandable in spite of the many theoretical issues involved.

2 Gross (that is, total) corn production will then be C+K.

3 The distinction between gross and net marginal product is needed for capital: the net marginal product of one more unit of capital is the increase in corn output, minus the one unit needed to replace the used-up unit of corn-capital.

4 The italicized sentence points to an important difference between traditional marginalist discussions of the time-consuming adjustments argued to bring equilibrium about, and the contemporary analyses of stability based on the fiction of the 'auctioneer', a hypothetical institution that blocks the economy, proposes prices,

invites each agent to communicate demand and supply promises at those prices, calculates excess demands on the several markets, and then, unless equilibrium has been reached on all markets, declares all promises void, proposes new prices (higher where excess demand had been positive, lower where negative), and collects new promises, repeating the procedure until general equilibrium is reached, with no exchange or production allowed until then (which means the adjustments must be assumed close to instantaneous). What interests us now is that in this 'Walrasian tâtonnement' it is always assumed that consumers have a spendable income equal to the value of the factors they plan to supply. But this can only be legitimate in the fairy-tale world of the auctioneer, where demand intentions are hypothetical and only to be respected in equilibrium. In the real world, only factor supplies which have found purchasers generate an income for their owners; this is particularly important in the labour market. Only by admitting this fact can the neoclassical economist determine the situation generated by a real wage kept persistently above its equilibrium level by law or trade unions: the unemployed labourers, having no income, have no purchasing power, hence they cannot demand the product; the demand for the product equals the income earned by the employed factors, which is equal to the value of the product; hence the product market is in equilibrium and the sole market not in equilibrium is the labour market. Therefore with this more realistic treatment of consumer incomes (which is the one adopted by Keynes too) it is possible to have disequilibrium in only one market.

5 Note that the adjustment toward equilibrium here described does not assume the auctioneer-guided tâtonnement; it can be viewed in realistic terms. When a decrease in the rental of a factor induces firms to employ more of it, incomes increase by as much as output, so there is again equilibrium in the output market. The abandonment of this realistic picture in favour of the totally unrealistic auctioneer-guided tâtonnement has reasons that will be pointed out later.

6 On the contrary, consumer choice as to how much to supply of factors is rather a cause of difficulties for the approach, since it can cause factor supply curves to be 'backward-bending', which can cause instability.

7 Example: suppose the economy produces corn, strawberries and meat, and corn is only used as a capital good. The net product of the economy consists of strawberries and meat (i.e. corn production simply replaces the used-up corn-capital; the economy is stationary). Production is in yearly cycles. Assume production of a unit of corn (which is the numéraire good) requires 0.2 units of corn-capital and 1 unit of labour; production of a unit of strawberries requires 1 unit of corn-capital and 5 units of labour; production of a unit of meat requires 6.2 units of corn-capital and 1 unit of labour. Wages are paid at the end of the year. If the wage rate (measured in corn) is $w=0.7$ then rate of interest or rate of profits in the production of corn, and hence in the other industries too, is $r=50\%$, the price of strawberries is $p_s=5$ and the price of meat is $p_m=10$. If the real wage goes down to $w=0.6$, then $r=100\%$, $p_s=5$, $p_m=13$: meat, the more capital-intensive good, rises 30% relative to strawberries. Plausibly, the neoclassical economist argues, the composition of consumption will change in favour of strawberries and against meat. 'Plausibly', because this result is not guaranteed, owing to income effects. But I neglect this issue here, in order to concentrate on the problems connected with capital goods.

8 The labour embodied in a commodity is the labour directly and indirectly employed to produce it (labour directly employed, plus labour directly employed to produce the capital goods utilized, plus labour directly employed to produce the capital goods utilized to produce those capital goods ...). Differently paid labour times are reduced to 'simple labour' time in proportion to wages; so the labour embodied in a

commodity should be more correctly called the *wages* embodied in its cost, that is, directly and indirectly paid for its production. If the rate of interest or of profit is zero, cost coincides with wages embodied, and then the long-period equality of price and cost implies relative prices equal to relative wages embodied. Unfortunately, as the example in the text shows, the latter equality no longer holds (except in very special cases) the moment a positive rate of interest or of profit enters cost.

9 This is easily seen in the simple case of corn as the sole product, produced by labour and corn seed. Assume the production of 1 unit of corn at the end of the year requires 0.2 units of corn as seed at the beginning of the year, and 4 labour-years. Corn is the numéraire. Then the rate of profits, with the yearly wage w paid at the end of the year, is determined by $1 = (1+r)0.2 + 4w$. The maximum rate of profits, corresponding to w=0, is 400%.

10 If there are scarce natural resources, one also needs the quantities produced to determine land rents. We cannot stop on this here; see Garegnani (1983) for the different role of demand in the neoclassical and in the classical approach. The tendency of technical choice to the outer envelope of wage curves shows that Marx was wrong to believe in a *tendency of the rate of profit to fall* due to mechanizing technical progress; see Petri 2016b 'Capital Theory', or more extensively *Microeconomics for the Critical Mind* (Petri 2018, ch. 1). A new process will be introduced only if the new wage curve is not inside the old one; unless the new process concerns nonbasics, it will create room for a rise in the rate of profit *or of the real wage* – which helps explain the historical evidence that shows an indubitable secular rise of real wages with no reduction in profit rates.

11 An important change of the meaning of 'profits' occurs with the advent of the marginal/neoclassical approach. In it, labour and capital (and land) are just factors of production, with rentals determined by the same mechanism; this symmetry makes it natural for the marginalists to consider both wages and interest as part of production costs; then profit is redefined to mean the revenue of the entrepreneur in excess of costs that *include* interest payments; while, for the classicals, interest payments are part of profits. So zero-profit prices for the marginalists are prices that cover costs inclusive of a rate of return on capital equal to the rate of interest. A classical author would call them prices such that the rate of profits is equal to the rate of interest. In this chapter, the meaning of 'profit' is the classical one; the neoclassical meaning is rendered by 'entrepreneurial pure profit'. Neglecting risk, rate of profits and rate of interest can be treated as equal. But to help readers accustomed more to Marshallian than to classical language, I have used 'cost' of a product neoclassically as including also the normal rate of return on capital, which the classicals did not treat as a cost but rather as a surplus appropriated by the capitalist.

12 Since consumers differ in tastes and endowments, the supply curve of a factor depends on how the total endowment of that factor and indeed of each factor is distributed among consumers, but I will neglect this dependence. The problem I intend to point out concerns total endowments of capital goods and would arise even if consumers were all identical in tastes and in factor endowments.

13 Given preferences, given production possibilities, and given factor endowments (on which see the previous footnote) are the three groups of data needed to determine the general equilibrium, both in its long-period and in its neo-Walrasian versions, these, as will be explained, differ in how they specify the endowment of capital goods but not in the need for these data. We concentrate on the capital endowment because that is where the greatest problems arise.

14 See Wicksell (1936 [1898], p. 80). *This* is the conception of capital that justifies the assumption of smooth substitutability in production functions. If capital goods physically specified are treated as distinct factors in production functions, the cases

when one can vary the proportion between the same factors are very rare. Generally a different production method requires *different* capital goods. With capital a quantity of value as the factor other than labour, and with given prices, isoquants with labour and capital as inputs can be construed by asking, for each amount of labour, what is the minimal 'quantity of capital' (value of capital goods) that allows the given output to be produced? Implicitly, different vectors of capital goods will be associated with different points of the same isoquant. But this derivation of the isoquants is based on *given* prices of the several capital goods; and this destroys the usefulness of these isoquants, because if the rate of interest or the real wage changes, all relative prices change and isoquants shift, so we cannot use the old isoquants to determine the change in capital-labour proportion; neither is the way isoquants shift easily ascertainable. How the capital-labour proportion will change can be ascertained via different tools, and what emerges, as explained later in the text, is that things can change in ways totally contrary to neoclassical beliefs.

15 A detailed demonstration of this point would require the study of the equations of some long-period general equilibrium (for instance the one in Wicksell's *Lectures*, or the one in my 1978 article mentioned later), and we don't have time for that. But at least this can be pointed out — suppose there are n kinds of capital goods; relative to treating their n endowments as given as if they were lands, to turn these endowments into (stationary) variables adds n unknowns to the system of equilibrium equations. But the condition of uniform rate of return on their supply prices adds n−1 equations that state that the rate of return on capital goods 2, 3, etc. must be equal to the rate of return on capital good 1. There remains one degree of freedom, 'closed' by the equation establishing equality between the total endowment of 'capital' the single factor, and the demand for it.

16 Therefore the answer to a question like "Why was capital traditionally measured as a quantity of value by marginalist economists?" must include, first, the reason why capital had to be conceived as a single factor of variable 'form' (answer: adjustments take time, therefore the adjustments that according to this approach bring to equilibrium include changes in the endowments of the several capital goods. Therefore these endowments must be treated as variables, and then, without this given quantity of capital, the single factor limiting these endowments, the equilibrium is indeterminate and the system of equations remains with a degree of freedom, see fn. 15), and second, the reason why this single factor had to be measured in value terms (answer: just given in the text).

17 As the determination of the value of capital associated with each technique (see later) illustrates, each way of producing the consumption good includes several processes in succession, that is, presumes the existence of several industries, each one with its production method; therefore it is a distinct technique.

18 If all capital were circulating capital, entirely renewed each period, investment and demand for capital would *coincide* because each period the entire labour force would be combined with entirely new capital goods. This is the case in Samuelson's example interpreted as applying to choice of techniques.

19 Note also that as r rises above 100% (and the wage decreases), the switch is from technique 'W', that uses 8 units of labour per unit of net output, to 'C' that uses 7 units of labour: the wage decrease induces the use of *less* labour per unit of net output. Again, substitution can work the opposite to neoclassical beliefs.

20 If the w(r) curve is strictly concave, along it the value of capital increases with r. This is not given great importance by neoclassical economists because as r rises, generally the optimal technique changes often, and then the important thing is how the value of capital changes owing to technical change.

21 Thus taking up again Walras's specification of the capital endowment, which had remained isolated among the founders of the marginal approach. But Walras's numerous grave inconsistencies, which we cannot discuss here, suggest that he was still trying to determine a long-period equilibrium; see Petri (2004, ch. 5; 2016a). On the contrary the starters of the neo-Walrasian approach (Lindahl, Hayek, Hicks) knew that a long-period equilibrium must determine the composition of capital endogenously, and that they were moving to a different notion of equilibrium.

22 For the determination of the demand curve for labour, the impermanence problem means that it is illegitimate to try to determine this curve on the basis of a given vector of endowments of capital goods, because this vector will quickly change during disequilibrium and therefore cannot be the one on the basis of which one can determine the effect of different levels of the real wage. So the capital endowment without which a labour demand curve cannot be determined is indeterminable both in the long-period and in the neo-Walrasian versions of the neoclassical approach, because neither the value of capital nor the vector of capital goods can be taken as given.

23 See Dvoskin and Petri, 2017, for evidence that this is indeed how modern neo-Walrasian economists reason.

24 Joan Robinson and John Eatwell, *An Introduction to Modern Economics* (1973), Samuel Bowles and Richard Edwards, *Understanding Capitalism* (1985), Malcolm C. Sawyer, *The Challenge of Radical Political Economy* (1989), are elementary introductions to this approach, whose reading is recommended to start grasping how one reasons inside such an approach. An advanced comprehensive textbook introducing the approach at a level comparable with, say, David Romer's textbook on mainstream macro theory is still missing. But an attentive reading of K. Bharadwaj and B. Schefold (1990) introduces most facets of the approach and debates within and around it. Also consult the Working Papers of Centro Sraffa. Garegnani (2007) is the most detailed explanation of his view of the difference between the classical and the neoclassical approach. Stephen Marglin and Juliet Schor (1990), and Philip Armstrong, Andrew Glyn and John Harrison (1991), give a taste of how the approach allows a different perspective on the evolution of modern capitalism. A good broad survey of non-neoclassical perspectives is Marc Lavoie (2014).

25 If there are non-basic commodities, one leaves them temporarily out of the price equations and of the choice of numéraire and determines prices and income distribution without them; then the costs of all the inputs to non-basic commodities are determined, and one easily determines their prices.

26 We do not specify whether it is a right or left eigenvector because the statement, although traditionally intended for right eigenvectors, in fact applies to either, since a left eigenvector is a right eigenvector of A^T, the transpose of A, again a square non-negative indecomposable matrix and with the same eigenvalues as A.

27 A matrix having a non-repeated eigenvalue of modulus strictly greater than the modulus of all other eigenvalues is called *primitive*. The last result in (i) can be expressed as: every positive indecomposable matrix is primitive. But a matrix of technical coefficients is generally not positive; it contains zeros. An *imprimitive* non-negative indecomposable matrix A, that is, having a second eigenvalue equal in modulus to λ^*, can, by renumbering rows and columns, be brought to this structure: all elements are zero except $a_{12}, a_{23}, a_{34}, \ldots, a_{n-1,n}, a_{n1}$. That is, industry i only needs inputs from industry i−1 (except for industry 1 that closes the circle by needing inputs only from industry n).

28 'Semipositive' means non-negative and with at least one positive element.

References

Armstrong, Philip, Andrew Glyn and John Harrison, 1991, *Capitalism since 1945*. Oxford, UK: Basil Blackwell.

Bharadwaj, Khrishna, and Bertram Schefold, 1990, *Essays on Piero Sraffa*. London: Unwin Hyman.

Blaug, Mark, 1958, *Ricardian Economics*, 1973 reprint, Westport, CT: Greenwood Press.

Carey, H. C., 1848, *The Past, the Present and the Future*. London: Longman.

Dvoskin, Ariel, and Fabio Petri, 2017, "Again on the Relevance of Reverse Capital Deepening and Reswitching", *Metroeconomica*, 4, doi: 10.1111/meca.12137.

Garegnani, Pierangelo, 1983, "The Classical Theory of Wages and the Role of Demand Schedules in the Determination of Relative Prices", *American Economic Review*, 73(2), 309–313.

Garegnani, Pierangelo, 1990, "Quantity of Capital", in J. Eatwell, M. Milgate, and P. Newman, eds., *The New Palgrave: Capital Theory*. Basingstoke, UK: Macmillan.

Garegnani, Pierangelo, 2012, "On the Present State of the Capital Controversy", *Cambridge Journal of Economics*, 36, 1417–1432.

Harcourt, G. C., 1972, *Some Cambridge Controversies in Capital Theory*. Cambridge, UK: Cambridge University Press.

Heal, Geoffrey, Gordon Hughes and Roger Tarling, 1974, *Linear Algebra and Linear Economics*, London: Macmillan.

Kalecki, Michal, 1943, "Political Aspects of Full Employment", *Political Quarterly*; as revised by the author and published in M. Kalecki, *Selected Essays on the Dynamics of the Capitalist Economy 1933–1970*. Cambridge, UK: Cambridge University Press, 138–145.

Kurz, Heinz D., and Neri Salvadori, 1995, *Theory of Production*. Cambridge University Press.

Lavoie, Marc, 2014, *Post-Keynesian Economics: New Foundations*. Cheltenham, UK: Edward Elgar.

Mainwaring, Lynn, 1984, *Value and Distribution in Capitalist Economies. An Introduction to Sraffian Economics*. Cambridge, UK: Cambridge University Press.

Marglin, Stephen, and Juliet Schor, 1990, *The Golden Age of Capitalism: Reinterpreting the Postwar Experience*. Oxford, UK: Oxford University Press.

Pasinetti, Luigi L., 1977, *Lectures on the Theory of Production*. London: Macmillan.

Petri, Fabio, 1978, "The Difference between Long-Period and Short-Period General Equilibrium and the Capital Theory Controversy", *Australian Economic Papers*, 17, 246–260.

Petri, Fabio, 2004, *General Equilibrium, Capital and Macroeconomics*. Cheltenham, UK: Edward Elgar.

Petri, Fabio, 2015, "Neglected Implications of Neoclassical Capital-Labour Substitution for Investment Theory: Another Criticism of Say's Law", *Review of Political Economy*, 27(3), 308–340.

Petri, Fabio, 2016a, "Walras on Capital: Interpretative Insights from a Review by Bortkiewicz", *Contributions to Political Economy*, 35(1), 23–37.

Petri, Fabio, 2016b, "Capital Theory", in G. Faccarello and H. D. Kurz, eds., *Handbook of the History of Economic Analysis* vol. III. Cheltenham, UK: Edward Elgar.

Petri, Fabio, 2017, "The Passage of Time, Capital, and Investment in Traditional and in Recent Neoclassical Value Theory", *OEconomia. History, Methodology, Philosophy* [Online], 7–1, 111–140, https://journals.openedition.org/oeconomia/2596.

Petri, Fabio, 2018, "Microeconomics for the Critical Mind", unpublished provisional ms, https://sites/google.com/site/fabiopetripapers/home.

Robinson, Joan, 1953–4, "The Production Function and the Theory of Capital", *Review of Economic Studies*, 21(1), 81–106.

Samuelson, Paul A., 1966, "A Summing-Up", *Quarterly Journal of Economics*, 80, 568–583; as reprinted in G.C. Harcourt and N.F. Laing (eds), *Capital and Growth*. Harmondsworth, UK: Penguin, 1971, pp. 233–250.

Smith, Adam, 1776, *Wealth of Nations*. There are several good editions; to help readers to trace quotations without having to have recourse to a specific edition, quotations are generally indicated (as in this chapter) by book, chapter and paragraph rather than by page.

Sraffa, Piero, 1960, *Production of Commodities by Means of Commodities*. Cambridge, UK: Cambridge University Press.

Wicksell, Knut, 1934, *Lectures on Political Economy, vol. I*. London: Allen & Unwin (1st ed. originally published in Swedish in 1901; the translation is from the posthumous 3rd ed., 1928).

Wicksell, Knut, 1936 [1898], *Interest and Prices*, London, Macmillan (originally *Geldzins und Güterpreise bestimmenden Ursachen*, Jena: G. Fischer).

5 The modern revival of the Classical surplus approach

Implications for the analysis of growth and crises

Sergio Cesaratto

1. Introduction

Sraffian economics has recovered the surplus approach to the theory of value and distribution developed by the Classical economists and Marx, and later obscured by the emergence of marginalist economics in the second half of the 19th century. It has also laid the foundations for a robust capital-theoretic critique of the marginalist theory of distribution. By virtue of this twofold contribution, Modern Classical Theory (MCT), also known as the Classical-Keynesian approach, is well suited to absorb and reinforce the more revolutionary insights of Keynes' legacy and to spur economic research in alternative and critical directions. The chapter suggests some implications for modern macroeconomics and the interpretation of the global and European crises. Given that the capital-theory controversy is illustrated by Fabio Petri's chapter in this volume (Chapter 4), I will extend my own contribution considering some other heterodox approaches in the light of MCT. The chapter intends to stimulate interest in MCT especially in young scholars interested in heterodox economics.

As said, MCT has two constituents:

A) Recovery of the Classical "surplus" theory of distribution. This approach entails a conflict (non-harmonic) theory of distribution and identifies the roots of the crises in income distribution inequalities and in the consequent problems of lack of aggregate demand.
B) Criticism of neoclassical capital theory. This undermines the microfoundations of modern macroeconomics (*pars destruens*) and saves the most revolutionary of Keynes' *General Theory* propositions (*pars construens*).

MCT tends to stick to the traditional method in economics of long-period equilibria (better defined as long-period positions) of the Classical economists and Marx (and of the early marginalists). This is one of the least understood aspects of MCT, often seen as an element of conservatism. As shown also by Petri, the opposite is true, and the necessity to dispel this frequent misunderstanding motivates the critical consideration given to some heterodox approaches in the final part of this chapter.

We begin from point A.

2. Pills of the surplus approach

Central to the Classical theory is the concept of social surplus encapsulated by the equation:

$$S = P - N \qquad\qquad (1)$$

where S is that part of the physical net social product P (net of the reproduction of the means of production) which is left once workers' "necessities" (or wage goods), N, are paid. The social surplus can be defined as the part of the social product that remains once society has put aside what is necessary to reproduce the social output at least at the same level and that can thus safely be used for any other purpose. The simplest example is that of an agricultural society. In this case, we may assume that P and N have the same physical composition, say corn. Using equation (1) we can easily calculate S.

2.1 Social surplus and civilizations

In *Guns, Germs, and Steel: The Fates of Human Societies* (1997), the US multi-disciplinary biologist Jared Diamond argued that about 10,000 years ago, some material conditions occurred in certain regions of the world that permitted the emergence of modern civilisation.[1] By this, we mean that humans overcame the nomad status of hunter-gatherers living for the day and organised themselves into a residential society endowed with a political organisation and a social stratification – say, working-class, aristocracy, soldiers, priests, artists and so on. Those material circumstances mainly refer to the possibility, for geographical reasons that materialised only in specific regions, of growing a basket of "domesticable" vegetables and animals. This permitted a per-capita output in the agricultural sector rich enough, in quantity and quality (nutritional value), to permit the survival and reproduction of the peasant-class, leaving a surplus to maintain the other social classes.

In other words, in spite of the enormous variety of vegetable and animal species, only a few are easily and conveniently cultivable or tamed; moreover, these "domesticable" species were originally present only in a few regions, where they made advantageous the transition from the human stage of hunter-gatherers to agriculture. The existence of a social surplus also allows the expansion of the economy when part of the surplus is invested, e.g. used as seeds to extend cultivated land in which to employ, for instance, the slaves captured after a successful war.

Equation (1) encapsulates this reasoning. In the early stages of civilisation, therefore, the emergence of a social surplus allowed humans to detach a segment of the population from the daily need of collecting the means of subsistence, so that this section could dedicate itself to political organisation, knowledge, war or just idleness. Unfortunately, this did not happen in a democratic way, and we can thus realize that the surplus approach is associated with a conflict view of social relations, in particular between the social classes that control the social surplus and those who produce it (see Svizzero and Tisdell (2016) for an anthropological review of the issue).

It is interesting to note that Diamond does not quote any economist in his book. This suggests two things. First, he likely found "modern" neoclassical theory useless to study the emergence of civilisation. Second, he did not realise that various generations of economists up until Ricardo anticipated his reasoning. A number of mercantilists, and most clearly Petty (Aspromourgos 1996), alluded to equation (1) when interpreting the origin of the wealth and power of a nation. Had Diamond been exposed to Classical Political Economy, he would have recognised the ancestors of his theory in Turgot (and Smith), who advanced a surplus-based "stage theory" of growth (Meek 1971, 1976). The French Physiocrat François Quesnay (1694–1774) proposed a sophisticated model that showed the circulation of the surplus among the various sectors of the economy. The later most sophisticated classical economists such as Adam Smith, David Ricardo and their notable critic, namely Karl Marx, adopted the scheme to interpret modern capitalism.[2]

2.2 The surplus in a more advanced society and the rate of profits

The existence of a physical surplus is very visible in agriculture, but what about the manufacturing and service sectors? Before getting into this very complicated question, let us consider an intermediate situation and assume, as Ricardo did in his *Essays on Profits* (1815), the existence of both an agriculture and a manufacturing sector, with the important proviso that wages in both sectors, and the (circulating) capital stock C_a in agriculture, still consist of agricultural commodities (corn) only.[3] In this case, we may still use equation (1) to calculate the agricultural surplus and the rate of profit in this sector as:

$$r_a = \frac{P_a - (N_a + C_a)}{N_a + C_a}$$

(2)

Where P_a is the *gross* agriculture product and N_a and C_a are, respectively, the necessities and circulating capital (where "circulating" means used-up in a single utilisation, e.g. seeds), both part of the capital stock anticipated by the agrarian capitalists. Suppose now $C_a = 0$ for simplicity (so capital consist of anticipated wages only). We can write N_a as wL_a, that is the wage rate (remember, defined in physical terms) times the number of workers in agriculture (L_a). Equation (2) becomes:

$$r = \frac{P_a - N_a}{N_a} = \frac{P_a - wL_a}{wL_a} = \frac{P_a}{wL_a} - 1$$

(3)

Given P_a that depends on the stage of capital accumulation, and given the productive techniques in use, we can easily calculate L_a. Equation (3) will thus define a downward sloping relation between w and r that we call the wage-profit curve. The reader can easily verify that when $w = 0$, then $r = \infty$, and that when $r = 0$, then $w = P_a/L_a$. The latter shows the case of a product democratically distributed among the peasants (that can trade part of it with manufactured products). Any other solution to the social conflict over distribution is possible along the curve, although we may presume that wages cannot fall below a subsistence level.

We must now answer two questions:

(a) How is the profit rate in the manufacturing sector determined?
(b) How is actual income distribution determined – that is, which circumstances affect the point of the line in which the economy actually ends up?

The answer to (a) is easy. Competition will lead capitalists to move their investment from less to more profitable employments (this may be a slow process, but it sets a tendency). So, given that the profit rate in agriculture is regulated by equation (2), if the profit rate in manufacturing is higher, say $r_m > r_a$, then capitalists will tend to disinvest in agriculture and move their investment to manufacturing. This will imply a larger supply of manufacturing goods and a falling profit rate in that sector until $r_m = r_a$.[4] We leave the reader to work out the case $r_a < r_m$. Note also that, if a coalition of workers of both sectors obtains a higher real wage, the profit rate will fall in agriculture and, therefore, in manufacturing too.

Before examining the case in which N and C_a also include manufacturing products, let us first consider the determinants of real wages according to the Classical economists.

For answer (b) and summing up the various theories (see Stirati 1994), according to the Classical economists real wages depend on the relative bargaining strength of workers and capitalists. This relative power depends in turn on the level of unemployment, which is lower when capital accumulation is faster and vice versa. The amount of "necessities", however, cannot be below the amount necessary for workers to survive, i.e. to maintain a certain level of physical efficiency and to reproduce themselves. Indeed, the necessities must also cover the expenses to raise the next generation of workers (to complete the assimilation of workers to machinery, necessities must perhaps also include the costs of scrapping older workers – that is pensions). Moreover, whenever a wage rise is persistent, consumption of new and better quality goods becomes a new habit (second nature). This is what Classical economists mean by subsistence wage, the historically determined wage rate that would assure a socially acceptable decent life for workers and their families. A long rise in subsistence wages took place, for instance, during the full employment "golden age" years (the *trente glorieuses*, roughly spanning the period 1950 to 1979). Symmetrically, prolonged depressions or economic decline may slowly erode the social perception of what is a decorous wage: the current case of Greece is only the tip of the iceberg of a process that is currently eroding the subsistence-wage standard in all industrialised countries.

2.3 The measurement problems

We have so far measured P_a and N_a (and C_a) in the agricultural sector as two homogeneous magnitudes of known physical quantities, so that S_a could be determined as well in physical terms and the rate of profits r_a calculated as a "material ratio". Let us now assume that wages (and C_a) consist of both agricultural and manufacturing goods, say corn and cloth. In this case, although we can measure, for instance, the physical wage basket per unit of labour (per unit of time, say per week), say 10 kilos of corn and 10 metres of cloth, we cannot assign a unique exchange value to it since we must know prices in advance. For instance, if the price of corn is €1 per kilo and that of cloth €2 per metre, the weekly wage-rate will be €30. If the number of labourers is 1 million, we can easily calculate N, which will be €30 million (per week). Assuming also that the given quantities of P and C are composed of corn and cloth, we may calculate their value and finally the profit rate. There is a problem, however – we are reasoning in circle. To know the price of goods we must first know the profit rate;[5] but, as we have just seen, we cannot calculate it if we do not know prices first, since they are necessary to measure P, N and C in *value*. The reader will recognise that this measurement problem is similar to the one that the Marginalist school encounters when measuring capital in value (see Petri, Chapter 4 this volume).

Both Ricardo and Marx understood this problem (much less the intellectual rigour we find in modern marginalists). In *Principles* (1821) and *Capital* (1974 [1867]), respectively, they found a solution by measuring the value of each commodity (and of their aggregations P, N, C and S) in the labour time needed, directly and indirectly, to produce it. Suppose a spade is produced with one unit of steel produced one period earlier, which is then transformed into a spade by one week of current labour (direct labour). Suppose also that the unit of steel is produced by half a week of unassisted labour ("indirect" labour in the production of the spade). In total, the labour-content or labour-value of the spade is $0.5 + 1 = 1.5$ weeks of labour. If we put the value of the weekly wage as equal to 1, the price of a spade will be 1.5. If we take another commodity, say a smartphone, produced with three weeks of unassisted direct labour, its price will be 3. If our magnitudes, N, C and P consist of spades and smartphones, we can now easily measure them in value (labour content) and calculate the profit rate.

There is another problem, however. The capitalist that produces the spade anticipates the salary to the worker who produces the steel one period earlier. On this anticipated capital, she wants it to yield a profit rate (r), otherwise she would have preferred to invest it in some safe asset earning a positive interest rate. This means that if we put again the value of the weekly wage as equal to 1 the price of the spade is $0.5 (1 + r) + 1$. Unfortunately, we do not know r, and we are again in a vicious circle. The labour theory of value would be valid only under the very restrictive assumption that all commodities are produced with the same technique, that is with the same proportion of direct and indirect labour.[6] For instance, if the smartphone was produced with one week of indirect labour and two of direct labour, its price would be $1(1 + r) + 2$. It can be seen that the relative price of the two commodities is equivalent to their relative pure labour-content (the price of the smartphone is double that of the spade, and so is their respective labour-content). We can thus easily calculate r: if P consists of one spade and one smartphone, and N of one smartphone, then $r = (P - N)/N = (3 - 2)/2 = 0.5$ or 50%.

Fortunately, Sraffa's contribution shows the validity of the surplus approach under more general assumptions, but this entails the abandonment of the labour theory of value (Garegnani 1984). This has led radical economists to endless debates.[7] Garegnani maintains that the labour theory of value was functional to measuring the magnitudes of equation (2) until the emergence of a more robust solution. No doubt, both Garegnani and Sraffa disdained a mystical interpretation of the labour theory of value. They would have perhaps shared Abba Lerner's assimilation of the labour theory of value to the marginalist's conception of saving:[8]

> This blessed word and symbol exuded thick fog of mystical mischief in much the way that the concept of "value" has in Marxian economics. There, "value" is conceived of as a fluid (aptly called "sweat" by Champernowne . . .) which is absorbed into the product from the laborers who worked at it, in proportion to the number of hours of labor applied.
>
> (Lerner 1974, p. 38)

Sraffa was very keen that in capitalistic production labour is on an equal footing with packhorses (with subsistence wages assimilated to hay). Therefore, there is nothing special that labour transmits to the value of commodities (on Sraffa's rejection of the subjective elements contained both in the marginal notions of utility and disutility, and in the labour theory of value, see Garegnani, 2005; Kurz, 2012; Fratini 2016). After all, this is faithful to Marx's idea that in capitalism labour is a commodity, produced, operated, maintained, scrapped and reproduced as any other input.

It makes little sense here to discuss Sraffa's solution to the problems left open by Ricardo and Marx. It will be enough to say that Sraffa autonomously completed a solution to which Marx was very close (Garegnani 1984, 2005; and Petri, Chapter 4 this volume).

To conclude this section, I want to remark that distribution theory shapes the way we think of society. MCT suggests that we cannot begin social analysis from the single individual. In this regard Marx forgave the Classical economists for their "robinsonades", a term Marx used to describe methodological individualism, the naïve idea that society can be interpreted by analysing the representative individual.[9] A class structure is clearly discernible in the surplus approach shared by the Classical economists, despite their liberal ideology, that no doubt Marx considered as a positive step in the liberation of human-kind from religious and feudal social ties. Social classes are indeed implicitly present also in neoclassical economics, for instance when they analyse labour and wages. In open contrast with the historical experience, however, labour is seen as a collection of individuals, while its organized representatives, e.g. trade unions, are seen as violations to a deeper, natural competitive order. Symmetrically, "capital" is seen as an ethereal, mystical "factor of production" resulting from individual thriftiness and cooperating with labour, and not as a social relation of production based on the private property of the means of production.

3. Macroeconomic implications: capital accumulation, money and crisis

Notoriously Keynes (1936, p. 32) looked at Marx with some contempt and did not clearly distinguish Ricardian economics and Marginalism. The two constituents of MCT permit us to put things straight. On the one hand, the recovery of the surplus approach firmly anchors the Keynesian demand-side determination of output to a consistent distribution theory; on the other, the capital critique clears Keynes of his marginalist legacy.

3.1 The surplus approach and the criticism of Say's law

Past generations of students of economics were taught "Say's Law", named after the French economist Jean-Baptiste Say that formulated it in the early 19th century. The "Law" claimed that capitalism does *not* suffer from problems of aggregate demand (AD). In its original formulation, Say's Law conveyed the idea that production generates income that in turn is spent in its entirety. Saving would not be an obstacle to the closure of the income-expenditure circuit, since decisions to save were identified with decisions to invest. Note, however, that Say's Law does not by itself demonstrate that the economy tends to full employment (but only that it does not suffer from problems of AD). Ricardo believed in Say's Law, but Marx was much more skeptical about it.

Referring to equation (1), we may think of social output as composed of necessities (N) that are demanded by workers, and investment goods and luxu-ries (both contained in S) that are purchased by "capitalists". Suppose then that S is so large that capitalists (and the ancillary social classes) do not demand and consume all of it. Part of the output is unsold and this generates a problem of AD. One solution would be, of course, to increase N, but each capitalist would like to see the *other* capitalists pay higher wages while paying the lowest wages possible to its own employees, as Marx pointed out. Another solution is that capitalists decide to invest systematically the whole surplus they do not consume themselves. Productive capacity would constantly increase, but as long as capitalists continue to invest all that they save (and the availability of labour or land does not create problems), the problems with AD are overcome. Science fiction? No, this is the solution envisaged by Tugan-Baranowski, a Russian economist of the beginning of last century. Michal Kalecki – a great Polish economist with a Marxist background who, in the early 1930s, reached autonomously the same result later published by Keynes – appreciated Tugan-Baranowski's idea that the satisfaction of human needs is not the purpose of capitalism: production of capital goods by means of capital goods would be fine as long as this leads to the absorption of the social surplus (Kalecki 1967). The problem, as Kalecki sees it, is that a systematic investment of all saving would require some economic planning, but "Now capitalists do many things as a class but they certainly do not invest as a class" (ibid., p. 152), he explained in one of his most famous aphorisms. Following Rosa Luxemburg, Kalecki envisaged in the "external markets" the solution: endogenous money creation (see later) would finance public spending, autonomous consumption and demand from foreign markets that would absorb the part of the social surplus that capitalists do not consume themselves.[10]

The surplus approach leads us to reject Say's Law, as Marx promptly recognised. Yet, marginalist economists later proposed a complex demonstration of the validity of the Law, that also included the claim that free market capitalism tends to full employment, deeply based on their capital theory. It is therefore necessary to show why this demonstration is wrong. This has been elegantly shown by Petri (see Chapter 4, this volume); thus, in the next subsection I will limit myself to recall the devastating consequences of the capital critique for modern macroeconomics.

3.2 The role of the capital theory critique

In a marginalist general equilibrium perspective there are two fundamental markets to look at: the labour and the capital market, respectively. In both markets, the existence of downward sloped factors' demand curves guarantees that both the labour and the capital supply are fully employed.

To appreciate the importance of this proposition, let us look at the labour market first. All the claims from many governments and international organisations (e.g. EU, OECD, IMF, etc.) that labour market flexibility is the key to full employment are based on the simple idea that free competition allows unemployed workers (often called outsiders) to exercise pressure on employed workers (insiders) to accept lower wages. The existence of a decreasing labour demand curve assures that at lower wages, both the insiders and the outsiders will find a job. So, the main causes of unemployment are the laws that protect the insiders and their shop stewards.

The importance of the capital market will be appreciated once we realise that the demand curve for investment is derived from the demand curve for capital: they are indeed the same curve, the former in terms of flows and the latter in terms of stock. If you assume that all capital is circulating capital – that is destroyed in one production period – then the two curves would even coincide.[11]

Given the saving supply (drawn in connection to full employment income), a demand function for investment negatively elastic to the interest rate assures that all saving supplied at the equilibrium interest rate is absorbed. Say's Law is demonstrated even if each capitalist does not invest all her savings, as naïvely assumed in the original formulation of Say's Law. There is a market in which saving supply and investment demand, each calculated assuming that output is at full employment, meet at an equilibrium (or natural) interest rate.

It is unfortunate that Keynes accepted the neoclassical investment demand function in the *General Theory*, which exposed him to be reduced to a particular case of market failure. To show the existence of non-full employment equilibria he had to rely on the obstacles that the monetary authority would meet in driving the interest rate to its full employment equilibrium level: the liquidity trap. This case has gained renewed attention after Larry Summers (2012) revived the concept of Secular Stagnation. The idea is that various causes have lowered the propensity to invest and raised the propensity to save – including slower population growth and ageing, declining technical change and increasing inequality. As a result, saving and investment functions, both drawn assuming that output is at full employment, would meet only at a negative real interest rate. Paul Krugman (2014b) particularly stressed the difficulty for monetary authorities in achieving negative long-term real interest rates once the nominal interest rate has reached the so-called zero-lower-bound and inflation is persistently low if not negative.

The results of the capital theory controversy allow us to say that the mainstream view of these two widely discussed policy issues, labour market flexibility and the Secular Stagnation, are wrong. The fact that both labour and capital demand curves do not behave as Marginalists would like (see Petri, Chapter 4 this volume), lead us to conclude that:

- Labour market flexibility and lower real wages do not increase employment and, by rendering income distribution more unequal, they weaken AD.
- Since investment does not depend on the interest rate, even negative real interest rates do not boost them, and different investment theory and policies are necessary. We may for instance suspect that investment is induced by expected AD, the time-honoured accelerator theory, while the interest rate influences autonomous consumption and residential investment.[12]

It should be appreciated that these results affect all modern macroeconomics, including the concept of a natural unemployment rate (Stirati 2016), Solow's growth model (Cesaratto 1999) and international trade models (Steedman 1979). One primary implication is also the critique of the neoclassical duality between a real and a monetary sector, the idea that expansionary monetary policy is not effective unless there is "monetary illusion". In this view, central banks must be independent and pursue price stability in order to maintain the economy at the non-accelerating inflation rate of unemployment (or NAIRU).

The implications of this criticism for the European monetary constitution are devastating (Cesaratto 2017). We shall return to the issue of money later.

Let us just note here that in the Classical-Keynesian approach, independent central banks are the watchdogs of income distribution. In the German model, for instance, the Bundesbank was the *Convitato di pietra* in the wage bargaining between trade unions and industrialists (you can guess siding with whom) (Cesaratto and Stirati 2011, pp. 73–74). There is no reason to argue that at the "natural unemployment rate" there is no involuntary unemployment. This rate is just the rate at which inflation is constant (i.e. non-accelerating). The fact that a fall in unemployment is associated with higher inflation does not depend on the necessity to cheat workers (as long as they suffer from monetary illusion), as in the Monetarist textbook tale. It originates instead in the fact that a higher employment rate – a lower industrial reserve army, in Marx's terminology – entails a stronger bargaining power of workers. In this view, monetary policy – particularly if associated with fiscal policy – is effective, but the fall in the industrial reserve army leads to higher real-wage claims and inflation.[13]

3.3 The Sraffian supermultiplier

We noted earlier that capitalism needs "external markets" to function. This is so because capitalists do not spend all their profits. In current economic jargon, "external markets" are defined as "autonomous/non-capacity creating components" of AD. According to many exponents of the MCT, the autonomous components of AD – autonomous consumption (*A*), government spending (*G*), exports (*E*) and in the short-run (when its capacity-creating role is neglected) investment (*I*) – are the determinants of the degree of capacity utilisation in the short run, and of the growth rate of the economy in the long run (cf. Bortis 1997; Cesaratto 2015; Freitas and Serrano 2015). Specifically, they refer to two equations:

(a) The first is the traditional determination of output in the short run through the Keynesian multiplier. The autonomous components regulate AD (Y_D), given the marginal propensity to consume *c*, the average tax rate *t* and the marginal propensity to import *m*:

$$Y_D = \frac{1}{1-c(1-t)+m}(\bar{A}+\bar{I}+\bar{G}+\bar{E})$$

(4)

Keynes' belief was that in capitalist economies AD is not on average sufficient to fully utilise productive capacity, such that the level of output *X* and the degree of capacity utilisation adjust to the level of Y_D, that is $X = Y_D$.

(b) In the long run, however, capacity tends to adjust to expected effective demand (ED)[14] and not the other way round as in neoclassical theory. In particular, capitalists will not invest blindly, but on the basis of expected ED. This is expressed through an induced investment function based on the *accelerator*.

$$I = v_n g^e Y_D \tag{5}$$

in which $g^e Y_D$ represents the expected growth of ED and v_n is the capital-output coefficient, that is, the desired quantity of capital per unit of output (we also assume that all capital is fixed and there is no depreciation). Using the same textbook procedure used to obtain equation (4), and taking equation (5) into account, we thus obtain an equation similar to equation (4) in which the fraction is named *supermultiplier* (SM), after Hicks (1950):

$$Y = \frac{1}{1 - c(1-t) - v_n g^z + m}(\overline{A} + \overline{G} + \overline{E}) = \frac{1}{1 - c(1-t) - v_n g^z + m} Z \tag{6}$$

where Z and g^z are the level and rate of growth of the autonomous/non-capacity-creating components of AD, respectively, and investment is an induced and not an autonomous component of AD, as it must be in a long-run growth model. In writing the equation we assumed $g^z = g^e$. It can be shown that within reasonable assumptions the actual and expected rates of growth tend to adjust to the growth rate of autonomous demand Z (Freitas and Serrano 2015). We may say that the Sraffian SM is a modern reformulation of Luxembourg-Kalecki external markets.[15]

3.4 Policy implications of the Sraffian supermultiplier

The SM suggests the idea that it is final demand (external markets) that sustains output and investment (via accelerator), and that saving is generated by the fuller exploitation of existing capacity (in the short run) and by the creation of new capacity (in the long run).

An example of the role of autonomous consumption financed by consumer credit in driving a prolonged phase of economic growth is the recent US "Great Moderation" era, which went from mid-1980 until the financial crisis of 2007. In this period, increasing inequality in income distribution was compensated by expansive monetary policy that promoted consumer debt and a residential investment bubble (Barba and Pivetti 2009). An example of export-led/mercantilist growth is Germany. Since the 1950s, and more markedly after the introduction of the euro, Germany's economic policy has been characterised by the compression of wages and domestic demand in order to find a vent-for-surplus in external markets (Cesaratto and Stirati 2011), as Adam Smith would have called it. Finally, government spending sustained growth during the full-employment golden-age years.

In a market economy, *private* "external markets" (autonomous consumption and foreign markets) may only temporarily solve the realisation problem. These markets are normally financed by purchasing power creation by the banking sector (e.g. consumption credit and foreign loans), and we see here an important field of convergence with the heterodox literature on "endogenous money" (see next subsection). Purchasing power creation feeds the external markets that absorb the capitalists' surplus that returns to the capitalists' hands as profits. Ultimately, therefore, capitalists become creditors of those "markets" (that is of households and foreign countries). Debt-driven growth is a major source of instability of capitalism, as both the US and Eurozone crises have shown. We see here some convergence with the Minskian tradition of the financial instability of capitalism. Government spending is a more solid solution, either if sustained by progressive taxation or by government debt in fully monetary-sovereign countries (Wray 1998).[16]

3.5 Endogenous money and the neoclassical duality

It is characteristic of autonomous expenditure that it is not financed out of income revenues, e.g. out of wages as in the case of workers' induced consumption; it must therefore be financed by credit creation. This leads us to the theory of endogenous money. In short, conventional textbooks (e.g. Mankiw 2015) still try to convince us that banks intermediate savings (this was labelled by D.H. Robertson as "loanable fund theory"). This is not so, however, as an increasing number of economists working at respected central banks (e.g. McLeay et al. 2014) are acknowledging.[17] When banks receive a request for a loan from a trusty customer (households or firms), they will never refuse it and will consequently open a deposit in her favour. In other words, banks create money (bank deposits) on request. This capacity to lend does not depend on having received savings a few minutes before, or even on having enough reserves to back the newly created deposit. Reserves are indeed created on request of commercial banks by the central bank. The idea of the textbook *deposit multiplier* that says that the amount of deposits the banking system can create depends on the *exogenous* liquidity supply by the central bank is deadly wrong. The central bank, given the demand for credit that the market advances at the prevailing interest rates, endogenously creates reserves. Are central banks then only passive creators of reserves? Not at all. They fix the (short-period) interest rate at which they provide reserves. This rate influences the longer-period interest rates in the economy and, therefore, autonomous spending, for instance the demand for mortgages. What endogenous money theory contends is that at the interest rate of her choice, the central bank provides all the reserves requested by the market.

In neoclassical theory, the interest rate targeted by the central bank is the "natural" one at which full capacity saving[18] is absorbed by investment, in order to assure a natural unemployment rate and price stability. After the capital theory controversy, the existence of a natural interest rate is indefensible. In a Classical-Keynesian view, the central bank will fix the interest rate following political choices. As seen earlier, for instance, during the so-called "Great Moderation" decade that preceded the recent financial crisis, lax monetary policy both in the US and in the Eurozone accommodated debt-driven growth, while in other historical junctures central banks have used restrictive policies to tame the social conflict. Accordingly, in the Classical-Keynesian approach, there is no duality between monetary and real sectors, and sustainable growth relies on the cooperation between monetary and fiscal policies. Inflation, a manifestation of social conflict, should be tamed by social compromise.

4. Modern Classical Theory and other heterodox approaches

In this final section, we shall discuss the relation of MCT to some other major heterodox schools. Saltwater (neo-Keynesian) and freshwater (Monetarist) mainstream macroeconomists notoriously dissent on policy issues, but they are unanimous in the belief in standard economic theory. Heterodox economists, on the other hand, generally converge on policy issues but often disagree on basic theory. At the risk of severe oversimplification, I single out and briefly consider here five heterodox schools: Post-Keynesian, neo-Schumpeterian, neo-Kaleckian, Circuitists and Modern Monetary Theory (MMT). There a few others of course, like institutionalists, which I shall not discuss.[19] It should also be considered that boundaries between the schools are often blurred. Moreover, for reasons of space, my comments will be rather trenchant and in need of further discussion.

4.1 The uncertain Post-Keynesians

Post-Keynesianism (PK) broadly refers to a school of mainly Anglo-Saxon economists, inspired by Joan Robinson and Paul Davidson, identified by the strong emphasis on "uncertainty" as the main characteristic of capitalism. "Animal spirits" and "expectations" are related, favourite expressions. There is little doubt that the ancestor to this approach and terminology is Keynes' *General Theory* (1936). By "fundamental uncertainty", PK authors mean that decision takers find it difficult to assign a probability to the possible outcomes of their choices. Individuals will therefore hold expectations that are the opposite of the rational expectations of mainstream economics, based on a reasonable knowledge of how the economy works. Decisions are instead taken based on animal spirits, "a spontaneous urge to action rather than inaction", as Keynes (ibid., p. 161) defined them. Instability of investment – and therefore of capitalism – is consequently explained along these lines.

An important discussion on this subject, unfortunately only available in Italian, took place in 1976 between Garegnani and Joan Robinson (Garegnani 1979, pp. 120–143). In short, Garegnani argued that Joan Robinson limited her criticism of Marginalism to the obstacles that, allegedly, uncertainty and expectations (or those due to the lack of "malleability" of capital) place in the adjustment of the economy to full employment equilibrium, neglecting the more substantial criticism of the very existence of that equilibrium, forthcoming from the capital theory critique. In this regard, Garegnani denounces the support that this PK position can inadvertently lend to the modern neo-Walrasian approach which, as explained by Petri (Chapter 4 this volume), abandons the method of long-period positions to avoid the problems of capital theory. Although other PK economists are more ready to acknowledge the importance of the capital theory critique, they still attribute primary importance to uncertainty and expectations to explain unemployment and the instability of capitalism.

In this respect, I should like to quote the Cambridge economist Dennis Robertson who, in his earliest heterodox writings on trade cycles, worked closely with Keynes. Despite this closeness, he was strongly critical of theories that attributed the cycle to the ebb and flow of optimism and pessimism, rejecting any subjective explanation of trade cycles based on the "state of confidence" and arguing that:

> Granted that [the entrepreneurs'] states of mind are immediately responsible for industrial dislocation, it does not follow that they are spontaneously generated; it seems only natural, in absence of proof, to give him the benefit of the doubt, and assume that they are at least induced, however irrationally, by external facts. Hence this objection also to the search for such facts fall to the ground.
>
> (Robertson 1915, p. 9)

Robertson, like Sraffa, did not like subjectivism in economics, suggesting that we must find the objective facts that guide the formation of expectations. Smith's "discovery" of the invisible hand, that is of the role of long-period prices in guiding economic decisions, marked, after all, the birth of modern economics. What distances heterodox from conventional economics is not so much the denial of this role of the price mechanism, but rather whether this guide leads to full employment in the absence of a public *visible* hand. The study of the policy context that affects autonomous demand and, via the accelerator, investment, is, for instance, a good direction for objective investigation at the macro level of both the visible and invisible hands. Robertson (1915) found the main tangible explanation of trade cycles in technical progress, and this leads us to the second school considered here, the Schumpeterian/evolutionary school.

4.2 Schumpeter versus Smith

As known, Schumpeter (1911, 1939) attributed business cycles to swarms of innovations, following major technological breakthroughs. Central to his theory is the figure of the innovative entrepreneur who transforms a technical invention into a commercial innovation. Schumpeter did not break with neoclassical theory, which, however, he regarded as only able to explain states of rest of the economy, but not the phenomenon of economic change that, in his view, assumed the shape of cyclical strorms of "creative destructions". He was also firmly critical of Smith and Keynes.

Smith proposed in fact a very different theory of technical change. In his view, innovation depends on the division of labour, i.e. the specialisation of functions, which in turn depends on the size of the market. The reference to market size places technical change in a macroeconomic context, because innovations brought about by production on a larger scale would not be profitable in a stagnating market, while increasing market size triggers "the competition of producers":

> The increase of demand . . . encourages production, and thereby increases the competition of the producers, who, in order to undersell one another, have recourse to new division of labour and new improvements of art, which might never otherwise have been thought of.
>
> (Smith 1976 [1776], p. 748)

According to Schumpeter, Smith and the Classical economists looked at economic change as an automatic process that excluded the innovative role of the entrepreneur. For instance, he wrote:

> With A. Smith [division of labour] is practically the only factor in economic progress . . . Technological progress, "invention of all those machines" – and even investments – is induced by it and is, in fact, just an incident of it . . . Division of labour itself is attributed to an inborn propensity to truck and its development to the gradual expansion of markets . . . It thus appears and grows as an entirely impersonal force, and since it is the great motor of progress, this progress too is depersonalised.
>
> (Schumpeter 1954, pp. 187–188)

A "creative response" is juxtaposed with the "adaptive" one envisaged by the Classical economists and "accordingly, a study of creative response in business becomes coterminous with a study of entrepreneurship" (Schumpeter 1947, p. 222). As Schumpeter repeatedly stated: "entrepreneurship . . . is essentially a phenomenon that comes under the wider aspect of leadership", although he also recognised that, especially in modern times, "the entrepreneurial function need not be embodied in a physical person and in particular in a single physical person" (Schumpeter 1949, p. 261), a step in a Smithian direction.

According to the Classical economists, on the contrary, individual and organizational capacities are seen as social developments. For instance, Smith famously regarded individual ingenuity not "so much the cause, as the effect of the division of labour" (1976 [1776], p. 28), and outcome of the cooperation of the "variety of talents", so that "dissimilar genius are of use to one another" and "every man may purchase whatever part of the product of other men's talents he has occasion for" (ibid., p. 30). The role of class structure is recalled by Marx: "It is not because he is a leader of industry that a man is a capitalist; on the contrary, he is a leader of industry because he is a capitalist" (Marx 1974 [1867], p. 314). We meet again here the contrast between, on the one hand, subjective factors and methodological individualism, and on the other, the investigation of the social nature of economic evolution and technical change.[20]

Schumpeter's downplay of the Keynesian criticism of Say's Law (e.g. 1936) provides additional arguments for a critical evaluation of his approach. The emphasis that Schumpeter put on "entrepreneurship", or on the innovating firm, as the primary cause and main unit of analysis of economic growth finds another blow in the existence of limits to growth on the demand side. The only bound to entrepreneurship envisaged by Schumpeter is on the financial credit side, again a supply side factor. As a result, in Schumpeter, not less than in Marginalism, growth is seen as a supply side phenomenon, and demand does not play much of a role. This view has been picked up by major neo-evolutionary scholars of technical change like Nelson and Winter (1982, p. 220), who construct their models assuming that Say's Law is always verified.

To be sure, other modern Schumpeterians are more skeptical of Say's Law (e.g. Dosi et al. 2010). They point to an integration of the demand and the supply side of technical change (Dosi 1982) and assign centrality to the State in the generation of new technologies (Mazzucato 2013). I would argue that rather than in a subjective Schumpeterian tradition, scholars like Mazzucato move within an objectivist underground economic tradition that originates from Mercantilism, and through Friedrich List and the German historical school, arrive at the modern concepts of the entrepreneurial State and of national systems of innovations. This "Other Canon", as some Baltic scholars have named it, I regard as part of the Classical-Keynesian tradition (Cesaratto 2013).

4.3 The not-so-Kaleckian neo-Kaleckians

At odds with some Schumpeterians, most non-orthodox economists share the centrality of what Nicholas Kaldor called the "Keynesian Hypothesis" – the idea that investment is, in both the long and the short run, independent of the savings that would be forthcoming from the normal utilisation of productive capacity. Keynes showed that, within the limits of the existing capacity utilisation, it is investment that determines savings rather than the other way around. As seen earlier, the outcomes of the capital theory controversy have reinforced this conclusion (Garegnani 1978–79). How to extend the Keynesian Hypothesis to the long run is, however, controversial.

During the 1960s and 1970s, the so-called *Cambridge Equation*, proposed by Kaldor, Joan Robinson and Luigi Pasinetti, was hegemonic. In short, the idea was that capitalists decide the rate of accumulation; since a higher investment rate implies a higher saving rate, and given that profits are the main source of saving, a faster accumulation rate must be associated with a higher profit rate. This entails that, when capitalists decide the rate of growth, they also determine income distribution. Suppose that productive capacity is fully utilised and that, inspired by a wave of optimism, capitalists desire to grow faster. Armed with the purchasing power creation of banks (endogenous money) in support of their demand for additional investment goods, capitalists are able to induce a diversion of production from wage-goods to capital-goods. Given nominal wages, the price of consumption goods (whose production has fallen) rise, and real wages fall. As a result the normal profit rate will be higher. Since profits are the main source of saving, the higher profit rate lets the economy grow at a faster rate along a new equilibrium path, with saving matching the larger share of investment on income.

Both Sraffian and so-called neo-Kaleckian (NK) authors objected that the association of higher growth rates with a change of income distribution in favour of profits is not particularly robust. If anything, real wages tend to rise during periods of faster accumulation because tighter labour markets lead to an increase in workers' bargaining power. Wages would instead tend to fall during downswings when the "industrial reserve army" increases. Moreover, both NK (notably Rowthorn 1981) and Sraffian authors (notably Garegnani 1992) have criticised the Cambridge equation approach on the grounds that capitalism can accommodate an upsurge in the rate of capital accumulation by utilising productive capacity more fully, above the normal degree of capacity utilisation, without the necessity for changes in income distribution.[21]

As seen earlier, many Sraffian authors (and recently even some NK) see in the autonomous components of aggregate demand – or Luxemburg-Kalecki's external markets – the ultimate determinant of investment decisions. Unfortunately, traditional NK models do not consider these components. Following the seminal paper by Marglin and Bhaduri (1990), these models typically envisage two growth regimes, *wage-led* and *profit-led*.

Wage-led growth identifies a cooperative form of capitalism. In this regime, a rise of real wages leads to a higher demand for consumption goods to an above-normal degree of capacity utilisation *and* to a high *actual* profit rate. The intuition behind this, is that an above-normal degree of capacity utilisation implies that capitalists are extracting more profits from the installed capacity than expected; in other words, the actual or *realised* profit rate is higher than the expected or *normal* profit rate. This regime, the NKs conclude, would thus make both workers and capitalists happier. In other words, a rise in real wages by leading to an above-normal degree of capacity utilisation would also benefit capitalists by a higher actual profit rate, making cooperative capitalism possible. Crucially, NK economists assume that this regime, characterised by an above-normal degree of capacity utilisation, would be associated with a persistently higher accumulation rate because of an *endless, but never accomplished* attempt to *restore*, through higher investment, a normal degree of utilization.

Profit-led growth entails that investments are quite sensitive to the profit-share; a rise in the wage-share, for instance, is supposed to lead to an "investment strike" and to a lower accumulation rate.[22]

On *wage-led growth*, MCT would object that wages are by definition an *induced* component of income and cannot therefore be the *primum movens* of growth, a role that the SM approach more consistently assigns to the autonomous component of AD (Cesaratto 2015). Indeed, the SM model shows that a larger wage-share has, *ceteris paribus*, a *level* but not a *growth* effect on income. Looking at equation (6), a larger wage-share would increase the marginal propensity to consume with, *ceteris paribus*, a positive level effect on income. However, it would not affect the income rate of growth that would remain anchored to the growth rate of autonomous demand. Second, the NK explanation of wage-led growth is based on the peculiar association of growth *without* normal capacity utilization and an endless attempt to regain the normal degree of utilization (Vianello 1989; Cesaratto 2015).

As to *profit-led growth*, MCT tends to share the idea that gross investment is determined by expected effective demand. Variations of the normal rate of profit, as such, have no mechanical influence on gross investment. For instance, an *increase* in the normal rate of profit would have a *negative* effect on investment if associated with lower workers' consumption. Likewise, a lower *normal* rate might leave gross investment unaffected, as long as single capitalists fear the loss of market shares to competitors if they do not invest (Cesaratto 2015, pp. 167–169).

The controversy has relevance for the interpretation of the golden age of capitalism, the full employment period between 1950 and 1979. Garegnani rejects the NK interpretation of the golden age as a wage-led regime in which the interests of capitalists and workers were aligned (Cavalieri et al. 2004). In Garegnani's view, the profit rate relevant for capitalists is not the *ex post*, realised one, but the *ex-ante*, normal one, i.e. the rate they expect to earn on newly installed equipment. A rise in the real wage rate, given the techniques in use, must lead to a fall in the *normal* profit rate. It is possible that in certain historical circumstances – as happened in the golden age after the Soviet Union challenge – capitalists acquiesce to such a fall without resorting to economic policies aimed at widening the industrial reserve army; but in these circumstances we should talk of a *compromise* between clashing interests rather than of a *coincidence* of interests.

We must finally note that current attempts by NK authors to explain the recent experiences of household debt-driven growth or mercantilist export-led regimes clash with the difficulty of inserting autonomous demand within their model (Pariboni 2016) that, also in this regard, underperforms compared to the SM ability to absorb the Kaleckian insights about "external markets". Not surprisingly, NK economist are now interestingly looking at the SM model which, as kindly put by Lavoie, "has been unfairly neglected by heterodox authors . . . over the last 20 years" (Lavoie 2017, p. 194).

4.4 Circuitists and MMT

Monetary Circuit Theory (CT) stresses the role of endogenous money creation by banks in financing capitalists' production decisions (e.g. Graziani 1990). In this regard, Schumpeter's preoccupation with the financial side of innovations is seen as a forerunner of the approach. According to the CT, credit mainly consists of anticipations of money wages. These are later either spent in consumption goods or saved. The emphasis of the approach is on the power of capitalists and banks of deciding "unilaterally" production levels. This is suggestive, but deceiving.

Firms (and banks that finance them) decide production levels looking at expected aggregate demand, not in a vacuum. In the CT, however, AD is reduced to wage spending only. While no explanation of production decisions is provided, it is also not clear how capitalists and banks can realise expected profits (who buys the surplus?). Circuitists, like Graziani, respond that firms are integrated, as if in the economy only one big firm existed, so the only fictional capitalist trades with herself. However, in this way Keynesian and Kaleckian theories of effective demand are lost and, indeed, although circuitists express support for these theories, there is no clear, analytical integration between them and the CT. Indeed, endogenous money creation is mainly seen as functional to supply-side production decisions and not to sustain autonomous demand (an attempt to integrate some insight from CT in the SM approach is made by Cesaratto 2016a).

MMT has one central proposition, that the State spends before taxing or issuing debt. It cannot but be so in a Keynesian world in which it is State spending that, *inter alia*, determines the level of income and, therefore, tax revenues and saving (used to buy public debt bonds). MCT welcomes this view (Cesaratto 2016b), although a number of dividing policy issues still remain, particularly about the degree of freedom that full monetary sovereignty leaves to peripheral countries to overcome the balance of payments constraint.

5. Conclusions

The widely recognised rigour of its main exponents, the mutual consistency of its various elements (conflict-based value and distribution, demand-led accumulation theory, refusal of subjective approaches), its inclusiveness of historical and institutional explanations, assign to MCT a central role in heterodox economics. The capital theory critique has been the only challenge to the mainstream that has been taken seriously by orthodox economists (Kurz 2013), and this created the necessary space for the birth of heterodox economics (Lavoie 2011). I do not believe that, however, MCT is self-sufficient in the challenge to the mainstream. Its analytical core should, however, serve as a catalysts for heterodox research both in methodology – keeping the critical economists along the robust tracks indicated by the great Classical economists and Marx – and in analysis, with its robust and consistent theories of distribution and accumulation and openness to serious historical and institutional work.

Notes

1 Diamond refers mainly to Mesopotamia and China. Analogous conditions materialised only later and to a lesser degree in Latin America.
2 In a lively debate in *The New York Review of Books* (June and August 2012), Diamond criticised the influential study by Acemoğlu and Robinson (2012) for the role it

attributes to the "right institutions" in setting the correct incentives to individual entrepreneurship and growth. According to Diamond, developmental institutions are the *outcome* of the geographical circumstances that permitted the emergence of a surplus, not the other way round. According to Meek (1976), Turgot and Smith held a similar view.

3 We also assume that fertile land is overabundant, and hence a free good, so that we can neglect rent.

4 We are assuming that r_a remains constant in spite of the change in the scale of the agricultural sector.

5 As clearly shown by Adam Smith, to know natural or long-period prices, we must know the natural profit and wage rates.

6 In Marx's parlance, the organic composition of capital must be the same in all industries.

7 See Mongiovi (2002) for a clear critical introduction to the debate (cf. also Petri 2015). One victim of the abandonment of the labour theory of value is Marx's *Law of the Tendency of the Rate of Profit to Fall*. This tendency is due to the progressive substitution of machinery (that incorporates past or "dead" labour) for living labour. Since living labour is the only source of surplus value, any rise of real wages that would stimulate the substitution of dead with living labour would thus negatively affect the profit rate and depress the stimulus to accumulate. The analysis of the choice of techniques recalled by Petri in Chapter 4, this volume, would however suggest that in general the introduction of a new technique is never accompanied, in free competition, by a fall in the profit rate, given the real wage. Moreover, if the innovation concerns the wage-good sector, the profit rate will increase for a given real wage.

8 Those who have fully understood Keynes know that something called "saving" is not a "fluid" that has an existence independent of investment that originated them.

9 "There is no such thing as society", as Margaret Thatcher famously said.

10 "Internal markets" are those created out of the income flow generated by production decisions.

11 Analogously, Marginalists regard the capital stock as a fund of savings (a fund of foregone consumption) and gross saving as the flow that maintains and beefs up the stock. In the capital market, we draw the demand and supply of capital in stock terms; in the saving-investment market the demand and supply of capital in flow terms. The shapes of the functions are, however, similar (Cf. Petri, Chapter 4 this volume).

12 Krugman (2014a) confessed the "dirty little secrets" that "monetary policy ... normally works through housing, with little direct impact on business investment". More consistently, one should acknowledge then that Secular Stagnation "stem[s] from sustained inadequacy of domestic demand resulting from worsening functional distribution of income (in particular the declining wage share of national income in many countries). The attempts to address this shortfall essentially through monetary and credit expansion does not induce firms to invest in productive activities, but rather encourages more investment in financial assets [or construction bubbles], thereby adding to the further concentration of wealth [financial instability] and continued stagnation of incomes of most people in the society" (Chandrasekhar and Ghosh 2015, p. 3, my additions).

13 The condition of zero (or constant) inflation at the natural rate on unemployment allows mainstream economists to determine the natural interest rate, which would otherwise be unknown. There is nothing "natural" in these rates; they are just those that correspond to an unemployment rate (or industrial reserve army) large enough to keep inflation at bay. An alternative solution to reconcile full employment and price stability is in some social compromise in which the working class barters wage moderation with full employment and substantially lower income inequality.

14 This is defined as the amount of AD forthcoming at normal or long-period prices.
15 Some Sraffians prefer not to formalise the role of autonomous demand through the SM. Garegnani (2015 [1962]) is, however, a common antecedent of all sorts of Sraffian views (see Cesaratto and Mongiovi 2015).
16 In this regard, the balanced budget theorem assumes that government spending is expansionary even if fully compensated by a corresponding taxation.
17 This shows that endogenous money is not sufficient to criticize conventional theory: the endogeneity of money is a fact rather than a theory (Jakab and Kumhof 2015, p. 4).
18 Full capacity saving is the amount of saving offered when output and capacity are adjusted to the natural unemployment rate.
19 A review of heterodox schools is proposed, among others, in chapter 1 of Lavoie (2014).
20 The great historian of technical progress, Nathan Rosenberg, was openly sympathetic with the Smithian tradition and critical of Schumpeter (e.g. Rosenberg 1976, p. 292, n. 19).
21 The idea is that firms normally desire some spare capacity to meet peaks in demand in order not to leave customers dissatisfied.
22 An analogous conclusion is drawn by the believers in Marx's Law of the *Tendency* of the *Rate of Profit to Fall* (see above n. 7). These views clash with the idea that inequality is the basic cause of the lack of aggregate demand in capitalism and that there is, at least in principle, a political space for reconciling higher wages and economic growth.

References

Acemoğlu, D. and Robinson, J.A. (2012) *Why Nations Fail: The Origins of Power, Prosperity and Poverty*, Crown Business, New York.

Aspromourgos, A. (1996) *On the Origins of Classical Economics: Distribution and Value from William Petty to Adam Smith*, Routledge, London.

Barba, A. and Pivetti, M. (2009) Rising Household Debt: Its Causes and Macroeconomic Implications – A Long-period Analysis, *Cambridge Journal of Economics*, 33(1), 113–137.

Bortis, H. (1997) *Institutions, Behaviour and Economic Theory*, Cambridge University Press, Cambridge, MA.

Cavalieri, T., Garegnani, P., and Lucii, M. (2004) Anatomia di una sconfitta, *La rivista del manifesto*, 48, 44–50.

Cesaratto, S. (1999) Savings and Economic Growth in Neoclassical Theory: A Critical Survey, *Cambridge Journal of Economics*, 23(6), 771–793.

Cesaratto, S. (2013) Harmonic and Conflict Views in International Economic Relations: A Sraffian View, in Levrero, E.S., Palumbo, A. and Stirati, A. (eds) *Sraffa and the Reconstruction of Economic Theory*, vol. II, *Aggregate Demand, Policy Analysis and Growth*, Palgrave Macmillan, Basingstoke, UK.

Cesaratto, S. (2015) Neo-Kaleckian and Sraffian Controversies on the Theory of Accumulation, *Review of Political Economy*, 27(2), 154–182.

Cesaratto, S. (2016a) Initial and Final Finance in the Monetary Circuit and the Theory of Effective Demand, *Metroeconomica*, 68(2), 228–258.

Cesaratto, S. (2016b) The State Spends First: Logic, Facts, Fictions, Open Questions, *Journal of Post Keynesian Economics*, 39(1), 44–71.

Cesaratto, S. (2017) Alternative Interpretations of a Stateless Currency Crisis, *Cambridge Journal of Economics*, 41(4), 977–998.

Cesaratto, S. and Mongiovi, G. (2015) Pierangelo Garegnani, the Classical Surplus Approach and Demand-led Growth. A Symposium, *Review of Political Economy*, 27(2), 103–110.

Cesaratto, S. and Stirati, A. (2011) Germany in the European and Global Crises, *International Journal of Political Economy*, 39(4), 56–87.

Chandrasekhar, C.P. and Ghosh, J. (2015) Understanding "Secular Stagnation", www.networkideas.org.

Diamond, J. (1997) *Guns, Germs, and Steel: The Fates of Human Societies*, Norton, New York.

Dosi, G. (1982) Technological Paradigms and Technological Trajectories: A Suggested Interpretation of the Determinants and Directions of Technical Change, *Research Policy*, 11, 147–162.

Dosi, G., Fagiolo, G., and Roventini, A. (2010) Schumpeter Meeting Keynes: A Policy-Friendly Model of Endogenous Growth and Business Cycles, *Journal of Economic Dynamics and Control*, 34(9), 1748–1767

Fratini, S.M. (2016) Sraffa on the Degeneration of the Notion of Cost, *Cambridge Journal of Economics*, 42(3), 26 April 2018, 817–836.

Freitas, F. and Serrano, F. (2015) Growth Rate and Level Effects: The Adjustment of Capacity to Demand and the Sraffian Supermultiplier, *Review of Political Economy*, 27(3), 258–281.

Garegnani, P. (1978–79) Notes on Consumption, Investment and Effective Demand, Parts I & II, *Cambridge Journal of Economics*, 2(4), 335–353 and 3(1), 63–82.

Garegnani, P. (ed.) (1979) Appendici (With Papers by Garegnani and J.Robinson), in *Valore e domanda effettiva*, Einaudi, Torino.

Garegnani, P. (1984) Value and Distribution in the Classical Economists and Marx, *Oxford Economic Papers*, 3, 291–325.

Garegnani, P. (1992) Some Notes for an Analysis of Accumulation, in Halevi, J., Laibman, D., and Nell, E. (eds) *Beyond the Steady-State*, Macmillan, Basingstoke, UK.

Garegnani, P. (2005) On a Turning Point in Sraffa's Theoretical and Interpretative Position in the Late 1920s, *The European Journal of the History of Economic Thought*, 12(3), 453–492

Garegnani, P. (2015 [1962]) The Problem of Effective Demand in Italian Economic Development: On the Factors That Determine the Volume of Investment, *Review of Political Economy*, 27(2), 111–133.

Graziani, A. (1990) The Theory of the Monetary Circuit, *Économies et Sociétés*, 24(6), 7–36.

Hicks, J.R. (1950) *A Contribution to the Theory of the Trade Cycle*, Clarendon Press, Oxford, UK.

Jakab, Z. and Kumhof, M. (2015) *Banks are Not Intermediaries of Loanable Funds: And Why This Matters*, Bank of England, Working Paper No. 529.

Kalecki, M. (ed.) (1967) The Problem of Effective Demand with Tugan-Baranowski and Rosa Luxemburg, in *Selected Essays on the Dynamics of the Capitalist Economy 1933–1970*, Cambridge University Press, Cambridge, UK.

Keynes, J.M. (1936) *The General Theory of Employment, Interest and Money*, Macmillan, Basingstoke, UK.

Krugman, P. (2014a) Notes on Easy Money and Inequality, *New York Times*, 25 October.

Krugman, P. (2014b) Four Observations on Secular Stagnation, in Teulings, C. and Baldwin, R. (eds) *Secular Stagnation: Facts, Causes, and Cures*, VoxEU.org, eBook.

Kurz, H.D. (2012) Don't Treat Too Ill My Piero! Interpreting Sraffa's Papers, *Cambridge Journal of Economics*, 36(6), 1535–1569.

Kurz, H.D (ed.) (2013) *The Theory of Value and Distribution in Economics. Discussions between Pierangelo Garegnani and Paul Samuelson*, Routledge, London.

Lavoie, M. (2011) Should Sraffians Be Dropped Out of the Post-Keynesian School? *Économies et Sociétés*, série Oeconomica, 45(7), 1027–1059.

Lavoie, M. (2014) *Post-Keynesian Economics: New Foundations*, Edward Elgar, Cheltenham, UK.

Lavoie, M. (2017) Prototypes, Reality and the Growth Rate of Autonomous Consumption Expenditures: A Rejoinder, *Metroeconomica*, 68(1), 194–199.

Lerner, A. (1974) From The Treatise on Money to the General Theory, *Journal of Economic Literature*, 12(1), 38–42.

Mankiw, G.N. (2015) *Principles of Macroeconomics*, 7th ed., Cengage, Stamford, CT.

Marglin, S. and Bhaduri, A. (1990) Profit Squeeze and Keynesian Theory, in Marglin, S. and J. Schor (eds) *The Golden Age of Capitalism: Reinterpreting the Postwar Experience*, Clarendon, Oxford, UK, 153–186.

Marx, K. (1974 [1867]) *Capital. A Critical Analysis of the Capitalist Production*, Lawrence & Wishart, London.

Mazzucato, M. (2013) *The Entrepreneurial State: Debunking Public vs. Private Sector Myths*, Anthem, London.

McLeay, M., Amar, R., and Ryland, T. (2014) Money Creation in the Modern Economy, Bank of England, *Quarterly Bulletin*, No. 1, 1–14.

Meek, R.L. (1971) Smith, Turgot and the Four Stages Theory, *History of Political Economy*, 3(1), 9–27.

Meek, R.L. (1976) *Social Science and the Ignoble Savage*, Cambridge University Press, Cambridge, UK.

Mongiovi, G. (2002) Vulgar Economy in Marxian Garb: A Critique of Temporal Single System Marxism, *Review of Radical Political Economics*, 34(4), 393–416.

Nelson, R.R. and Winter, S.G. (1982) *An Evolutionary Theory of Economic Change*, Harvard University Press, Cambridge, MA.

Pariboni, R. (2016) Household Consumer Debt, Endogenous Money and Growth: A Supermultiplier-Based Analysis, *PSL Quarterly Review*, 69(278), 211–234.

Petri, F. (2015) On Some Modern Reformulations of the Labour Theory of Value, *Contributions to Political Economy*, 34(1), 77–104.

Ricardo, D. (1815) An Essay on the Influence of a Low Price of Corn on the Profits of Stock, in *The Works and Correspondence of David Ricardo*, P. Sraffa (ed.) (with M. Dobb), Cambridge University Press, 1951, vol. IV.

Ricardo, D. (1821) *On the Principles of Political Economy and Taxation*, in *The Works and Correspondence of David Ricardo*, P. Sraffa (ed.) (with M. Dobb), Cambridge University Press, 1951, vol. I.

Robertson, D.H. (1915) *A Study of Industrial Fluctuation*, P. S. King & Son, London (Series of Reprints of Scarce Works on Political Economy No. 8, London School of Economics 1948).

Rosenberg, N. (1976) *Perspectives on Technology*, Cambridge University Press, Cambridge, UK.

Rowthorn, R. (1981) Demand, Real Wages and Economic Growth, *Thames Papers in Political Economy*. Autumn TP/PPE/81/3.

Schumpeter, J.A. (1911) *The Theory of Economic Development: An Inquiry into Profits, Capital, Credit, Interest and the Business Cycle*, Transaction Publishers, New Brunswick, NJ and London.

Schumpeter, J.A. (1936) Review of the *General Theory, Journal of the American Statistical Society*, repr. in Schumpeter *Essays* (1989), 160–164.

Schumpeter, J.A. (1939) *Business Cycles: A Theoretical, Historical, and Statistical Analysis of the Capitalist Process*, McGraw-Hill, New York.

Schumpeter, J.A. (1947) The Creative Response in Economic Theory, *Journal of Economic History*, repr. in Schumpeter *Essays* (1989), 221–231.

Schumpeter, J.A. (1949) Economic Theory and Entrepreneurial History, in *Change and the Entrepreneur*, prepared by the Research Center in Entrepreneurial History, Harvard University Press, repr. in Schumpeter *Essays* (1989), 253–272.

Schumpeter, J.A. (1954) *History of Economic Analysis*, Oxford University Press, Oxford, UK.

Schumpeter, J.A. (1989) *Essays*, Clemence, R.V. (ed.), Transaction Publishers, New Brunswick, NJ.

Smith, A. (1976 [1776]) *An Enquiry into the Nature and Causes of the Wealth of Nations*, Cambell, R.H. and Skinner, A.S. (eds), Oxford University Press, Oxford, UK.

Steedman, I. (1979) *Trade amongst Growing Economies*, Cambridge University Press, Cambridge, UK.

Stirati, A. (1994) *The Theory of Wages in Classical Economics: A Study of Adam Smith, David Ricardo and Their Contemporaries*, Edward Elgar, Aldershot, UK.

Stirati, A. (2016) Real Wages in the Business Cycle and the Theory of Income Distribution: An Unresolved Conflict between Theory and Facts in Mainstream Macroeconomics, *Cambridge Journal of Economics*, 40(2), 639–661.

Summers, L. (2012) Secular Stagnation, speech at 14th Annual IMF Research Conference, Washington, DC, November.

Svizzero, S. and Tisdell, C.A. (2016) Economic Evolution, Diversity of Societies and Stages of Economic Development: A Critique of Theories Applied to Hunters and Gatherers and their Successors, *Cogent Economics & Finance*, 4(1), 1161322. https://doi.org/10.1080/23322039.2016.1161322.

Vianello, F. (1989) Effective Demand and the Rate of Profits: Some Thoughts on Marx, Kalecky and Sraffa, in Sebastiani M. (ed.) *Kalecki's Relevance Today*, Macmillan, Basingstoke, UK.

Wray, L.R. (1998) *Understanding Modern Money: The Key to Full Employment and Price Stability*, Edward Elgar, Cheltenham, UK.

6 A Marx 'crises' model

The reproduction schemes revisited

Marco Veronese Passarella

1. Introduction

The US financial crisis of 2007–2008 and the crisis of the Euro Area which has been taking place since the end of 2009 have arguably been triggered and then fostered by a multiplicity of factors. Several radical and other 'dissenting' analyses of the historical causes of western countries' economic and financial distress have been developed ever since. This is not surprising. Quite a few, alternate, theories of crisis can be found in or built upon Marx's works (see, among others, Shaikh 1978, and Clarke 1990). The long-run fall in the rate of profit (resulting either from the rising organic composition of capital or from the depletion of the reserve army of labour), the thinning of the costing margin due to class struggle (either overdistribution or overproduction), the lack of aggregate demand (meaning the tendency to overproduction that may result in a 'realisation' crisis), and the rise of sectoral imbalances (or 'disproportionalities'), are all mentioned by Marx as inner forces or tendencies of capitalism.

This chapter aims neither to endorse explicitly any of these explanations nor to provide a brand new interpretation or theory of crisis. Rather it builds upon the Marxian enlarged reproduction schemes to test the effects of some recent developments in the most advanced capitalist nations on an artificial two-sector or 'two-department' growing economy. It shows that, simplified though they are, the Marxian reproduction schemes may allow the redefining and comparing of a variety of theories of crisis within a coherent analytical framework. The method chosen is quantitative. Different causes of crisis are treated as specific shocks, meaning changes in parameters and exogenous variables of a formal difference equation model. Their dynamic impact on key endogenous variables is then analysed through numerical simulations. These shocks, in turn, are meant to reproduce the most apparent 'stylised facts' – to steal an expression from Nicholas Kaldor – of the current phase of capitalism. This method is consistent with the accounting approach used by Marx in the second volume of *Capital*. In fact, baseline parameters and initial values of variables are usually taken from Marx's own examples.

The rest of the chapter is organised as follows. Sections 2 and 3 set up the benchmark model and define the reproduction (or balanced growth) conditions of the system. The resemblance of the Marxian approach to the Cambridge School of Economics and other recent post-Keynesian theories is briefly discussed. In Section 4 an extended Marxian 'enlarged reproduction' model is developed, aiming to account for the effect of financial markets and institutions on the creation of social value and surplus value. In Section 5 a number of experiments are performed to test the impact of some 'stylised facts' (distilled from recent developments in real-world highly financialised countries) on an artificial two-department growing economy. Key findings are discussed further in Section 6.

2. The benchmark model

The view of the economic system as a circular flow of interconnected acts of production and circulation of commodities and money is deeply rooted in the history of economic thought. Its inception can be traced back to the pioneering work of François Quesnay and other French Physiocrats of the eighteenth century.[1] The Physiocrats (and, at least to some extent, David Ricardo and the Classical political economists) focused on the process of creation, circulation, and consumption of the *produit net* of an agriculture-based economy. Marx built upon that line of research and focused on the process of creation, circulation, and destruction of the monetary surplus value in a manufacturing-based capitalist system (Veronese Passarella 2017). The so-called 'reproduction schemes' are developed in the second volume of *Capital* as a logical tool to analyse this process (Marx 1885, chapters 20 and 21). The reproduction schemes are accounting matrixes where Marx defines the theoretical equilibrium conditions of the economy in terms of interdependences between 'departments' – meaning the net flows of commodities that must be produced and circulated among the productive macro-sectors to meet the respective demands of inputs.

While Marx never engaged with a formal model of enlarged reproduction, he provided several notes and numerical examples that may well be turned into a system of difference (or differential) equations. In fact, there is a well-established tradition of dynamic modelling carried out by Marxist economists since the 1970s, inspired by the Marxian reproduction schemes (see, among others, Harris 1972; Bronfenbrenner 1973; Morishima 1973; more recently, Olsen 2015; Cockshott 2016). This section draws from that tradition and cross-breeds it with other current heterodox approaches, particularly with post-Keynesian macro-monetary modelling.[2] This allows the setting up of the formal benchmark model of a growing capitalist economy that moves forward in time, t, and is made up of two sectors or departments: a sector producing capital or investment goods (called 'department I' by Marx), defined by the subscript 'i'; and a sector producing consumption goods (named 'department II'), defined by the subscript 'c'.[3] For the sake of simplicity, it is assumed that each production process takes a fraction $1/n_j$ (with $j = c, i,$) of the reference period, t, where n_j is a parameter accounting for the sectoral intra-period turnover rate.[4] Commodities are produced by means of capital goods and labour inputs.

Labour supply is plentiful and does not form a binding constraint on the level of employment (see Appendix 1). A net product arises (both in real and monetary terms) in each sector and is distributed as wages to workers and surplus value (or profit) to capitalists.

As is well known, Marx's analysis of value relies upon the distinction between the variable component of capital and its constant component. The former roughly corresponds to the wage bill paid by the industrial capitalists to the workers in exchange for their labour power. This sum covers the part of the total working day that is devoted to the production of 'subsistence' for workers.[5] Under a growing economy, the two sectoral investment plans in variable capital inputs are, respectively:

$$V_i = V_{i,-1} + \frac{S_{i,-1} \cdot \theta_{i,-1}}{1 + q_i}$$
(1)

and

$$V_c = V_{c,-1} + \frac{S_{c,-1} \cdot \theta_{c,-1}}{1 + q_c}$$
(2)

where S_j is the surplus value created in the j-th department (with $j = i,c$), θ_j is the sectoral rate of saving or retention of capitalists, $q_j = C_j / V_j$ is the sectoral organic composition of capital (OCC),[6] and C_j is the sectoral constant capital, meaning the amount of capital inputs (i.e. fixed and circulating capital net of wages) accumulated in the j-th department.

Equations (1) and (2) show that a share θ_j of the surplus value created in the j-th sector is reinvested in the same sector in the subsequent period.[7] The ratio of constant capital to variable capital is defined by the OCC, which is taken as an exogenous variable of the model. Accordingly, the constant capital advanced in the production can be worked out as:

$$C_i = V_i \cdot q_i$$
(3)

and

$$C_c = V_c \cdot q_c$$
(4)

According to Marx, it is only the variable capital that valorises in the production sphere, as the wage-earners work well beyond the time necessary to cover the exchange value of their own labour power. As a result, the 'masses' of surplus value created in each sector in a certain period are, respectively:

$$S_i = V_i \cdot \varepsilon_i \cdot n_i$$
(5)

and

$$S_c = V_c \cdot \varepsilon_c \cdot n_c \tag{6}$$

where ε_j is the sectoral rate of surplus value (mirroring the composition of the total working day and hence the rate of exploitation of workers) and n_j is a parameter reflecting the sectoral intra-period turnover rate.[8]

Equations (5) and (6) show that the mass of surplus value created in the j-th sector across a period – say, a quarter or a year – is a direct function of the variable capital invested in that sector, the rate of surplus value, and the turnover rate, meaning the number of times the same capital is reinvested within the period. In principle, capitalists can either consume the non-retained surplus value or divert it towards their own personal saving. Accordingly, the capitalists' unproductive expenditures are, respectively:

$$F_i = (1-\theta_i) \cdot S_i \cdot (1-\sigma_{i1}) + (1-\sigma_{i2}) \cdot H_{i,-1} \tag{7}$$

and

$$F_c = (1-\theta_c) \cdot S_c \cdot (1-\sigma_{c1}) + (1-\sigma_{c2}) \cdot H_{c,-1} \tag{8}$$

where σ_{j1} and σ_{j2} (with $j = i,c$) are the marginal propensities to save (hoard) out of income and wealth, respectively, and H_j is the stock of financial wealth amassed by j-sector capitalists. The latter can be defined as follows:

$$H_i = H_{i,-1} + \sigma_{i1} \cdot (1-\theta_i) \cdot S_{i,-1} \tag{9}$$

and

$$H_c = H_{c,-1} + \sigma_{c1} \cdot (1-\theta_c) \cdot S_{c,-1} \tag{10}$$

Accordingly, the realised total values of sectoral outputs are, respectively:

$$Y_i = C_i + V_i + \theta_i \cdot S_i + F_i \tag{11}$$

and

$$Y_c = C_c + V_c + \theta_c \cdot S_c + F_c \tag{12}$$

If capitalists spend their all their income, either through productive investment or through consumption, then $Y_j = C_j + V_j + S_j$, meaning that the overall monetary value realised (by the capitalists) on the market matches or 'validates' the overall value created *in potentia* (by the workers) in the production sphere. Similarly, the realised sectoral profit rates are, respectively:

$$r_i = \frac{S_i \cdot \theta_i + F_i}{V_i + C_i}$$

(13)

and

$$r_c = \frac{\theta_c \cdot S_c + F_c}{V_c + C_c}$$

(14)

Finally, the sectoral rates of accumulation can be defined as:

$$g_i = \frac{\dfrac{S_i \cdot \theta_i}{1 + q_i}}{V_i} = \varepsilon_i \cdot \theta_i \cdot n_i \cdot \frac{1}{1 + q_i}$$

(15)

and

$$g_c = \varepsilon_c \cdot \theta_c \cdot n_c \cdot \frac{1}{1 + q_c}$$

(16)

Each sectoral rate of growth is a direct function of the retention rate, the exploitation rate, and the intra-period turnover rate parameter, and an indirect function of the organic composition of capital of the j-th sector.

3. The reproduction conditions

3.1 Simple reproduction

As has been mentioned, Marx (1885) defines the equilibrium conditions for a capitalist economy in terms of the necessary interdependences between macro-sectors, meaning the theoretical requirements allowing the overall system to reproduce smoothly over time.[9] Marx analyses the equilibrium conditions under a simple reproduction regime (namely, a stationary-state economy) and then under an enlarged or expanded reproduction regime (meaning a growing economy). Capitalists' hoarding is assumed away, so that $\sigma_{1j} = 0$ and hence $H_j = 0$. In addition, sectoral rates of retention are all null under a simple reproduction regime ($\theta_j = 0$), and so are accumulation rates ($g_j = 0$). Investment and consumption goods markets clear when:

$$Y_i = C_i + C_c$$

and

$$Y_c = V_i + V_c + F_i + F_c$$

Using equations (11) and (12) in the equalities above, one gets the well-known Marxian reproduction condition for a stationary-state economy:

$$C_c = V_i + F_i = V_i + S_i \tag{4B}$$

After some manipulation, one also obtains:

$$\frac{V_i}{V_c} = \frac{q_c}{1+\varepsilon_i} \tag{4C}$$

Equation (4B) shows that the neo-value of output of the i-sector (right-hand component) must match the capital input needs of c-sector's capitalists (left-hand component). Equation (4C) shows that the equilibrium distribution of variable capital across sectors depends on the c-sector OCC and the i-sector exploitation rate. When this condition is met, the economy finds itself in the simple reproduction equilibrium position. By contrast, if $V_i + S_i > C_c$ there is a lack of demand for capital goods. According to Marx, market prices of capital goods will tend to fall short of reproduction values. As a result, both the (expected) profit rate and the real investment fall. Similarly, if $V_i + S_i < C_c$ there is an excess of demand for investment goods. Market prices exceed reproduction values. Both the profit rate and the real investment rise. Sooner or later the lack (excess) of demand for capital goods ends up reducing (increasing) the supply of capital goods.[10]

However, Marx does not advocate any inner adjustment mechanism of capitalist economies. Under a free market regime, nothing ensures that the change in the supply of capital goods – resulting from capitalists' individual decisions – exactly matches the supply-demand gap. For Marx, once capitalists' investment plans are out of equilibrium, individual expectations and behaviours (meaning competition between capitalists) drag prices and quantities away from their own reproduction values. In real-world capitalist economies, 'supply and demand never coincide, or if they do so, it is only by chance and not to be taken into account for scientific purposes: it should be considered as not having happened' (Marx 1894, p. 291). In principle, the equilibrium condition may be regarded as a long-run attractor, but cyclical fluctuations and crises are an inherent feature of capitalism. These recurring phenomena could prepare the ground for a radical undermining of the system. However, the final collapse of capitalism is anything but *necessary*. The contradictions of capitalism, including the one between the drive towards the unlimited expansion of production and limited consumption, 'testify to its historically transient character, and make clear the conditions and causes of its collapse and transformation into a higher form; but they by no means rule out either the possibility of capitalism' (Lenin 1908, chapter I, section VI, p. 57). In other words, the reproduction schemes show that capitalism 'proceeds though crises rather than being rendered an impossibility because of them' (Patnaik 2012, p. 374).

3.2 Enlarged reproduction

Things get slightly more complicated when one considers a growing economy. Now the reproduction conditions are met if and only if capitalists' production and accumulation plans are mutually consistent. Following Marx, one can assume that it is the rate of accumulation in the consumption goods sector that varies to ensure the smooth reproduction of the system (see Olsen 2015). In other words, the *c*-sector demand for investment goods is assumed to adjust to match the net supply by the *i*-sector. In formal terms, the accumulation of constant capital in the *c*-sector is:

$$S_c \cdot \theta_c \cdot \frac{q_c}{1+q_c} + C_c = Y_i - C_i - S_i \cdot \theta_i \cdot \frac{q_i}{1+q_i}$$

Similarly, the accumulation of variable capital in the *c*-sector is:

$$S_c \cdot \theta_c \cdot \frac{1}{1+q_c} = \left[Y_i - C_i - S_i \cdot \theta_i \cdot \frac{q_i}{1+q_i} - C_c \right] \cdot \frac{1}{q_c}$$

Finally, the equilibrium rate of growth of the *c*-sector can be worked out as follows:

$$g_c = \frac{S_c \cdot \theta_c \cdot \frac{q_c}{1+q_c}}{C_c} = \frac{Y_i - C_i - S_i \cdot \theta_i \cdot \frac{q_i}{1+q_i}}{C_c} - 1$$

This condition ensures the consistency of *c*-sector capitalists' accumulation plans with *i*-sector capitalists' production (and investment) plans. In other words, it assures the long-run gravitation of the economy towards the 'reproduction equilibrium'. Such a state is extremely unlikely to be matched (and maintained) in practice. In fact, the reproduction schemes allow Marx to argue that real–world capitalist economies always work in disequilibrium.[11] They also allow for shedding light on the adjustment paths of key variables of the model. This is the reason equation below is used hereafter:

$$g_c = \left[\frac{Y_i - C_i - S_i \cdot \theta_i \cdot \dfrac{q_i}{1+q_i}}{C_c} - 1 \right] + g_\xi$$

(16B)

where g_ξ is a random component accounting for 'exogenous shocks' to the c-sector growth rate.[12]

Notice that g_c may well differ from g_i in the short run. However, the former converges towards the latter in the long run (due to the constancy of OCCs), i.e. $\lim_{t \to +\infty} (g_{c,t}) = g_i$. As a result, the economy-wide 'balanced growth' rate is:

$$g = g_c = g_i = \varepsilon_i \cdot \theta_i \cdot n_i \cdot \frac{1}{1+q_i} = \theta_i \cdot r_i$$

(17)

Using equation (16) in (17), the equilibrium solution can be redefined as:

$$\frac{\theta_c}{\theta_i} = \frac{\varepsilon_i}{\varepsilon_c} \cdot \frac{n_i}{n_c} \cdot \frac{1+q_c}{1+q_i}$$

(17B)

Equation (17B) is the dynamic counterpart of equation (4C), meaning that the equilibrium requires that the ratio between sectoral retention rates be a direct function of the ratio between sectoral OCCs – given turnover and exploitation rates. Since these ratios are independent of each other, there is nothing to ensure that equation (17B) holds true in fact. A balanced growth is a theoretical possibility, as the expansion of production in one sector enlarges the market for the other. However, 'the rate of growth of production in the various branches of production is determined primarily by the uneven development of the conditions of production, rather than by the different rates of growth of the markets for their products' (Clarke 1990, p. 458). This leads to a disproportional development of the two sectors, which is the form taken by the inner tendency of capitalism to overaccumulation and crisis.

Similarly, equation (17) shows that enlarged reproduction conditions are matched if sectors grow all at the same pace. It bears a strong resemblance to the Cambridge distributive equation, interpreted as a dynamic investment function and rearranged for a two-sector economy (see Lavoie 2014).[13] Equation (17) shows that the economy-wide rate of growth is a direct function of both the retention rate of i-sector capitalists and the i-sector rate of profit. This means that, while the i-sector retention rate is exogenous, the retention rate of the c-sector is determined endogenously as follows:

$$\theta_c = g_c \cdot (1 + q_c) / (e_c \cdot n_c)$$

(18)

Equation (18) shows that the retention rate of the c-sector adjusts endogenously to guarantee the enlarged reproduction of the system.[14] The convergence of sectoral growth rates, and the necessary adjustment of the c-sector retention rate, are shown by charts A and B (in Figure 6.1), respectively. Chart C shows the (increasing) trend in sectoral outputs and hence in total output. Finally, chart D shows the sectoral profit rates and the general rate of profit of the economy. While the sectoral profit rates do not converge towards a uniform rate, the general or average profit rate of the economy declines in the first few periods and then stabilises because of the asymmetric adjustment in the sectoral stocks of capital.

4. The amended model

Simplified though they are, the Marxian reproduction schemes provide a refined explanation of the fragility of unregulated capitalist economies. In fact, Marx's grim predictions fit well with the economic, political, and social instability that marked early-industrialised countries from the end of the Victorian era to the Second World War. They also implicitly account for the stabilising function that has historically been performed by the government sector since the 1930s. However, there is no room in the reproduction schemes for the effect of the development in the banking and financial sector on the creation of social value and surplus value. The increasing importance of financial markets, institutions, assets, and motives – namely, the 'financialisation' process – is one of the most apparent aspects of modern economies and should be explicitly accounted for. In addition, the reproduction schemes do not take into consideration the long-run impact of the competition between capitalists on sectoral profit rates and prices. In fact, no price-setting mechanism is established, as prices are just assumed to be proportional to labour contents of commodities. The fact is that the reproduction schemes are discussed in the second volume of *Capital*, whereas the so-called 'equalisation' of the profit rate and the formation of production prices are covered by Marx in the third volume. While the manuscripts that comprise the third volume were written by Marx before those comprising the second one, the former logically follows the latter as the degree of abstraction gets lower as the analysis proceeds. The effect of competition (and market forces) on reproduction conditions can only be discussed after those conditions have been worked out under the hypothesis of exchange of equivalent values.

The current section aims to bridge these gaps. For this purpose, three amendments are made to the benchmark model. First, it is assumed that the retention rate and hence the investment undertaken by i-sector capitalists are a non-linear function of the expected rate of profit. Drawing from Robinson (1962), it is assumed that any increase in the propensity to invest (i.e. capitalists' rate of retention in this simplified model) requires ever larger increases in the expected rate of profit. If adaptive expectations are hypothesised, the equation defining the rate of retention in the i-sector can be defined as:

$$\theta_i = \theta_{i0} + \theta_{i1} \cdot \ln\left(1 + r_{i,-1} + r_\xi\right)$$

$$(19)$$

where r_ξ is a random or shock component of profit expectations incorporating capitalists' 'animal spirits', whereas parameters θ_{i0} and θ_{i1} are defined in such a way that: $0 \le \theta_i \le 1$.

Similarly, it is assumed that the parameter defining the sectoral intra-period turnover rate is a function of the share of surplus value which is diverted from productive scopes to financial assets and services (Veronese Passarella and Baron 2015). More precisely, F_j (with $j = i, c$) is redefined to include both the amount of (unproductive) capital invested in financial assets and the expenditure for financial services. This is the second amendment to the benchmark reproduction model. If a positive but decreasing impact of finance on the turnover is assumed, sectoral turnover rates can be defined as follows:

$$n_i = n_{i0} + n_{i1} \cdot \ln\left(F_{i,-1}\right)$$

$$(20)$$

and

$$n_c = n_{c0} + n_{c1} \cdot \ln\left(F_{c,-1}\right)$$

$$(21)$$

where $n_{i0}, n_{i1}, n_{c0}, n_{c1} \ge 0$. Equations (20) and (21) state that any increase in the sectoral rate of turnover requires ever larger increases in the past expenditure for financial assets and services. Notice that now θ_i defines i-capitalists' preference for productive investment against non-productive expenditure, while parameters σ_{1j} and σ_{2j} in equations (7) and (8) define the speed or pace of 'financialisation'.

Furthermore, competition between capitalists under a *laissez faire* regime entails the cross-sector levelling of profit rates in the long run (Marx 1894). While profit equalisation should only be regarded as a tendency, it allows the pointing out of, first, the dominance of capital-intensive sectors over labour intensive sectors (as the former 'steal' surplus value from the latter), and second, the consistency of the general law of creation of value (meaning that social value arises from the exploitation of living labour in the production sphere) with the specific law of distribution of value (meaning the prevailing price setting, including the one defined by the competition hypothesis). Notice that the general rate of profit can be split into two components, notably the profit share of net income and (the inverse of the) total capital to net output ratio.[15] In formal terms, the wage share of net income is:

$$\omega = \frac{V_i + V_c}{Y_i + Y_i - \left(C_i + C_c\right)}$$

$$(22)$$

The profit share is:

$$\pi = \frac{\theta_i \cdot S_i + \theta_c \cdot S_c + F_i + F_c}{Y_i + Y_c - (C_i + C_c)} = 1 - \omega$$

(23)

Finally, the total capital (including the wage-bill) to net output ratio is:

$$a = \frac{V_i + V_c + C_i + C_c}{Y_i + Y_c - (C_i + C_c)}$$

(24)

The general (realised) rate of profit is therefore:

$$r = \frac{\theta_i \cdot S_i + \theta_c \cdot S_c + F_i + F_c}{V_i + V_c + C_i + C_c} = \frac{\pi}{a}$$

(25)

As is well known, this is the profit rate that would prevail across sectors if capitalists were free to invest their own capitals wherever it is more convenient for them. Sectoral outputs can now be expressed in terms of prices of production. They are, respectively:

$$\hat{Y}_i = C_i + V_i + r \cdot (C_i + V_i) = C_i + V_i + \theta_i \cdot P_i + F_i$$

(11B)

and

$$\hat{Y}_c = C_c + V_c + r \cdot (C_c + V_c) = C_c + V_c + \theta_c \cdot P_c + F_c$$

(12B)

where $P_j = r \cdot (C_j + V_j)$ is the total mass of profit realised in the j-th sector.[16]
Notice that sectoral OCCs do not converge to a uniform ratio, as they depend on a variety of sector-specific technological and institutional factors. As a result, sectoral production prices usually differ from sectoral values. Growth rates, in contrast, still converge in the long run to meet the criteria for a balanced growth, and the same goes for sectoral retention rates (see charts E and F in Figure 6.2). In formal terms:

$$g_i = \frac{\theta_i \cdot P_i}{C_i + V_i} = \theta_i \cdot r$$

(15B)

and

$$g_{c,t} = \frac{\hat{Y}_i - C_i - \theta_i \cdot P_i - C_c}{C_c + V_c} = g = g_i \text{ for } t \to +\infty$$

(16C)

where P_j is the mass of profit realised by j-sector capitalists and r is the general rate of profit arising from the competition between capitals.

Since both the accumulation rate and the profit rate are uniform across sectors in the long run, sectoral retention rates must converge too:

$$\theta_{c,t} = \theta = \theta_i \text{ for } t \to +\infty$$

and hence:

$$g = g_c = g_i = \theta \cdot r \tag{17B}$$

where θ is the long-run uniform rate of retention on profits (or rate of retention out of capital incomes).

In addition, using equation (25) in equation (17B) one gets:

$$g = \frac{\theta}{a} \cdot \pi \tag{17C}$$

The latter calls to mind a familiar result in Keynesian macroeconomic dynamics of the 1930s to 1940s, that is, the Harrod-Domar warranted rate of growth (Harrod 1939; Domar 1946).[17] Given the profit share, the economy-wide equilibrium growth rate depends on the capitalists' retention rate and (the inverse of) the capital to output ratio.

Notice, finally, that charts G and H in Figure 6.2 confirm the well-known Marx's finding that capital-intensive sectors 'steal' surplus-value from labour-intensive sectors. Given the sectoral demand schedules, production prices of investment goods are higher than (or more than proportional to) values, whereas production prices of consumption goods are lower than (or less than proportional to) values. This happens because a higher OCC has been assumed in the i-sector compared to the c-sector.

5. Some experiments: shocking Marx

In this section some comparative dynamics exercises are performed. The aim is to see how the main endogenous variables of the amended model react following a shock to key exogenous variables and parameter values. The adjustment process from the old equilibrium position (meaning the initial balanced growth rate) to the new one is then analysed. Such a methodology is akin to the current post-Keynesian approach to macro-monetary modelling (e.g. Lavoie 2014). In particular, the impacts of the following shocks are tested:

(a) An increase in the OCC. This is the standard Marxian assumption underpinning the alleged tendency for the general profit rate to fall. For Marx, each individual capitalist finds it profitable to replace workers with machines (and other constant capital components) to increase labour productivity and reduce the bargaining power of workers. While this is a rational behaviour for the individual capitalist, it ends up reducing the source that social surplus value is extracted from, thereby affecting the general profit rate of the economy.

(b) A fall in the economy-wide propensity to consume, leading to a lack of aggregate demand and hence to a realisation crisis. This experiment is coherent with the well-known Marx's claim that:

> [t]he last cause of all real crises always remains the poverty and restricted consumption of the masses as compared to the tendency of capitalist production to develop the productive forces in such a way that only the absolute power of consumption of the entire society would be their limit.

> (Marx 1894, p. 88)[18]

(c) A fall in the rate of retention out of profits, reflecting a fall in capitalists' propensity to invest in productive assets, or a higher reliance on financial markets to fund production plans, or a higher pressure to pursue shareholder value maximisation in the short run. This is a way to test some of the recent developments associated with financialisation in our simplified artificial economy.

(d) A change in the rate of turnover of capital, reflecting the 'bell-shaped' impact of the developments in the banking and financial sectors on the 'manner' of extraction of living labour from workers in the production sphere (Veronese Passarella and Baron 2014). This experiment is an alternate way to test the impact of financialisation within a Marxian model.

(e) The rise (or the worsening) of imbalances between departments, roughly mirroring the effect of external imbalances between national economies. This experiment aims to account for the 'uneven and combined development' of nations, which is another well-known concept in Marxist tradition of thought.

While experiments (a) and (b) have been the focus of long-lasting debates among the Marxists and between the Marxists and other economists, experiments (c) and (d) are somewhat original. They are meant to echo the recent developments in highly financialised economies, preparing the ground for the US financial crisis of 2007–2008. Similarly, experiment (e) can be regarded as a first step towards a formal Marxian model aiming to account for the impact of external imbalances between the members of a certain economic area. The model tested is made up of equations (1) to (15), (16B), and (18) to (25). Equation (16B) provides the long-run attractor of the system. The analysis is focused on the medium-run readjustment dynamics triggered by specific shocks to exogenous variables and parameter values. Consequently, the profit equalisation effect generated by competition between capitalists is assumed away.[19] Shocks are all run in period 20.

Focusing on the first experiment, Figure 6.3 shows the impact of a 10% increase of i-sector OCC on growth rates, profit rates, and income shares. As one would expect, the impact is negative on both the economy-wide accumulation rate (chart I) and the i-sector rate of profit (chart L). The average rate of profit declines as well, but this does not affect the c-sector rate of profit if cross-sector capital movements are not allowed. Finally, the relative reduction of wages paid in the i-sector is not associated with a change in the economy-wide wage share and hence in the overall profit share in net income (chart M). As is well known, the fall in the rate of profit due to the increase in the organic composition of capital is regarded by Marx as the most important inner law of motion of capitalism. In fact, some contemporary Marxists regard financialisation as being a result of the fall in profitability of western economies since the 1970s. Yet, that trend is regarded by other Marxist authors as a long-run secular tendency (acting as the economic equivalent of the law of gravitation) that does not provide the ground for a theory of crisis – meaning that can neither explain the *necessity* of the crisis nor account for each specific cyclical turn.

So, unsurprisingly, only a few authors have traced the recent crises back to the tendency for the profit rate to fall. Most Marxist, radical, and post-Keynesian economists (and also some New Keynesians) have focused on income inequality and other financial factors as the main triggers of the US crisis of 2007–2008 and the current crisis of Euro Area's member-states. Figure 6.4 shows the impact of a fall in i-sector propensity to consume on growth rates, profit rates, and income shares.[20] The negative effect on the accumulation rate of the c-sector is apparent, though temporary (chart N). The fall in aggregate demand, in turn, affects negatively the economy wide profit rate and the profit share in net income (charts O and P). In other words, the realisation crisis turns into a profitability crisis for the capitalist class.[21] Notice that the lack of demand (and the overproduction) may well be the outcome of an increase in income inequality, involving a rise in the economy-wide marginal propensity to save (hoard), as is usually claimed by the Keynesians.

As mentioned, the possible link between income inequality and crisis has been stressed by many heterodox and 'dissenting' orthodox economists since the start of the US financial crisis. Popular though it is, the 'inequality' interpretation neglects some of the most notable developments of highly financialised capitalist economies in the last few decades. Two of them are worth stressing here: the fall in the rate of retention on corporate profits, and the impact of the financial sector on the turnover rate of capital. A fall in the retention rate of capitalists depresses the economy-wide accumulation rate, even though the initial impact on the c-sector growth rate is positive (chart Q in Figure 6.5), because of the increase in current consumption. Sectoral profit rates remain unchanged, but a somewhat paradoxical positive effect on the average profit rate arises, because of the increasing weight of the c-sector (chart R in Figure 6.5). Finally, there is no aggregate impact on income distribution.

The association between growing income inequality and increasing short-termism of corporations has been one of the most important features of highly financialised Anglo-Saxon economies since the 1990s. However, the analysis of the causes of the initial success of such a finance-led capitalism is as important as the examination of its own flaws. Notice that, from a Marxian perspective, the amount of capital invested in financial assets and businesses is unproductive. Finance may well circulate the already created value but cannot create value for the macro-economy, let alone surplus value. However, financial markets, banks, and other financial institutions are all but unnecessary. In fact, they allow the industrial capitalists to fund their own production and investment plans.[22] In addition, financialisation (meaning the stronger and stronger dominance of financial markets, agents, motives, and culture) ends up affecting the 'form' of the extraction of surplus labour from workers, leading to a 'real subsumption of labour to finance' (Bellofiore 2011). It is not coincidence that the increasing weight of finance is usually associated with 'reforms' of the labour market and a change in the corporate governance.

Such an indirect impact of finance on the creation of surplus value is captured by the turnover rate of capital in the Marxian theory. Particularly, it seems to be reasonable to assume that the absolute impact on the (intra-period) turnover rate of the investment in financial assets or services is positive, at least during 'normal times', whereas its marginal impact is negative.[23] The effect on accumulation, profitability, and net income distribution, of an increase in the autonomous component of the i-sector turnover rate function − n_{i0} in equation (20) − is shown in Figure 6.6. The growth rate of the economy increases (chart T) and so does the average profit rate (chart U). These effects arise, in turn, from the increase in the mass of social surplus value. The profit share in net income augments too (chart V), thereby confirming the negative influence of financialisation on distributive equality. The opposite happens in 'times of distrust', when the impact of finance on capital valorisation fades away or even becomes negative.[24] These features are all consistent with the available empirical evidence about the effect of financialisation on advanced economies since the late 1980s.[25]

The last experiment deals with the effect of a positive but temporary shock to the c-sector autonomous accumulation on sectoral growth rates and the output gap (meaning the difference between i-sector output value and c-sector one). It shows that the readjustment process can be rather painful for the 'dependent' sector or economy (chart W in Figure 6.8). A catching up process initially shows up, but the output gap keeps on increasing in absolute terms and remains unchanged in relative terms in the long run (chart X). Clearly, the current model is too simplified to be applied to the analysis of real-world capitalist economies. However, this simple experiment shows that a further refinement of the Marxian reproduction schemes could allow for accounting for the impact of external imbalances between national economies, or between an individual country (which is likened to the dependent sector, i.e. the *c*-sector) and the rest of the world (which is likened to the *i*-sector). In fact, the limits to domestic growth arising from the state of world-wide demand for import may well be regarded as a natural extension of the Marx's two-sector model that bears a resemblance to current post-Keynesian balance of payments constrained growth models (Thirlwall 2014).

6. Final remarks

The aim of this chapter was to recover and develop the reproduction schemes to test the impact of some of the most apparent 'stylised facts' of current capitalism on an artificial two-sector growing economy. For this purpose, the key features of Marx's schemes have been stressed and discussed. The strong family resemblance to early and current post-Keynesian models of growth has been highlighted and discussed as well. In addition, some simple amendments have been made to Marx's benchmark schemes to make them suitable for the analysis of the impact of finance on accumulation, profitability, and income distribution. It has been shown that the Marxian reproduction schemes allow for the framing of a variety of radical, post-Keynesian, and other dissenting theories of crisis of advanced countries with a flexible and sound analytical model. Clearly, the preliminary findings presented here are just of a qualitative nature. The model is still too simplified to provide a quantitative assessment of recent developments in real-world capitalist economies. Besides, some analytical aspects should be further discussed and refined (particularly, the functional form of turnover and retention rates). Finally, numerical simulations should be coupled with a sensitivity analysis (or an empirical estimate of parameter values) to check the robustness of results. However, the preliminary findings look consistent with the available empirical evidence and they may well open the way to future research.

Table 6.1 Key to symbols and values

Symbol	Description	Kind	Value	Symbol	Description	Kind	Value
a	Net output to total capital ratio	En		r_c	Rate of profit in consumption sector	En	
C_c	Constant capital in consumption sector	En		r_i	Rate of profit in investment sector	En	
C_i	Constant capital in investment sector	En		r_ξ	Random component of profit expectations	X	ξ^{**}
F_c	Unproductive spending from consumption sector	En		S_c	Surplus value in consumption sector	En	

F_i	Unproductive spending from investment sector	En		S_i	Surplus value in investment sector	En	
g	Economy-wide rate of accumulation	En		V_c	Variable capital in consumption sector	En	750*
g_c	Rate of accumulation in consumption sector	En		V_i	Variable capital in investment sector	En	1000*
g_i	Rate of accumulation in investment sector	En		Y_c	Value of output of consumption sector	En	
g_ξ	Random component of consumption sector growth rate	X	ξ^{**}	$\hat{Y}_c$	Price of production of output of consumption sector	En	
H_c	Consumption sector capitalists' wealth (stock)	En		H_i	Value of output of investment sector	En	
H_i	Investment sector capitalists' wealth (stock)	En		$\hat{Y}_i$	Price of production of output of investment sector	En	
L	Total direct labour spent by workers	En		α	Propensity to consume out of wages	X	1.00
L_c	Direct labour in consumption sector	En		δ	Depreciation rate of constant capital	X	1.00
L_i	Direct labour in investment sector	En		ε_i	Rate of exploitation in investment sector	X	1.00
m	Monetary expression of labour time	X	$\overline{m}$	ε_c	Rate of exploitation in consumption sector	X	1.00
n_c	Turnover rate in consumption sector	En		θ_c	Retention rate in consumption sector	En	
n_{c0}	Parameter in consumption sector turnover function	X	1.00	θ_i	Retention rate in investment sector	En	

(continued)

Table 6.1 (continued)

Symbol	Description	Kind	Value	Symbol	Description	Kind	Value
n_{cl}	Parameter in consumption sector turnover function	X	0.00	θ_{i0}	Parameter of investment sector retention function	X	0.50**
n_i	Turnover rate in investment sector	En		θ_{i1}	Parameter of investment sector retention function	X	0.00
n_{i0}	Parameter in investment sector turnover function	X	1.00	π	Profit share of total net income	En	
n_{i1}	Parameter in investment sector turnover function	X	0.00**	σ_{cl}	Consumption sector capitalists propensity to save out of income	X	0.00
P_c	Mass of profit in consumption sector	En		σ_{c2}	Consumption sector capitalists prop. to save out of wealth	X	0.95
P_i	Mass of profit in investment sector	En		σ_{i1}	Investment sector capitalists prop. to save out of income	X	0.00**
q_c	OCC in consumptions sector	X	2.00	σ_{i2}	Investment sector capitalists prop. to save out of wealth	X	0.95
q_i	OCC in investment sector	X	4.00**	ω	Wage share of total net income	En	
r	General rate of profit	En					

Notes: En = endogenous variable. X = exogenous variable or parameter. * Starting values for stocks and lagged endogenous variables. ** Shocked parameters: $\theta_{i0} = -50\%$ (scenario 1); $q_i = +10\%$ (scenario 2); $\sigma_{i1} = 0.01$ (scenario 3); $n_{i1} = 0.001$ (scenario 4); $g_g = +0.01$ (scenario 5).

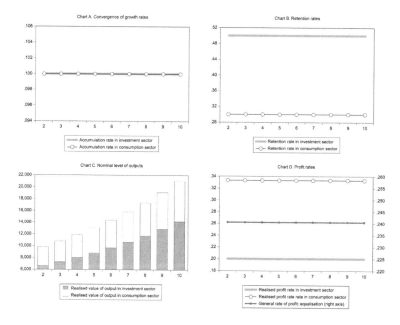

Figure 6.1 Adjustment to the balanced growth path: baseline (no equalisation).

Notes: Initial conditions are: $V_i = 1000$, $V_c = 750$, $q_i = 4$ (or $C_i = 4000$), $q_c = 2$ (or $C_c = 1500$), $\varepsilon_i = \varepsilon_c = 1$, and $\theta_i = \theta_{i0} = 0.5$ (see Table 6.1). These values are drawn from Marx (1885) and are commonly used in the literature on the enlarged reproduction schemes (cfr. Luxemburg 1913, Olsen 2015).

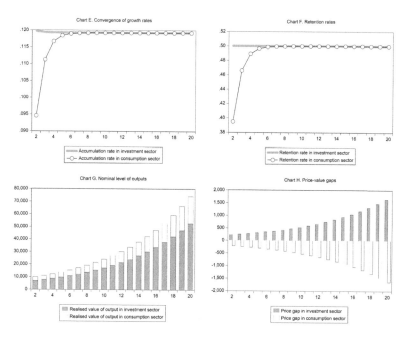

Figure 6.2 Adjustment to the balanced growth path: profit equalisation.

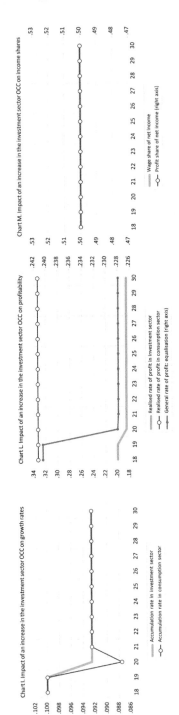

Figure 6.3 An increase in the organic composition of capital invested in *i*-sector.

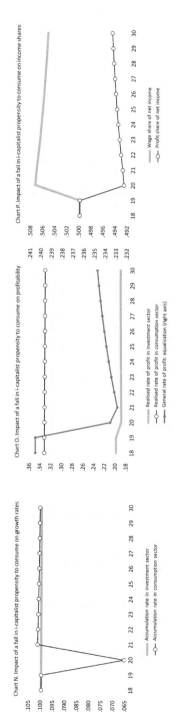

Figure 6.4 A fall in *i*-sector capitalists' propensity to consume.

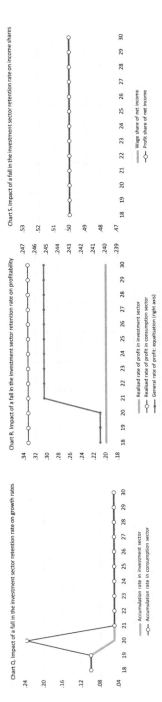

Figure 6.5 A fall in *i*-sector capitalists' retention rate.

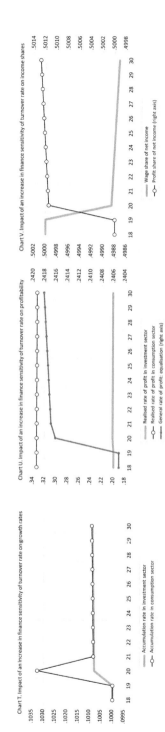

Figure 6.6 An increase in finance sensitivity of *i*-sector turnover rate.

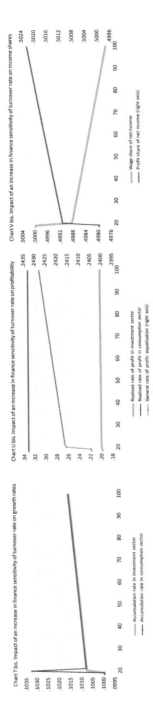

Figure 6.7 Long-run impact of an increase in finance sensitivity of *i*-sector turnover rate when a parabolic turnover function is used.

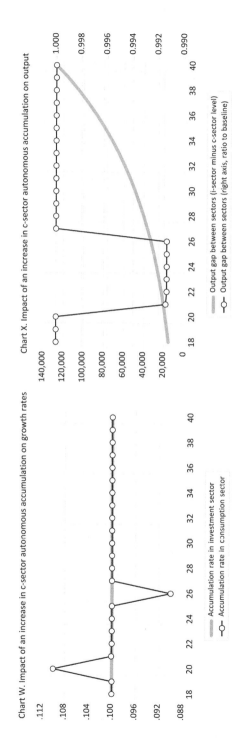

Figure 6.8 Impact of a temporary (i.e. 5-periods) increase in the autonomous component of *c*-sector accumulation rate.

Appendix 1: The monetary expression of social labour time

In this chapter a 'simultaneous' and 'single-system interpretation' of the Marxian labour theory of value is implicitly adopted, in the wake of Duménil and Foley (2008). As a result, a fixed ratio between units of money and units of direct social labour is assumed. This ratio, named 'the monetary expression of labour time', is defined as the ratio of the monetary value added of the economy (say, the domestic net product at current prices) to the direct productive labour expended in the production process over a certain period. In formal terms, one gets:

$$m \equiv \frac{V_i + V_c + S_i + S_c}{L} = \bar{m} \tag{A1}$$

The main strength of this hypothesis is that it allows for the equating of the monetary accounting with the labour accounting, in spite of the specific price-setting system of the economy. In addition, since m is given, equation (A1) defines the quantity of labour inputs (say, the number of working hours or the employment level) demanded by the capitalists:

$$L = \frac{V_i + V_c + S_i + S_c}{\bar{m}} \tag{A2}$$

For the sake of simplicity, it is assumed that the supply of labour is plentiful and does not form a binding constraint on the level of employment. In other words, the capitalist class can count on an abundant 'reserve army' of unemployed workers. Accordingly, the allocation of labour inputs across sectors mirrors their own relative weights:

$$L_i = L \cdot \frac{V_i + S_i}{V_i + V_c + S_i + S_c} \tag{A3}$$

and:

$$L_c = L - L_i \tag{A4}$$

where L_j (with $j = i,c$) is the sectoral employment level determined by the autonomous production plans of the capitalists.

Appendix 2: Simple reproduction condition – a disaggregated formulation

Once Marx's equations are conveniently disaggregated, the two-fold clearing condition of goods markets can be redefined as follows:

$$\lambda_i \cdot y_i = \lambda_i \cdot \left(c_i + c_c \right)$$

and

$$\lambda_c \cdot y_c = v \cdot (L_i + L_c) + F_i + F_c$$

where λ_i is the unit value of capital goods (say, inventories or one-period last-ing machines), λ_c is the unit value of consumption goods, and v is the unit value of the labour power (corresponding to the money wage rate). Notice that both output, y_j, and constant capital (homogenous) inputs, c_j, are expressed in real terms (with $j = i, c$).

Similarly, the reproduction values of sectoral outputs are:

$$\lambda_i \cdot y_i = \lambda_i \cdot c_i + v \cdot L_i + \theta_i \cdot S_i + F_i \tag{11B}$$

and

$$\lambda_c \cdot y_c = \lambda_i \cdot c_c + v \cdot L_c + \theta_c \cdot S_c + F_c \tag{12B}$$

where: $S_j = \varepsilon_j \cdot v \cdot L_j$ (with $j = i, c$).

The Marxian reproduction condition for a stationary-state economy becomes:

$$\lambda_i \cdot c_c = v \cdot L_i + S_i \tag{4D}$$

and hence:

$$\frac{L_i}{L_c} = \frac{q_c}{1 + \varepsilon_i} \tag{4E}$$

Equation (4E) shows that the equilibrium distribution of labour across sectors depends on the c-sector OCC and the i-sector exploitation rate. Equation (4D) redefines the equilibrium condition in terms of equilibrium values (or prices), allowing for three possible scenarios:

(a) $\lambda_i = (v \cdot L_i + S_i)/c_c = p_i$, the demand for capital goods matches the supply, so that the market price of capital goods (call it p_i) equals the reproduction value (λ_i) and the system reproduces smoothly.
(b) $\lambda_i = (v \cdot L_i + S_i)/c_c > p_i$, there is a lack of demand for capital goods, so that market prices tend to fall short of reproduction values, thereby leading to a reduction in the production of capital goods.
(c) $\lambda_i = (v \cdot L_i + S_i)/c_c < p_i$, the demand for investment goods exceeds the supply, so that market prices tend to exceed reproduction values, thereby leading to an increase in the production of capital goods.

Notice that here the adjustment affects market prices in the short run, whereas it involves a change in quantities in the long run (through a change in profit expectations).

Notes

1 See Marx 1885, chap. 19, pp. 435 ff., and chap. 20, pp. 509–513.
2 The resemblance of the Marxian approach to the current post-Keynesian macro-monetary literature shows up particularly when an 'endogenous' rendition of Marx's monetary theory is adopted (Hein 2006).
3 Notice that upper case letters are associated with endogenous variables expressed in monetary units, unless otherwise stated. Lower case letters stand either for percentages or for parameter values expressed in monetary units. The key to symbols is provided by Table 6.1.
4 This possibly controversial assumption is discussed further in footnote 8. Notice that $n_j = 1$ in the baseline model. As a result, each production process takes exactly one period, unless otherwise stated.
5 This should be better defined as the 'unallocated purchasing power' of workers (Duménil and Foley 2008), meaning the quantity of direct labour expressed by the commodities bought by the wage earners on the market. For the sake of simplicity, this issue is neglected hereafter. The reader is referred again to Appendix 1.
6 Notice that Marx defines the 'organic composition of capital' as the ratio of constant capital (made up of plants, equipment, buildings, raw materials, inventories, and other capital and intermediate goods) to variable capital (used to hire workers).
7 For the sake of simplicity, capital depreciation is assumed away. Following Marx, we also ignore cross-sector investment (see Marx 1885, chap. 21, pp. 568–581). This can be regarded as a strong simplifying assumption. In fact, it seems at odds with the hypothesis of competition, which requires free mobility of capital between sectors (Robinson 1951; Harris 1972). However, it does not affect the main findings of this chapter.
8 Under an enlarged reproduction regime, the mass of surplus value created in a certain period should be better defined as: $S_j = V_j \cdot \varepsilon_j \cdot \sum_{\tau=1}^{n_j} (1 + \vartheta_j \cdot \varepsilon_j)^{\tau-1}$, where the subscript τ defines the sub-periods, n_j is the number of turnovers, and θ_j is the intra-period retention rate. This expression accounts for the reinvestment of variable capital within the same period (see Veronese Passarella and Baron 2015). However, such a complication is ignored hereafter. Notice that this expression collapses to $S_j = V_j \cdot \varepsilon_j \cdot n_j$ under simple reproduction (i.e. for $\theta_j = 0$). Consequently, enlarged accumulation described in Section 3.2 takes place *across* periods but not *within* periods in this simplified model.
9 Notice, however, that the equilibrium interpretation of the Marxian reproduction schemes is anything but uncontroversial (see Fine 2012).
10 Notice that variables are all 'expressed in terms of value aggregates and as such can provide only the conditions for aggregate equilibrium' (Harris 1972, p. 190). To discuss the effect of the disequilibrium conditions on prices and physical magnitudes (such as real supplies and employment levels), respectively, it is necessary to refine further the analysis – see Appendix 2.
11 Balanced growth 'is itself an accident' (Marx 1885, p. 571).
12 It is worth noticing that the adjective 'exogenous' should only be used to refer to the formal model (i.e. the system of difference equations) not to its 'subject' (i.e. capitalist economies).
13 The Cambridge distributive equation is the main pillar of the theory of distribution endorsed by most prominent post-Keynesian economists (such as Nicholas Kaldor, Joan Robinson, and Luigi Pasinetti) in the mid-1950s and early 1960s. It relates the macroeconomic rate of profit (r) to the growth rate of the economy (g), given capitalists' propensity to save (θ). The standard formulation is $r = g/\theta$, entailing a causality from g to r.

14 When the State is included in the analysis, the government sector may well be regarded as the 'buffer' of the economy. Economic planning to eliminate cross-sector disproportionalities and crises was advocated historically by Tugan-Baranowsky and Hilferding (see Shaikh 1978). Today the stabilisation function of government is advocated by the post-Keynesians and other heterodox economists. However, this view was criticised by Luxemburg (1913) and is still questioned by most Marxists. The reason is that disproportionalities are not regarded as 'the contingent result of the "anarchy of the market", which can be corrected by appropriate state intervention; they are the necessary result of the social form of capitalist production' (Clarke 1990, p. 459).

15 In principle, each sectoral capital to net output ratio could be expressed, in turn, as the product of the inverse of the sectoral actual rate of utilisation of plants and the sectoral capital to full-capacity net output ratio. For the sake of simplicity, and in line with the Marxian tradition, both rates of utilisation are assumed to be constant.

16 Notice that now P_j replaces S_j n equations (7) and (8).

17 That resemblance has been stressed by many authors, notably Robinson (1951), Harris (1972), and more recently Olsen (2015). It seems no coincidence that the Harrod-Domar model was pioneered by a Marxist author, i.e. Feldman (1928).

18 However, there is here a noteworthy difference with respect to Marx's statement. Since the Classical hypothesis is adopted (meaning that the propensity to consume out of wages is assumed to be unity), we test a reduction in the propensity to consume out of non-labour incomes $(1-\sigma_1)$.

19 This does not affect the main qualitative findings of the model in any way.

20 The reader is referred again to footnote 19.

21 Notice that here the fall in the rate of profit is the result of the realisation crisis, as claimed by the 'underconsumptionist' branch of Marxism. By contrast, experiment (a) assumes that the fall in the rate of profit (following a rise in the OCC) is the cause of the crisis, as advocated by most Marxist theories of the 1970s (see Clarke 1990).

22 For a thorough analysis of the different functions performed (within a financially sophisticated capitalist economy) by banks and other financial institutions, respectively, see Sawyer and Veronese Passarella (2017).

23 'The rationale is that the higher the degree of development of the banking and finance sector … the higher the speed at which manufacturing firms (or their owners/shareholders) could re-invest the initial capital. At the same time, beyond a given historically determined threshold at least, "diseconomies" are expected to arise as the (relative) dimension of the banking and finance sector increases' (Veronese Passarella and Baron 2014, pp. 1435–1436).

24 If, following Veronese Passarella and Baron (2014), a parabolic turnover function is used, then both accumulation and profitability collapse in the long run, whereas income shares fluctuate over time (see Figure 6.7).

25 A full review of recent literature about financialisation is beyond the purpose of this chapter.

References

Bellofiore, R. (2011) "Crisis Theory and the Great Recession: A Personal Journey, from Marx to Minsky", in Zarembka P. and Desai R. (eds.), *Revitalizing Marxist Theory for Today's Capitalism* (Bingley, UK: Emerald Group Publishing), pp. 81–120.

Bronfenbrenner, M. (1973) "The Marxian Macro-Economic Model: Extension from Two Departments", *Kyklos*, 26(4), pp. 201–218.

Clarke, S. (1990) "The Marxist Theory of Overaccumulation and Crisis", *Science & Society*, 54(4), pp. 442–467.

Cockshott, W. P. (2016) "Marxian Reproduction Prices Versus Prices of Production: Probability and Convergence", University of Glasgow, unpublished working paper.

Domar, E. (1946) "Capital Expansion, Rate of Growth, and Employment", *Econometrica*, 14(2), pp. 137–147.

Duménil, G. and Foley, D. (2008) "The Marxian Transformation Problem", in S. N. Durlauf and L. E. Blume (eds.), *The New Palgrave Dictionary of Economics*, 2nd edition (Basingstoke, UK: Palgrave Macmillan).

Feldman, G. A. (1928) "On the Theory of Growth Rates of National Income", translated in N. Spulber (ed.), *Foundations of Soviet Strategy for Economic Growth* (Bloomington, IN: Indiana University Press, 1964).

Fine, B. (2012) "Economic Reproduction and the Circuits of Capital", in B. Fine, A. Saad-Filho and M. Boffo (eds.), *The Elgar Companion to Marxist Economics* (Cheltenham, UK: Edward Elgar), pp. 111–117.

Harris, D. J. (1972) "On Marx's Scheme of Reproduction and Accumulation", *Journal of Political Economy*, 80(1): 505–522. Republished in: M. C. Howard and J. E. King (eds.), *The Economics of Marx* (London: Penguin Books, 1976), pp. 185–202.

Harrod, R. F. (1939) "An Essay in Dynamic Theory", *The Economic Journal*, 49(193), pp. 14–33.

Hein, E. (2006) "Money, Interest and Capital Accumulation in Karl Marx's Economics: A Monetary Interpretation and Some Similarities to Post-Keynesian Approaches", *The European Journal of the History of Economic Thought*, 13(1), pp. 113–140.

Lavoie, M. (2014) *Post-Keynesian Economics: New Foundations* (Cheltenham, UK: Edward Elgar).

Lenin, V. I. (1908) "The Development of Capitalism in Russia", in *Collected Works*, III (Moscow: Progress Publishers, 1964), pp. 37–69. Downloaded from: Marxists Internet Archive (www.marxists.org/archive/lenin/works/1899/devel/).

Luxemburg, R. (1913), *Die Akkumulation des Kapitals*. Translated by A. Schwarzschild, *The Accumulation of Capital* (New York: Monthly Review Press, 1951).

Marx, K. (1885) *Capital: A Critique of Political Economy, Volume II* (London: Penguin Books, 1978).

Marx, K. (1894) *Capital: A Critique of Political Economy, Volume III* (London: Penguin Books, 1981).

Morishima, M. (1973) *Marx's Economics: A Dual Theory of Value and Growth* (Cambridge, UK: Cambridge University Press).

Olsen, E. K. (2015) "Unproductive Activity and Endogenous Technological Change in a Marxian Model of Economic Reproduction and Growth", *Review of Radical Political Economics*, 47(1), pp. 34–55.

Patnaik, P. (2012) "Vladimir I. Lenin", in B. Fine, A. Saad-Filho and M. Boffo (eds.), *The Elgar Companion to Marxist Economics* (Cheltenham, UK: Edward Elgar), pp. 373–378.

Robinson, J. (1951) "Introduction", in R. Luxemburg, *The Accumulation of Capital* (New York: Monthly Review Press).

Robinson, J. (1962) *Essays in the Theory of Economic Growth* (Basingstoke, UK: Macmillan).

Sawyer, M. and Veronese Passarella, M. (2017) "The Monetary Circuit in the Age of Financialisation: A Stock-Flow Consistent Model with a Twofold Banking Sector", *Metroeconomica*, 68(2), pp. 321–353.

Shaikh, A. (1978) "An Introduction to the History of Crisis Theories", in Editorial Collective Union for Radical Political Economics (eds.), *U.S. Capitalism in Crisis* (New York: Union for Radical Political Economics Press), pp. 219–241.

Thirlwall, A. P. (2014) "The Balance of Payments Constraint as an Explanation of the International Growth Rate Differences", *PSL Quarterly Review*, 32(128), pp. 45–53.

Veronese Passarella, M. (2017) "Monetary Theories of Production", in T. Jo, L. Chester and C. D'Ippoliti (eds.), *Handbook of Heterodox Economics* (London: Routledge), pp. 70–83.

Veronese Passarella, M. and Baron, H. (2015) "Capital's Humpback Bridge: Financialisation and the Rate of Turnover in Marx's Economic Theory", *Cambridge Journal of Economics*, 39(5), pp. 1415–1441.

7 High wages and economic growth in a Kaldorian theoretical framework

Guglielmo Forges Davanzati[1]

1. Introduction

Nicholas Kaldor is often associated with a long list of authors classified as Post-Keynesians, meaning that their contributions expand the basic Keynesian theory as formulated in the *General Theory* (cf. Harcourt, 2006). However, many important sections of Kaldor's theory depart from the Keynesian tradition. In particular, unlike Keynes's *General Theory*, Kaldor supported an endogenous money theory, rejected the assumption of perfect competition[2] to emphasize the importance of firm size and imperfect competition, and stressed the importance of the territorial dimension of economic processes (Thirwall, 1987; Targetti, 1992). Moreover, Kaldor also departed from the standard Keynesian picture of the functioning of the labour market, mainly because he focused on the effects of variations of aggregate demand not only on employment but above all on labour productivity. As will be shown, Kaldor's theory of the labour market can also account for the fact that wage increases can generate increased labour productivity. Kaldor's contribution can therefore be conceived as a variant of the so-called high wage theory (cf. Lavoie, 1992; Forges Davanzati, 1999).[3]

Historians of economic thought have devoted little attention to these topics, even though the issue is also highly relevant to the current macroeconomic debate. It is well known that the dominant view supports the idea that policies designed to deregulate the labour market are necessary in order to reduce the unemployment rate and are also effective in improving firms' competitiveness in foreign trade. Evidence suggests that these outcomes are not always in operation (cf. European Commission, 2014),[4] and the Post-Keynesian reaction mainly focuses on the necessity to replace the wage moderation policy with expansionary fiscal policies. In a standard Keynesian model, these policies are supposed to increase the level of employment via the increase in aggregate demand. A re-reading of Kaldor's theory of the links between wages and productivity may also help to improve the current Post-Keynesian policy suggestions. Economic policies which redistribute income to the benefit of workers also have a positive effect on the dynamics of labour productivity, thus generating a process of systematic interaction between aggregate demand

and aggregate supply,[5] with endogenous money, where the outcome of this interaction crucially depends on the dynamics of the credit supply. As a matter of fact, one can see that Kaldor's theory reflects the specific historical and institutional setting in which he was writing. In the current scenario of financialization and globalization combined with the marked decline of workers' bargaining power (both in the labour market and in the political arena), his *policy prescriptions* are very difficult to implement. Nevertheless, it can be argued that his analysis of the determinants of economic growth is still valid. As will be shown later, Kaldor's technical production function can still be used to explain the decline of labour productivity due to the processes of financialization, globalization and the decline of workers' bargaining power. The basic transmission mechanisms assumed in Kaldor's model remain unaltered.

The aim of this chapter is to provide a reconstruction of Kaldor's theory of the functioning of the labour market. In particular, special attention will be paid to i) Kaldor's view that wage increases stimulate increases in the rate of growth of labour productivity for the individual firm; and ii) Kaldor's view that this effect can also be generated on the macroeconomic plane. As regards this second point, an extension of Kaldor's theory will be proposed, where the link between wages and productivity basically depends on banking policy, assuming that credit supply is endogenous. In so doing, a "continuist reading" of Kaldor will be put forward: Kaldor's theory of growth, elaborated in the 1950s–1960s, can be integrated with his theory of endogenous money, elaborated in the 1970s–1980s.

The exposition is organized as follows. Section 2 provides a reconstruction of Kaldor's view that wage increases incentivise the increase in labour productivity for the individual firm. Section 3 provides a re-reading of Kaldor's thesis that policies designed to increase wages generate economic growth, via the accelerator effect. Section 4 concludes.

2. The high wage theory

The idea that wage increases stimulate increases in labour productivity and in profits has a long tradition in the history of economic thought (cf. Petridis, 1996; Forges Davanzati, 1999), and it is reconsidered in some recent developments of Post-Keynesian economics (cf., among others, Lavoie, 1992). From Adam Smith to Alfred Marshall, most economists considered that wage increases could foster an increase in labour productivity. Francesco Saverio Nitti, an early 20th-century Italian economist, can be considered one of the most important referents for this approach (cf. Nitti, 1893; Forges Davanzati and Patalano, 2015).

First of all it must be stressed that the high wage theory differs profoundly from the contemporary efficiency wage, for two main reasons. First, the efficiency wage approach is based on the idea that, since workers' effort (and thus labour productivity) increases as wages rise, it is *profitable* for the individual firm to set a level of wages higher than the "equilibrium wage" (i.e. the market clearing wage) in order to maximize profits (cf., among others, Akerlof and Yellen, 1986). This theory aims at providing an explanation of involuntary unemployment derived from wage rigidities within a Neo-Keynesian theoretical framework (Shapiro and Stiglitz, 1984), where the Neoclassical inverse relation between wages and employment is supposed to occur. By contrast, the high wage theory is not based on the supposed Neoclassical inverse relation between wages and employment. A wage rise does not determine an increase in unemployment but only raises the rate of economic growth via higher labour productivity. Second, the efficiency wage approach is based on the belief that the sole determinant of labour productivity is individual effort. By contrast, as will be shown, Kaldor focuses on two different determinants of labour productivity: technical progress and the quality of the workforce. Kaldor maintains that a deregulated market economy tends spontaneously to generate low wages and that low wages are associated to labour productivity's tendency to decline over time. His view is therefore not confined to a purely microeconomic approach, such as that of the efficiency wage theory. This conclusion derives from the rejection of the Neoclassical conviction that the functioning of the labour market can be analysed on the microeconomic plane, so that the levels of employment and wages are determined by the interaction of a downward labour demand schedule and a upward labour supply curve. Accordingly, all the "imperfections" introduced in the Neoclassical analysis are considered irrelevant (cf., for instance, Pissarides, 2011).

The author deals with the links between wages and productivity on two distinct planes. At the level of the individual firm, Kaldor explains the positive relation between wages and productivity assuming that the high wage effect i) mainly operates in the manufacturing sector and ii) is more intense in big firms. The rationale for the high wage effect to be in operation lies in the following logical steps:

1   In the manufacturing sector (and in big firms) union density is higher than in other sectors and in small firms. "Union negotiators", Kaldor (1989) observes, are "the leading group" in this sector. They are:

> [i]n a particularly favourable bargaining position: it may, for example, be in an industry in which productivity growth has been exceptionally rapid; similarly, it may be in an industry or firm where profits have increased significantly; or it may be a group of skilled workers the demand for whose services has risen sharply.
>
> (p.122)

Wage claims are designed to preserve (or to increase) *relative wages*: "the key group continue to press for what they regard as their justified claim for higher *relative* wages" (p.122).

2   Big firms have higher internal financing than small firms and, as a result, they *can* pay their employees higher wages: "the leading sector will feel

entitled to higher wages, and their employers will probably go far in meeting the union wage demand" (p.122).

3   Under the pressure of *social conflict*, being in the position to pay high wages, big firms in the manufacturing sector may find it profitable to increase wages to the benefit of their employees. The increase in wages reflects the increase in productivity and, in turn, pushes a further increase of labour productivity:

> [Big firms] are keen to pay their workers more than they can obtain elsewhere and to raise their wages in line with the increase in the value of output. Indeed, they are anxious that everyone should share in the prosperity of the enterprise and they reap the reward in terms of good *labour relations* . . . Under conditions of a high degree of unionization, the wage increases granted by successful oligopolies will set the standard to which the average enterprise will be under pressure to conform.
>
> (Kaldor, in Targetti and Trirlwall, 1989,
> p.123, italics added)

4   Finally, high wages mean high productivity via the improvement of labour relations.

Therefore, to Kaldor, *social conflict drives wage rises and wage rises drive increases in labour productivity*. As shown, the basic preconditions if this sequence is to hold is that firms have high internal funds, which mainly applies to what Kaldor calls "successful oligopolies" (i.e. big firms) operating in the manufacturing sector, and that there is a high degree of union density. One can expand this argument by observing that, in contrast, in economies populated by small firms operating in non-manufacturing sectors, both because of low union density and low internal funds, the rate of growth in labour productivity is at its minimum level.

It must be pointed out that in Kaldor's approach, variations of labour productivity ultimately depend on factors related to *motivation* and the *quality of the workforce*, i.e. workers' propensity to vary their labour intensity in response to firms' wage policies. On the macroeconomic ground – as shown in the next section – Kaldor maintains that the path of labour productivity mainly depends on factors related to *technology* and capital accumulation.[6]

3. Kaldor's second law revised

This section is devoted to reconstructing the macroeconomic effects of wage increases, based on Kaldor's view. This exercise aims to provide a variant of Kaldor's basic schema of economic growth, where the independent variable which drives the growth of labour productivity is the wage share and not, as in Kaldor, the rate at which output grows. In line with the so-called Neo-Kaldorian view, the basic idea is that a productivity regime is wage-led (cf. Boyer, 1988; Setterfield and Cornwall, 2002). Kaldor did not explicitly deal with this issue, although it can be consistently inserted into his macroeconomic model of economic growth. He did not consider this effect because he maintained that money wage increases are translated by firms into price rises. Kaldor (in Targetti and Thirlwall, 1989, p.123) stresses that: "The rise in money wages invariably tends to exceed the average rise in the productivity of labour, though it is likely to be less than the increase in the productivity of labour in most 'dynamic' firms or industries". In other words, it is the claim for preserving *relative* wages, independently of the path of labour productivity in different industries, which is the ultimate cause of inflation.

However, it can be argued that this effect reflects specific past conditions where unions had strong bargaining power and inflation (not deflation) was the problem. Moreover, Kaldor saw that inflationary pressures in European countries in the 1970s derived from "the changed distribution of power between Capital and Labour, under full employment" (Kaldor, in Targetti and Trirlwall, 1989, p.97), which is, of course, a very specific condition in the dynamics of capitalist reproduction. A generalization of Kaldor's model should also consider the cases (as in the present context) where the opposite conditions occur: low worker bargaining power and deflation. At a higher level of abstraction, Kaldor's theory of the determinants of labour productivity can be generalized assuming that wages *can also* affect them. As Fejio and Lamonica (2013, p.117) point out, the high wage theory is fully consistent with Kaldor's view on the links between the path of wages and that of labour productivity: "When wages grow faster than productivity, profits will decrease and entrepreneurs will be stimulated to invest in new machinery in order to increase productivity and the share of profits". Based on Kaldor, they show that less productive machines are replaced (thus giving rise to technical advancement and structural change) as a result of wage rises: "The entrepreneur must replace the machine to recover its profitability, as the investment in new and . . . more advanced machinery will increase labour productivity above the average wage" (ibid., p.112). Implicitly, this effect can increase firms' profits on condition that the elasticity of productivity with respect to wages is higher than one.

The revision of the Kaldor effect proposed here is based on his view that the effects of wage rises depend on the distribution of political power between Labour and Capital. Kaldor wrote in a period where wages were relatively high, as was union density. In this context, wage rises produced inflationary pressures which "exerted a strong deflationary influence (in terms of *real* demand)" (Kaldor, 1989, p.97). A change in the distribution of political power between Labour and Capital modifies this effect, since the decline in wages helps to generate disinflation and lower the rate of growth of labour productivity. Accordingly, the possibility that wage increases produce inflation is to be excluded in the case where the political power of Capital is significantly higher than that of Labour: otherwise, (moderate) inflation may be desirable for the sake of stimulating investment. More importantly, the possibility of wage rises requires a redistribution of political power to the benefit of workers and, following the Kaldor effect, proves to be an efficacious instrument in achieving higher rates of economic growth.

Starting from this consideration, a revised Kaldorian schema of the macroeconomics of high wages will be proposed, taking Kaldor's contribution in the field of monetary economy into consideration, in the belief that this contribution cannot be isolated from his theory of economic growth (cf. Forges Davanzati, 2015). As we know, Kaldor supported the view that money supply is endogenous and demand driven (cf. Bertocco, 2000).[7] In this respect, this view is at the basis of the contemporary monetary theory of production (MTP).[8] The MTP basic schema involves three macro-agents: banks, firms and workers. The banking sector creates money *ex nihilo* (in accordance with the idea that loans make deposits); firms buy inputs and produce commodities; and workers supply labour power. The circular process of the monetary economy starts with bargaining in the money market between banks and firms. Banks supply firms with initial finance; firms need money in order to buy labour power and to start production. Firms use bank finance to purchase labour power, paying workers the previously negotiated money wages. After the production process has taken place, firms fix the price level so that real wages are known *ex-post* (Graziani, 2003).

Kaldor refers to the positive relation between the rate of growth of output and labour productivity in the manufacturing industry, with causality running from the former to the latter, due to the accelerator effect and the operation of increasing returns.[9] In other words, he develops his theory of economic growth based on the "accelerator" effect. Following Perri and Lampa (2014), this relation can be reformulated, substituting the rate of growth of output with the rate of growth of aggregate demand. Kaldor named this effect "the Verdoorn Law" in his Cambridge Inaugural Lecture in 1966. It is also known as the Kaldor-Verdoorn Law or Kaldor's Second Law:

> [t]he growth of real incomes was not determined by the growth of "factor supplies" because, on account of increasing returns, higher rates of production growth were invariably associated with higher rates of growth of productivity.
>
> (Kaldor, in Targetti and Trirlwall, 1989, p.87)

And:

> [t]he growth of productivity will be greater the more technological change is "activated" through new investment.
>
> (Kaldor, in Targetti and Trirlwall, 1989, p.28)

This is what the author calls the "technical production function".[10]

In dealing with the link between wages and productivity on the macroeconomic plane, one can assume, in line with Kaldor, that i) workers' propensity to consume is higher than that of capitalists (cf. Kaldor, 1955); ii) the path of labour productivity depends on that of investment; and iii) the dynamics of investment depend on that of aggregate demand, due to the accelerator effect.

Based on these assumptions, the following effects derive, assuming, for the sake of simplicity, a closed economy. A policy of income redistribution to the benefit of workers expands aggregate demand for two reasons. First, an increase in money wages increases the demand for consumption goods. Second, this effect is amplified by the high propensity to consume on the part of low-income households (cf. Pressman and Holt, 2008). In view of assumption iii), firms react by increasing investment, and this, in turn, generates an increase in the rate of growth of labour productivity. This dynamic can be formalized as shown in equations 1, 2 and 3.

Although Kaldor maintained that the most important component of demand is the growth of exports, it is legitimate to isolate the effects of the increase of work-ers' consumption on the growth of aggregate demand. In simple formal terms, the effects of wages on labour productivity can be derived as follows. One can write:

$$I_t = \beta(D_{t-1}), \text{ where } D_{t-1} = cW_{t-1}, \; \beta \geq 0 \tag{1}$$

Equation (1) establishes that the dynamics of investment (I) depend on that of demand (D), involving a time lag which is required in order to produce more capital goods, where β is a coefficient of acceleration. For the sake of simplic-ity, D equals workers' consumption, given by their propensity to consume (c) and the wage bill (W).

Moreover, the investment decision is affected by the availability of internal financing (S_k) and by the degree of bank accommodation (θ):

$$I_t = (\vartheta, S_k), \; f_\theta' > 0, \; f_{sk}' > 0 \tag{2}$$

where $0 < \theta < 1$ is the degree of bank accommodation (excluding the non-realistic case where banks do not finance investment at all, i.e. $\theta = 0$). Hence the productivity function becomes:

$$\pi_t = f[\beta(D_{t-1}), S_k, \vartheta] = f[\beta(cW_{t-1}), S_k, \vartheta)], f_\beta' > 0, f_D' > 0, f_{sk}' > 0, f_\theta' > 0 \tag{3}$$

Equation (3) establishes that the rate of growth of labour productivity rises i) the higher the wages; ii) the higher the propensity to consume; iii) the higher the banks' degree of accommodation; and iv) the higher β. Note also that the rate of growth of labour productivity grows as firms' internal funds grow, which establishes that economies populated by small firms, with high dependence on the banking system, tend to experience lower productivity growth than economies populated by bigger firms. On the formal plane, equation (3) also captures Kaldor's rejection of the Neoclassical aggregate production function and the consequent rejection of the decreasing marginal productivity assumption. The technological setting is dynamic in essence, insofar as production involves historical time.

A similar result has recently been reached by Storm and Naastepad (2012, p.1), in a working paper of the International Labour Office, who find that "Higher real wages provide *macroeconomic benefits* in terms of increased demand (if the economy is wage-led) and higher labour productivity growth and more rapid technological progress". Moreover, the higher the firm's propensity to invest (and/or the degree of unused capacity), the more labour productivity grows, which caputures the Kaldorian accelerator effect.

Note that it is a widespread conviction that the accelerator effect can be in operation only in a context of full employment. Although this is true in its basic formulation, one can maintain that this condition does not necessarily hold. If involuntary unemployment exists, firms can react to the increase in the demand for consumer goods by increasing their demand for labour (cf. Thirwall, 1987). The consequent increase in employment generates further wage rises, due to the increase in workers' bargaining power, pushing firms to stay competitive (i.e. avoiding a price rise) via the increase in labour productivity. The latter effect may not be in operation if one considers the standard Kaldorian view that, on the assumption of full employment, firms react to the increase in money wages by raising prices, with the consequent reduction in real wages. However, since Kaldor considers that it is social conflict which drives wage rises, this effect may be counterbalanced by successful union claims, which are even more probable in a condition of full employment. Moreover, for the operation of the Second Kaldor Law, this leads to the increase in the labour productivity growth rate. As a result, *the higher the employment rate, the higher the labour productivity growth rate.*[11]

It may be pointed out that a State intervention aimed at regulating the labour market is needed to reach this result (unlike the efficiency wage theory). This occurs for two reasons. First, the increase in productivity resulting from the wage rise takes time, while the individual firm is forced by competition to obtain profits in a short-term perspective (cf. Forges Davanzati and Pacella, 2013). Time is required because the increase in productivity derives from investment in new machines and workers need time to learn to use them. Second, firms will never find it convenient to raise wages if this entails a short-term decline in profits. Moreover, insofar as wages are (partially) paid via indebtedness to the banking sector, an increase in wages would be associated with increasing financial costs, which grow as the money interest rate goes up, thus amplifying the reduction of short-term profits.

It is worth pointing out that the arguments presented here only aim at providing a *theoretical* extension of Kaldor's theory, considering that Kaldor's policy prescriptions are very difficult to implement in modern economies where globalization and financialization are important features and where Capital dominates over Labour. In the current context, firms can react to the increase in wages via delocalization and the consequent decline of investment, which affect firms' propensity to invest. Second, firms may lack financing partly because banks may find it profitable to divert money to financial activities, which affects banks' degree of accommodation. Moreover, the decline of workers' bargaining power makes it more difficult to raise wages. In view of equation (3) these phenomena negatively affect the path of labour productivity. In formal terms, financialization involves both a reduction of firms' propensity to invest and of banks' degree of accommodation. Since it is often associated with deindustrialization, it produces a further negative effect on the growth rate insofar as, based on Kaldor, economic growth is driven by the increase in productivity of big firms operating in the manufacturing sector. The decline of workers' bargaining power reduces the rate at which wages and consumption grow and, as a result, it also contributes to the reduction of the rate of growth of labour productivity. These considerations may make Kaldor's policy prescription appear useful in the Golden Age of Capitalism, which does not mean that his analysis must be rejected today. The augmented version of Kaldor's Second Law proposed here can be used to interpret the current reduction of the labour productivity growth rate in the Eurozone, particularly in the Mediterranean countries. This can (also) be explained by using Kaldor's model, suggesting that the decline in aggregate demand combined with wage moderation produces such an outcome. Accordingly, Kaldor's theory can be used *a contrario*, i.e. not to identify the factors triggering labour productivity and economic growth but to find the variable which – in the contemporary capitalist dynamics – reduces them.

4. Concluding remarks

This chapter dealt with Kaldor's view on the links existing between wages and labour productivity. It has been shown that Kaldor maintains that a high wage policy stimulates increases in labour productivity. He stresses that, in an economy populated by big firms operating in the manufacturing sector, high union density is associated with social conflict, which, in turn, generates wage rises and, via better labour relations, higher labour productivity. The same results are obtained by the operation of the "accelerator" effect.

Notes

1 I thank Giancarlo Bertocco, Giorgio Colacchio, Andrea Pacella, the participants in the session on "Monetary circuit and the crisis" at the Italian Economics Society (Naples, 22–24 October 2015) and an anonymous referee for their useful suggestions. The usual disclaimer applies.

2 Kaldor was fully convinced that Keynes, in the *General Theory*, assumed that markets are perfectly competitive. However, this is a very controversial point (see, among others, Chick, 1983; Kregel, 1987; Davidson, 2000).

3 Lavoie (1992) defines the high wage theory as the "Webb effect", insofar as the Webbs also elaborated a positive relation between wages and productivity.

4 Especially for firms operating in the peripheral areas of the Eurozone.

5 In line with Kaldor's view that "In a monetary economy … aggregate demand can be a *function* of aggregate supply (both measured in money terms) without being *equal* to it" (Kaldor, 1989, pp.49–50).

6 In this respect, Kaldor mainly refers to what Salter (1962) called net investment (different from replacement investment and gross investment), insofar as net investment is determined essentially by new demand.

7 Bertocco (2000) emphasizes that Kaldor maintains that banks tend, as a norm, to restrict credit supply (an argument that is relevant to the later discussion). In a similar vein. Musella and Panico (in Musella and Panico, 1995, p.56) state that "the content of Kaldor's later writings makes it difficult to argue that for him the supply of loans is a *non-discretionary* variable for the individual bank". This is because of his reference to "variations in the creditworthiness of potential borrowers", which led him – according to the authors – to conclude that "The reserve ratios . . . tend to vary over the trade cycle and to be unstable with respect to the interest rate". Musella and Panico (1995, p.57) maintain that "a horizontal money supply represents . . . the simplest (and probably the most convenient) hypothesis".

8 See Forges Davanzati (2015).

9 In this respect, Kaldor criticizes the Neoclassical view that as output increases this implies an increase in the *number* of firms. As markets are not perfectly competitive, the *existing firms* react to the increase in output by increasing their size in order to increase their market share. Kaldor also criticizes Marx's view that it is competition which stimulates innovations, arguing that, as a norm, they are produced in oligopolistic market structures.

10 Kaldor's theory of increasing returns reflects both the heritage of Allyn Young and that of Gunnar Myrdal. It is interesting to observe that Kaldor considered Young his "first real teacher in economics" (Kaldor, in Targetti and Thirlwall, 1989, p.14).

11 Note that this result is in contrast to the "discipline effect", which predicts that labour productivity will increase, via the increased effort, as the unemployment rate grows (see Shapiro and Stiglitz, 1984). This difference can be imputed to the different views on the determinants of labour productivity with Neoclassical scholars emphasizing the role of individual effort and PostKeynesians emphasizing the crucial role of capital accumulation.

References

Akerlof, G.A. and Yellen, J.L. (1986). *Efficiency wage models of the labor market.* Cambridge, UK: Cambridge University Press.

Bertocco, G. (2000). *Is Kaldor's theory of money supply endogeneity still relevant? Metroeconomica*, 52(1), pp.95–120.

Boyer, R. (1988). *Formalizing growth regimes*, in G. Dosi, C. Freeman, R. Nelson, G. Silverberg and L. Soete (eds.), *Technical change and economic theory.* London and New York: Pinter Publishers, 608–630.

Chick, V. (1983). *Macroeconomics after Keynes.* Oxford, UK: Philip Allan.

Davidson, P. (2000). Three major differences between Kalecki's theory of employment and Keynes's general theory of employment, interest and money. *Journal of PostKeynesian Economics*, 23(1), 3–25.

European Commission (2014). Labour costs pass-through, profits and rebalancing in vulnerable Member States, *Special Topic on the Euro Area Economy*, vol. 12, n.3.

Fejio, C.A. and Lamonica, M.T. (2013). A Kaldorian approach to catch-up and structural change in economies with a higher degree of heterogeneity. *PSL Quarterly Review*, 66(265), 107–135.

Forges Davanzati, G. (1999). *Salario, produttività del lavoro e conflitto sociale [Wages, labour productivity and social conflict].* Lecce, Italy: Milella.

Forges Davanzati, G. (2015). Nicholas Kaldor on endogenous money and increasing returns, PostKeynesian Economics Study Group. Working paper n.1505, March.

Forges Davanzati, G. and Pacella, A. (2013). The profits-investments puzzle: A post-Keynesian-Institutional interpretation. *Structural Change and Economic Dynamics*, 26, pp.1–13.

Forges Davanzati, G. and Patalano, R. (2015). The economics of high wages and the policy implications: Francesco Saverio Nitti's contribution. *History of Economic Ideas*, XXIII(2), 73–98.

Graziani, A. (2003). *The monetary theory of production.* Cambridge, UK: Cambridge University Press.

Harcourt, G. (2006). *The structure of post-Keynesian economics.* Cambridge, UK: Cambridge University Press.

Kaldor, N. (1955). Alternative theories of distribution. *The Review of Economic Studies*, 23(2), 83–100.

Kaldor, N. (1989). *Further essays on economic theory and policy.* London: Duckworth, edited by F. Targetti and A.P. Trirlwall, p.123.

Kregel, J.A. (1987). Keynes's given degree of competition: comment on McKenna and Zannoni. *Journal of PostKeynesian Economics*, 9(4), 490–495.

Lavoie, M. (1992). *Foundations of PostKeynesian economics.* Aldershot, UK: Edward Elgar.

Musella, M. and Panico, C. (eds.) (1995). *The money supply in the production process.* Aldershot, UK: Edward Elgar.

Nitti, Francesco Saverio. (1893). *I problemi del lavoro [The problems of labour]*, prolusione al corso di Economia Politica fatta il 4 dicembre 1893 all'Università di Napoli, in "Estratto della nuova rassegna".

Perri, S. and Lampa, R. (2014). Il declino e la crisi dell'economia italiana: dalla teoria ai fatti stilizzati [The Italian economic decline: from theory to stylized facts], in R. Cerqueti (ed.), *Polymorphic crisis. Readings on the Great Recession of the 21st century.* Macerata, Italy: Edizioni Università di Macerata.

Petridis, R. (1996). Brasseys' Law and the economy of high wages in nineteenth-century economics. *History of Political Economy*, 28(4), 585–605.

Pissarides, C. (2011). Equilibrium in the labor market with search frictions. *The American Economic Review*, 101(4), 1092–1105.

Pressman, S. and Holt, R.P.F. (2008). Nicholas Kaldor and cumulative causation: Public policy implications. *Journal of Economic Issues*, XLII(2), 367–373.

Salter, W.E.G. (1962). Marginal labour and investment coefficients of Australian manufacturing industries. *The Economic Record*, XXXVIII, 82, June.

Setterfield, M. and Cornwall, J. (2002). A neo-Kaldorian perspective on the rise and decline of the Golden Age, in M. Setterfield (ed.), *The economics of demand-led growth: Challenging the supply-side vision of the long run.* Cheltenham, UK: Edward Elgar, 67–86.

Shapiro, C. and Stiglitz, J.E. (1984). The equilibrium unemployment as a worker discipline device. *The American Economic Review*, 74(3), 433–444.

Storm, S. and Naastepad, C.W.N. (2012). Wage-led or profit-led supply: Wages, productivity and investment. *International Labour Office*, working paper n.36.

Targetti, F. (1992). *Nicholas Kaldor: The economics and politics of capitalism as a dynamic system.* Oxford, UK: Clarendon Press.

Thirlwall, A.P. (1987). *Nicholas Kaldor: Economist and adviser.* Brighton, UK: Wheatsheaf.

8 Financial crises and sustainability

Competing paradigms and policy implications[1]

Alessandro Vercelli

1. Introduction

This chapter discusses the implications of alternative visions of the economic process for the link between financial crises and sustainability. The critical assessment of this controversial issue is articulated in three parts. The first part sketches the path that leads from the early reflections on money to the recent insights on financialisation, focusing on the basic conceptual options and their implications. The analysis starts from the quantitative aspects of money that have been a crucial object of economics for a long time. Section 2 sketches a bird's eye view of the mainstream approach from Hume to Woodford, then Section 3 outlines the parallel evolution of some of the heterodox points of view from Marx to Minsky. Section 4 discusses the main views of orthodox and heterodox economists on money as structure. Section 5 investigates why the different paradigms mentioned earlier lead to different understandings of the meaning and role of financialisation.

The second part sketches the conceptual path that leads from the early reflections on economic crises to different understandings of the great crises and to contrasting views on the sustainability of the economic system. Section 6 discusses foundations and implications of these views on business-cycle crises, while Section 7 considers the main approaches to understanding and controlling great crises. Finally, Section 8 examines the concepts of sustainability associated with these paradigms.

The third part investigates the interaction between financialisation and sustainability from the synchronic point of view (Section 9), and from the diachronic point of view (Section 10), focusing on their broad policy implications. The concluding remarks in Section 11 emphasise that the vision of scholars and policy-makers matters not only in the pre-analytic stage of research, as maintained by Schumpeter, but in all its stages, as well as in the subsequent use of its results for decision making.

PART 1: FROM MONEY TO FINANCIALISATION

This part of the chapter presents the recent process of financialisation (since the 1970s) as the latest stage in an evolutionary process that has progressively shaped the structure and functioning of the economic system (Vercelli 2017). At the same time, this part reconstructs the parallel evolution of the theory worked out to understand and control it. To this end, a sharp distinction has to be introduced between two aspects of money that are often confused: (i) money as quantity that is created, multiplied, hoarded and utilised to transact and invest; and (ii) money as technological and institutional structure that determines the forms of exchange, circulation and accumulation of goods, services and value, deeply affecting the way in which capitalism works in a certain time and space. Rarely has mainstream economics, in its different varieties, taken into account the role of money as technological and institutional structure, or at least it did not embed it in the core of economic theory and policy. On the other hand, even within the heterodox paradigms, the absence of a clear distinction between the two basic aspects of money has often been a source of serious confusions and misunderstandings.

2. Money and the real economy in mainstream economics: a bird's eye view

The quantity theory of money (henceforth QTM) may be considered to be the first mainstream view on the relationship between quantity of money and economic activity. The reconstruction of its origin and early development is very controversial because of the persistent confusion between "Equation of Exchange" (henceforth EQE) and QTM. As was clarified by Fisher (1911), the EQE is an identity equating the aggregate quantity of money in circulation M multiplied by its velocity of circulation V, to the total of goods and services transacted T multiplied by the general index P of their prices: $MV = PT$. The QTM is a particular causal interpretation of the EQE based on the assumption of the exogeneity of money and the invariance, or at least slow and autonomous variability, of its velocity of circulation (Fisher, 1911). The most influential early version of the QTM is that of Hume (1752). In his view, an unexpected increase in the quantity of money may stimulate the real economy but only in the short run; in the longer run the expansionary effect translates into proportionally higher prices while the real economy gradually recedes to the previous level that is determined exclusively by real forces. This analysis is based on key concepts that will continue to characterise classical macroeconomics. First, money is assumed to be neutral in the long run, although not necessarily in the short run. In this view, the expansionary effect of an increase in money supply is a transitory phenomenon that fades away in consequence of the progressive adaptation to new circumstances. If one compares long-term positions, nominal prices fully reflect the effects of variations in the quantity of money leading to a dichotomy between the real system and the monetary system (henceforth "classical dichotomy").

Adam Smith, the reputed founder of economics as an autonomous scientific discipline, is not specifically remembered for his contributions to monetary economics (apart from his sketch of a monetary theory of balance of payments).

However, he enters into the present narrative because he was the first economist who clarified the nature of the long-run positions (described by the QTM as equilibria) in a sense similar to that of Newtonian physics (gravitation centres). In modern economics, the long period is conceived as a stable equilibrium, while the transition period characterised by non-neutrality of money is believed to be just a transitory process. This new perspective has an important policy implication. Smith's most famous contribution is his argument showing that the gravitation centre of a competitive market coordinates the activity of economic agents in the best possible way as if it were performed by a providential "invisible hand" (Smith, 1776). The alleged optimality of long-run stable competitive equilibria and their independence of money provided the two main building blocks of classical monetary theory in opposition to the mercantilist vision that had dominated national states' policies in the 17th and 18th centuries.

Marshall (1890) added further insights. First, he reformulated the QTM as a demand function of cash balances, putting it in a less mechanical perspective. Second, he introduced the distinction between aggregate demand and supply, arguing that demand is particularly important in the short period, while the long period ultimately depends on supply forces.

A few years later, Wicksell (1898) emphasised the importance of money as technological and institutional structure showing that a credit economy works differently from a simple monetary economy, enhancing the short-term non-neutrality of money. First, he argued that in a credit economy the indirect effects of interest rates are more important than the direct effects of money supply. Elaborating on this link, he distinguished between the real rate of return on new capital (called the "natural rate of interest") and the actual market rate of interest. He argued that whenever the market rate of interest lies below the natural rate, the amount of loans demanded would increase and the amount of saving supplied would fall. Investment, which equalled saving before the interest rate fell, would exceed saving at the lower rate. The increase in investment would boost overall spending, thus driving up prices. This "cumulative process" would stop only when banks' reserves had fallen to their legal or desired limit, whichever was higher.

As mentioned before, Fisher (1911) was the first to work out a rigorous version of the QTM as a particular causal interpretation of the EQE. In his view the growing importance of credit does not change the picture because its quantity is seen as depending on exogenous money (later called "monetary base" or "high-powered money") via the credit multiplier. This approach was later resumed and developed by Friedman (1960).

The young Keynes contributed to the QTM in the Cambridge version worked out by Marshall, focusing on the demand for money within a less mechanical approach (see, in particular, Keynes, 1924). He focused on the non-neutralities characterising the short run in the belief that the "long run is a misleading guide to current affairs" (ibid., p.65). In particular, he stressed that the velocity of circulation and the demand for money are significantly endogenous.

The Great Depression seriously questioned the validity of the classical point of view inducing a growing number of economists, led by Keynes and his followers, to reject the QTM also in the long run (see next section). Mainstream Keynesianism ruling in the Bretton Woods period (often called "neoclassical synthesis") restored long-term neutrality although it mainly focused on the short-run theory characterised by non-neutrality. This was ascribed to the institutional features of capitalism that cannot be mended through monetary policy. The foundations of this point of view were provided by Modigliani (1944), Samuelson (1947), and Patinkin (1956) who argued that the convergence to long-period equilibrium may be too slow unless an apt policy strategy intervenes to quickly recover full employment. This particular variety of Keynesianism became mainstream in the 1950s and retained a strong, though fading, influence until the late 1970s.

In the meantime, the critique to mainstream Keynesianism was kept alive by the monetarist school led by Milton Friedman on the basis of an updated version of the QTM (Friedman, 1960; Friedman and Schwarz, 1963). Since the late 1960s, the dominant battle between mainstream Keynesians and Monetarists was fought mainly on the battleground of the Phillips curve (Phillips, 1958). Friedman (1968) pointed out that the Phillips curve, interpreted by the Keynesians as a long-run relation between wage inflation (a crucial money variable) and unemployment rate (a crucial real variable), violates the classical dichotomy between monetary and real systems and the long-run neutrality of money. He maintained that the long-run relationship between inflation and unemployment must be represented as a vertical line (expressing the long-run neutrality of money and the classical dichotomy), crossing the abscissas axis in correspondence to the value of the "natural rate of unemployment" (Friedman, 1968). At the same time, he argued that the empirical evidence on the trade-off between money wages (or nominal prices) and unemployment was consistent with the long-run neutrality of money taking into account the accelerating increase of inflation expectations whenever the rate of unemployment is lower than the natural rate. In the 1960s and 1970s, a growing number of economists maintained that the empirical evidence appeared to be consistent with Friedman's hypothesis rather than with the Keynesian interpretation. A few Keynesians tried to rescue the Phillips curve by interpreting it as a short-term relation that may be shifted by extra-economic factors such as the contemporaneous struggles in the market of labour and the oil shocks occurring in 1973 and 1979. They did not succeed, however, to convince the majority of economists and policy makers that this view of the Phillips curve was not ad hoc.

In the 1970s, a group of economists of the younger generations led by Lucas (1972, 1976, 1981) accepted the policy implications of the criticism advanced by Friedman, but tried to provide more solid and updated foundations to his classical paradigm rooting it in stochastic general equilibrium theory as worked out by Arrow and Debreu (see, in particular, Debreu, 1959). The new version of the classical paradigm made the contrast with the Keynesian paradigm much more radical than before. In this view, the economy is always in a state of full unemployment equilibrium. This does not exclude small fluctuations triggered by exogenous factors, in particular the disturbances induced by Keynesian interventionist policies. However, the new paradigm implies money neutrality also in the short run sweeping away the rationale for countercyclical policies.

This new stream of the classical paradigm, called by Lucas and his followers "New Classical Economics", became rapidly (by the end of the 1970s) the new mainstream school in macroeconomics (Vercelli, 1991). The new classical paradigm underwent updating and refinements but did not change its basic methodology and policy implications. However, the monetarist explanation of business cycles accepted by Lucas, based on the so-called "monetary equilibrium business cycle" model was soon ousted by the non-monetarist "real business cycle" model that accepts Lucas's methodology but reverses the causal link between the real and the monetary economy and explains business cycles as a consequence of random technological shocks (Kydland and Prescott, 1982).

Keynesian economists tried to respond to the "new classical revolution" by showing that small modifications to the New Classical assumptions are sufficient to produce Keynesian results and policy implications. Therefore, the so-called New Keynesian economists accepted rational expectations and intertemporal maximization. They also, however, introduced into the general equilibrium model a variety of market imperfections (such as monopolistic competition, coordination failures, price rigidities and asymmetric information), implying the short-run non-neutrality of money and re-asserting the superiority of Keynesian policies under more realistic assumptions (Mankiw and Romer, 1991; Goodfriend and King, 1997). The second generation of this school strived to build on these micro foundations full-fledged dynamic stochastic general equilibrium (DSGE) econometric models capable of assisting policy makers and supervising authorities. New Keynesian economics has significantly contributed to reducing the methodological and policy gap between the current versions of Classical and Keynesian paradigms. This has led a few influential economists to identify the new mainstream economics in the late 1990s and early 2000s as a "New Consensus", that is a combination of elements drawn from the Classical and Keynesian traditions with a significant Wicksellian flavour (see, in particular, Woodford, 2003). This alleged consensus is based on the agreement that money is neutral in the long period but not in the short period.

However, as had happened before during the great crisis of the 1930s and that of the 1970s, the great crisis started in 2007 questioned the neutrality of money also in the long period and produced a polarisation between different schools of thought, breaking the fragile consensus shared in more tranquil times.

3. Money as quantity and the real economy

Marx was the first to develop a radical critique of the QTM. The main argument was that it ignores that the goods exchanged have an intrinsic value in terms of labour time. Notwithstanding this and other critiques, the QTM continued to play the role of ruling monetary theory until the Great Depression. The blatant contradiction between this theory and the empirical evidence made evident by the Great Depression convinced the late Keynes to reject it by refusing the neutrality of money both in the short and long period. Keynes argued that the long period is nothing but a sequence of short periods that is path-dependent (Keynes, 1936). In his view, a real economy is:

> [a]n economy in which money plays a part of its own and affects motives and decisions and the course of events cannot be predicted in the long period or in the short without knowledge of the behaviour of money between the first state and the last.
>
> (Keynes, 1973, pp.408–409)

In the GT he considered the QTM a special theory working only in conditions of full employment but failing in all the other cases. While the supporters of the Neoclassical Synthesis reverted to the position of the young Keynes (1924), accepting in principle the long-run neutrality of money though de-emphasising its relevance for current decisions, the Post Keynesians made a more radical rejection of the QTM by clarifying that in modern capitalism money is endogenous, since most money is credit money created by banks in response to demand for it from the private sector. In particular, post Keynesians showed:

> [t]hat the existence of a credit multiplier, as a result of some exogenous control by the monetary authorities, does not necessarily imply a causality running from high-powered money (monetary base or central bank money) to the money stock. On the contrary, causality runs from higher credit needs, to higher bank deposits, to higher required reserves.
>
> (Lavoie, 1984, pp.776–777)

The recent empirical findings are not favourable to the QTM. For example, De Grauwe and Polan summarise in the following way the results of their study:

> First, when analysing the full sample of countries, we find a strong positive relation between the long-run growth rate of money and inflation. However, this relation is not proportional. Our second finding is that this strong link between inflation and money growth is almost wholly due to the presence of high-inflation or hyperinflation countries in the sample. The relation between inflation and money growth for low-inflation countries (on average less than 10% per year over 30 years) is weak, if not absent.
>
> (De Grauwe and Polan, 2005, p.256)

The recent great crisis dramatically confirmed the unreliability of the monetarist approach. For example, Koo (2011) showed that, although during the ongoing Great Recession central banks increased the monetary base at an unprecedented rate by resorting to massive quantitative easing measures, the money in circulation remained stagnant in consequence of the breakdown of the money multiplier, and credit money did not increase notwithstanding near-zero interest rates.

4. Money as evolving technological and institutional structure

The structural dimension of analysis is not altogether absent in classical theory. However, the distinction between different monetary regimes usually does not go much beyond the basic distinction between a barter economy and a monetary economy. A monetary economy is argued to be much more efficient than a barter economy as it relaxes the strictures of "double coincidence of wants". At the same time, however, the systematic diffusion of monetary exchange introduced the germs of economic instability. According to the traditional mainstream point of view, the trade-off between efficiency and stability is overcome by forcing a monetary economy to behave as a barter economy, anchoring it to a solid peg (such as the gold standard) and to an orthodox budget policy.

The process of financialisation, which spread and intensified in the second half of the 19th century until WWI, progressively changed the functioning of capitalism giving a growing importance to credit. The increasingly endogenous process of money creation on the part of the banking system became more and more inconsistent with the QTM, but this seemed to pass unnoticed by most classical economists. Significant exceptions may be found in the contributions of a few forward-looking classical economists in the most innovative part of their contributions: Wicksell (cumulative process, 1898), Fisher (debt-deflation, 1933), Schumpeter (theory of economic development, 1934 [1911]). In all these cases, the compromise with classical theory was sought through a dichotomy between an institutional framework consistent with classical theory and one inconsistent with it: monetary economy-pure credit economy (Wicksell), circular flow-development (Schumpeter), ordinary crises-great depressions (Fisher).

Each of these institutional dichotomies captures how the crucial economic role assumed by credit since the late 19th century has altered the functioning of capitalism in a way increasingly inconsistent with traditional monetarism. According to Wicksell (1898), in a credit economy circulating money is endogenous and crucially depends on the interest rate rather than on its exogenous supply. Schumpeter (1934 [1911]) emphasised the crucial role of credit allocated to innovative entrepreneurs in promoting the process of capitalist development. Fisher (1933) showed that the spontaneous fluctuations of a credit economy may lead to over-indebtedness and deflation, triggering a vicious circle that may degenerate into a great depression.

The role of money in capital circulation plays a crucial role in identifying different forms and phases of capitalism. In Marx (1867) the simplest steps in the evolution of mercantile forms are:

Barter: C–C,

Simple mercantile society: C–M–C′,

Commercial capital: M–C–M′,

Industrial capital: M–C–. . .P. . .–C′–M′,

Financial capital: M–M′,

where C stands for commodity, M for money, P for productive process and the dash for a surplus value.

Hilferding updated Marx's insights on the financialisation of capitalism, interpreting it as the transformation of competitive "liberal capitalism" into monopolistic "finance capital" (Hilferding, 1981 [1910]). In his opinion, finance capital has unified the industrial, mercantile and banking interests under the leadership of big finance. This structural transformation has also altered the relationship between market and state, since finance capital sought a "centralised and privilege-dispensing state" intervening in the interest of wealth-owning classes, reversing the earlier liberal pressure towards the reduction of the role acquired by the state in the mercantilist era. This process eventually led to the Great Depression of the 1930s. After this disaster, a growing number of economists under the leadership of Keynes started to analyse the consequences of the process of financialisation.

Keynes resumed the traditional distinction between barter economy and monetary economy but argued that the second cannot be forced to work as a barter economy just through monetary means (Keynes, 1936). The trouble with classical economics is that it assumes axioms are fit for a barter economy (C–M–C) where money plays the role of means of exchange, while in a monetary economy (M–C–M′) the accumulation of money value is the goal of the exchange.[2] As Minsky clearly put it:

> [w]hereas classical economics and the neoclassical synthesis are based upon a barter paradigm . . . Keynesian theory rests upon a speculative-financial paradigm . . . the relevant paradigm is a City or a Wall Street where asset holdings as well as current transactions are financed by debt.
>
> (Minsky, 1975, pp.57–58)

This view represents well the standpoint of post-Keynesian economics. In particular, Minsky builds on Keynes, Kalecki and Fisher (debt deflation theory) to show that one has to distinguish different stages of a monetary economy: his "Financial Instability Hypothesis" refers not to a generic monetary economy but to a "sophisticated monetary economy", namely a mature stage of the evolution of capitalism where credit and finance play a crucial role. Even a "sophisticated monetary economy" undergoes a significant evolution: "recurrent financial instability has had consequences so devastating as to induce significant institutional changes that have, in turn, altered the dynamics of capitalist growth itself" (Minsky, 1975, p.68). The last stage examined by Minsky is the "money market capitalism" characterised by a wider scope of finance and an increasing difficulty in regulating it and preserving the stability of the system.

The Second financialisation, like the First, increased the power of oligopolies able to manipulate the market and to affect governmental policies in favour of finance and wealth-owner interests. However, the new policy strategy, often called neoliberal or neoconservative, aimed to weaken the role of the state through systematic privatisation and deregulation, advocating a more decentralised and competitive market (see Vercelli, 2017).

5. The process of financialisation in the long run

The insights on the evolution of money rapidly recalled in the preceding section suggest that one may identify a secular tendency towards financialisation, in the broad sense of the increasing importance and sophistication of money, credit and finance in shaping the modalities of the process of capital circulation and accumulation. This process has always strictly interacted with the long-term development of trade and markets. The driving force for this evolutionary process is rooted in a continuous flow of financial innovations meant to remove the existing obstacles to the flexibility of exchanges. For example, the adoption of money as a medium of exchange has removed the strictures of the double coincidence of wants, while the concession of credit relaxes the cash-in-advance constraint. As these examples suggest, financial innovations aim to extend the set of exchange options in time and space for the decision maker that introduces it. Their systemic effects, however, often turn out to have negative implications such as financial instability, unemployment, underinvestment in the real sector and stagnation. When these consequences accumulate beyond a certain threshold and become unbearable, the remedy may be sought in self-regulation, regulation by law, or sheer financial repression.

The secular tendency towards a progressive financialisation of the economy has also developed very slowly, because it has often been repressed for religious, ethical and political reasons. A case in point is the hostility toward the rate of interest in the ancient world and in the middle ages. Therefore, one may observe periods of acceleration of the process when financial repression is relaxed and deceleration, even regression, of the process when financial repression is strengthened (Vercelli, 2017). The latter, however, never succeeded in interrupting the process for a long period of time.

Focusing on the period after the industrial revolution, one may observe two periods of financialisation. The "First financialisation" occurred in the second half of the 19th century and the beginning of the Great Depression, while the "Second financialisation" started after the end of the Bretton Woods period (in 1971). Though their immediate causes, modalities and consequences are different, being intertwined with the contemporaneous processes of their age, it is possible to find a few significant analogies.

It is interesting to observe that the First and Second financialisations broadly overlap with the First and Second globalisations (Vercelli, 2017). This is not surprising since the process of financialisation may thrive only if the spatial constraints of exchange are removed, while the process of globalisation may be implemented to the extent that it is supported by internationalised finance. Second, both the process of financialisation and globalisation need a common permissive condition: the liberalisation of cross-country flows of goods, services and capital. The First globalisation and financialisation have been made possible by the systematic liberalisation of the industrialised economies implemented since the 1850s. The two processes were interrupted, and to some extent repressed, in the Bretton Woods period by the adoption of a policy strategy, influenced by Keynes, strengthening the public control on the economy and finance. The unilateral repeal by Nixon in 1971 of dollar convertibility started a new era soon characterised by the adoption of neoliberal policy strategies that greatly accelerated both the process of globalisation and financialisation.

The different views on money as technological and institutional structure are strictly related to different views on the process of financialisation. According to the classical point of view, the process of financialisation is a physiological stage of evolution of capitalism spontaneously developed by the market to increase its efficiency. According to the Keynesian mainstream, financialisation is a stage of evolution of capitalism having both physiological and pathological aspects. According to most heterodox schools, financialisation is mainly a pathological stage of evolution of capitalism that requires either its radical reform or its supersession. I intend now to analyse in some detail the rationale and implications of these different understandings of the process of financialisation from the point of view of their sustainability. However, in order to analyse the nexus between financialisation and sustainability, one has to grasp the rationale and implications of different understandings of the crises, the occurrence of which have been greatly affected by the process of financialisation itself.

PART 2: FROM CRISIS TO SUSTAINABILITY

The concept of crisis is strictly related to that of sustainability. A crisis is the interruption of a process or a radical change in its direction. Though the effects of a crisis may be temporary and reversible, their occurrence questions the sustainability of the process, that is its viability and persistence. This challenge may be more or less significant according to the nature of the crisis.

First of all, one has to distinguish the typical crisis that characterises one phase of business cycles from the "great crises" that are rarer but much more profound. The time scale of the fluctuations to which the crisis is related is in the first case in the order of a few years (from about three to eight) and in the second case of a decade or more. As is well known, the latest great crises happened in the 1930s (the Great Depression), in the 1970s (the Great Stagflation) and since 2007 (the Great Recession). Although from the point of view of the empirical evidence this distinction is accepted by most economists and economic historians, it very rarely plays an explicit role in economic theory. The main reason for this neglect is that mainstream theories do not have a general explanation for great crises that are seen as exceptions (black swans) to be understood *ex-post* case by case.

One of the few mainstream economists who made a clear distinction between the two categories of crisis and suggested different explanations for them was Fisher (1933). It is difficult to find a fully fledged theory that explains both kinds of crisis and why they occur. A remarkable exception among heterodox economists is Minsky who explains why business cycles tend to deteriorate in consequence of the growing temporal distance from the last great crisis and the ensuing progressive weakening of a new dramatic crisis fear (Minsky, 1982).

6. Different visions of business cycles crises

Let us first survey very briefly the main explanations of business cycle crises. The crucial distinction here is between exogenous causes and endogenous causes. The classical economists who believe in the self-regulating virtues of unfettered markets struggle to interpret the crises as the consequence of exogenous shocks disturbing market equilibrium. There are two versions to this point of view. According to the traditional version, the external shocks have the power to disturb the equilibrium path of the economy. In this view, business cycles are the consequence of the interaction between the disequilibrating effects of external shocks and the equilibrating effects of market forces. According to the much more extreme new classical perspective systematically adopted by Lucas and his followers, the exogenous shocks do not have the power to displace the economy from equilibrium but only to shift it.[3] This idea provided the basic inspiration for the influential "equilibrium business cycle" approach. However, in order to produce persistent wave-like oscillations, the equilibrium approach has to add in the model endogenous mechanisms, such as an acceleration principle or a learning mechanism, that are inconsistent with the crucial assumption of persistent equilibrium (see Vercelli, 1991). Lucas and his followers claimed that the endogenous propagation processes could play a role only if triggered by unexpected exogenous shocks. The equilibrium approach aims to show that a market economy always brings about optimal results that cannot be improved by exogenous interventions. In this view, countercyclical policies – as those implemented by Keynesian policymakers – cannot stabilise the economy as policy interventions add instead further shocks that contribute to the observed fluctuations.

The alternative view pursued by economists of heterodox inspiration is that business cycles are endogenous processes occurring in disequilibrium. This justifies countercyclical policies aimed at stabilising the economy by mitigating the systematic factors underlying disequilibrium fluctuations.

An intermediate position was that of Friedman (1968). He analysed the propagation process in terms of adaptive expectations, but he claimed that the process is triggered by the disturbing interference of Keynesian policies on market processes. In this view, a predetermined – and thus predictable – monetary policy, coupled with a *laissez faire* policy strategy, would eliminate the impulses triggering the business cycle so that the economy would rapidly converge towards the equilibrium corresponding to the natural rate of unemployment. The monetarist point of view was based on the traditional classical principles (short-term non-neutrality and long-term neutrality of money). Since these principles were also shared by mainstream Keynesians, the comparative assessment of the two theories was discussed mainly in terms of statistical or econometric parameters such as the relative stability of the monetary and real multipliers, a criticism strategy that proved to be weak and questionable. This is a crucial reason why Lucas struggled to provide different foundations in the 1970s, radically different from all the Keynesian schools including the "neoclassical synthesis". Disequilibrium was declared meaningless, and thus endogenous fluctuations and crises were also condemned to be meaningless (Vercelli, 1991). However, this is one crucial reason why the dominant approach since the late 1980s has proved to be unable to provide an explanation of great crises. That of the 1930s was ascribed to mistakes in the monetary policy that transformed a routine crisis into a great recession (Friedman and Schwarz, 1963), but its repetition was considered impossible since the policy authorities had learned from past mistakes.

After the New Classical Revolution, mainstream Keynesians (often called "New Keynesians") tried to defend their policy conclusions, showing that it was enough to introduce some plausible imperfections in the Lucas-style models to open the road to wealth improving policy interventions. As anticipated in Section 2, this led to a New Consensus that became dominant in the decades before the Great Recession. However, the New Consensus did not obtain the support of all the prominent New Keynesians. Since the deep financial crisis in South East Asia that questioned the assumptions of the New Consensus, many of them took an increasingly radical point of view, introducing into the analysis many structural and behavioural elements inconsistent with the Consensus approach (Stiglitz and Krugman are cases in point). Finally, the consensus broke up completely during the Great Recession. As has already happened in the 1930s and in the 1970s, great crises enhance the conflict between different approaches.

7. Alternative understandings of the "great crises"

The alternative visions of great crises may be classified in three broad categories that span a large part of the conceptual space of economic research. Each of them is an ideal type that may be useful to classify the main schools of thought, with the proviso that none of them may be simply identified by the thoughts of single researchers with all their complexities and peculiarities.

According to the view that is typically entertained by mainstream economists, the recent great crisis, as the preceding ones, has been defined as a black swan whose sight could not be predicted (Taleb, 2008). In this opinion, events of this sort are extremely rare ("occur once in a century" as Greenspan asserted) but, in principle, there is nothing one can do to predict the next one and very little to prevent it. In this view, a future great crisis is likely to happen only in a distant future beyond the reach of our competence and responsibility. The problem is thus only that of getting out of the crisis as soon as possible and resuming a sustained path of growth along the same guidelines of the preceding development paradigm.

According to the second viewpoint, typically entertained by heterodox economists, great crises are rather seen – so to say – as "grey swans", since crises of this sort characterise recurring phases of accelerated structural change.[4] The underlying laws have a limited degree of persistence that do not exclude recurrent, though not very regular, long-run fluctuations (Goodwin et al., 1989). The Kondratief cycle is the prototype of this view, elaborated by Schumpeter and further developed by his followers (see, in particular, Perez, 2002; Freeman, 2008). In this case, the same underlying regularities may encompass both the periods of crisis and the periods of financial tranquillity (Minsky, 1982). The distinction between ordinary crises and great crises depends on conditions largely endogenous to the above regularities.

According to the third point of view, adopted by evolutionary approaches, the recent Great Recession is a particularly deep and persistent instance of an event that has been ubiquitous in industrial and financial capitalism since its inception. Thus, in order to explain this crisis, one has to understand the intrinsic features of capitalism and its evolution since the early 19th century. This point of view does not deny the specificities of the recent crisis but claims that even the latter may be understood on the basis of common features.

Most heterodox economists combine the "grey swan" with the "evolutionary" points of view: great crises have something in common but their actual development depends on a host of structural and institutional circumstances that vary in different times and countries (see e.g. Vercelli, 2017). According to the black swan point of view, the crisis is the consequence of exogenous factors, while according to the other two points of view the causes are essentially endogenous, which does not necessarily exclude a role for exogenous disturbances. The latter, however, are conceived not as random shocks having a small (in some versions infinitesimal) size but as sizable and historically determined shocks.

A finer classification should distinguish different variants between each of these three broad categories, but that goes beyond the scope of the present chapter.

8. Different concepts of sustainability associated to the paradigms analysed earlier

The great crises question the sustainability of the existing model of development in a much more radical way than the shorter and milder crises associated with business cycles. In the history of Political Economy one finds three basic concepts of sustainability: dynamic stability of a steady state or path, viable reproduction of an economic (or socio-economic) structure, and resilience (or structural stability).[5]

In neoclassical economics, the only concept of sustainability systematically analysed is the very limited one of steady state. The classical economists entertained a much broader concept of sustainability that also took into account the relationship between growth of food and population (in particular Malthus, 1798; Ricardo, 1817; Stuart Mill, 1848; Wicksell, 1898), and the relationship between growth and the availability of energy sources (Jevons, 1865). This led them to believe that the only sustainable state is stationary. This point of view may be considered as the ancestor of the recent concept of sustainable development, although the latter in many versions does not imply stationarity.

In the 19th century, however, the exponents of uncritical *laissez faire* maintained that unfettered markets would have spontaneously corrected whatever factors of unsustainability could emerge. This simplistic point of view became very influential with policy makers but was never shared by the most reputed economists (see on this and related issues Robbins, 1952).

Marxian reproduction schemes clarified the conditions under which the capitalist process results are sustainable (Marx, 1867, 1885). The scope of this approach raised many controversies and misunderstandings. A widespread but ungrounded belief, probably inspired by the actual experience of "real socialism", maintains that Marx's focus on economic conditions led him astray, clouding the importance of further sustainability dimensions such as the social and environmental conditions. However, Marx is fully aware that the reproduction schemes are only the starting point of a fully fledged analysis of capitalist evolution. In his view, to study its sustainability one has to investigate also the conditions of reproduction of social relations as well as those of the relations between the capitalist process and nature. Social relations are increasingly unsustainable in capitalism as they are progressively submitted to mercantile relations and therefore alienated from their sources. The relationship between individuals and society on the one side and nature on the other is also progressively submitted to the market logic as use value becomes more and more subordinated to exchange value. In this view, the unsustainability of capitalism is thus not so much related to the tendency of the profit rate to fall but also to a much more comprehensive analysis of the complex relationships between individuals, society and nature. Within this broader framework, the Marxian insights on sustainability are still a source of inspiration (see e.g. Bellamy Foster, 2002).

At the turn of the century, the updated liberalism of Marshall and his followers (in particular Pigou, 1920) clarified why the markets cannot in principle realise the optimal allocation of natural resources: the widespread existence of externalities, i.e. costs and benefits that are not registered by the market. Their existence is implied by the incompleteness of markets and brings about market failures which jeopardise the sustainability of development. Only their thorough internalisation would allow the market to make its job of efficient coordination of economic activity. This basic insight still provides the foundations for environmental economics as developed since the late 1960s.

Keynes pointed out a different, macroscopic, market failure: the inability of unfettered markets to keep, or quickly restore, full employment. Within the subsequent Keynesian schools, sustainability assumed the meaning of full employment steady growth that requires apt countercyclical measures. The opponents of Keynesianism maintained instead that unfettered markets are able to sustain a continuous process of full-employment steady growth. As for social and environmental sustainability, the Keynesian paradigm struggled to integrate them within its models introducing the analysis of the environmental and social externalities (see e.g. Vercelli, 2017). The New Classical paradigm maintained instead that unfettered markets did not need social and environmental policies to improve the welfare of citizens.

The hegemony of the New Classical schools since the 1970s led to a widespread confusion between growth and development shared also by many Keynesian economists, although not all of them. This confusion is based on five crucial assumptions. First, it is assumed that per capita income is a fairly reliable measure of individual welfare. Second, it is assumed that the inequality of income may be increased by the process of modernisation but in the long period recedes as a consequence of the process of growth according to the "Kuznets Curve" (Kuznets, 1955). Moreover, it was believed that the distribution of income is substantially invariant in the long period so that poverty may be reduced only by increasing aggregate income. As for environmental sustainability, it is claimed that the process of modernisation may increase the negative impact on the environment in the short period, but this trend will eventually be reversed by the process of growth according to the so-called environmental Kuznets Curve (see, for example, the critical survey in Borghesi and Vercelli, 2008). It is possible to show that none of these widespread beliefs is supported by the available evidence (ibid.).

PART 3: FINANCIALISATION AND SUSTAINABILITY

In the final part of this chapter, I connect the results obtained in the two preceding parts, discussing the foundations of the main understandings of the interaction between financialisation and sustainability, with their policy implications. I consider the main paradigms from the synchronic point of view (Section 9), and then from the diachronic point of view (Section 10). The concluding remarks in Section 11 emphasise that the vision of researchers matters in all stages of research as well as in the use of its results for decision making.

9. Synchronic views on the interaction between financialisation and sustainability

I have to distinguish two basic points of view (synchronic and diachronic) and three main "visions" (orthodox, heterodox and evolutionary). Within the orthodox point of view, I distinguish three main branches: mainstream (neo and new) classical economics, (neo and new) Keynesian synthesis and (neoclassical) environmental economics.

According to mainstream classical economics, in principle the process of financialisation does not jeopardise the sustainability of the system (in the narrow sense of steady growth) if financial innovations are introduced and spread by unfettered markets. In this view, the sustainability of steady growth is undermined by the unjustified interference of policy makers and market supervisors. Within mainstream classical economics one can distinguish between two streams that have different policy implications. The fundamentalist point of view relies on the optimality of unfettered markets and rejects any form of bailout even in favour of the biggest and most connected banks. In addition, it argues in favour of budget orthodoxy under all circumstances including a deep and persistent depression. The pragmatist point of view maintains that great crises occur under extreme circumstances that require the adoption of unorthodox remedies. In particular, under these circumstances, the bailout of banks that are too big or too interconnected to fail may be justified to thwart the process of financial contagion that could otherwise ravage the economy. Analogously, a policy of abundant provision of liquidity to the private sector could also be justified, even by resorting to the massive use of unorthodox measures such as quantitative easing interventions.

According to the Neoclassical Synthesis, one has to distinguish the positive consequences of the financialisation process from its negative implications. In this view, the process of financialisation has significantly increased the liquidity of assets and the efficiency of the investment process (Brainard and Tobin, 1968). However, at the same time, financialisation has increased the instability of the system that may permanently oscillate around a position characterised by involuntary unemployment. This depends mainly on the increasing weight of speculation propped up by a continuous flow of ad hoc financial innovations. Sustainability, conceived merely as full-employment steady growth, may thus be seriously impaired by market-led financialisation. The remedy is seen in a series of policy measures aimed at keeping full employment, or restoring it, through countercyclical policies and stricter supervision and control of finance, also by adopting some sort of Tobin tax (see in particular Tobin, 1978).

According to neoclassical environmental economics, the sustainability of development (often confused with steady growth) is jeopardised by externalities that depend on the incompleteness of markets. The role of financialisation seen from this point of view is ambiguous. It may be beneficial as it may contribute to complete the markets and to relax the limits to growth. At the same time, the process of financialisation may be a source of new externalities distorting growth towards short-term objectives. The emphasis of environmental economics is on the internalisation of environmental externalities and on the use of financial markets to improve this process. Internalisation is sought mainly through market-based instruments such as green taxation and/or tradable permits systems.

Within the second ("grey swan") point of view, the great crises are recurring episodes marking the end of long historical phases or long cycles. In these cases development may be sustained only through a process of comprehensive structural change able to maintain a new cycle of development.

For example, Schumpeter understood great crises as crucial turning points of long waves (Schumpeter, 1934 [1911]; Goodwin et al., 1989; Perez, 2002). In these cases, development may be resumed only through a technological and institutional revolution that establishes a new model of development. Finance plays a crucial role in facilitating this radical structural change, provided that credit goes to innovating entrepreneurs. The process of financialisation does not, however, seem to have improved this role of the financial system.

Minsky himself has a long-wave interpretation of great crises (Minsky, 1982, 1986). Business cycles are typically characterised by financial crises at the end of the boom. They are mild after a great crisis since the fear of a new one is still alert, but the more the latest great crisis recedes in time, the more this fear fades away paving the way for a new severe crisis.

10. Diachronic views on the interaction between financialisation and sustainability

Heterodox economists maintain that the crisis is the consequence of market failures aggravated by the orthodox policies of privatisation, deregulation and austerity. The way out is sought in radical reforms that modify the working of the economy. The nature of these reforms depends on the complex intertwining between economic vision and political vision of decision makers. A satisfactory analysis of this nexus would require an extensive investigation going much beyond the limits of this chapter. Therefore, I briefly mention here only some relevant implications of Marx's and Keynes's vision.

Although Marx saw only the beginning of the First financialisation, he still grasped many of its implications for the sustainability of capitalism. He emphasised in particular the basic contradictions introduced by money and finance in a capitalist economy, namely higher efficiency and flexibility of exchanges coupled with a growing potential of disequilibrium, instability and crises. In his view, this contradiction progressively reaches unprecedented degrees of intensity that pave the way for the breakdown of capitalism. The process of financialisation may counteract in the short period the tendency to a fall in the rate of profit but only by strengthening the tendency to increasingly devastating financial crises. Some followers of Marx systematically developed insights contained in Marx's writings, interpreting "Finance Capital" as the last stage of Capitalism (see, in particular, Hilferding, 1981 [1910]). Marx also understood the strict link between financialisation and globalisation as promoted by imperialist powers in the 19th century, a link that has been confirmed, though in a different form, by the recent Second financialisation. The consequences of Marx's analysis are uncompromisingly radical. A sustainable process of flourishing human potential requires the abandonment of capitalism and the instauration of a different mode of production.

According to Keynes and his more faithful followers, free-market capitalism cannot survive without radical reforms that mend the most macroscopic and intolerable market failure: the inability of the unregulated capitalist market to maintain full employment. The unsustainability of steady full-employment growth in an unfettered market economy depends on the monetary nature of capitalism and is progressively aggravated by the unchecked process of financialisation. Sustainable full employment growth may be reached through a radical reform of the policy strategy aiming to tame the financial system through the so-called "financial repression" based on better regulation and supervision. The control of the process of financialisation must be complemented, on the side of the real economy, by countercyclical policies, socialisation of investment, redistribution of income and the progressive build-up of an efficient welfare state. Keynes did not see with his eyes the recent evolution of capitalism, but his analysis of the consequences of financialisation, as developed in particular in chapters 12 and 17 of the *General Theory* (Keynes, 1936), was forward looking and fits the current world as shaped by the Second financialisation even more than the pre-WWII world as moulded by the First financialisation.

The scope of Keynes's and Marx's analysis was not restricted to the economic aspects of society as some followers or critics seemed to suggest. The social aspects are of course central in Marx but play a crucial role also in Keynes. Moreover, though the environmental aspects of their analysis have been almost completely neglected by early followers and interpreters, one can find in their writings important insights that have been recently rediscovered and further developed (see e.g. Vercelli, 2017).

In particular, ecological economics has clarified that the ongoing evolution of capitalism is inconsistent with the preservation of the fundamental equilibria of the biosphere. This point of view, differently from that of (neoclassical) environmental economics, is sceptical on the contribution that market-based instruments (such as green taxation or tradable pollution permits) may provide to establish a new relation, sustainable even in the very long run, between the economic and financial system on the one side and the biosphere on the other.

Mainstream economists themselves emphasise the nexus between a great crisis and the structural features of capitalism and often advocate more or less radical structural reforms to reduce the risk of a new great crisis or to mitigate its effects. Most of them in this case emphasise that the real markets are quite different from perfect competition markets and require reforms that reduce the crucial gap between them. One has to distinguish, as we did before, between fundamentalist and pragmatist mainstream economists. According to fundamentalist economists, the ultimate cause of the crisis is related to the persistent interference of the state in the markets that continues to distort their functioning. Therefore, the ultimate remedy to escape from the crisis preventing new ones in the future is seen in a further, much more radical, liberalisation and deregulation of markets. To the extent that public intervention is required (mainly in the fields of defence and justice), the discretionary power of policy authorities should be limited as far as possible by strict rules based upon monetary and budget orthodoxy. In particular, the fundamentalists insist on the necessity of an effective market discipline that excludes any sort of bailout of virtually bankrupted units, even in the case of too-big-to-fail banks. Pragmatist mainstream economists are more focused on the immediate resumption of growth in the business-as-usual version and to obtain this result are prepared to compromise with their neoliberal principles advocating the bailout of big financial firms, public support to the economy and unorthodox monetary measures. In both cases the structural reforms advocated by mainstream economists go in a direction that is opposite to that advocated by heterodox economists. However, the existing markets are considered by pragmatist mainstream economists as a good approximation to competitive markets, good enough to justify the confidence in their ability to recover a satisfactory steady growth in the near future.

11. Concluding remarks

The complex taxonomy of the main different meanings that have been attributed to money, financialisation, crisis, sustainability and their mutual relations has shown that the "vision" (general paradigm) of the capitalist process and its long-term evolution matters as it affects the socio-economic theories suggested to understand and control it. This chapter has been drafted in the conviction that the vision matters not only in the pre-analytic stage of research, as maintained by Schumpeter, but also in the analytic stage that pretends to be independent of such broad preconceptions (Vercelli, 2017). The vision has thus also a crucial impact on decision making by economic agents and politicians, as it is often deeply influenced by the results of research in economics and finance.

The different meanings of the basic concepts discussed in this chapter are worked out and adopted by researchers and decision makers according to their vision of the capitalist process and lead them to divergent conclusions on the connections between finance and sustainability. The awareness of the complex set of cognitive and pragmatic options may be alerted by a taxonomic approach such as that pursued in this chapter and is important for several reasons. First of all, it could foster communication and mutual understanding. Second, it could promote scientific and political pluralism. And finally, it may play the role of an antidote to the authoritarian and depressing belief that "there is no alternative", showing that one can, and should, pursue better alternatives in economics and finance that may guarantee economic, social and environmental sustainability.

Notes

1 A preliminary draft of this chapter was completed as a contribution to the research FESSUD (Vercelli, 2014). This research has received funding from the European Union Seventh Framework Programme (FP7/2007–2013) under grant agreement n° 266800.
2 Keynes (1979, p.81) uses here the distinction made by Marx (e.g. in 1867, pp.248–257) recognising that it captures well the crucial difference of a monetary economy as compared to previous stages of the economy.
3 Frisch (1933) was the first who claimed that exogenous shocks impinging on a stable system could produce persistent oscillations. He never gave a proof of this claim and it was eventually shown to be wrong (see Chen, 2000).

4 This metaphor is based on the well-known fact that the colour grey characterises a specific phase in the life cycle of swans.
5 The concept of sustainability is discussed in more detail in Chichilnisky et al. (1997).

References

Bellamy Foster J., 2002, Marx's ecology in historical perspective, *International Socialism Journal*, 96, pp.1–16.

Borghesi, S. and Vercelli, A., 2008, *Global Sustainability. Social and Environmental Conditions*, Basingstoke, UK and New York: Palgrave Macmillan.

Brainard, W. and Tobin, J., 1968, Pitfalls in financial model building, *American Economic Review* (Papers and Proceedings), 58(2), pp.99–122.

Chen, P., 2000, *The Frisch Model of Business Cycles. A Spurious Doctrine, But a Mysterious Success*, Discussion Paper, China Center for Economic Research, No.c1999007, Peking University.

Chichilnisky, G., Heal, J., and Vercelli, A., 1997, *Sustainability: Dynamics and Uncertainty*, Dordrecht, the Entherlands: Kluwer.

Debreu, G., 1959, *Theory of Value*, New York: Wiley.

De Grauwe, P. and Polan, M., 2005, Is inflation always and everywhere a monetary phenomenon? *Scandinavian Journal of Economics*, 107(2), pp.239–259.

Fisher, I., 1911, *The Purchasing Power of Money. Its determination and Relation to Credit, Interest and Crises*, New York: A.M. Kelley, 2nd revised ed. 1922, reprinted 1963.

Fisher, I., 1933, The debt-deflation theory of the Great Depression, *Econometrica*, 1(4), pp.337–357.

Freeman, C., 2008, *Systems of Innovation: Selected Essays in Evolutionary Economics*, Cheltenham, UK: Edward Elgar.

Friedman, M., 1960, *A Program for Monetary Stability*, New York: Fordham University Press.

Friedman, M., 1968, The role of monetary policy, *The American Economic Review*, 68(1), pp.1–17.

Friedman, M. and Schwarz, A.J., 1963, *A Monetary History of the United States, 1867–1960*, Princeton, NJ: Princeton University Press.

Frisch, R., 1933, Propagation and impulse problems in dynamic economics, in *Essays in Honour of Gustav Cassel*, London: George Allen and Unwin.

Goodfriend, M. and King, R., 1997, The new classical synthesis and the role of monetary policy, in Bernanke, B. and J. Rotemberg, eds., *NBER Macroeconomics Annual 1997*, 12, pp.231–296.

Goodwin R., Di Matteo, M. and Vercelli, A., 1989, *Social and Technological Factors in Long Term Fluctuations*, New York: Springer.

Hilferding, R., 1981 [1910], *Finance Capital*, London: Routledge and Kegan Paul.

Hume, D., 1752, *Political Discourses*, 12th ed. of 1777 reprinted in Hume, D., *Writings in Economics*, London: Thomas Nelson, 1955.

Jevons, W.S., 1865, *The Coal Question*, Basingstoke, UK: Macmillan.

Keynes, J.M., 1924, *Tract on Monetary Reform*, Basingstoke, UK: Macmillan.

Keynes, J.M., 1936, *The General Theory of Employment, Interest and Money*, Basingstoke, UK: Macmillan.

Keynes, J.M., 1973, A monetary theory of production, in D. Moggridge, ed., *The Collected Writings of John Maynard Keynes, Vol. 13, The General Theory and After, Part I – Presentation*, Cambridge, UK: Cambridge University Press.

Keynes, J.M., 1979, *The Collected Writings of John Maynard Keynes, Vol. 29, The General Theory and After: A Supplement*, Cambridge University Press, UK: Cambridge.

Koo, R.C., 2011, The world in balance sheet recession: Causes, cure, and politics, *Real World Economic Review*, 58(12), pp.19–37.

Kuznets, S., 1955, Economic growth and income inequality, *American Economic Review*, 45(2), pp.1–28.

Kydland, F.E. and Prescott, E.C., 1982, Time to build and aggregate fluctuations, *Econometrica*, 50, pp.1345–1370.

Lavoie, M., 1984, Endogenous flow of credit and the Post Keynesian theory of money, *Journal of Economic Issues*, 18(3), pp.771–797.

Lucas, R.E. Jr., 1972, Expectations and the neutrality of money, *Journal of Economic Theory*, 4(2), pp.103–124.

Lucas, R.E. Jr., 1976, Econometric policy evaluation: A critique, *Carnegie-Rochester Conference Series on Public Policy*, 1, pp.19–46.

Lucas, R.E. Jr., 1981, *Studies in Business Cycle Theory*, Cambridge, MA: MIT Press.

Malthus, T.R., 1798, *An Essay on the Principle of the Population*, London: J. Johnson.

Mankiw, N.G. and Romer, D., eds., 1991, *New Keynesian Economics*. Vol. 1: *Imperfect Competition and Sticky Prices*; Vol. 2 *Coordination Failures and Real Rigidities*, Cambridge, MA: MIT Press.

Marshall, A., 1890, *Principles of Economics*, Basingstoke, UK: Macmillan.

Marx, K., 1867, *Capital*, Vol. I, Harmondsworth, UK: Penguin 1976.

Marx, K., 1885, *Capital*, Vol. II, Harmondsworth, UK: Penguin 1978.

Minsky, H.P., 1975, *John Maynard Keynes*, New York: Columbia University Press.

Minsky, H.P., 1982, *Can "It" Happen Again?* Armonk, NY: M.E. Sharpe.

Minsky, H.P., 1986, *Stabilizing an Unstable Economy*, New Haven, CT: Yale University Press.

Modigliani, F., 1944, Liquidity preference and the theory of interest and money, *Econometrica*, 12(1), pp.45–88.

Patinkin, D., 1956, *Money, Interest and Prices: An Integration of Monetary and Value Theory*, Evanston, IL: Row, Peterson and Co.

Perez, C., 2002, *Technological Revolutions and Financial Capital: The Dynamics of Bubbles and Golden Ages*, Cheltenham, UK: Edward Elgar.

Phillips, A.W., 1958, The Relationship between Unemployment and the Rate of Change of Money Wages in the United Kingdom 1861–1957, *Economica*, 25(100), pp.283–299.

Pigou, A.C., 1920, *The Economics of Welfare*, Basingstoke, UK: Macmillan.

Ricardo, D., 1817, *On the Principles of Political Economy and Taxation*, London: John Murray.

Robbins, L., 1952, *The Theory of Economic Policy in English Classical Political Economy*, Basingstoke, UK: Macmillan, reprint 1961.

Samuelson, P.A., 1947, *Foundations of Economic Analysis*, Cambridge, MA: Harvard University Press.

Schumpeter, J.A., 1934 [1911], *The Theory of Economic Development*, Eng. trans., New Brunswick, NJ and London: Transaction Publishers.

Smith, A., 1776, *An Inquiry into the Nature and Causes of the Wealth of Nations*, London: Methuen, ed. Edwin Cannan, 1904. Fifth edition.

Stuart Mill, J., 1848, *The Principles of Political Economy: with some of their applications to social philosophy*, London: John W. Parker.

Taleb, N.N., 2008, *The Black Swan: The Impact of the Highly Improbable*, Harmondsworth, UK: Penguin.

Tobin, J., 1978, A proposal for international monetary reform, *Eastern Economic Journal*, 4(3–4), pp.153–159.

Vercelli, A., 1991, *Methodological Foundations of Macroeconomics. Keynes and Lucas*, Cambridge, UK: Cambridge University Press.

Vercelli, A., 2014, Implications of different understandings of financial crises for divergent conclusions on the connections between finance and sustainability, FESSUD Working Paper No.46.

Vercelli, A., 2017, *Crisis and Sustainability. The Delusion of Free Markets*, Basingstoke, UK: Palgrave Macmillan.

Wicksell, K., 1898, *Interest and Prices*, Eng. trans. 1936, New York: Sentry Press.

Woodford, M., 2003, *Interest and Prices: Foundations of a Theory of Monetary Policy*, Princeton, NJ: Princeton University Press.

9 Finance is not the dark side of the force

Anna Maria Grazia Variato

1. Introduction

The expression dark side recalls a number of alternative pictures. The one implicitly assumed in the title evokes the movie *Star Wars*, where "the Dark Side of the Force" is the evil against which the Good Side is supposed to fight. In this particular perspective, the one where finance is supposed to play the role of evil, the sentence in the title can be taken as an assertion. Indeed there is no need to assume as a normative principle that the financial side is a negative lever of macroeconomic dynamics. Neither one could imply that the financial side alone may affect resource allocation (hence efficiency) more badly than the real side.

But there is another fairly recurrent image contrasting light and darkness, and this is the well-known yin-yang representation of interacting forces. Differently from the previous *Star Wars*-like standpoint, this picture is not implicitly marked by any normative preconception; in contrast it can be used as a symbolic tool meant to depict both complementary matters or interactions. More precisely, the image can be employed as a symbol of the complementarity of elements of human existence or Nature, and also as a two-dimensional representation of a dynamic process whose character is both endogenous and cyclical. Nonetheless, it has to be noticed that both static and dynamic symbolisms require a holistic/organicist conception of reality. Then a fundamental question arises. If one subscribes such a view, what kind of role is it expected to give to finance, and in particular to the idea of financial instability?

Questions of this kind are too often ruled out from an explicit account, as they belong to the realm of method; nevertheless no scientist could leave aside the assumption of a preferred perspective: it will act as an implicit framework through which reality is given a meaning. Though methodological reflections are always relevant in the processes of interpretation, they have a different degree of relevance according to different environmental conditions. In the presence of strong conventional views and tranquil times, methodological discussions are perceived as less urgent to the attention of non-methodologists. Not surprisingly, non-methodologists usually emphasize the importance of implicit perspectives under two conditions: first, when they individually want to underline the relevance of a position which turns out to be critical with respect to the conventional view; second, when there is a perception that "times have changed", hence convention amendments might be needed too. So the enduring effects of the financial crisis of 2007 can be taken as both evidence of an economic crisis and as a symptom of a crisis of ideas (Roncaglia, 2010a, 2010b). Whether such a crisis was just a "moment", or the result of a "process", is one of the core issues in the present chapter.

In this chapter the yin-yang picture is used as a simplifying pedagogical tool, in order to address both methodological and empirical issues. Indeed, this pictorial example is employed as an unconventional starting point to sustain the main thesis, meanwhile addressing a debate revived by recent recurrent episodes of financial instability. Such events put on the stage two relevant questions: (1) Is it correct to blame finance as the primary cause of recent crises? (2) If one tries to use a theoretical paradigm in order to satisfactorily represent ongoing phenomena, does it eventually connect to the mainstream–neoclassical paradigm, or to a quite radically different theoretical tool?

Basically, the thesis suggested in this contribution focuses on three pieces of argumentation. First, it underlines that the representation of the role of finance in the economy is not simply an epistemological matter, but rather it stems from a deeper methodological foundation. In other words, any model/ theory (representation) on the role of finance in the economy is not a neutral description of objects (static) or objective relationships (dynamics); in contrast it is the effect of a specific interpretation of reality, whose hidden nature is subjectively chosen by the one who suggests the model itself (Schumpeter, 1954; Heilbroner, 1990; Hodgson, 1993).

Second, it points out that even if it may be correct to state that, for example, the recent sub-prime crisis had a "financial trigger", it would be quite misleading to represent what has happened from 2008 until now as the effect of a "unique culprit" named finance. Putting it differently, it is one thing is to say that the financial side has been the place where the impulse of the crisis started, and quite another to suggest that without such an impulse a crisis like 2008 would not have happened.

Third, it seems fair to say that neoclassical/mainstream theory is not tailored to take into account phenomena like systemic crises, especially if they show up as systemic financial crises (Minsky, 1991; Kotz, 2009; Parguez and Thabet, 2013). So, in the face of more recurrent, more contagious and persistent cycles dominated by financial factors, it is quite natural to look for alternative explanatory/representative views. These explanations have a long tradition in the history of economic thought. They belong to a heterogeneous (nowadays also heterodox) body that could be labelled "critical finance" (Toporowski, 2005). This chapter attempts to move from the historical/factual dimension of the recent financial crisis to support the thesis that a unifying theoretical paradigm can be built using the concept of financial economy of production which naturally connects to Hyman Minsky's approach and vision.

The chapter is divided into four parts. The second section deals with methodological aspects; the third section addresses empirical evidence, and the performance of the mainstream models in representing/predicting historical events are addressed; and the fourth section compares the emergent pillars of a paradigm of endogenous (financial) instability with the foundations of the neoclassical mainstream paradigm, giving a definition of financial economy of production. The final section concludes.

2. Method and finance in the macro-economy: using the yin-yang metaphor to highlight the role of subjective pre-analytic visions

Before going into the detail of alternative interpretations of the yin–yang image, one of its fundamental features needs to be underlined. It entails a notion of systemic equilibrium in the interaction among forces, and it also involves the idea of cycles. The choice is not a casual one because it is indicative of the extreme interpretative dialectics surrounding the macroeconomic events after 2007: namely the vision of an exceptional but temporary nature to the crisis, as opposed to the view of its complexity (hence not full predictability) and recurrence.

Though the view I want to suggest implies that the concept of equilibrium cannot be dismissed as a fundamental principle, one has to be careful in this respect. As already known, equilibrium can be attributed very different meanings: for the purposes of the present chapter, the emphasis is on the difference between normative and positive uses of the equilibrium concepts (Vercelli, 1992). In the normative perspective, equilibrium is considered preferable to disequilibrium; that is, equilibrium conditions are assumed to be the more suitable, producing well-being, prosperity, enhancement and so on. Hence equilibrium is a value. In contrast, according to the positive perspective, the notion of equilibrium acts as a matter of fact. In other words it is an intrinsic property or tendency of the system. One may add that the positive perspective on equilibrium is more reductionist than its normative counterpart, as it does not embody disequilibrium as a twin matter of fact; as a result though, disequilibrium exists in a positive view: it is only temporary and autonomously fades away. The thesis I am going to argue is that such a specific difference in the methodological meaning given to the notion of equilibrium couples with holistic/independence views as a further (likely implicit) precondition of radical distinction among contrasting interpretative macro-perspectives. Hence, the black and white yin-yang parts can be specifically interpreted as the forces embodying dynamic macro-processes. Consistent with the opening statement of the chapter, white (yin) represents the real side of the economy (or, in a different couple, expansion during a business cycle), while black (yang) denotes the financial side (or contraction).

2.1 Reading the picture with a positive economics perspective: the world as it is

The first way to understand the yin-yang picture is to see it as a representation of the world as "it is" (positive economics). Furthermore, one may look at the components using two criteria (likely implicit, but far from being innocuous in the effects) of separation and mutual symmetry. The first criterion is consequential to the fact of not possessing (assuming) a holistic perception of reality; the second criterion is consequential to the mere observation of the picture, evaluated from an "as a matter of fact" standpoint.

Let's select the real/financial couple in order to express the resulting interpretation of the picture as a narrative of the interaction between the two systemic economic components. It would sound more or less like the following. A dynamic macro-process, in principle, is either started by real or financial sides of the economy (the two big parts of the picture). Forces are symmetrical and complementary; furthermore they are independent from one another. From time to time, eventually, they may come into conflict, giving rise to instability. This is more likely to happen the bigger the role of one dimension becomes with respect to the other. The tension is sharp and evident when a financial (real) shock disrupts a real (financial) expansion. Thus the two dots in the picture can be understood as the exogenous shocks (whose nature can be equally either real or financial) and the big parts become the transmission mechanisms of such shocks.

In this way, to give meaning to the picture, the economic system is neither supposed to fall apart (i.e. experiencing a disruptive internal conflict), nor is it sensitive to the scale of the system itself. The possibility of one side overcoming the other is ruled out if the picture is given a positive economics interpretation. Furthermore, if the criteria of separation (independence) and symmetry become assumptions, they turn into sufficient conditions to ensure that any dynamic process is self-containing and coherent (or dynamically stable).[1]

This interpretation, while apparently appropriate to tell a story, as long as reality is assumed as a matter of fact, turns out to be compatible with a quite limited number of dynamic processes. More specifically, this way of looking at the picture may become incompatible with most historical processes involving qualitative change and evolution. Somehow, through this interpretation, one confronts a self-referential sketch of the fundamental forces leading the order of the economy (Variato, 2008).

2.2 Reading the picture with a normative economics perspective: the world as it should be

The second way to describe the yin-yang picture uses the concept of equilibrium just as a normative principle. In other words, the picture is an interpretative tool meant to represent reality as "it should be" (i.e. the ideal state of things, given a selected framework). Furthermore without a criterion of separation, the forces, while still symmetric, are intertwined. They interact with each other, they are embraced: dots are like hooks representing the idea that one force comes into the other without the possibility of separating one from the other. It must be emphasized that in this normative perspective, symmetry has a normative significance too. As a result, the tale spelling out the sense of the image would emphasize that each force can lead dynamics (as in the previous description); but where it differs from it is in the organic nature of the relationships that makes the picture comprise only two parts (instead of four) and gives rise to a different conception of conflict and instability (Vercelli, 2000). In fact, in the positive economics perspective, conflict was the effect of separation; in contrast it turns out that, in this normative view, conflict is the cause of disequilibrium and then the cause of instability. Furthermore, while the idea of exogenous shock is not an evident part of the picture, the idea of equilibrium as the effect of compensation among forces is the main normative feature intrinsic to it. But the balancing of the forces can be attained through different kinds of dynamic interaction. And the normative interpretation of the imagination would just select the preferred one.

So, given the nature of the system under analysis (made up of just two forces), we have three kinds of possible dynamics. The first type implies a perfect (instantaneous) compensation of forces. Technically speaking, the system follows a path of endogenous linear-dynamic equilibrium. This kind of dynamics is not the one that the picture shows up.

The second kind of dynamics, the one evident in the picture, is the one giving rise to endogenously stable cycles. Here the two components become temporarily dominant (leading) one over the other. In this case, one does not need necessarily to suggest powers competing against each other (in a perspective of conflict, when one part becomes bigger, the other is bound to retreat); one simply has to concede that during the dynamic interaction, forces whose nature is heterogeneous do not change at the same speed, at the same time. Nevertheless, under this second scenario, the organic nature of forces implies that the bigger the divergence among them, the stronger the power of the self-equilibrating mechanism led by the temporarily dominated force. In other words, if we look at the picture, the faster or the bigger the white (black) part becomes with respect to the black (white) one, the bigger the black (white) hook grows, which eventually overturns the dynamic interaction between the parts. The forces in this case balance at the systemic level but do not even out at each point in time.

The third kind of dynamics is the one leading to runaway paths. Here the forces do not balance at the systemic level, and eventually one of them seizes the other. The symmetry in the picture falls apart. Taking expansion/contraction as the couple under observation, explosions or implosions are possible if the notion of equilibrium is given a normative meaning only. Then, disruptive conflict and untamed instability are the expression of a particular kind of endogenous interaction of interdependent forces: the one due to excessive disequilibrium or asymmetry in the dynamic power of forces.

Each of the three dynamics embodies a significant conception of moments and processes. In fact the whole picture is the logical representation of a process, while the dots (hooks) are the logical representation of moments. Using the picture as the representation of the daily cycle between light and darkness (process), the moments would obviously be dawn (when darkness turns into light) and dusk (when light turns into darkness). For the purposes of this chapter, if one takes the picture as the logical representation of positive and negative phases of a business cycle, then it must imply that inside any expansionary phase there is the seed for the next contraction, because inside any contraction is the seed for the next expansion. In this case, obviously moments are the turning "points". Cycles are naturally emergent in this perspective; nevertheless, if a cycle shows up, persisting through time, this means that some systemic self-equilibrating mechanism is already at work.

As long as a normative view is undertaken, the picture showing a sequence of self-equilibrating systemic cycles has to be justified as the preferred state of the system. Let's suppose this conjecture is proved correct. It becomes especially interesting if the interpretation of the picture is the one entailing the use of the endogenous-stable cycle referring to the interaction between real and financial sides of the economic system. The implicit vision would lead us to describe such interaction as the compensation–alternation of powers. As a result, the real side couldn't be perceived as dominant/leading in principle over the financial side. The converse is also not possible. The opposite of such a view, it is quite natural to observe that the two sides could become dialectic (instead of harmonic), giving rise eventually to sharp and strong contradictions. In this particular case, implying that the economic system is involved in a deep crisis (or, on the opposite in a euphoric boom), no "individual culprit" can be found: one can neither blame the financial (real) side for moving too quickly with respect to the real (financial side), nor can one blame the real (financial) side for moving too slowly with respect to the real (financial side). In other words, there is no "dark side" in the economy at the ground level of ontological principles.

It is easy to observe that the methodological tenets explicitly emphasized in order to compare the views on the yin-yang picture interpretation are also the ones assumed by the extreme economic paradigms; namely, mainstream/ neoclassical, as opposed to heterodox alternatives rooted in heterogeneous traditions. Furthermore, given the particular couples selected for the comparison (expansion/contraction and real/financial), it also becomes evident as the rationale for the selection of Minsky as the natural paradigmatic reference author: the four elements are at the core of his original exposition of the Financial Instability Hypothesis. Indeed, if one were to describe Minsky with a maxim, it would probably be: "stability is destabilizing" (Minsky, 1994, p.7, footnote 12).

3. Facing financial crises of the past

As long as the ontological level of reflection does not allow one to come to a conclusive answer with respect to correctness or truthfulness of visions, reality behaviour becomes the discriminant criterion for indirect validation. So the pillars of the ontological vision become axioms at the epistemological level of representation. There one builds theories and models, runs experiments or collects evidence in order to falsify theoretical implications. Focusing on the specificity of this contribution, the events connected to the 2007 financial crisis become a suitable experimental laboratory to provide validation.

3.1 Empirical evidence: contrasting facts and theoretical implications

In this section I will mention empirical facts only indirectly and using the contribution by Reinhart and Rogoff (2008). Their article was published right at the beginning of the crisis. Nevertheless, it shows all the critical elements that lately have become customary in the empirical evaluation of financial instability. As the title (using irony) correctly suggests, the 2007 crisis was not so different from other crises, especially if one focuses upon the interpretation of causes, recurrence and persistence. In other words, empirical evidence challenging theoretical mainstream implications was present long before 2007; as a result, it would be quite problematic to consider the events afterwards as just an occasional historical accident.

In their contribution, the authors present a number of considerations and pictures summarizing data related to more than 100 countries in the world and focusing in particular on the period from 1800 to 2006. The main suggestion emerging from their paper is that financial crises are not unusual or exceptional. This evidence determines the first point of strong contradiction of mainstream assumptions: financial disturbances are not rare, are not insignificant, do not belong to underdeveloped countries only, but most of all they are complex and not idiosyncratic (i.e. sort of systematic as well as systemic) (Crotty, 2009b).

The second indication relates to the supposed beneficial effects of capital markets' integration. The mainstream view holds that the higher the capital market integration at the international level, the lower the possibility of a pervasive financial crisis. A standard corollary of this argument is that more sophisticated financial markets are especially suited to prevent banking crises, which are believed to be the expression of the weakness of less sophisticated (hence less developed or at least evolved) economies. In contrast, Reinhart and Rogoff (2008, figure 3) suggest that higher capital mobility coupled with higher frequency of bank crisis is a sort of stylized fact.

The third evidence comes from their figure 6 where the authors split the time-series 1800–2006 relating to the duration of the default episodes (frequency of occurrence, percent) into two parts: before and after 1946. Obviously, the implicit idea under investigation is to visualize whether the institutional change due to the Bretton Woods system constituted a structural break leading to higher financial stability. It appears that in the period 1815–1945 (130 years) 127 episodes of financial crisis happened lasting on average 6 years; while during the period 1946–2006 (50 years) the episodes have been 169, lasting on average 3 years. Financial crises have become more frequent but do not last as long. One cannot infer causal relationships from the figure. But at least the evidence opens up a further interpretative puzzle.

Finally, the authors show that usually a financial crisis lasting on average five years, does not present itself with just one symptom (only debt default, only banking, only currency crash, . . .); on the contrary, it evolves through different ones (exchange rate + bank; or bank + sovereign default; and so on). As economists are accustomed to handling even complex matters using the *ceteris paribus* criteria, their models (while addressing macroeconomic issues) mostly manage one symptom at a time. Specifically, we may find in the literature models able to successfully face each of the individual types of financial crisis. One may prefer one model or the other according to the side-effects the solution of the crisis implies (for example inflation outbursts). When a financial crisis is characterized by different triggers (it does not matter whether they arise together, or in a sequence taking a relatively short time to develop), the difficulty emerges that the solutions we know are no longer solutions; in fact the instruments intended to solve one type of crisis may happen to be the very same ones to avoid in order to face the other type of crisis. Incidentally, this is another sign of the need to think of macroeconomic processes in a perspective of irreducible complexity.

3.2 Attempts to rationalize puzzling evidences related to financial crises

The attempt to rationalize puzzling evidence necessarily implies the collection (selection) of relevant elements and the building of a network of causal relationships. A careful look at the literature devoted to the interpretation of financial crises shows that there are a few recurrent privileged focuses. Assembled in a unifying perspective, they really appear as not independent but integrated with one another. Not many authors confront the issue of a unifying theory of crisis as a theoretical need (a significant exception is Dymski, 2009). Nevertheless it is possible to find, at the very least, a common starting point for criticism of the neoclassical mainstream: the excess of reduction is the critical factor leading to fallacious implications.

The choice of the set of relevant research themes is not casual. In fact the critical accounts against the mainstream focus on the allegedly too simplistic representation of: (1) credit (either at international and/or internal level); (2) individual behaviour (rationality, imitation, power, information); (3) risk evaluation (and related notion of uncertainty) and varieties of financial instruments (especially derivatives); (4) liquidity; (5) institutions (in the strictest sense but also in political/sociological views) and prior events (evolution, irreversibility and causative role of the real side).

Let's explore in greater detail the exposition made on the interaction between international capital mobility and the banking crisis. In the standard view, the first channel for stabilization induced by higher capital mobility is higher liquidity for the system. Liquidity reduces the likelihood of a banking crisis, both directly (as firms have access to different instruments to finance themselves) and indirectly. This second aspect is more articulated: external funds allow banks to collect liquidity when firms or lenders become insolvent. So bank liquidity is a condition that reduces the risk of a bank becoming involved in the contagion default mechanism due to the clients (asset side). Furthermore, liquidity reduces the likelihood of a deposit run (liability side): the access to external liquidity enables banks to face even sudden and drastic withdrawals. Also, the fact that depositors know they are going to be repaid probably makes them more tranquil (i.e. less prone to withdraw and hence to "run").

Another fundamental argument advanced in order to justify the beneficial implication of higher capital market mobility is related to the issue of risk reduction. This is a third stabilizing channel. As long as the existence of a huge variety of (financial) risks is acknowledged, the reduction of overall risk may be pursued if one can find an adequate presence of financial instruments in the market. In other words, financial instruments are supposed to be quantitatively and qualitatively differentiated (not simply "many" different types, but many within the same category). Differentiation of financial instruments leads to the possibility of handling risk diversification; but it also leads to specialization among financial intermediaries, which are supposed either to deal with specific risks, or to manage the portfolios of specifically tailored customers. In other words, according to the mainstream view, customization (which means complex financial instruments and many types of specialized financial intermediaries) implies the possibility of equipping the market with contracts closer to state-contingency, hence entailing a higher likelihood of approaching efficiency. Here we have the fourth stabilizing channel.

A corollary of the approach is that sophisticated and mature economies have equally sophisticated and mature financial systems. Therefore, the presence of a high proportion of banks in the system of financial intermediaries is taken as a symptom of backwardness. Banks are not particularly appreciated in this view, as they are represented as comparatively less efficient: they manage too many risks (targets) without the due instruments to control them. Lack of specialization means higher specific risk for this kind of intermediary. Not surprisingly, the operative suggestion stemming from this corollary is to either reduce the relative importance of banks in the system and/or to make the surviving banks bigger. In other words, if banks have to survive as banks (i.e. a distinctive financial intermediary), they need to be sufficiently big to have highly differentiated portfolio segments (i.e. both assets and liabilities need to be highly differentiated quantitatively and qualitatively). Otherwise, they are supposed to be forced to quit the market, or to outsource a great amount of their activity to other specialized financial intermediaries. This is the fifth stabilization mechanism.

The striking contrasting evidence depicted in Reinhart and Rogoff (2008, figure 3), basically suggests that at least one of the stabilizing channels does not work in the way implied by the mainstream paradigm. Any heterodox view would start emphasizing that the mainstream causal description is at best partial, and is substantially silent with respect to the fact that (financial) crises have relevant qualitative impacts on systems (Acemoglu et al., 2015). As the contending literature is vast, in what follows I will just summarize the key concepts in a schematic way. The different criticisms address the alternative undervalued/overlooked destabilizing processes. These processes develop simultaneously with the ones just described as characterizing the mainstream description.

Credit lever

Not disputing that higher capital mobility leads to higher liquidity, it conversely means higher potential credit; but higher potential credit, if matched with a real side of the economy approaching its own present potential (full use of resources that can be utilized in the present, which is different from full utilization of available resources) will give rise to a "toxic expansion". In other words, higher credit will transform into higher debt eventually, instead of being the leading variable behind growth.[2] From a systemic point of view, if the issue under scrutiny is causality, it does not matter whether the debt is held by firms, households or sovereign states. Furthermore, the absolute amount/change of liquidity is not the problem; liquidity comparative dynamics is the issue with respect to the simultaneous pace of the real side of the economy. Empirical evidence suggests that there exist different historical experiences, varying according to the diverse stage of economic development and/ or degree of State intervention in the economy. It does not matter whether such dynamics are determined by the private sector (mainly firms) or by the public sector (also by means of a lack of adequate institutional reforms). What counts is the emergence of a difference between the speed of the financial gear (giving rise to a higher potential aggregate outcome) and the speed of the real gear which is not able to generate timely matching opportunities to transform such potential into an effective outcome.

The other empirical sign of this discrepancy is the accelerating dynamics of internal credit expansion (normally antecedent to financial crises). Again the availability of credit becomes incongruent (too much) with respect to the absorption capabilities of the real side of the economy. This is fairly recurrent in mature economies, especially those already experiencing a lower systemic productivity in comparison with economies at the same stage of maturity. The divergent dynamics should increase the attention of the authorities to prevent the crisis from starting (either credit control and/or structural reforms), but the expansionary phase of the business cycle usually leads to an underestimation of the dangers. As a result, the authorities either tend to bring forward the weight of structural reforms, or do not constrain financial expansions at all.

Indeed, it may be that the opposite happens, that credit expansion is possible exactly because monetary authorities increase liquidity in the markets, under the hypothesis that this will stimulate the real economy via the interest rate channel. Given that the economy fluctuates between expansions and recessions, it is likely that reforms will be unavoidable during a time of recession, which is the worst environment for the design of any structural change (resources are less available or mobile, spending constraints are more binding, even current public expenditure could not be totally financed).

Though a deep contraction may not come, the mechanism described above builds up to an increasingly systemic financial fragility.

Individual behaviour: risk attitude, rationality, imitation and power

The emergence of a financial crisis in this case is traced back to the analysis of individual behaviour. The recognition of a framework where information limits are relevant and in the form of both asymmetric information and fundamental uncertainty, make substantive rationality a too restrictive representative criteria (i.e. one should not use strict maximization as a technical tool to represent the micro-foundation of individual decision processes). Using the *ceteris paribus* methodology, information limits are usually treated separately. Asymmetric information is faced in a framework without uncertainty (at most risk); uncertainty is usually treated with heterogeneous, but equally informed, agents (for a different perspective see Fazzari and Variato, 1994, 1996; Variato, 2004).

Focusing on the destabilizing role of information limits, three aspects are worth stressing. First, prices are no longer sufficient statistics to convey relevant information to individuals. Then individual behaviour leads to macroeconomic incoherence. Furthermore, financial markets give rise to particular chains of fallacies of composition.

With respect to macroeconomic incoherence, a crucial concept is convention. As long as informative limits are recognized in any form by individuals, their rational response is to undertake informative actions. The main consequences of these different actions are either the diffusion of conventional views and behaviours, or the increase of power of those who are supposed to possess relevant information (Akerlof and Shiller, 2009).

Conventional behaviours are homologative in nature, i.e. they reduce the intrinsic heterogeneity of systems due to individual variety. The reduction of complexity operates at the three stages of economic analysis: individual, market, system. At the individual level, the agent accepts conforming to an already existing behavioural model, instead of relying on his or her own representative model of reality. This reduces the effort to validate the model; this is the more likely choice the lower the level of confidence the individual has with respect to his or her own capabilities to understand complex phenomena (Brock and Hommes, 1997). Applied to the specific framework of financial decisions, this means that individuals (even quite sophisticated ones) apply benchmarking techniques.

The market level homologation process involves interaction between individuals (contract design). Agents adopting the same model do not query behaviours whose features follow the shared model, but they become suspicious (hence less prone to interaction) if behavioural diversity becomes somehow extreme. In this case the choice to behave unconventionally requires not only self-confidence but also availability of resources. Inside financial markets, one may think about two opposite situations where customization leads to negative effects (for example, inefficient amount of credit supply). One is the financing of bad projects under moral hazard and the other is credit rationing for those who cannot demonstrate their good nature (as a model for their type does not exist).

The third level of homologation is systemic and involves model representativeness. The higher the number of individuals accepting conventional views and behaviours (hence imitating the conventional prescriptions), the higher the self-validating properties of the convention (i.e. the likelihood of the success of the conventional view) and the higher the representative power of the model implied by the convention (i.e. subjective representation seems like objective representation). When a shared model becomes a systemic reference paradigm, it is extremely difficult for any individual to act unconventionally. Not only does self-confidence become virtually irrelevant, one has also to "endure" and become resilient to processes of systemic invalidation.[3] In other words, it may be the case that being unconventional in a framework of strong conventional views one risks his or her own survival. The European banking system might be considered an example of this kind of systemic effect. As the institutional paradigm is built around profit-seeking banks, for truly mutualistic banks the survival in good times becomes quite a difficult task.

Given the above considerations, the implication is that conventional behaviours and views cannot be considered stabilizing or destabilizing per se. Their common premise is the reduction of uncertainty (so the intent is a stabilizing one), but in the end they turn out to be (potentially) destabilizing. It is quite interesting to note that the destabilizing power of conventions increases during tranquil (stable) times and does not necessarily need to show up in abrupt phenomena such as euphoria and panic, or herd behaviours.

If conventions do not have a definite effect on system stability, the existence of chains of fallacies of composition leads to destabilization. The ones selected in what follows specifically apply to financial markets and to the context of the 2007 financial crisis. The chain involves four microeconomic principles that are usually assumed to be able to bring equilibrium and efficiency in a mainstream perspective: (i) savers are rational (in financial markets individuals are assumed to be utility maximizers who select optimal returns conditional to risk); (ii) financial markets are competitive (the specificity of the markets is such that similar portfolio managers are supposed to be able to assure their customers of at least equal portfolio returns); (iii) financial markets reward innovative behaviour (innovation is supposed to be a beneficial process; in financial markets innovation has been mainly addressed to increase market liquidity; directly this induced securitization; indirectly it determined the emergence of a huge variety of sophisticated, even exotic, derivatives); (iv) if portfolio managers (agents) are rewarded with productivity premiums, their attitude towards customers (principals) improves (instead of reducing principal-agent distortions, in financial markets this produces risk propagation in two main ways: first, if the premium is simply related to the amount of sales, as in the case of "blue-collar" traders, because they are directed by the employer to sell particular financial instruments; second, if the premium is related to portfolio returns, as in the case of "white-collar" traders, because they are rewarded if the return is positive, but they do not share in the losses) (King and Maier, 2009; Allen, 2005).

Hence one way of depicting the build up to the 2007 financial crisis starts by emphasizing the issue of individuals' appetites (greed) for return and their risk perceptions, in a framework where portfolio returns were declining and savers were not being fully informed about portfolio compositions and their intrinsic risks (Taleb, 2004; Bracha and Brown, 2013). As a result, on one side savers were asking for the high returns (no longer compatible with macroeconomic conditions); on the other side, portfolio managers, in order to keep their clients, moved towards riskier portfolio selections (higher risks, at the beginning, meant higher returns). During the expansionary phase the more prudent-honest portfolio managers were punished by the market because their performance was lower than their riskier-hazardous competitors. Meanwhile, riskier competitors maintained their own liquidity by issuing new financial instruments (securitization) (Gino and Ariely, 2011; Hochman et al., 2014). Those trading with these new instruments were rewarded with premiums (Crotty, 2009a). As being prudent was equal to being unconventional, there was no individual incentive to contain risk. Therefore the result of increasing systemic risk, and increasing financial fragility, was unavoidable.

The composition effects of the different fallacies of composition turned out to be a powerful destabilizing systemic mechanism (Shiller, 2000, 2008; Ariely, 2008). Furthermore, they were reinforced exactly because financial markets had been provided with high liquidity (in search of a return higher than the one compatible with such an amount of liquidity).

Risk reduction and varieties of financial instruments or intermediaries

In this case the emphasized destabilizing argument is a technical one. One could address the issue starting from a methodological foundation, criticizing the very definition of risk. The reference to Post-Keynesian literature devoted to the definition and implication of fundamental uncertainty would come naturally; but also other traditions grounded on subjectivist approaches to probability would be equally suitable to sustain the critical assessment. Nevertheless, destabilization may arise even when adopting a mainstream conception of probability. Obviously, one has to specify the conditions justifying a violation of order implications in financial markets. The first relates to the far from negligible dimension of systemic risk (Duffey, 2011); the second is connected to the wrong evaluation (measurement) of risk. Both problems stem from the same methodological issue: to put into question the ergodic nature of the data-generating processes characterizing financial markets. If processes are not ergodic, distribution tails can be "fat", skewed and/or flatter than normal.

The problem hence emerges because of a representation choice. In this case, paradoxically, the insurgence of the financial crisis is not related to the fact that some people (less informed) were purposefully deceived by more informed ones who wanted to gain their own advantage. In contrast it is the effect of a "sophisticated ignorance": the one leading to the undervaluation of the relevance of non-ergodicity in economic processes.[4] This particular ignorance, incorporated and coupled with institutional frameworks prone to create incentives for higher diversification of financial instruments and intermediaries, brought about another destabilizing channel due to financial relationships. Furthermore, the fact that, basically, agents mistook uncertainty for risk, assuming that it could be managed with the quantitative methods of finance (when the crucial reason for this mistake is the social environment creating a particular perception of risk and its evaluation), connects this technical point to the previous two, supporting the argument for a union between the different critical channels of endogenous instability (Dymski, 1988).

Liquidity

Financial crises have shown many times that liquidity which is considered a property of the functioning of the economic system is not a certain (sure, deterministic) variable at all. In particular it can dissolve suddenly when a crisis sets in. The argument is rooted in the *General Theory* (1936), where Keynes emphasized the particular fallacy of composition due to liquidity: it does not exist at macroeconomic level (unless an agent accepts becoming extremely illiquid and buying all existing liquidated assets). In modern terms liquidity requires the presence of market makers. Traditionally this function was exercised by central banks. But in a world where financial markets are connected and there is a global dimension, national central banks become virtually powerless, both for their relative dimension and their institutional span of action. As a result, financial market integration (which has allowed the increase in the dimension of financial intermediaries and their evolution into super-national institutions) has become a channel through which liquidity can drain more quickly, not the opposite (Wagner, 2007; Han and Lee, 2012). One crucial point to be noted is that liquidity can move more quickly and even multiply through the presence of varieties of financial intermediaries and instruments. The shadow banking system, in this respect, has been of fundamental relevance in the evolution of the recent financial crisis (Nersisyan and Wray, 2010). On the other hand, the power to originate the monetary base still belongs only to central banks. As a result, the critical account emphasizing the issue of liquidity calls for a reflection on the new roles of monetary institutions in a worldwide network of transactions where financial markets "never go to sleep".

Institutional framework and prior events

These aspects connect to the recognition of the historical nature of macroeconomic processes. As long as time is no longer a logical category, it appears that history (society and politics) and evolution matter. Up to this point it should be quite evident that the methodological vision adopted in this chapter subscribes to this very position. Just two elements of the related literature are then occasioned.

From the point of view of policy intervention, institutionalist literature produces evidence of the non-neutral (and endogenous) role of institutions in affecting the stability properties of macro-dynamics. As a result, the persistence and recurrence of crises can be connected to the choices (at times unwise or mistaken) of policy authorities (Montanaro and Tonveronachi, 2012; Tropeano, 2012).

From the point of view of causation, authors mainly connected to the Marxian tradition, while not disputing that 2007 implied a disruptive financial disturbance, emphasize that the destabilizing process had started before and was grounded in an over-accumulation of productive capacity (basically a real antecedent cause) (Bellofiore and Halevi, 2011; Chesnais, 2014).

Two observations emerge from this specific remark. On the one hand, the attempt to figure out the "exact timing" of the beginning of the crisis is not necessarily a signal of substantial attention towards the role of history and causation. Causation claims are coherent with a positive interpretation of events, but they are not necessarily correct in the normative interpretation, especially if phenomena under evaluation do not evolve following linear stable paths. Causation requires a sequence and a functional relation. It is meaningful in a context such as the beginning of one history, or it is useful when the determinant variable is not affected (even indirectly) by the changes in the variables it causes (Vercelli and Dimitri, 1992). Systemic phenomena are both cause and effect of the passage of time, and most of their change comes from within rather than from external causes (or surprises). As a result, the choice of a particular point in time, which one can call a moment, is nothing but a convenient beginning, just a convention at work. The understanding of the nature of the underlying process (which is the same, regardless of the conventional starting point one may choose) is more relevant if the dynamic path is cyclical. When dynamic processes are cyclical, the concept of causation becomes labile.

On the other hand, if the process of interaction between real and financial variables is endogenously cyclical, the focus on destabilizing financial triggers (moments) is anyway of fundamental importance. Adopting a financial perspective in the interpretation of crises, it is possible to show that the real sensitivity of the economy to the crisis is not an intrinsic feature of the real side of the economy. In contrast the sensitivity of income and other real variables to the crisis is related to level of financial fragility of the economy as a whole. So the higher the financial fragility of the economy, the higher the real impact of the financial crisis if it sets in.

Focusing on a real explanation for instability, in the end one risks not enriching too much the mainstream interpretative tools. The power of alternative perspectives comes if finance and institutions (history, society, politics) are not neutral to macro-dynamic stability, not only as transmission mechanisms but also as autonomous forces.

4. Building a paradigm of endogenous financial instability: naïve sketch

This part of the chapter is an attempt to face the task to suggest a theoretical framework of endogenous instability where finance is given a substantive place. It is methodologically close to Toporowski (2005), but it differs in two respects.

First, it takes a comparative/thematic perspective instead of a historical one. Second, it specifically addresses the issue of paradigm building. The main shared idea is that not every approach to money and finance is compatible with a theory of endogenous financial instability. Even facing sophisticated capitalistic economies, where finance plays a non-negligible role to foster dynamics, one needs a particular notion of money and finance in order to have the latter be responsible for endogenous crises. There exists a variety of explanations concerning financial instability. In many cases they substantially overlap; however, they are not fully compatible. This means one may attempt to build a unifying theory, but the result cannot be unique. Anyway, if finance is crucial to the representation of dynamic processes, it cannot be left (as it usually happens) in the background (another way to see the meaning of "dark side") while money stands at the front. A complex notion of money is only coherently connected with a complex notion of finance.

Thus, while Toporowski (2005) calls for a method of *critical finance*, in the present chapter the macroeconomic emergent system, both as historical matter and as theoretical framework, would be qualified as a *financial economy of production*. As a result, the needs arise to elicit the meaning of critical finance and to explain what a financial economy of production is.

4.1 Critical finance and financial economies of production as emergent features of complex capitalism

The attempt to give a rationale for the existence and role of money (and later finance) can be considered as a sort of anthropological feature. In some ways the reflection (whether in the form of intuitions, or more articulated) is pervasive. Furthermore, it becomes inescapable if the focus of the analysis is addressed to the functioning of the economic system as a whole. Taking a historical-evolutionary perspective, one may see that the attributions of money and finance have changed according to the stage of advancement of economic systems. An increasing degree of economic complexity has always been joined with an increasingly complex definition of money and finance (Mason, 1996; Wray, 1998; Clower, 1999).

Naturally, this factual observation leads to the core question about the causal role connecting systemic complexity and money-finance attributions, for it implies the assessment on the casual link involving money-finance and growth, and also an evaluation of the impact on the stability of this relationship (Arestis and Chick, 1995; Arestis and Sawyer, 2001; Shaikh, 2016). The unavoidable issue is the evaluation of the relationship between money and finance. In a sophisticated capitalistic system, money in the strict sense becomes a smaller component of total money.

Money endogeneity prevails over the exogenous control of the central bank, and money as financial asset is much more driven by financial markets in order to face the liquidity needs of the economy. In this view more (an excess of) money means more (an excess of) liquidity, which transforms into more credit (inflation credit, not price inflation). Furthermore, the process is not necessarily symmetrical (Semmler and Sieveking, 1993). And this consideration becomes crucial from the perspective of the evaluation of the effects of monetary policies. In fact, money relative restriction does not necessarily mean less liquidity. As shown by recent history, the need for further liquidity prior to the financial crisis in 2008 led to financial innovation and the emergence of derivatives such as CDOs and ABSs.

Thus the emphasis on finance does not imply that money is not relevant, but it drives the attention to the fact that if one wants to understand the crucial elements of macro-dynamics one cannot leave finance in the background, The relevant pairing becomes the real vs. financial side, instead of the real vs. money side.

The definition of critical finance

Consistently with this representation, Toporowski (2005) distinguishes three different ways to give a role to finance: neutral, reflective and critical, but he leaves unexplored the corresponding role of money working behind these frameworks: this link is naïvely elucidated here.

Neutral finance involves a system where events affecting the financial side are not supposed to have a permanent impact on the real side of the economy. Thus neutrality has to be understood as in the standard interpretation used with respect to money, and obviously it applies to dynamic processes. It can be said that the environment compatible with money neutrality is the one in which the above distinction between monetary and financial economies of production does not matter. When money is neutral so is finance, as the system degenerates into a trivial case which is nothing but a sophisticated barter economy. In other words, money neutrality is the equivalent of financial neutrality. Furthermore, given the fact that the necessary and sufficient conditions for money neutrality are identified in the Arrow-Debreu-Mantel theorem (as well as in the Modigliani-Miller theorem for finance), they turn out to be necessary and sufficient for financial neutrality too: one can have neutral finance if and only if money is also neutral.

The framework of reflective finance is the one in which financial disturbances may magnify fluctuations, but the structural source of instability is mainly real. The world of reflective finance can be linked to the literature portraying the financial side of the economy as a transmission mechanism of disturbances. Nevertheless in this framework the role of finance and money are not the same as in the case of neutrality. In fact it may be that reflective finance goes together with reflective money. If so, obviously, the only reason for endogenous instability is real. But it may also be that reflective finance pairs with critical money. As a result, though finance is just a transmission mechanism, money can affect the stability of the system determining the path of real variables. Here we have a set up where monetary economies of production (as usually understood in the literature) emerge. Furthermore, one may say that this corresponds to a stage of primitive financial capitalism.

Finally, the context of critical finance is the one where financial events are able to originate instability, permanently affecting the dynamic path of the economy (hence real variables). In other words, in this framework, finance is no longer a servant of the economy and becomes a dominant force (Toporowski and Michell, 2012). This is the context of a financial economy of production too. Toporowski qualifies as critical "an approach to finance which does not presume that finance is benign, but shows how, notwithstanding the virtues of its intermediary function, finance may systematically disturb the functioning of the modern capitalist economy and aggravate fluctuations in the real economy" (2005, p.3). Indeed, a financial economy of production does not necessarily always need finance to disturb the real side of the economy; it simply requires such a potential to be an emergent feature of the macroeconomic system.

In particular, it turns out that neutral finance is methodologically consistent with a positive vision of the interaction between real and monetary forces. In contrast critical finance seems compatible only with a holistic normative perspective. Therefore, if the final target is to have a theoretical basis for endogenous financial instability, looking at the history of economic thought, one would select only authors who held a conception of critical finance.

The meaning of financial economy of production

The paradigm of critical finance shows a precise incompatibility: the one that implies neutrality and independence at different stages of the functioning/evolution of the economic system. In other words, critical finance is an alternative to the neoclassical mainstream. But then it implies a substantial compatibility with a broad class of non-neoclassical paradigms: the underlying holistic vision that imposes the reciprocal causal interaction between parts at the same time does not provide a measure to the force and/or to the change of such interactions. More specifically, Post-Keynesian, Institutionalist and Austrian approaches (just to mention the most obvious) would easily fit into the context of critical finance; Marxian and Schumpeterian would not, according to Toporowski, as they have at most an implicit notion of critical money (there are similar accounts from a different perspective in Godley and Lavoie, 2007).

Critical finance breadth has an ambivalent value. The negative side is represented by the fact that focusing on it one does not come up with a parsimonious paradigmatic selective criteria. In contrast, the positive side is represented by the possibility of having a theoretical framework that is intrinsically pluralist. This observation directly leads to the explanation of why the concept of financial economies of production has been introduced. What makes a financial economy of production different from a monetary economy of production? Why insist upon finance if one recognizes the endogeneity of money and its financial nature? A number of authors in the Post-Keynesian field would likely find the issue simply a semantic choice, especially those connected to Minsky's (1989) concepts who defined the capitalism emerging around the end of the 20th century as "money-manager capitalism" (Whalen, 2010; Wray,

2011; Tymoigne and Wray, 2014). Even I would not deny that, at present and empirically, financial economies of production are indistinguishable from money-manager capitalism. In other words, as historical matters, the two things are substantially the same. Furthermore, whatever the definition of financial economy of production may be, it cannot leave aside Hyman Minsky's ideas.

It has to be pointed out that the wording is not original per se. In fact, the same term can be found in a couple of papers by Fumagalli and Lucarelli (2010, 2011). These articles are interesting as they help to underline the specific meaning I give to the expression. Even connecting to different schools of thought (such as French Regulation, Circuitist and Schumpeterian), the authors, as for money-manager capitalism, portray the financial economy of production as a particular evolution of a capitalistic system where finance becomes the endogenous determinant of the path followed by the economy. Then it is a sort of degenerated capitalism.

Two structural implications come from the argument. First, one (stemming from Classic literature) leads to the conclusion that the contradictory nature of capitalism is bound to a sophisticated self-destruction unless an outside (public/institutional) intervention puts an end to the endogenous increasingly destabilizing mechanisms. Second, the implication is that the operation of free markets does not lead to a pervasive diffusion of perfect competition: money-manager capitalism implies big international corporations and market power, hence powerful engines able to increase inequality. Again this calls for an institutional intervention, in order to fix the failure.

I don't mean to reject these aspects. I intend to justify the financial economy of production using a structural claim as well. But the emphasis is different. As long as the financial economy of production is taken as an interpretative theoretical framework, it is no longer a point (an existing system, at a particular time), nor a moment (a phase of the system). It becomes the most general structure one is supposed to use in order to explain the essence of capitalism. Mature capitalism implies the possibility of fully using this framework; earlier stages of capitalism (the ones in which finance does not play a dominant role) simply allow the use of less complex interpretations (i.e. simpler representations or reductions). So the structural argument in my view applies to the generality of the representative vision. It docs not apply to the historical realization of capitalistic dynamics: what has happened since the 1980s, just to fix a conventional point, came neither by chance (as in the orthodox view), nor by destiny (as in the structuralist view). The power of finance never grew autonomously outside the capitalistic system. On the contrary, it developed because of particular institutional frameworks inducing specific individual behaviours. Worldwide financial instability was not inescapable as a natural law. Once certain paths are undertaken, markets can reach the point of no return (hence a sort of negative predictability) as finance is an extremely powerful and subtle macroeconomic force.

Bringing finance under the spotlight allows a comprehensive understanding of the contradictory nature of capitalistic dynamics. In particular it gives a different evaluation of the degrees of freedom economic policy has (its power together with its failure). Thus I have three reasons to refer to financial economies of production. The first obviously comes from what has just been said, that the monetary and financial systems are methodologically identical (i.e. both money and finance are critical), but the dominant force is different. In a monetary economy the dominant force is money, while in the financial economy the dominant force is finance.[5] A financial economy of production is intrinsically more fragile (and likely more unstable) than a monetary economy of production. Indeed, the power of finance relates to the expansion of present opportunities based upon trust that in the future the outcomes of actions will validate such trust. Monetary and financial worlds differ even without addressing the well-known aspect relating to objective/deterministic dimension as opposed to subjective/probabilistic dimension for the definition of decisional parametric space. In fact, in order to validate a circuit of finance one needs increasing liquidity; in contrast, in order to validate a circuit of money one needs increasing income (in the aggregate production).[6] Furthermore, money never expires, while financial assets do. Finance comes from a market convention; money comes from a systemic convention. Liquidity cycles (usually) are shorter than production circuits: the enhancement of possibilities due to the existence of finance is exactly due to this fact. More precisely, liquidity cycles may open and close more than once while a productive cycle takes place (especially at the micro level).

Hence, the recognition of a dimension where capitalism evolves into financial capitalism is fundamental in order to show the difference between the concepts of liquidity and solvency, which are features pointing to the underlying microeconomic structure of dynamic interaction. Conventional approaches in general fail to appreciate the difference and basically lead to the equivalence between the logic of the flows of income (leading to solvency) and the logic of the cash flows (leading to liquidity) (as a remarkable exception, see Vercelli, 2011; for methodological deepenings, see also Vercelli, 2010).

Similarly to critical finance, the reference to financial economies of production underlines the fact that the beneficial attitude towards finance is not separate from the attention to its opposite potential power. If finance just feeds itself without giving rise to a proper amount of real stimulus, it is just a matter of time before there is a (serious) systemic crisis. As a result, the concern of policy authorities should be focused on detecting whether or not finance and the real economy move consistently (not too divergent one from the other). Incidentally, this also explains why the name of the system contains the term production: it is a way to recall that the economy under study implies an organic interaction between real and financial forces.

The second reason to denote a financial economy of production is less evident but still fundamental and consequential to the above statement. There is another relationship that can be expressed as a pairing interaction, and this is the duo of state-market. Again, there is a difference between a monetary economy of production and a financial economy of production.

The capitalistic phase of a monetary economy of production involves the possibility of market failure which can be counterbalanced by a successful state intervention. The state comes in, joins the market where the market cannot go, and leads the economy out of the crisis. At the opposite extreme, the phase of a financial economy of production is the one in which the market may fail, but the state may not have enough power to bring the system out of the crisis. It happens for many reasons: because there is a lack of a proper institutional design; because the level of financial interaction is no longer national and then the macroeconomic dimension would require "a bigger macro-economy"; because the financial dimension is internally complex: not simply credit, not simply derivatives, but also institutions, conventions, and power in many directions and levels. As long as finance is dominant over money, implicitly the market is dominant over the state as well; then policy design cannot be conceived of as in the framework where money is dominant.

The third reason to speak of financial economies of production is to suggest a constructive road towards an alternative paradigm for economic policy. The concept of the monetary economy of production somehow belongs to the capitalism of the past. It was the one suitable to Keynes' age; it has been of fundamental importance granting theoretical support to New Deal policies. Nowadays capitalism (due also to the abandoning of the Keynesian paradigm in favour of the neo-liberalist one) is quite different. Though the nature of the system has not changed (the forces are always the same), the proposal of policies close to a newer edition of a New Deal would likely be a failure, as these policies have failed in the proposal of austerity measures. What I am suggesting is that the exit from stagnation calls for a radical change in the approach to economic policy, and this would require the puting together of the efforts of different schools of thought. It may be the case that the reference to a monetary economy of production does not help, because it directly points just to a specific school of thought, leaving other relevant contributions in the shade. "New" words may help to have a more pluralist and effective framework.

4.2 What kind of theory are we really looking for? The peculiar complexity of Minskian vision

In recent years a number of authors have emphasized the need for a paradigmatic change, with a specific focus on the theme of economic policy conduct. This implies a fundamental turn in macroeconomics. Before the 2007 crisis contributions appeared occasionally; lately they have become more recurrent.[7] The likely features of an alternative paradigm to the neoclassical mainstream imply both a change in the pedagogy of macroeconomics and the conduct of macroeconomic policy, having a privileged focus on finance.

Up to this point five elements have emerged as determinant pillars of an alternative paradigm, and they can also be used as selective criteria to find reference authors in the history of economic thought. The starting point concerns the basic methodological conception: holism, organicism, critical realism, which are all compatible with the idea that reality is complex either with respect to its own essence (ontology) or in terms of a representation (epistemology) involving economies conceived as open systems. The second issue relates to the way macroeconomics is conceived: it has to be substantive macroeconomics, something which is methodologically incompatible/inconsistent with strict microfoundation.

Once substantive macroeconomics is in place, one needs to go a step further, because the third criteria requires one to focus just on financial economies of production. Hence one is supposed to face the workings of the overall economic system, while at the same time emphasizing the complexity/peculiarities of the financial side of the economy and the endogenously unstable cyclical nature of dynamic processes.

The fourth and fifth features are not necessary foundations, in terms of the completeness of paradigm building. They are just pillars. I personally prefer the opposite alternatives. Indeed, whenever revolutions take place in the history of economic thought they involve the disappearance and marginalization of relevant pieces of existing knowledge, just because they belong to "defeated" visions. Throughout this chapter I quote from interpretations of events which are the expressions of different intellectual traditions. I would prefer the next revolution to be able to merge such different visions instead of making one victorious against the other. Hence my preference for eclectic visions.

Then finally comes the attitude towards economic policy. If in many respects macroeconomics is a purposeful representation meant to be addressed to the ones who have to face the burden of political choice (select and grade priorities and targets), then the theoretical reference framework I would prefer is the one where it is possible to find pragmatic suggestions for action. Even more preferable would be if such advices are endowed with a far-sighted vision of state intervention.

Given such premises, Minsky appears quite naturally as a reference author. It is possible to see quickly[8] his views on each of the five aspects mentioned, comprising the issue of macroeconomic complexity in each of the dimensions faced in this chapter, spanning from method to economic policy suggestions. This view appears as the ideal prototype for a financial economy of production (Foley, 2001).

That Minsky had a holistic perspective comes from different contributions (Minsky, 1981, 1982, 1986, 1992). In short, the capitalistic system is intrinsically dynamic, incoherent and unstable (Minsky, 1980). These three features, while logically identifiable as separate, act in the system as interconnected elements determining its irreducible complexity and are at the root of its endogenous tendency to fallacy.

The structural fallacy of capitalist economies becomes evident through two fundamental limits: the inability to maintain tight full employment over time (Minsky, 2013, p.3) and the tendency of financial components to give rise to debt deflation crises (Minsky, 1993, 1995). These fallacies cannot be eradicated from capitalism because this is a particular organization of society requiring liabilities to be created in advance with respect to the revenue flows (usually determined upon expectations which can be disappointing *ex-post*). Then the seed of instability arises that belongs to the very nature of capitalism, as long as one understands such organizations as a financial economy of production.

Minsky definitely sees macroeconomics in a substantive way: not just instability arises as an effect of there being no dichotomy between the real and financial sides of the economy. The presence of fallacies of composition, institutions determined to direct the evolution of change and his own representation are original because they can be summarized by another triad of concepts. First, in order to depict the system, starting from a microeconomic foundation, the representative unit is a "bank"; second, the complexity of individual heterogeneity is reached through the use of a limited (discrete) number of types essentially connected to financial positions and/or variables; third, the relevant dynamic interactions that imply the non-separable nature of cycles and growth. It is interesting to point out that this triad acts at different levels or stages of representation: the ground level of individual representation, then the meta-level of the market, and finally the systemic and most aggregate level. Then one of the ways Minskian complexity sets in is through a stratification of arguments (which are nested, not simply one on the top of the other).

It is noteworthy to point out that by referring to units as "banks" there is a fundamental departure from mainstream representation. Instead of using the so-called *homo economicus* (rational maximizer), the agent is depicted through his or her balance sheet position. One does not need to assume substantive rationality; one simply has to apply the basic principles of accounting. Second, one can depict the functioning of the system just by connecting all the balance sheets. As a result there is an objective way through which the analysis can move from an individual level towards the market and then systemic levels (Variato, 2016). Furthermore, the choice of accounting language reveals exactly the organic nature of systemic relations, as technically speaking accounting measures are not homogeneous of degree one with respect to space and time.

Also, the particular conception of the cycle-growth integration enables us to show why Minsky is interesting as an author embedding different interpretative perspectives (Ferri, 2011; Fazzari et al., 2013). The idea that the interaction between forces produces instability in the midst of stability (i.e. stability is destabilizing), especially due to the interaction among conventions and expectations, directly shows the Keynesian root of his claims.

But other two possible intellectual roots become evident while depicting crisis whose nature is complex and not idiosyncratic: these two elements are, in fact, usually summarized as qualifying the crisis as structural. In this respect one can connect to Marxian and Schumpeterian traditions as well (Minsky, 1990).

Finally come the considerations about attitude towards policy intervention. Though Minsky's popularity is related to the financial instability hypothesis, his early writings focused more on the issue of full employment. His peculiar mark in this respect is the definition of the concept of "tight full employment", which leads to original evaluations about the effectiveness of economic policy and the priority of targets it is supposed to reach.

This issue can be easily appreciated thanks to the work of Papadimitriou and Wray, who published the posthumous Minsky book *Ending Poverty: Jobs Not Welfare* (2013). Using the language of 2017, instead of the one of the late 1960s, it is possible to say that the first unconventional point addressed by Minsky was the inseparable nature of economic policies meant to reach full employment and the ones meant to combat inequality (Dymski, 2009). Another unconventional observation was the distinction between full employment as a point and full employment as a process (in his definition, tight full employment). Here, if the system can automatically reach instantaneous full employment through market adjustments, it cannot maintain full employment indefinitely without the active intervention of the State, which is supposed to come to fix this specific market failure by acting as an employer of last resort. Minsky was also unconventional while objecting to the policy makers of the 1960s over their choice of incorrect policy instruments. His pragmatic critique suggested alternative measures. The most vigorous claim was the one in favour of job creation, as opposed to transfer policies granting people money to spend without the dignity of a place in the society. Furthermore he was clearly aware of the dangers coming from considering labour as a homogenous good/service.

As the optimistic Cassandra described by Chick (2001), Minsky left a fruitful intellectual heritage but also a normative vision where both State and Economists are seen as the ultimate good instruments to grant enduring prosperity despite the unavoidable contradictions of the capitalistic system. His peculiar paradigm of critical finance widens the representative languages, while at the same time suggesting a complex modelling where cycles are nested and which is able to capture the qualitative nature of dynamic processes. Nevertheless, the Minskian view tells us that if we conceive capitalistic systems as financial economies of productions, this is more like a starting point than an achievement.

5. Concluding remarks

The span of the chapter covered methodological, epistemological and policy issues, in order to discuss the relevance of the financial side in economics. At the methodological level, it addressed the reasons to prefer holism and equilibrium as a normative principle as opposed to the mainstream view grounded on principles of independence, symmetry and a positive notion of equilibrium.

Contrasting empirical evidence and epistemological alternative representations in the chapter showed that paradigms using just money together with risk and arbitrage are different representative reductions of capitalism. In particular they turn out to be a too simplistic case with respect to paradigms treating explicitly (critically) finance in the presence of uncertainty and then speculation. Thus the narrative representation of a world where shocks are exogenous, have just temporary effects, long-term changes are possible only if the structure of the system changes etc. is the consequence of a particular reduction of economic complexity (the one also implying the independence between cycle and growth dynamics). Such a description is not the reflection of the inner nature of the capitalistic system (i.e. it doesn't come as natural law).

Furthermore, not all dynamic processes contain evolution and not all evolutionary processes imply complexity. So it may be the case that a system whose basic foundations and nature do not change, transforms through time becoming something radically different from the beginning. The child that grows old becomes an elder, but the caterpillar that grows old becomes a butterfly. In some sense the neoclassical mainstream perspective treats capitalism as it evolves as a human, while the alternative perspective presented in the chapter conceives of capitalism as more like a butterfly: more beautiful in its maturity (though radically different from youth), but much more fragile.

Then the alternative view suggested throughout the chapter is one according to which not only the change is relevant per se but also the relative speed of change matters: any process is characterized by a quantitative-qualitative dimension giving rise to largely irreducible measurement problems. Complexity and difficult analytical representation also come from the organic nature of relations, suggesting that the methods of microeconomics and macroeconomics probably cannot be the same.

These considerations do not represent a novelty in the so-called heterodox field. The specificity of this chapter is that it emphasized the role of finance, trying to show that deep financial crises are not exogenous accidents due to some dark uncontrolled force. But if finance is not a culprit, it has nonetheless to be treated as a critical force. At the moment a literature on financial instability is growing trying to connect modelling and critical reflections on macro effects of financial behaviours (Asada, 2012; Bhattacharya et al., 2015). While considering this reflection worthwhile and fruitful, this chapter addressed the further methodological issue that a complete (alternative) paradigm requires a systemic approach as opposed to a partial approach where finance "simply" substitutes for the real side as a leading force. In this respect a lot of work still needs to be done.

Starting from the deepest foundation elements of economic thinking, the chapter attempted to reach the ambitious goal of showing that paradigmatic views holding finance as a critical (causative) variable enable us to give a better interpretation of capitalism as it is nowadays, leading to a richer rationale for economic policy conduct. In a perspective of critical constructivism, the chapter took a particular position with respect to the selection of relevant representative pieces. It also suggested that the possibility of having a radical change in Economics does not require us "to reinvent the wheel", as we already have all the foundational pieces of knowledge we need. The strong standpoint taken is that the Minskian paradigm can be used as a keystone of such an alternative paradigm: a stone connecting and giving equilibrium to other relevant stones of economic knowledge.

Quite often, over the last few years I have been reading papers saying that we are on the verge of a paradigmatic change (a number of them are quoted in this chapter). Yet, at the moment, nothing really revolutionary seems to have happened. This chapter did not explore the surely relevant historical, sociological, political reasons involved in such an apparent enduring paradox. But at least it suggested a general interpretative rationale, implied a forecast and adopted a constructive perspective. With respect to the general rationale, even the interaction between opposite schools of thought can be understood as endogenously cyclical (Van den Berg, 2012). But as long as the moment of change is becoming more lengthy, the forecast is that eventually the change in paradigm will probably spread through the use of extreme language and concepts (i.e. the change would be comparatively less prone to accept the coexistence of plural views). In terms of the constructive perspective, the forecast is not a prophecy; in other words, the path of change can be transformed. In a sense this would be the authentic revolution with respect to past experience. This constructive perspective starts from the recognition of the intrinsic value of the different and often contrasting pieces of economic knowledge, as the recognition of the existence of relevant differences is the fundamental step towards opening the mind to evolution and change.

The real challenge, as it always happened in the history of economic thought, is to find "an equilibrium in the middle ground between absolutism and relativism" (Foshee and Heath, 2010). One could ask where the true dark side of the force comes from. If a dark side is at work, it is not finance, but rather anything hindering this time of epochal change to become a new era of scientific enhancement, opportunity and discovery.

Notes

1 This does not mean that the system cannot change (the system may be obviously open, so not self-contained). Nevertheless, it implies that the initially given proportions among parts do not change over time.
2 The mechanism is quite complex, but it is exactly due to the relative speeds of adjustments. In fact, even if expectations about potential growth are on average correct (imagine that the system really goes towards full employment of available resources), it nonetheless means that the speed of convergence is lower. Hence, *ex-post*, the actual behaviour of individual income will be lower than expected (even correct on average), giving rise to a need to access external funds (just to keep things as simple as possible) in order to meet repayment needs. At the beginning the increase in indebtedness is not systemic, so the dynamics simply mean that we have a redistribution of resources from borrowers (the ones who made a "mistake" on the actual behaviour of income) to lenders (who just have excess liquidity to use).
3 If the conventional view is successful, this is quoted as merit; if the unconventional view is successful, it is considered a curiosum, not generalizable.
4 This is another example of over-reduction where a result (the generalization of the central limit theorem) is used as a dogmatic premise in modelling.
5 Using the yin-yang metaphor, one may imagine that dynamically the relationship between money and finance alternates the dominance of one element over the other. As a result, the complementarity between money and finance at the macroeconomic level contains a dynamic-cyclical relationship where the two forces do not have the same power while time elapses. If one takes the yin-yang metaphor,

he also understands why in some sense it is pointless to "quarrel" about monetary vs. financial economies of production, as they are the same thing, seen at different stages of the same process. The process has to be the financial-monetary interaction, i.e. a subset of the macro-economy.

6 This crucial difference is one of the distinctive traits of Minskian analysis.

7 See, among others, Crotty (1994, 2002); Piegay (2000); Lawson (2005); Beinhocker (2006); Tropeano (2010); Roncaglia (2012); Weeks (2012).

8 The purpose of the paragraph is simply to justify the opening statement. It is not to be taken as a review of Minsky's contribution.

References

Acemoglu, D., A. Ozdaglar, and A. Tahbaz-Salehi (2015) "Systemic Risk and Stability in Financial Networks," *American Economic Review*, 105, 564–608.

Akerlof, G. A., and R. J. Shiller (2009) *Animal Spirits: How Human Psychology Drives the Economy, and Why It Matters for Global Capitalism*. Princeton, NJ: Princeton University Press.

Allen, F. (2005) "Modelling Financial Instability," *National Institute Economic Review*, 192, 57–67.

Arestis, P., and V. Chick (1995) *Finance, Development and Structural Change: Post-Keynesian Perspectives*. Cheltenham, UK: Edward Elgar.

Arestis, P., and M. Sawyer (2001) *Money, Finance and Capitalist Development*. Cheltenham, UK: Edward Elgar.

Ariely, D. (2008) *Predictably Irrational. The Hidden Forces That Shape Our Decisions*. London: Harper Collins.

Asada, T. (2012) "Modeling Financial Instability," *Intervention: European Journal of Economics and Economic Policies*, 9, 215–232.

Beinhocker, E. D. (2006) *The Origin of Wealth: Evolution, Complexity, and the Radical Remaking of Economics*. Boston, MA: Harvard Business School Press.

Bellofiore, R., and J. Halevi (2011) "A Minsky Moment? The Subprime Crisis and the 'New' Capitalism," in *Credit Money and Macroeconomic Policy*, ed. by C. Gnos and L. P. Rochon. Cheltenham, UK: Edward Elgar, 20–32.

Bhattacharya, S., C. A. E. Goodhart, D. P. Tsomocos, and A. P. Vardoulakis (2015) "A Reconsideration of Minsky's Financial Instability Hypothesis," *Journal of Money, Credit, and Banking*, 47, 931–973.

Bracha, A., and D. J. Brown (2013) "(Ir)Rational Exuberance: Optimism, Ambiguity and Risk," Cowles Foundation for Research in Economics, Yale University, Cowles Foundation Discussion Papers: 1898, 20.

Brock, W. A., and C. H. Hommes (1997) "A Rational Route to Randomness," *Econometrica*, 65, 1059–1095.

Chesnais, F. (2014) *Fictitious Capital in the Context of Global over-Accumulation and Changing International Economic Power Relationships*. Cheltenam, UK: Edward Elgar.

Chick, V. (2001) "Cassandra as Optimist," in *The Economic Legacy of Hyman Minsky*, ed. by R. Bellofiore, and P. Ferri. Cheltenham, UK: Edward Elgar, 35–46.

Clower, R. (1999) "Post-Keynesian Monetary and Financial Theory," *Journal of Post Keynesian Economics*, 21, 399–414.

Crotty, J. (1994) *Are Keynesian Uncertainty and Macrotheory Compatible? Conventional Decision Making, Institutional Structures, and Conditional Stability in Keynesian Macromodels*. Ann Arbor, MI: University of Michigan Press.

Crotty, J. (2002) *Trading State-Led Prosperity for Market-Led Stagnation: From the Golden Age to Global Neoliberalism*. Armonk, NY: M.E. Sharpe.

Crotty, J. (2009a) "The Bonus-Driven 'Rainmaker' Financial Firm: How These Firms Enrich Top Employees, Destroy Shareholder Value and Create Systemic Financial Instability," University of Massachusetts Amherst, Department of Economics, Working Papers.

Crotty, J. (2009b) "Structural Causes of the Global Financial Crisis: A Critical Assessment of the 'New Financial Architecture'," *Cambridge Journal of Economics*, 33, 563–580.

Duffey, R. B. (2011) "The Quantification of Systemic Risk and Stability: New Methods and Measures," National Bureau of Economic Research, Inc, NBER Working Papers: 17022.

Dymski, G. A. (1988) "A Keynesian Theory of Bank Behavior," *Journal of Post-Keynesian Economics*, 16, 49–54.

Dymski, G. A. (2009) *Does Heterodox Economics Need a Unified Crisis Theory? From Profit-Squeeze to the Global Liquidity Meltdown*. Routledge Advances in Heterodox Economics. London and New York: Routledge.

Fazzari, S., P. Ferri, E. Greenberg, and A. Variato (2013) "Aggregate Demand, Instability and Growth," *Review of Keynesian Economics*, 1, 1–21.

Fazzari, S. M., and A. M. Variato (1994) "Asymmetric Information and Keynesian Theories of Investment," *Journal of Post Keynesian Economics*, 16, 351–369.

Fazzari, S. M., and A. M. Variato (1996) "Varieties of Keynesian Investment Theories: Further Reflections," *Journal of Post Keynesian Economics*, 18, 359–368.

Ferri, P. (2011) *Macroeconomics of Growth Cycles And Financial Instability*. Cheltenham, UK: Edward Elgar.

Foley, D. (2001) "Hyman Minsky and The Dilemmas of Contemporary Economic Method," in *The Economic Legacy of Hyman Minsky*, ed. by R. Bellofiore, and P. Ferri. Cheltenham, UK: Edward Elgar, 47–59.

Foshee, A. W., and W. C. Heath (2010) "Between Absolutism and Relativism: The Economist's Search for a Middle Ground," *Journal of Economic Issues*, 44, 819–829.

Fumagalli, A., and S. Lucarelli (2010) "Cognitive Capitalism as a Financial Economy of Production," in *Cognitive Capitalism and Its Reflections in South-Eastern Europe*, ed. by V. Cvijanovic, A. Fumagalli and C. Vercellone. Bern: Peter Lang, 9–40.

Fumagalli, A., and S. Lucarelli (2011) "A Financialized Monetary Economy of Production," *International Journal of Political Economy*, 40(1), 48–68.

Gino, F., and D. Ariely (2011) "The Dark Side of Creativity: Original Thinkers Can Be More Dishonest," Harvard Business School, Harvard Business School Working Papers: 11–064, 47.

Godley, W., and M. Lavoie (2007) *Monetary Economics: An Integrated Approach to Credit, Money, Income, Production and Wealth*. New York: Palgrave Macmillan.

Han, L., and I. H. Lee (2012) "Optimal Liquidity and Economic Stability," International Monetary Fund, IMF Working Papers: 12/135, 22.

Heilbroner, R. (1990) "Analysis and Vision in the History of Modern Economic Thought," *Journal of Economic Literature*, 28, 1097–1114.

Hochman, G., S. Ayal, and D. Ariely (2014) "Keeping Your Gains Close but Your Money Closer: The Prepayment Effect in Riskless Choices," *Journal of Economic Behavior and Organization*, 107, 582–594.

Hodgson, G. M. (1993) *Economics and Evolution: Bringing Life Back into Economics*. Paperback reprint. Economics, Cognition and Society series. Ann Arbor, MI: University of Michigan Press.

Keynes, J. M. (1936) *The General Theory of Employment, Interest and Money*. New York and London: Harcourt Brace Jovanovich.

King, M. R., and P. Maier (2009) "Hedge Funds and Financial Stability: Regulating Prime Brokers Will Mitigate Systemic Risks," *Journal of Financial Stability*, 5, 283–297.

Kotz, D. M. (2009) "The Financial and Economic Crisis of 2008: A Systemic Crisis of Neoliberal Capitalism," *Review of Radical Political Economics*, 41, 305–317.

Lawson, T. (2005) "Reorienting History (of Economics)," *Journal of Post Keynesian Economics*, 27, 455–470.

Mason, W. E. (1996) *Classical Versus Neoclassical Monetary Theories: The Roots, Ruts, and Resilience of Monetarism – and Keynesianism*. Ed. by William N. Butos. Boston, MA; Dordrecht, the Netherlands; London: Kluwer Academic.

Minsky, H. P. (1980) "Capitalist Financial Processes and the Instability of Capitalism," *Journal of Economic Issues*, 14, 505–523.

Minsky, H. P. (1981) "Financial Markets and Economic Instability, 1965–1980," *Nebraska Journal of Economics and Business*, 20, 5–16.

Minsky, H. P. (1982) *Can It Happen Again?* New York: M.E. Sharpe.

Minsky, H. P. (1986) *Stabilizing an Unstable Economy*. Twentieth Century Fund Report series. New Haven, CT: Yale University Press.

Minsky, H. P. (1989) *Financial Crises and the Evolution of Capitalism: The Crash of '87. What Does It Mean?* New York: St. Martin's Press.

Minsky, H. P. (1990) *Schumpeter: Finance and Evolution*. Ann Arbor, MI: University of Michigan Press.

Minsky, H. P. (1991) *Financial Crises: Systemic or Idiosyncratic*. Annandale, NY: Levy Economics Institute, Bard College.

Minsky, H. P. (1992) *Taking Schumpeter's Methodology Seriously: Commentary*. Ann Arbor, MI: University of Michigan Press.

Minsky, H. P. (1993) *Finance and Stability: The Limits of Capitalism*. Annandale, NY: Levy Economics Institute, Bard College.

Minsky, H. P. (1994) "Longer Waves in Financial Relations: Financial Factors in the More Severe Depressions II," Levy Institute Archive, published (1995) in *Journal of Economic Issues*, 29, 83–96. Based upon the original contribution of (1964) "Longer Waves in Financial Relations: Financial Factors in the More Severe Depressions," *American Economic Review*, 54, 324–335.

Minsky, H. P. (1995) *The Creation of a Capitalist Financial System*. Aldershot, UK: Ashgate.

Minsky, H. P. (2013) *Ending Poverty: Jobs, Not Welfare*. Annandale, NY: Levy Economics Institute, Bard College.

Montanaro, E., and M. Tonveronachi (2012) "Financial Re-Regulation at a Crossroads: How the European Experience Strengthens the Case for a Radical Reform Built on Minsky's Approach," *PSL Quarterly Review*, 65, 335–383.

Nersisyan, Y., and L. R. Wray (2010) *The Global Financial Crisis and the Shift to Shadow Banking*. Annandale, NY: Levy Economics Institute, Bard College.

Parguez, A., and S. Thabet (2013) "The Twenty-First Century World Crisis: A Keynes Moment? A True Systemic Crisis Fitting Keynes's Prophecy," *International Journal of Political Economy*, 42, 26–39.

Piegay, P. (2000) "The New and Post Keynesian Analyses of Bank Behavior: Consensus and Disagreement," *Journal of Post Keynesian Economics*, 22, 265–283.

Reinhart, C. M., and K. S. Rogoff (2008) "This Time Is Different: A Panoramic View of Eight Centuries of Financial Crises," National Bureau of Economic Research, Inc, NBER Working Papers: 13882.

Roncaglia, A. (2010a) "Economic Policy Dilemmas in Front of the Crisis," *PSL Quarterly Review*, 63, 179–183.

Roncaglia, A. (2010b) "Le Origini Culturali Della Crisi," *Moneta e Credito*, 63, 107–118.

Roncaglia, A. (2012) "Economia Politica: Impostazioni a Confronto. (Economics: Comparing Paradigms. With English Summary)," *Moneta e Credito*, 65, 227–239.

Schumpeter, J. A. (1954) *History of Economic Analysis*. New York: Oxford University Press.

Semmler, W., and M. Sieveking (1993) "Nonlinear Liquidity-Growth Dynamics with Corridor-Stability," *Journal of Economic Behavior and Organization*, 22, 189–208.

Shaikh, A. (2016) *Capitalism: Competition, Conflict, Crises*. Oxford, UK: Oxford University Press.

Shiller, R. J. (2000) *Irrational Exuberance*. Princeton, NJ: Princeton University Press.

Shiller, R. J. (2008) *The Subprime Solution: How Today's Global Financial Crisis Happened, and What to Do About It*. Princeton, NJ: Princeton University Press.

Taleb, N. N. (2004) *Fooled by Randomness: The Hidden Role of Chance in Life and in the Markets*. New York: Thomson, Texere.

Toporowski, J. (2005) *Theories of Financial Disturbance: An Examination of Critical Theories of Finance from Adam Smith to the Present Day*. Cheltenham, UK: Edward Elgar.

Toporowski, J., and J. Michell (2012) *Handbook of Critical Issues in Finance*. Cheltenham, UK: Edward Elgar.

Tropeano, D. (2010) "The Current Financial Crisis, Monetary Policy, and Minsky's Structural Instability Hypothesis," *International Journal of Political Economy*, 39, 41–57.

Tropeano, D. (2012) Quantitative Easing in the United States after the Crisis: Conflicting Views. Cheltenham, UK: Edward Elgar, 16–242.

Tymoigne, E., and L. R. Wray (2014) *The Rise and the Fall of Money Manager Capitalism. Minsky's Half Century from World War Two to the Great Recession*. New York: Routledge.

Van den Berg, H. F. (2012) "Technology, Complexity, and Culture as Contributors to Financial Instability: A Generalization of Keynes's Chapter 12 and Minsky's Financial Instability Hypothesis," *Journal of Economic Issues*, 46, 343–352.

Variato, A. M. (2004) *Investimenti, Informazione, Razionalità*. Milan, Italy: Giuffré.

Variato, A. M. (2008) *Perchè Studiare La Macroeconomia?* Rome: Aracne editrice.

Variato, A. M. (2016) "Can We Say Minsky Moment When Households Matter?" in *Cycles, Growth and the Great Recession*, ed. by A. Cristini, S. Fazzari, E. Greenberg, and R. Leoni. New York: Routledge, 25–44.

Vercelli, A. (1992) "Il Declino Della Concezione Dinamica Di Equilibrio," *Economia Politica*, 9, 3–11.

Vercelli, A. (2000) "Structural Financial Instability and Cyclical Fluctuations," *Structural Change and Economic Dynamics*, 11, 139–156.

Vercelli, A. (2010) "Minsky Moments, Russell Chickens and Grey Swans: The Methodological Puzzles of Financial Instability Analysis," in *Minsky, Crisis and Development*, ed. by R. Tavasci, and J. Toporowski. London: St. Martin Press, Macmillan, 15–31.

Vercelli, A. (2011) "A Perspective on Minsky Moments, Revisiting the Core of Financial Instability Hypothesis," *Review of Political Economy*, 23, 49–67.

Vercelli, A., and N. Dimitri (eds) (1992) "Causality and Economic Analysis: A Survey," in *Macroeconomics: A Survey of Research Strategies*. Oxford, UK: Oxford University Press, 393–421.

Wagner, W. (2007) "The Liquidity of Bank Assets and Banking Stability," *Journal of Banking and Finance*, 31, 121–139.

Weeks, J. (2012) *The Irreconcilable Inconsistencies of Neoclassical Macroeconomics: A False Paradigm*. Routledge Frontiers of Political Economy. London and New York: Routledge.

Whalen, C. J. (2010) *A Minsky Perspective on the Global Recession of 2009*. New York: St. Martin's Press, Palgrave Macmillan.

Wray, L. R. (1998) *Understanding Modern Money*. Cheltenham, UK: Edward Elgar.

Wray, L. R. (2011) "Minsky's Money Manager Capitalism and the Global Financial Crisis," *International Journal of Political Economy*, 40, 5–20.

Part III

Alternative analyses and policies

10 Technological and productive systems facing the economic crisis

Heterogeneity, convergence and divergence in the European Union

Andrea Califano, Tommaso Gabellini and Simone Gasperin

1. Introduction

1.1 The general context

An animated debate over the effects of economic, financial and monetary integration in the European Union (EU) has captured the interest of a large spectrum of economists, political scientists and commentators. The discussion is usually focused on budget deficits, debt over GDP ratios, inflation rates, interest rates on government bonds, trade imbalances, capital flows, etc. However, little if no analytical attention has been given to the state and dynamics of indicators representing scientific, technological and productive capabilities. In fact, these variables have rarely been at the core of both theoretical and empirical scientific works aimed at explaining the distinct economic conditions and trajectories of EU countries.

With this chapter we will focus on indicators such as R&D expenditure, patents, number of researchers, manufacturing value added, high-tech exports, productivity growth relative to the economic performance of a selected group of EU member states. The result of this empirical investigation is two-fold. First, we have to deny the existence of a scientific and technological homogeneity at the EU level. Member states' systems of innovation and production appear to be intrinsically national in their quantitative and qualitative aspects. Second, it is possible to challenge the idea that the process of integration – celebrated in the EU treaties and in traditional economic literature on economic growth – would promote "spontaneous" convergence among countries with different initial levels of economic development. The underlying purpose of this chapter is to contribute, from a different perspective, to the critical assessment of the long-standing economic crisis in the EU.

1.2 Inside and beyond the debate on the "European Paradox"

The central motive of this chapter is to present the "relationships between science, technologies and their industrial exploitation"[1] as a potentially useful theoretical framework for better understanding the economic crisis in the EU. In doing so, we move from Dosi et al. (2006), whose work has sought to demystify the so-called "European Paradox". The latter consisted in the conjecture put forward by the European Commission (ibid., p. 1450): "EU countries play a leading global role in terms of top-level scientific output, but lag behind in the ability to convert this into wealth-generating innovations". On the contrary, the authors have presented descriptive evidence that the European weakness in industry, compared to international competitors such as the US and Japan, resides in its relative weakness in terms of "the generation of both scientific knowledge and technological innovation" (ibid., p. 1461).

However, this result rests on a high level of aggregation among countries belonging to this peculiar supranational organization (Fabbrini, 2007). As a matter of fact, EU member states still appear as being sovereign entities with distinct national features (e.g. systems of innovation) and different levels of economic development. Even in the above article on *Research Policy*, when disaggregated at the national level, some indicators present broad variations, with certain countries (e.g. Germany, Sweden, and the UK) performing comparably better than the US, while others (e.g. Italy and Spain) score well below the EU-15 or EU-25 average. This raises some doubts over the level of observation that needs to be adopted in order to perform international comparisons. It also suggests the existence of distinct national models of science and technology, as well as their application to the production process, not all producing the same results. This would imply the existence of structural differences (i.e. heterogeneity) within the EU itself, which might possibly contribute to a more complete explanation of the recent economic performances of its member states.

Thus, this chapter seeks to provide a preliminary investigation into the alleged heterogeneity in scientific, technological and other productive indicators of a significant group of EU countries. However, we will also claim that, beyond debating the existence of a "European Paradox", it would be important to discuss what might be defined as the "Paradox of the European Union". With this expression we would assert that, contrary to the hypothesis supported by the EU institutions and its official documents (Commission of the European Communities, 1990), the long-lasting process of integration among European countries has produced mixed results in terms of economic convergence. This could be seen not only with respect to macroeconomic variables but also relative to technological and productive capabilities.

1.3 The "Paradox of the European Union": a convergence puzzle

For almost three decades before the global financial crisis of 2007, a widespread consensus had characterized the analysis of economic, financial and monetary integration in the EU. Conventional economic theory had justified it as a necessary process that would have favoured convergence in the standards of living among its member states. A notable argument in favour of this view was put forward by Blanchard and Giavazzi (2002). They maintained that the current account deficits registered by Eurozone countries with lower levels of GDP per capita had to be seen as the natural outcome of financial and economic integration between economies with different levels of economic development (defined in terms of their capital-labour ratio, K/L). In a similar fashion, Modern Growth Theory (Barro and Sala-i-Martin, 2003) asserts that "conditional convergence" occurs when countries with a lower K/L ratio – therefore with higher marginal productivity of capital – increase domestic investment because of higher expected returns and, at the same time, reduce their domestic saving, since future growth will allow for the repayment of today's liabilities. Eventually, a higher rate of productivity growth in less developed economies would result in effectively catching up to the levels of more advanced countries.

In effect, before the crisis, and particularly in the immediate aftermath of the introduction of the single currency, this process of convergence seemed to be in place (Archibugi and Filippetti, 2013). The economies of southern Europe were performing relatively well,[2] while Germany was notably being labelled "the sick man of Europe" for its meagre economic performance (*The Economist*, 1999). Nevertheless, almost one decade after the onset of the crisis, things have radically changed, with northern European economies bouncing back and growing little but steadily, while peripheral countries have been enduring a severe economic depression from which they have not yet fully recovered.

A visual representation of this process is depicted in Figure 10.1, where per capita GDP has been indexed to the year 1995, thus showing its dynamic trend over the following 20 years. According to the literature on centre-periphery developments in the EU, pioneered by Simonazzi et al. (2013) and validated by a series of empirical studies conducted by the Vienna Institute for International Economic Studies (Stehrer and Stöllinger, 2015; Landesmann et al., 2015), a selected sample of relevant European countries have been grouped as follows: the group "Core" includes Germany, the Netherlands, Austria and Finland; the "Periphery" is composed of Italy, Spain, Greece, Portugal; with the "Semicore" we have labelled France and Belgium; finally, "Gersphere" indicates Poland, the Czech Republic, the Slovak Republic and Hungary.[3]

Figure 10.1 displays the convergence process in GDP per capita taking place between the central European economies and other long-time members of the EU.[4] At the beginning of the period, the Gersphere had a level of GDP per capita[5] which was less than half of the Periphery and much lower (41.7%) if compared to the advanced economies in the north of the continent. In 2016, Gersphere's GDP per capita was up to 81.8% relative to the Periphery and 60.8% relative to the Core.

A totally different story – one of failure – must be told with respect to the catching-up process of southern European economies. At the beginning of the period the level of GDP per capita in the Periphery was almost 87% relative to the Core, but with a very pronounced intra-group heterogeneity.[6] Before 2008, a limited tendency towards convergence between the Periphery and the

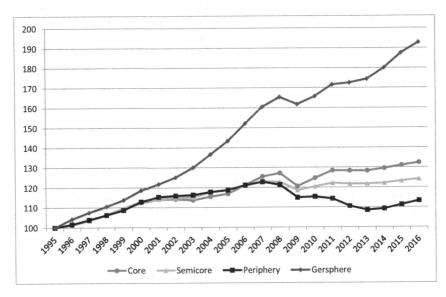

Figure 10.1 GDP per head weighted by GDP shares within each group (index 1995=100).

Source: authors' elaboration based OECD data.

northern European economies was effectively occurring, most notably driven by a within-group convergence of Spain, Greece and Portugal towards Italy's levels. The Eurozone crisis has nonetheless dramatically changed the picture after 2009, so that even in 2016 no single economy in the southern periphery had yet recovered to its 2007 level of GDP per capita, while every country[7] in the Core and in the Semicore has. In 2016, GDP per capita in the Periphery has fallen to 74.3% relative to the Core.

What is behind this "Paradox of the European Union"? In the central part of this chapter we will investigate this "convergence puzzle", adopting an alternative perspective to the usual macroeconomic focus on interest rates, current account imbalances, unit labour costs, inflation rates, capital flows, and so on (Franks et al., 2018). A selected set of indicators on the innovative and productive capabilities of those countries will be analysed and interpreted. Two distinct but related results seem to characterize our inquiry: first, the success of eastern European countries to converge towards higher levels of income per capita is accompanied by a significant improvement in their innovative and productive capabilities. Second, the failed economic convergence – which has effectively become *divergence* – of southern economies towards the levels of the most developed European countries is reflected by the negative dynamics of their technological and productive indicators.

2. The methodology

2.1 The groups

As already mentioned, figures on the "Paradox of the European Union" will be presented according to the following categorization: European "Core" (Germany, the Netherlands, Austria, Finland); European "Periphery" (Italy, Spain, Greece, Portugal); "Semicore" countries (France and Belgium); a handful of central and eastern European countries (Poland, the Czech Republic, the Slovak Republic, Hungary) which we named "Gersphere", due to their crucial role as providers of intermediate capital goods in Germany's supply chain (IMF, 2013; Sinn, 2006). The degree of integration in productive activities among Germany and other countries is measured by the foreign value added (or "import") content of Germany's exports – sometimes referred to as backward linkages in global value chains (OECD, 2015) – weighted by manufacturing value added of the country of origin. Each value presented in Table 10.1 illustrates the share of manufacturing value added of a given country which is exported to Germany by that country and then used by German firms in the production of final goods that are eventually exported.

Table 10.1 exposes the main rationale for establishing the group Gersphere: it is composed of countries which have stronger linkages with German-centred value chains. Austria has been excluded from this group and instead it has been included in the Core because of its status as an advanced economy. Slovenia has been dismissed from the analysis,[8] despite providing German exports with a significant amount of intermediate goods. We consider Slovenia as being a country with rather unique characteristics as compared to other members of the Gersphere group. Once the richest part of the former Yugoslavia, its level of GDP per capita in 1995 was much higher than the Slovak Republic, Hungary and Poland. Furthermore, it appears to enjoy much fewer political and historical similarities with its central and eastern European neighbours. Those countries are also part of an official political alliance called the 'Visegrad Group', constituted in 1991. They are strongly connected through common historical vicissitudes, and to many extents they share similar economic, cultural and social features. Denmark is another country whose exclusion from the analysis deserves a few clarifying words. Denmark's GDP per capita is comparable to the average level in Core countries. Across most of the time span, its value is even greater than in Germany, the Netherlands, Austria and Finland. However, for the sake of within-group homogeneity, we have preferred not to include Denmark in the Core category. This is due to its cultural and economic links with the Scandinavian economies of Sweden and Norway, and because of its decision not to adhere to the single currency. Both elements are indeed representative of an effectively higher extent of economic autonomy from Core countries (e.g. the import content ratio for Denmark confirms the relatively low degree of backward linkages with Germany, despite its geographical proximity).

Table 10.1 Import content ratio of Germany's exports (year 2011, latest available)

Country	Import content ratio of German exports (%)	Group
Czech Republic	7.86	G
Hungary	7.42	G
Slovak Republic	7.28	G
Austria	6.42	C
Slovenia	6.40	
Poland	4.61	G
Belgium	3.67	S
Netherlands	2.77	C
France	2.59	S
Italy	2.48	P
Finland	2.31	C
Denmark	2.23	
Spain	2.12	P
Portugal	1.94	P
Greece	1.65	P

Source: authors' elaboration based on OECD and UNIDO data.

2.2 The indicators

The core of this analysis is divided in two parts, broadly identified by the different nature of the two sets of indicators considered. The first, included in Sections 3.1 to 3.4, aims to capture the innovative performance of the chosen countries: R&D expenditure, patents, levels and quality of education and research. Complementary to them, Sections 4.1 to 4.3 move to a comparative exploration of productivity levels, export capacity in high-tech products and productive structures of selected countries (following Cimoli et al., 2009).

The choice of indicators relates to the conclusion reached by Abramovitz (1956) in his seminal study on the determinants of economic growth: almost one-half of it was essentially unexplained by the "known" inputs (capital and labour). The main variable causing increases in output was then classified as "total factor productivity", or what the author himself described as a "measure of our ignorance about the causes of economic growth" (ibid., p. 11). That admission and Solow's subsequent work (1957) marked the starting point for econometric studies seeking to explain why growth rates differ between countries. Nevertheless, most of such empirical analyses misrepresent the nature and role of innovation in the economic process.

Unless differently specified, the data on which we have based most of our elaborations come from the OECD Science and Technology Indicators database. We have adhered to the customary division between indicators of innovation input and innovation output, despite the wide range of complexities they raise. With respect to technology inputs, we present data on gross R&D expenditure over GDP (Section 3.1). Patenting activity has been used as a proxy for technology output, and in this regard we have employed the *triadic patent families* statistics provided by the OECD (Section 3.2). We have also included other indicators that go beyond the input/output dichotomy: the number of researchers on the labour force is at the same time the input for creating new scientific and technological knowledge and, to a large extent, the output of policies in the innovation field (Section 3.3); the European Innovation Scoreboard, being a composite index, gives us a general synthetic (albeit only quantitative) picture of the national systems of innovations in the analysed countries (Section 3.4). The data for the share of manufacturing over total value added (Section 4.1) and for high technology export as a percentage of manufacturing exports (Section 4.2) are related to the complex debate on the crucial role of manufacturing in modern advanced economies. Section 4.3 raises a few considerations on the productivity performance of the selected countries.

3. National technological systems

3.1 The input of innovation: gross R&D expenditure

Our first indicator of research intensity is the typical gross domestic expenditure on research and development (GERD). R&D measures were diffused as soon as data on the share of income spent on devising new production techniques, on new products and on human capital formation were available. Since then, innovation statistics have been standardized by the OECD in the *Frascati Manual* (OECD, 1963). Useful and widespread as they are, these proxies for innovation activity present severe limitations (Freeman, 1994) and therefore some caution is needed when interpreting the data. One of the main issues is that GERD is a good indicator of innovativeness only for certain countries and for particular sectors. In fact, industries such as car production, pharmaceutical and electronics have high R&D expenditure and can be defined as "science-based" (Pavitt, 1984). As a consequence, an economy which is quantitatively more specialized in these sectors will also show a higher level of the ratio between GERD and GDP, which is one of the most common indicators for cross-country comparison in terms of R&D intensity. On the contrary, sectors such as mechanics, food processing, basic chemicals and steel are characterized by a low degree of research intensity.[9] This is one of the reasons why, when doing international comparisons, it is important to consider countries which show similar characteristics in terms of their production systems.

In any case, the figures for GERD over GDP reveal sharp differences among EU countries and especially between the groups of countries as previously classified. Table 10.2 shows that the average rate of GERD over GDP in the years 1995–2015 has been systematically higher in Core countries

Table 10.2 Gross domestic R&D expenditure over GDP (average rates 1995–2015, weighted by a country's GDP share within its own group)

	Average (1995–2015)
Austria	2.31
Finland	3.19
Germany	2.51
Netherlands	1.82
Core	**2.42**
Belgium	1.98
France	2.14
Semicore	**2.12**
Greece	0.63
Italy	1.12
Portugal	0.99
Spain	1.08
Periphery	**1.06**
Czech Republic	1.30
Hungary	0.98
Poland	0.68
Slovak Republic	0.69
Gersphere	**0.86**

Source: authors' elaboration based on OECD data.

(except for the Netherlands), with Austria, Germany and Finland devoting between two and three times the amount of their resources (relative to GDP) that the Periphery invests in R&D. Countries in the Semicore show values for R&D expenditure relative to their GDP that are not so dissimilar from those of the Core. Finally, the Gersphere group presents substantial variation among its members, with the Slovak Republic and Poland scoring particularly badly, in line with Greece, while the Czech Republic performs better than any peripheral country.[10] Looking at the R&D indicator over such a long time period reveals the existence of a significant heterogeneity among EU countries, with a clear taxonomy which broadly reflects the division into our four groups.

Nevertheless, this remains a static picture of the case under investigation, which does not account for possible trends of convergence or divergence among those economies. An illustration of such trends is presented in graphical terms in Figure 10.2, which shows the persisting difference in the innovation efforts between the Core/Semicore and the Periphery. The period considered spans almost 20 years of harmonization policies which should have brought a faster pace of investment in innovation in relatively more backward countries. On the contrary, the average annual growth in total R&D expenditure showed by Core countries (2.82%) has been slightly higher than in the Periphery

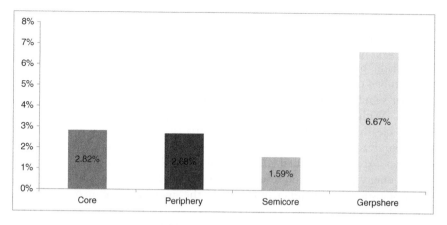

Figure 10.2 Compounded average annual rate of growth in GERD between 1995
and 2015 (weighted by a country's GDP share within its own group).
Source: authors' elaboration on OECD data.

(2.68%) despite the latter's marked lagging behind in R&D investment over
GDP in 1995 (0.82%) relative to the Core (2.05%). In fact, in the first 12 years
since then, the yearly growth rate of total GERD has been higher in peripheral countries with respect to both Core and Semicore countries. However,
when the economic crisis hit in 2008, the trend reversed, with Core countries increasing their expenditure in R&D faster than the Periphery and the
Semicore. On average, the Semicore has registered a remarkably weak growth
in R&D expenditure (1.59%) throughout the period, whereas Gersphere
countries' investment in innovation activities has grown at a considerable rate
(6.67%). Both Periphery and Semicore countries have, on average, increased
their total investment in R&D over time, but they have done so at a lower
rate relative to Core economies. Gersphere countries have instead constantly
increased their efforts in catching up with the most advanced economies. What
emerges from the dynamic pattern of the R&D indicator is divergence for the
Periphery and the Semicore with respect to the Core and strong convergence
for the Gersphere relative to every other group.

3.2 The output of innovation: patents

Measuring and assessing the outcome of R&D and other innovation policies is
a complex and far from uncontroversial task. Despite the complexities deriving
from different legal systems and other cultural and institutional country-based
biases, patents' records are usually employed to measure national technological output. The OECD developed "patent families" – gathering patents filed
in more countries – in an effort to enhance the usefulness of patent statistics.

Among them, the triadic patent family gathers those inventions filed in the three major patents offices (US, Europe and Japan), while recording the country of origin of the invention.

The average yearly values for the period 1995–2013 weighted by population (triadic patents by million) are reported in Table 10.3. The difference in the number of patents between Core (71.25) and Periphery (8.8) countries is rather significant. It would be even more so if it were not for Italy's value (13.47). Within the Core countries, Germany (74.01) and the Netherlands (75.17) clearly emerge as leaders, with Austria lagging behind at 40.67, which corresponds to the OECD average and is in line with the figure for Semicore countries (41.81). Structural, institutional and cultural considerations on the heterogeneity between countries, and on the resulting complexity in the use of this statistic, are not sufficient to dismiss the significance of such a wide gap between groups.[11]

Even in the case of this indicator on patents, considering the EU average value as a reliable benchmark for international comparisons might lead to ambiguous results. This remark holds in general for the entire period considered, as the ranking of the groups is stable through time: no significant variations occur, not even looking at the absolute number of patents registered. Gersphere makes for a partial exception, although there are a few further features of these figures

Table 10.3 Triadic patents by population in millions (average value 1995–2013). Average for each group is weighted by the share of GDP of the countries composing it

	Average 1995–2013
Austria	40.67
Finland	64.60
Germany	74.01
Netherlands	75.17
Core	**71.25**
Belgium	42.79
France	41.63
Semicore	**41.81**
Greece	1.26
Italy	13.47
Portugal	1.42
Spain	4.74
Periphery	**8.80**
Czech Republic	1.99
Hungary	3.90
Poland	0.68
Slovak Republic	0.83
Gersphere	**1.49**

Source: authors' elaboration based on OECD data.

which stand out and undermine the explanatory power of further insights to be obtained from the data. Most notably, the series shows a high inter-annual variability and is also highly correlated with the business cycle.

R&D and patent statistics show different aspects of a single process, that is the process of industrial innovation. This idea is based on Schumpeter's (1947) intuition that an industrial firm's competitiveness is mostly based on its *innovation* activities and not simply on its ability to create inventions. In this light, patents are considered as one of the means by which firms protect their innovations. Thus, a firm's innovative activity is not only captured by expenditure on R&D but also by patenting: both of them are positively related to firm-level innovativeness. Using patenting activities and R&D expenditure statistics has some advantages. At the country level of aggregation, both indicators are differently biased due to structural characteristics of the national economic system (Freeman, 1995). Institutional, cultural and social factors have an influence on patenting activities. R&D results may not be patented (e.g. in Northern Italy within the mechanical sector), whereas some innovative activities, though being performed outside formal R&D, may result in patenting activity (not to mention the different "patenting intensity" in product and process innovation). The robustness of using both of them is mutually enhanced by the high positive correlation shown in Figure 10.3.

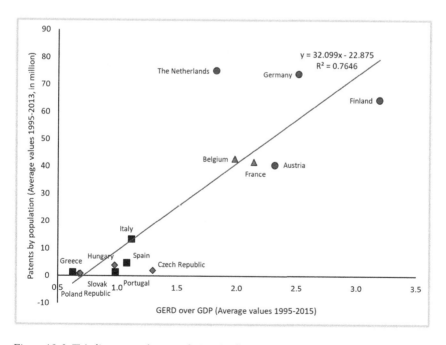

Figure 10.3 Triadic patents by population (millions) (average value 1995–2013) and GERD over GDP (average value 1995–2015).

Source: authors' elaboration based on OECD data.

3.3 Number of researchers

In this section, we present another indicator which is commonly used to describe and compare "national systems of innovation" – for instance in Dosi et al. (2006). As will be shown, once again it does not seem possible to aggregate country-level data in order to obtain figures which are reliable for the EU as a whole. Furthermore, this statistic may act as a "robustness check" of one of the hypotheses underlying this chapter, namely the idea that a good performance of the productive sector and the development of a highly innovative industrial sector tend to be matched by a coordinated effort in the development of science and investment in research.

Table 10.4 portrays the number of researchers per thousand labour force in four distinct years: 1995, 2001, 2007 and 2013. A visible separation emerges among the four groups as a clear indicator of within-EU heterogeneity. This time, Semicore is displaying slightly better results than Core, while Periphery and Gersphere lag significantly behind. It is interesting to note that Gersphere countries (excluding Poland), although starting from initial lower values, in 2013 essentially reached, and in some cases outperformed, the levels of the southern Periphery. A dynamic analysis reveals a generalized tendency to increase the number of researchers relative to their working population, although with similar growth rates, thus maintaining fairly constant the differential among them

Table 10.4 Total researchers per thousand labour force (average value for the groups weighted by the share of GDP of each country) (*=1997 value, ^=2002 value)

	1995	2001	2007	2013
Austria	4.94*	6.16^	7.68	9.32
Germany	5.87	6.66	6.99	8.50
Netherlands	4.67	5.51	5.82	8.53
Finland	n.a.	n.a.	14.47	14.54
Core	**5.62**	**6.43**	**6.85**	**8.57**
Belgium	5.40	7.42	7.67	9.37
France	5.97	6.72	8.01	9.31
Semicore	**5.88**	**6.83**	**7.95**	**9.32**
Greece	2.30	3.05	4.22	6.01
Italy	3.23	2.76	3.81	4.60
Portugal	2.44	3.32	5.09	7.16
Spain	2.89	4.43	5.47	5.31
Periphery	**3.01**	**3.36**	**4.51**	**5.12**
Czech Republic	2.31	2.90	5.36	6.46
Poland	2.95	3.23	3.64	4.12
Slovak Republic	3.93	3.64	4.66	5.42
Hungary	2.56	3.58	4.13	5.78
Gersphere	**2.82**	**3.26**	**4.18**	**4.93**

(with the exception of Portugal, which has more than doubled the number of researchers relative to its population in the past 15 years).

The fact that some Gersphere countries (the Czech Republic and Hungary in particular) are on a catching up trend matches other findings highlighted in this chapter. The relevance of labour force education for a given country's overall economic performance is in fact at the core of the works of Szirmai (2012), and most notably Szirmai and Verspagen (2015). Among other authors, they have been involved in the renewed debate on economic growth, mostly concerned with the econometric evaluation of largely debated results in the literature (e.g. Gerschenkron, 1962; Kaldor, 1966; Abramovitz, 1986; Baumol, 1986). Szirmai and Verspagen thus suggest using "education" as a proxy for the "absorptive capabilities" of a country, i.e. (simplifying a complex matter) the capacity of a country to exploit the "advantage of backwardness" (the possibility to "copy" what other more advanced countries have already done). Within that framework, the importance of investment in research clearly stands out; it is also evident that this sort of investment lies at the core of the interactions between industrialization and growth. The authors further denote that the impact of manufacturing on the economic performance of a country (the subject of Section 4.1) may be positive and significant only in the presence of a highly educated workforce – and when the country is comparatively less advanced.

3.4 The European Innovation Scoreboard 2016

The annual European Innovation Scoreboard (EIS) constitutes a comprehensive evaluation of the research and innovation performance of the EU member states, signalling relative strengths and weaknesses of their research and innovation systems. We have used the 2016 edition of the EIS, with data referring to the year 2015. The usual grouping has been made and the figures for the summary index, as well as for each single indicator, are visible in Table 10.5.

The "Summary Innovation Index" is composed of several indicators related to the innovation performance external and internal to the firm, as well as to the output effects of innovation activities. In the case of external sources, "Human resources" measures the availability of a highly skilled and educated workforce. "Research systems" estimates the international competitiveness of the science base. "Finance and support" indicates the amount of finance available for innovation programmes as well as governments' involvement in research and innovation activities. With respect to the internal dimension of firms, "Firm investments" reflects both R&D and non-R&D investments realized by private enterprises. "Linkages and entrepreneurship" captures the entrepreneurial efforts of innovative firms and their interaction with the public sector. "Intellectual assets" represents many different forms of Intellectual Property Rights, not only patents but also trademarks and designs, resulting from the innovation process. The output effects of innovation are accounted for by "Innovators", which proxy the number of firms that have introduced product or process as well as organizational or marketing innovations,

Table 10.5 Summary of results from the European Innovation Scoreboard 2016
(indicators based on 2015)

	Core	Semicore	Periphery	Gersphere
Summary Innovation Index	**0.629**	**0.564**	**0.359**	**0.333**
Human resources	0.601	0.600	0.407	0.551
Research systems	0.513	0.556	0.433	0.176
Finance and support	0.586	0.413	0.347	0.305
Firm investments	0.642	0.351	0.240	0.362
Linkages and entrepreneurship	0.643	0.514	0.346	0.184
Intellectual assets	0.690	0.636	0.305	0.351
Innovators	0.710	0.675	0.405	0.295
Economic effects	0.623	0.597	0.360	0.397

Source: authors' elaboration on European Innovation Scoreboard 2016 data, weighted by the share of GDP of each country within the respective group.

together with the number of fast-growing enterprises. Finally, "Economic effects" stands for economic implications of innovation in terms of employment, exports and revenues.

Looking at the results for each group of countries, it is possible to obtain a confirmation on the quality of the "Research systems" in Semicore countries. However, that appears to be the only dimension in which Core countries are outperformed by others. Hence, their leading is all but confirmed by the figures reported in Table 10.5. As a matter of fact, the hierarchical order is rather clear-cut: the Core group performs better than the Semicore group in any other element considered except in the "Research system" indicator. At the same time, the Semicore clearly outperforms Periphery and Gersphere, not just in the general index but also in every single indicator. The Periphery in turn classifies before the Gersphere in the summary index, but it lags behind when it comes to certain specific indicators. First, countries belonging to the Gersphere show superior results in "Human resources". Second, they appear to score better in some indicators directly linking research with production (e.g. "Firms investment"). Third, the overall economic effect of innovation policy is significantly stronger than in peripheral countries. In conclusion, even this summary table of innovation indicators within the EU points to a marked difference among the four groups, with the usual ranking.

4. National productive systems

4.1 Manufacturing value added

The first relevant indicator to be examined in the second part of this chapter is the share of manufacturing over total value added. In a 1967 lecture, Nicholas

Kaldor explained the reasons why the production of tangible goods has been the locus of most of the innovating activities being undertaken by private firms' R&D divisions (Kaldor, 1967). New innovative products and techniques diffuse out of the manufacturing sector and spread over to the service sector, thus increasing the overall productivity of the economy. One of the fundamental properties of the manufacturing sector is defined as dynamic returns to scale: the higher the growth of productivity in this particular economic sector, the faster the growth in its output. This relationship is known as Verdoorn's law and also posits that the faster the rate of growth of manufacturing output, the greater the rate of growth of labour productivity (Verdoorn, 1949). Both of these properties arise from learning-by-doing and learning-by-using effects, as well as by the network effect stemming from the diffusion of particular technologies such as computers and software. In turn, this raises the productivity of the other sectors so that the latter becomes endogenous to the growth of manufacturing productivity, which explains why the manufacturing sector can be thought as the "engine of growth" (Thirlwall, 1983). However, it would be misleading to think about these properties only from a supply-side perspective. Apart from the case of a country in an early stage of development, the growth of the manufacturing sector is not limited by the availability of inputs, but it is mainly influenced by aggregate demand, of which exports are the most important component. Thus, a relatively high growth rate in exports is capable of igniting a virtuous cycle of output growth.

The importance of including this section on manufacturing in our chapter is summarized by Table 10.6. It shows that, in all the countries here analysed, the share of business R&D which is performed within the manufacturing sector is

Table 10.6 Manufacturing R&D as a share of business R&D; last available data refer to 2013 unless specified (^=2012 data, *=2011 data)

Country	Manufacturing R&D as a percentage of BERD
Germany	86.13^
Italy	74.28^
Finland	71.33
Austria	63.69*
Belgium	62.93*
Hungary	62.72^
Netherlands	58.46
Czech Republic	57.57
Slovak Republic	57.43
Spain	55.14
France	50.21*
Poland	44.06
Portugal	41.01
Greece	39.22*

Source: OECD Science, Technology and Innovation Scoreboard 2015.

well over 50%, with the only exceptions being Poland, Portugal and Greece. These figures are even more relevant when taking account that in 2015 the share of manufacturing over total value added ranges from Greece's 9.14% to the Czech Republic's 27.06%. The most outstanding case is that of Germany: with a share of manufacturing over value added corresponding to 22.77% (in 2012), the investment in R&D performed by private manufacturing firms reaches the impressive level of 86.13% over total private investment in R&D in the same year.

Over the past 30 years, developed countries have been experiencing a rapid fall in the share of manufacturing value added, a sign that we are induced to interpret as representing a trend of de-industrialization. Given the theoretical background outlined above, a declining share of industry over total output may harm the ability of a country to benefit from the cumulative process of growth described by Kaldor. Figure 10.4 shows that manufacturing has been an important share of the economic activity for both the Core and the Gersphere all along the considered period, while the Semicore and the Periphery have been characterized by a tendency towards progressive de-industrialization. The correlation between the shares of manufacturing activities of the Core and the Gersphere can be regarded as evidence of the strong linkages in their production chains (IMF, 2013). Although since 2008 both groups of countries have experienced a decline in their share of manufacturing value added, the Core has almost recovered whereas the Gersphere has managed to fully attain

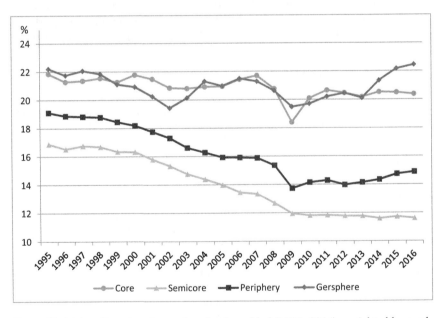

Figure 10.4 Manufacturing share of total value added (1995–2016), weighted by total value added within each group.

Source: authors' elaboration based on World Bank data.

the pre-crisis share, which was 22% of total value added. On the contrary, the difference in the manufacturing share of value added between the Core and the Gersphere on the one side, and the Semicore and the Periphery on the other, has been persistently widening. In 1995, manufacturing output in the Periphery and in the Semicore as a whole represented respectively 19.5% and 17% of their value added. The initial difference between the Germany-centred productive system and the peripheral industries has constantly increased since then, as the Periphery and the Semicore continued to experience a sharp decline in manufacturing value added which has accelerated during the great financial crisis. In fact, since the onset of the crisis, the difference has widened to unprecedented levels. In 2009, the Gersphere share of manufacturing over total value added fell to 18%. In the same year, the Periphery and the Semicore totalled a meagre 14% and 12% respectively, down by more than 5 percentage points with respect to the 1995 values. Thus, differences between the performance of the manufacturing sector of those countries linked to Germany's production system and the results obtained by the Periphery and the Semicore are very sharp. We regard this trend as further confirming our thesis of a process of divergence occurring among European countries.

4.2 High-technology exports

A significant aspect of the economic development of a country concerns its ability to endure a process of structural change towards highly specialized and sophisticated production activities. Ultimately, converging to higher levels of productivity requires both technological advancement in already existing productions and a sustained specialization in sectors and activities with higher productivity potentials (McMillan and Rodrik, 2011).

Moreover, the issue of specialization relates to the growth potential of a country from the demand side as well through its external competitiveness (Kaldor, 1971). International competitiveness is influenced by structural and supply factors in two distinct ways. First, it is generally associated with higher productivity growth, which enables lower unit production costs, thus lower prices. But internal price competitiveness is only one element of the export success of an economic area, and its importance has been decreasing in advanced countries, where more closely integrated value chains have implied higher import contents of manufactured exports (OECD, 2015). The other element is represented by "technological competitiveness". There is a long established tradition in the theory of economic growth which sees the structural and technological characteristics of the economy as crucial determinants of a country's international competitiveness (Dosi et al., 1990). The explanatory mechanism is to be found in the responsiveness of export and import growth to the growth in, respectively, external and internal demand (e.g. the elasticities of demand for exports and imports). McCombie and Thirlwall (1994) have argued that the growth rate of countries is eventually restrained by the balance-of-payments constraint, which in the end is determined by the rates of growth in domestic and external demand, as well as by the import and export elasticities. The higher the elasticity of demand for exports, the softer the long-run growth constraint, and vice versa with respect to the elasticity of demand for imports. Finally, more sophisticated exports with a higher knowledge and technological content generally present higher income elasticities and more inelastic price elasticities (Felipe et al., 2012).

Applications of this intuition have been elaborated with reference to the catching up process of developing countries in Latin America (Cimoli et al., 2010). In the European case that is presented here, the balance-of-payments constraint appears to be of little relevance, given that most of those countries are embedded in the institutional structure of the Eurozone, which effectively excludes the occurrence of typical balance-of-payment crises (Collignon, 2013). It is nonetheless important to consider the export specialization in high-technology products with respect to our groups of selected countries, as indicative of their technological competitiveness in external markets.

In this case, high-technology exports are defined as products with a high R&D intensity, in sectors such as aerospace, computers, pharmaceuticals, scientific instruments and electrical machinery. Single-country data on the share of high-technology exports in total manufactured exports have been grouped, and a weighted average[12] of their values has been computed for the years 1995, 2001, 2007 and 2013. The obtained results point to several interesting observations (see Figure 10.5). First, the share of high-technology exports over

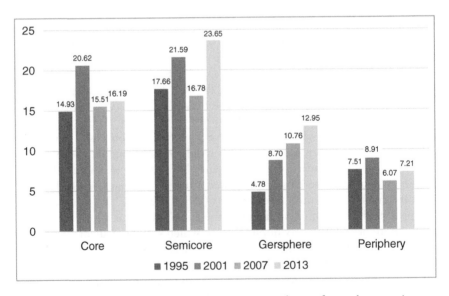

Figure 10.5 Share of high-technology exports over total manufactured exports in 1995, 2001, 2007, 2013, weighted by the share of GDP of each country within the respective group.

Source: authors' elaboration based on World Bank data.

manufactured exports has remained above 15% in both Core and Semicore countries, while the Periphery has never exceeded the 10% threshold. Second, and more importantly, those numbers are fairly constant over the 18 years under examination. There is no evident catching up of the Periphery towards Core or Semicore levels. If anything, the figure for 2013 (7.21%) is even lower than that of 1995 (7.51%), while Core and Semicore countries have slightly augmented it. Finally, a real convergence appears to be in place for the Gersphere group, which has increased its share of high-technology exports by almost three times between 1995 and 2013; each country in the group has overtaken any country in the Periphery. This process may have to do with the above-mentioned integration of the Gersphere group in the German manufacturing supply chain (Sinn, 2006). It has been noted that the trade linkages between Germany and those central European countries are several times higher – in proportional and sometimes also absolute terms – than the ones maintained with the Periphery (Simonazzi et al., 2013). Whether this evidence represents the main explanatory factor for the excellent performance of Gersphere countries in high-technology exports remains an issue to be further investigated.

4.3 Growth in labour productivity

It is widely recognized as a 'stylized fact' that "international differences in labour productivity quite closely correlate with differences in per capita income and, dynamically, so do labour productivity growth and income growth" (Dosi et al., 1994, p. 23). As a matter of fact, long-term productivity growth represents the main driver in the process of economic development. A country's rate of productivity growth relative to others significantly indicates whether it is "Catching Up, Forging Ahead, and Falling Behind" (Abramovitz, 1986).

Despite being also positively influenced by the rate of growth in demand (Kaldor, 1966), productivity growth is structurally dependent on the ability of firms to discover and adopt organizational and process innovation in their productive activities (Dosi, 1988), which is largely influenced by the nature and specificity of their respective national systems of innovation (Lundvall, 1992; Nelson, 1993). Some of the crucial determinants of these 'dynamic capabilities' (Teece and Pisano, 1994) have been identified by the scientific and technological indicators presented in previous sections of this chapter. In this case, real economic convergence (or divergence) among European economies has to be ultimately certified by the relative patterns of labour productivity growth.

The OECD's preferred measure of productivity is that of 'GDP per hour worked' – rather than output per employee – because it better approximates to the use of labour inputs. Thus, this definition of labour productivity can be written as:

$$\pi = \frac{GDP}{h} \tag{1}$$

where π defines hourly productivity, *GDP* stands for gross value added in market prices, and *h* is the total number of hours worked per employee. In dynamic terms the above expression becomes:

$$\frac{d}{dt}\pi = \frac{d}{dt}GDP - \frac{d}{dt}h \qquad (2)$$

which can be arranged as:

$$\frac{d}{dt}GDP = \frac{d}{dt}\pi + \frac{d}{dt}h \qquad (3)$$

This expression suggests that the growth rate of GDP – a proxy for economic convergence – can be accounted for by the growth in productivity and by the growth in the number of hours worked per employee.

Therefore, by looking at the performance of the countries grouped in our taxonomy, over the period 1995–2015 two observations emerge as relevant for the discussion on convergence patterns. First of all, as Table 10.7 shows, the annual compounded rate of growth in labour productivity has been substantially different between Gersphere countries and the other groups. Productivity growth in the first case (3.42%) has been almost three times higher relative to the Core (1.24%) and Semicore (1.15%). This might partially represent a confirmation of the 'convergence theory' (Abramovitz, 1986),[13] as the average productivity level of Gersphere countries in 1995 was about one-third that of the Core and the Semicore as a whole. Nevertheless, this does not seem to also apply to the less productive economies within the Periphery (0.58%), which register a dismal average rate of annual compounded labour productivity growth over those years. Here we must consider the Periphery's internal differences at the beginning of the period, where hourly labour productivity in Spain and Italy was only just below that registered in Core[14] and Semicore countries. At the same time, the productivity of Portugal and Greece was only slightly above those of the Gersphere members.[15] In this case, annual productivity growth in Portugal (1.21%) and Greece (1.24%) has not been as dissimilar but is still lower than almost any country in the Core, therefore showing no sign of convergence in productivity levels over that period. Spain and Italy have been the two poor performers of the group, with productivity growth rates as low as 0.65%[16] and 0.38% respectively, over the 20-year period. The most striking result perhaps is that economies in the Gersphere have almost or fully[17] bridged the gap in productivity levels with respect to Greece and Portugal.

Removing the Gersphere from the analysis and reviewing the remaining groups of countries[18] from a dynamic perspective reveals the evolution of labour productivity through time. It is also possible to discern the trend before and after the economic crisis of 2008–2009. Figure 10.6 illustrates how an

Table 10.7 Compound annual growth rate of hourly labour productivity between 1995 and 2015, in selected groups of countries. Figures for Core, Semicore, Periphery and Gersphere represent the average values of the countries belonging to each group, weighted by their respective share of GDP within each group

Compound labour productivity growth, 1995–2015	
Austria	1.45%
Finland	1.56%
Germany	1.22%
Netherlands	1.13%
Core	**1.24%**
Belgium	1.11%
France	1.16%
Semicore	**1.15%**
Greece	0.97%
Italy	0.38%
Portugal	1.23%
Spain	0.65%
Periphery	**0.58%**
Czech Republic	2.79%
Hungary	2.59%
Poland	3.76%
Slovak Republic	3.95%
Gersphere	**3.42%**

Source: authors' elaboration on OECD data.

evident divergence in labour productivity had already begun around 1998, well before the global financial crisis and even before the parities among previously existing currencies were irrevocably fixed in 1999, in preparation for the introduction of the single currency. By 2007, with respect to the beginning of the period in 1995, hourly labour productivity had grown by 22.7% and 22.3% in Core and Semicore countries respectively, while in the Periphery group it increased by a mere 6.2%. From 2008 onwards, notwithstanding the crisis and the double-dip recession, productivity differentials between those groups of countries have remained fairly constant, neither decreasing nor accentuating significantly.[19]

5. Conclusions

In this chapter we have attempted to explore some relevant aspects of the technological and productive systems since the late 1990s, relative to our sample of EU countries. The statistics presented need to be commented on in the light of the theoretical inquiries that were announced at the beginning.

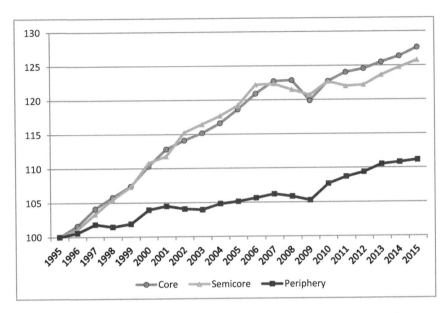

Figure 10.6 Evolution of hourly labour productivity in selected groups, over the period 1995–2015 (index 1995=100), weighted by the share of each country's GDP within its own group.

Source: authors' elaboration on OECD data.

First of all, the set of data presented highlight a profound and persistent heterogeneity in our selected indicators across the EU, with a more diffused homogeneity among certain countries, which have been grouped together accordingly. This would suggest that the "European Paradox" not only does not correspond to existing evidence as previously demonstrated (Dosi et al., 2006), but it also represents a misleading focal point for the analysis of scientific, technological and productive capabilities across the continent. Instead, previous findings in the literature about the local stickiness and cumulativeness of scientific and technological knowledge seem to find confirmation (Dosi et al., 1988, 1994). In line with the theoretical framework of the "National Systems of Innovation" literature (Lundvall, 1992; Nelson, 1993; Freeman, 1995), our descriptive evidence seems to confirm the existence of several different and specific national characteristics belonging to each EU member state. There exists a recurrent pattern by which Core countries on average perform better in every single indicator displayed, followed in order by the Semicore countries and by the Periphery and the Gersphere, although the latter two in interchangeable order depending on the indicator considered.

We argue that this result has two important implications. First, when it comes to technological innovativeness, it renders any international comparison with the EU as a whole a rather ambiguous exercise. If some degree of aggregation was needed, it would require to be made among economies with similar industrial structures and correspondent levels of economic and technological development. In this light, we argue that the grouping presented in this chapter may be suitable to compare the selected EU countries with respect to some standard indicators. More detailed work could be done by exploring, for instance, different uses and sources of R&D expenditure, or by performing a more disaggregated analysis of other variables (e.g. patents, educational systems, high-tech exports, productivity) at the sectoral level, so as to account for structural differences composing the aggregate figures. Second, heterogeneity in innovative and productive capabilities among EU member states implies that certain countries (classified in Core and Semicore) compete at a comparable level with the world leading innovators, whereas others (i.e. those belonging to the Periphery and Gersphere) seem to lag behind to a large extent. A further step has been to move beyond this static picture in order to assess whether the Periphery and the Gersphere have undertaken any significant process of convergence in those indicators, towards the levels of the more innovative and productive European economies.

The preliminary evidence that we have presented in the chapter tells a rather interesting story: one of success and one of failure. At the beginning of the period under observation, Gersphere countries performed worse than the Periphery in every single indicator. After two decades, the gap between the two groups has narrowed significantly with respect to R&D expenditure, patenting activities and productivity levels; indeed, it has also turned into an advantage for the Gersphere in the figures for total number of researchers and share of high-tech exports. Moreover, despite the inevitable process of structural change towards a higher weight of services in the economy, Gersphere countries have managed to maintain a significantly high share of manufacturing value added, while this figure has fallen in the Periphery. This set of elements seems to delineate a clear and univocal pattern: Gersphere countries have embarked upon a catch-up process in scientific, technological and productive activities. At the same time, the Periphery, despite showing a modest trend of convergence in GDP per capita before the 2007 global financial crisis, has not been able to narrow the gap in innovative and productive capabilities. If anything, the disparity has increased, especially in recent years.

Notwithstanding the financial nature of the economic crisis and the stagnation in domestic demand in the peripheral countries, one might argue that the persistent weakness in the above-mentioned structural aspects is an important explanatory factor for their recent dismal economic performance. On the contrary, the increasing success of countries grouped in the Gersphere could therefore be explained by their participation in the dynamic German production system. As hinted throughout the chapter, those countries have developed and organized a considerably strong manufacturing sector which produces mainly intermediate capital goods, later assembled in the Core, at much lower costs compared to the southern periphery. Indeed, the Periphery is much less integrated in the German industrial matrix of production.

This seems to confirm that there is no spontaneous mechanism of convergence that is propelled by simply integrating substantially different economies into a single market for goods and services, or by adopting a single currency. National differences persist and could potentially increase. The road to convergence remains a deliberate policy choice that is usually adopted at the most relevant decisional level: the national state. However, it would be very undesirable, and most likely ineffective, for countries in the Periphery to compete with central and eastern European economies by means of wage devaluations. Domestic demand has already been curtailed in peripheral countries, and it is very doubtful that lowering unit labour costs will result in productive competitiveness over their direct competitors. Beyond a much needed fiscal stimulus, those countries have only one sensible strategy for solving the "Paradox of the European Union": to reverse their structural trend of low scientific and technological capabilities' accumulation (if not actual decumulation), low productivity and harsh de-industrialization. This is not an easy process, and crucial political decisions will have to be adopted if some cohesion and cooperation among EU member states is to be preserved and enhanced.

Notes

1 From the title of the article mentioned just below.
2 With the marked exception of Italy.
3 The criteria underlying such distinction will be pointed out in the next section.
4 It is important to specify here that the Gersphere countries did not have a lower level of GDP per capita to begin with. They did not join the EU until 2004, and only the Slovak Republic has adopted the euro ever since (in 2009).
5 For each group, GDP per capita has been computed as a weighted average based on each country's share of GDP within its own group.
6 In 1995, the level of GDP per capita (measured in 2010 USD and PPP) in Italy ($32,121) was comparable to that of Germany ($32,832), but Spain ($24,652) was lagging behind; Greece ($20,860) and Portugal ($21,949) even more so.
7 With the notable exception of Finland.
8 The decision is also supported by the IMF (2013).
9 See Fagerberg (1988), in which some of the issues characterizing the relationship between R&D and patents statistics are highlighted as well.
10 The heterogeneity between the selected groups is evident also in relation to other international figures. Austria, Germany and Finland report values above the OECD average (2.19); Finland is the only one showing values above notable international competitors such as the US (2.6), Japan (3.19) and South Korea (2.86). By committing 2.11% of their GDP to R&D expenditure, Semicore countries locate themselves in line with the OECD average. On the contrary, countries belonging to the periphery and the Gersphere spend less than half as much as the OECD average.
11 Similarly, even allowing for a certain degree of "transportability" and sharing of knowledge, once we consider patents as a reliable indicator it would be difficult to neglect the existence of such a wide and neat gap.
12 Within the four groups each country has been weighted according to its relative share of GDP. Almost identical results are obtained by weighting by the goods export share of each country within its group.

13 The theory is rooted in Gerschenkron's (1962) famous argument on the "advantage of backwardness": growth in productivity is generally inversely related to the initial level of productivity. This has mainly to do with the level of technology embodied in a given country's capital stock. In leading countries the chronological age of the stock installed tends to be the same as the technological age, as those economic systems lie right at the technological frontier. Stock replacement will thus generate effects which are limited by the short time span between the introduction of the technology and its substitution. "Those who are behind, however, have the potential to make a larger leap" (Abramovitz, 1986, p. 386).

14 It is interestingly to note that in 1995, hourly productivity of labour, measured in 2010 US dollars at PPPs, was higher in Italy (44.4) and Spain (41.2) than in Austria (40.6) and Finland (37.2).

15 Labour productivity per hour worked in 1995 was 25.8 for Greece and 25.2 for Portugal, above the Czech Republic (20.0), Hungary (18.9) and the Slovak Republic (17.7), and almost double if compared to Poland (13.6).

16 However, in the case of Spain, productivity has been almost flat between 1995 and 2007. In fact, more than 70% of the growth in productivity in the period 1995–2014 is accounted for by the last few years, from 2008 onwards. Given the unstable pattern of Spain's GDP over the latter period (especially between 2009 and 2012), that surge in productivity has much to do with the significant fall in the number of hours worked per employee.

17 Labour productivity per hour worked in 2015 was higher in the Czech Republic (34.7) and the Slovak Republic (38.4) compared to Greece (31.3) and Portugal (32.3); the figures for Poland and Hungary are 28.4 and 31.4 respectively.

18 Importantly, these groups include all euro area members since the introduction of the single currency, or after 2001 in the case of Greece.

19 The Gersphere performance since the crisis has instead been quite satisfactory. After a fall in 2008, productivity growth has kept pace, being especially driven by the performance of Poland and the Slovak Republic.

References

Abramovitz, M. (1956). *Resource and Output Trends in the United States Since 1870.* NBER, 1–23. www.nber.org/chapters/c5650.pdf.

Abramovitz, M. (1986). "Catching up, forging ahead, and falling behind". *The Journal of Economic History*, vol. 46, no. 2, pp. 385–406.

Archibugi, D., and Filippetti, A. (2013). *Innovation and Economic Crisis: Lessons and Prospects from the Economic Downturn.* Oxford, UK: Routledge.

Barro, R. J., and Sala-i-Martin, X. (2003). *Economic Growth*, 2nd ed. Boston, MA: MIT Press.

Baumol, W. J. (1986). "Productivity growth, convergence, and welfare: what the long-run data show". *The American Economic Review*, vol. 76, no. 5, pp. 1072–1085.

Blanchard, O., and Giavazzi, F. (2002). "Current account deficits in the Euro area: the end of the Feldstein-Horioka puzzle?" *Brookings Papers on Economic Activity*, 2.

Cimoli M., Dosi G., and Stiglitz J. (eds.) (2009). *Industrial Policy and Development: The Political Economy of Capabilities Accumulation.* Oxford, UK: Oxford University Press.

Cimoli, M., Porcile, G., and Rovira, S. (2010). "Structural change and the BOP constraint: why did Latin America fail to converge?" *Cambridge Journal of Economics*, vol. 34, no. 2, pp. 389–411.

Collignon, S. (2013). "Macroeconomic imbalances and competitiveness in the Euro area". *Transfer: European Review of Labour and Research*, vol. 19, no. 1, pp. 63–87.

Commission of the European Communities (1990). "One market, one money. An evaluation of the potential benefits and costs of forming an economic and monetary union". *European Economy*, 44.

Dosi, G. (1988). "The nature of the innovative process", in Dosi, G., Freeman, C., Nelson, R., Silverberg, G., and Soete, L. (eds.) *Technical Change and Economic Theory*. London: Pinter, pp. 221–238.

Dosi, G., Freeman, C., and Fabiani, S. (1994). "The process of economic development: introducing some stylized facts and theories on technologies, firms and institutions". *Industrial and Corporate Change*, vol. 3, no. 1, pp. 1–45.

Dosi, G., Freeman, C., Nelson, R. R., Silverberg, G., and Soete, L. (eds.) (1988). *Technical Change and Economic Theory*. Brighton, UK: Wheatsheaf.

Dosi, G., Llerena, P., and Sylos Labini, M. (2006). "The relationships between science, technologies and their industrial exploitation: an illustration through the myths and realities of the so-called 'European Paradox'". *Research Policy*, vol. 35, pp. 1450–1464.

Dosi, G., Pavitt, K., and Soete L. (1990). *The Economics of Technical Change and International Trade*. Brighton, UK: Wheatsheaf.

Fabbrini, S. (2007). *Compound Democracies*. Oxford, UK: Oxford University Press.

Fagerberg, J. (1988). "International competitiveness", *The Economic Journal*, vol. 98, no. 391, pp. 355–374.

Felipe, J., Kumar, U., Abdon, A., and Bacate, M. (2012). "Product complexity and economic development". *Structural Change and Economic Dynamics*, vol. 23, pp. 36–68.

Franks, J., Barkbu, B., Blavy, R., Oman, W., and Schoelermann, H. (2018). "Economic convergence in the Euro area: coming together or drifting apart?" (No. 18/10), IMF Working Paper.

Freeman, C. (1994). "The economics of technical change". *Cambridge Journal of Economics*, vol. 18, no. 5, pp. 463–514.

Freeman, C. (1995). "The 'National System of Innovation' in historical perspective". *Cambridge Journal of Economics*, vol. 19, pp. 5–24.

Gerschenkron, A (1962). *Economic Backwardness in Historical Perspective: A Book of Essays*. Cambridge, MA: Belknap Press of Harvard University Press.

IMF (2013). "German-Central European supply chain-cluster report". *IMF Country Report No. 13/263*.

Kaldor, N. (1966). *Causes of the Slow Growth in the United Kingdom*. Cambridge, UK: Cambridge University Press.

Kaldor, N. (1967). *Strategic Factors in Economic Development*. New York: The New York State School of Industrial and Labor Relations.

Kaldor, N. (1971). "Conflicts in national economic objectives". *The Economic Journal*, vol. 81, no. 321, pp. 1–16.

Landesmann, M., Leitner, S., and Stehrer, R. (2015). "Competitiveness of the European economy". WIIV Research Report 401. www.wiiw.ac.at/competitiveness-of-the-european-economy-dlp-3629.pdf.

Lundvall, B. (1992). *National Systems of Innovation: Towards a Theory of Innovation and Interactive Learning*. London: Pinter.

McCombie, J. S. L., and Thirlwall, A. P. (1994). *Economic Growth and the Balance-of-Payments Constraint*. Basingstoke, UK: Macmillan.

McMillan, M. S., and Rodrik, D. (2011). "Globalization, structural change and productivity growth". *NBER* Working Paper No. 17143.

Nelson, R. R. (ed.). (1993). *National Innovation Systems: A Comparative Analysis*. Oxford, UK: Oxford University Press.

OECD (1963). *The Measurement of Scientific and Technical Activities. Proposed Standard Practice for Surveys of Research and Employment*. Paris: OECD Publishing.

OECD (2015). *OECD Science, Technology and Industry Scoreboard 2015: Innovation for Growth and Society*. Paris: OECD Publishing.

Pavitt, K. (1984). "Sectoral patterns of technical change: towards a taxonomy and a theory". *Research Policy*, vol. 13, no. 6, pp. 343–373.

Schumpeter, J. A. (1947). "The creative response in economic history". *The Journal of Economic History*, vol. 7, no. 2, pp. 149–159.

Simonazzi, A., Ginzburg, A., and Nocella, G. (2013). "Economic relations between Germany and southern Europe". *Cambridge Journal of Economics*, vol. 37, pp. 653–675.

Sinn, H. W. (2006). "The pathological export boom and the bazaar effect: how to solve the German puzzle". *World Economy*, vol. 29, no. 9, pp. 1157–1175.

Solow, R. M. (1957). "Technical change and the aggregate production function". *The Review of Economics and Statistics*, vol. 39, no. 3, pp. 312–320.

Stehrer, R., and Stöllinger, R. (2015). "The Central European manufacturing core: what is driving regional production sharing?" FIW Research Reports, No. 2014/15–02. www.fiw.ac.at/fileadmin/Documents/Publikationen/Studien_2014/Studien_2014_adapted_file_names_stoellinger/02_Stoellinger_FIW_Research_Report_The_Central_European_Manufacturing_Core_What_is_Driving_Regional_Production_Sharing.pdf.

Szirmai, A. (2012). "Industrialisation as an engine of growth in developing countries, 1950–2005". *Structural Change and Economic Dynamics*, vol. 23, no. 4, pp. 406–420.

Szirmai, A., and Verspagen, B. (2015). "Manufacturing and economic growth in developing countries, 1950–2005". *Structural Change and Economic Dynamics*, vol. 34, pp. 46–59.

Teece, D., and Pisano, G. (1994). "The dynamic capabilities of firms: an introduction". *Industrial and Corporate Change*, vol. 3, no. 3, pp. 537–556.

The Economist (1999). "The sick man of the Euro". 3 January. www.economist.com/node/209559.

Thirlwall, A. P. (1983). "A plain man's guide to Kaldor's Growth Laws". *Journal of Post Keynesian Economics*, vol. 5, no. 3, pp. 345–358.

Verdoorn, P. J. (1949). "Fattori che Regolano lo Sviluppo della Produttività del Lavoro", *L'Industria*, vol. 1, pp. 3–10.

11 Reshaping the economy

An industrial and investment policy for Europe[1]

Mario Pianta, Matteo Lucchese and Leopoldo Nascia

1. Policies for post-crisis Europe

1.1 Crisis and divergence

The current transformations of European economies – accelerated by the crisis started in 2008 and by the austerity policies imposed by EU institutions – are leading European countries towards a serious divergence in terms of economic activities, investment, productivity, employment and incomes. The divergence in manufacturing production and in the dynamics of private services is at the core of such a process. The group of economies that are closely integrated with the German production system have experienced limited losses of industrial production and are returning to growth. Southern European countries (France included) have suffered major losses in production capacity and risk new imbalances in current accounts alongside those in public budgets. Central-Eastern European economies have a differentiated pattern, with few cases of rapid but fragile growth, integrated in the "German production core" (e.g. Poland) and others suffering the economic and social effects of the protracted recession.[2] A clear risk of fragmentation of the EU exists and must be countered not just with macroeconomic policy changes – moving beyond austerity – as argued by other chapters of this book, but also with a reconstruction of production capacity in the weaker areas of Europe.

Figure 11.1 shows the divergent patterns of manufacturing production from January 2008 to December 2015 within EU countries, with Eastern economies experiencing rapid growth, Germany showing stable performance, the UK and France having poorer records, and Southern European countries experiencing a major loss of industrial production. In the EU as a whole, manufacturing production is now almost 10% lower than at the start of the crisis.

The evolution of manufacturing production between 2008 and 2015 in the main European countries is shown in Figure 11.2. The recovery from the 2008 crisis has been robust in Germany, while Poland has shown a major expansion of about 34%. In France, production has lost about 15%. Italy and Spain have experienced dramatic losses – about 25% – with the latter showing modest improvement since 2013.

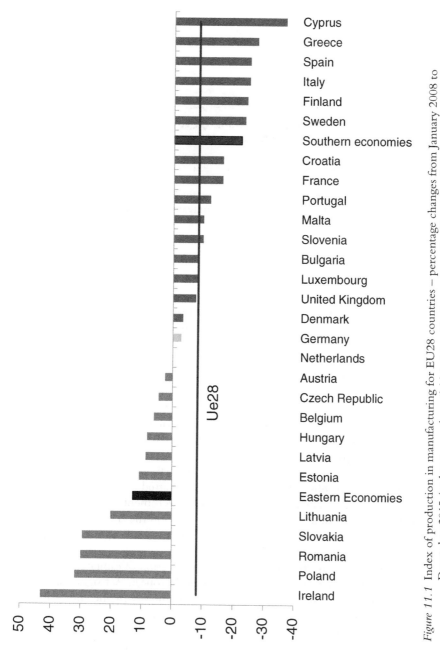

Figure 11.1 Index of production in manufacturing for EU28 countries – percentage changes from January 2008 to December 2015 (or latest month available). Monthly data, seasonally adjusted and adjusted by working days.

Source: Eurostat, Short-term business statistics, Industry.

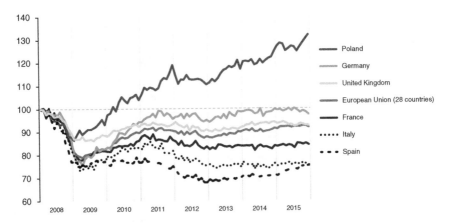

Figure 11.2 Index of production in manufacturing for EU28 and selected European
economies, January 2008=100. Monthly data, seasonally adjusted and
adjusted by working days.

Source: Eurostat, Short-term business statistics, Industry.

International production systems are thus moving towards a more hierarchical
and concentrated structure. Leading firms increase their oligopolistic market
power and control a wider network of outsourcing and offshoring activities,
distributed in a larger number of countries. Countries from the "periphery"
now have very few leading firms in global markets and experience a continuing loss of ownership of major firms to foreign investors whose commitment
to maintaining production, employment, R&D and managerial activities in
the periphery is at best uncertain. In this context, the challenge for Southern
Europe's industry is the very possibility of surviving as a European player,
which requires an active public policy role for defending and reconstructing
manufacturing capabilities.

The space for industrial and investment policy in Europe has steadily
declined since the 1980s, when neoliberal views started to dominate the economic policy debate. Their argument was that government failures are serious
and that markets are able to operate efficiently both in the short term (allocating given resources) and in the long term, when the challenge is developing
new activities, resources and markets.

Key steps in this trajectory included: the liberalisation of capital movements
in 1990; the liberalisation of finance; the Single European Act signed in 1986
establishing a Single Market in the European Community by the end of 1992,
eliminating trade barriers and regulatory differences, and opening up public
procurement, resulting in greater concentration and increased oligopolistic
power; and the Maastricht Treaty of 1992 opening the way to the creation of

the Euro with a deeply flawed institutional construction (see the other chapters in this book).

These policies have had a major impact on Europe's industry. Large State-owned firms were privatised in most countries (France is a partial exception), leading to the extensive closing down of capacity, foreign takeovers and greater market concentration. The space for industrial policy at the national level was drastically reduced, with policies that lost their selectivity and were limited to "horizontal" mechanisms, such as across-the-board tax incentives for R&D or for acquisition of new machinery, or incentives to producers and consumers of particular goods. The result has been a general loss of policy influence on the direction of industrial change and development in Europe. In most countries, this has meant a major loss of industrial activities.

In particular, the Single Market policy (European Commission, 1990) pushed back political involvement in industry and reduced the role of policy. Discretionary government measures favouring particular firms or industries were seen as "distorting" market competition. Public procurement was liberalised at the European level; the homogenisation of rules among member countries required an end to established policies that could provide selective (and therefore "unfair") support to national firms. A new consensus emerged against the State as a "producer", limiting its role to that of market "regulator". "Selective" industrial and technology policies, targeting particular fields, were to be abandoned as the market "knew best" which industries and firms were more efficient. "Horizontal" policies became fashionable, i.e. policies such as R&D tax incentives, which affect all firms in the same way.

Government action was conceptualised as "State aid"[3] and viewed with suspicion. Europe's statistics monitor such activities, documenting that between 1992 and 2013 for the 28 EU countries, State aid as a share of GDP fell from 1.2% to 0.5%, as shown in Figure 11.3 (European Commission, 2014). These data effectively summarise the retreat of policies in the field of production activities. The fall in State aid has slowed down during the crisis after 2008, but it played no counter-cyclical role in supporting demand and investment (Stöllinger et al., 2013).

Within this general reduction, Italy, Germany, Spain and Portugal are the countries that reduced State aid the fastest. In Germany, the adjustments in policy that followed unification explain much of this reduction. In Southern Europe, the long-established role of public enterprises and the extensive support that the State had provided to relatively weak private industry was rapidly reduced under the pressure of new European rules, contributing to the fall in industrial activities documented earlier.

There is evidence that the retreat of industrial policy in the last decades has left Europe with a poorer economic and technological base that is more polarised between "centre" and "periphery" and which has been unable to recover after the 2008 crisis. In the context of sluggish private investment and stagnating world exports, an active industrial policy is a necessary condition for a recovery in European economies.

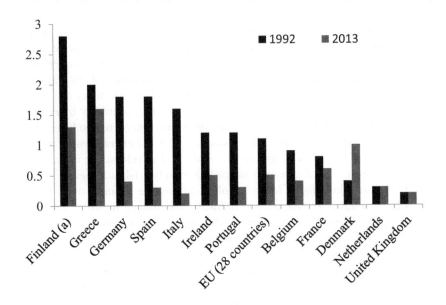

Figure 11.3 Non-crisis State aid as a percentage of GDP in European countries. State aid data excludes railways.

Note: 'Finland (a)' = 1995, 2013.

Source: State Aid Scoreboard 2014, DG Competition.

1.2 The evolution of EU policy

The liberalisation agenda of the EU has not slowed down after the 2008 crisis. A wide range of policies are extending rules based on the principles of competition, free trade and restraint of State intervention, making the emergence of a new industrial policy more difficult.

Since the late 1990s, a complex system of regulations enforcing market liberalisation has emerged, often enforced by the European Court of Justice. The general principle of EU legislation is the prohibition of any kind of selective government support providing any advantage to a firm over its competitors. However, EU legislation offers the possibility of implementing some specific derogation, as enlisted in Article 107 of the Lisbon Treaty. The inclusion of State Owned Enterprises in the notion of State aid introduced another obstacle to the implementation of national industrial policies.[4]

The Single Market for services and State aid

The strategy for a European Single Market of goods and services was launched in 2015, focusing on services that have remained somewhat "protected" by national rules and practices. The European Commission argues that persisting barriers to services have a significant cost and their removal through the systematic implementation of the Services Directive would increase EU GDP by 1.8%. The 2006 Services Directive concerns services that represent 46% of EU GDP, including retail trade, tourism, construction and business services. Sectors such as transport, telecommunications and energy are also included in the strategic document of the European Commission.

Liberalisation efforts also include public services, traditionally provided by a public monopoly. Current rules about State aid defined the notion of Services of General Economic Interest (SGEI) as a special case for State aid policies. SGEI are services relevant for the population that are not supplied by the market alone. The usual examples are transport networks, postal services and social services. The provision of SGEI from or by publicly subsidised private companies falls under the requirements of the State aid legislation with the exemption of the *de minimis* measures.[5] Social Services of General Interest (SSGI) are another group of public services, usually not provided by markets, that must comply with specific set of rules within State aid legislation. In 2012, the European Commission revised the set of regulations for SGEI and SSGI, extending their application. In 2003 the European Court of Justice, with the so-called Altmark judgment, formulated the four mandatory conditions that exclude State aid rules from application to social and general interest services.

After the 2008 crisis, the European Commission had to allow more space for emergency action by governments with temporary State aid measures for the financial sector and failing banks in particular, in derogation from the Treaties with the goal of ensuring financial stability. After 2013, these exceptions have been closed as the Banking Union has redefined rules for the financial sector, including "bail-in" regulations.

Finally, current State aid legislation ignores the impact of favourable tax treatment by EU member states. In fact, the global tax planning of transnational companies aiming to minimise tax payments represents a major "distortion of competition" that is ignored by the European Commission. A weakening of State aid rules and of the drive towards liberalisation is essential to create a policy space for new actions at the EU level for industrial and investment policy.

The Trade in Services Agreement (TiSA)

Constraints to public action also come from international treaties. The Trade in Services Agreement (TiSA) is a trade agreement being negotiated by 23 members of the World Trade Organization (WTO), accounting for 70% of world trade in services. The main objective of TiSA is the opening up of markets and improving rules in areas such as licensing, financial services, telecoms, e-commerce, maritime transport and professionals moving abroad temporarily to provide services. TiSA would enable a greater liberalisation of the trade in services through multilateralisation. In a first step, participants are negotiating a plurilateral agreement, which would then be extended to other countries.

The impact of TiSA will be particularly relevant for service sectors such as telecoms and financial services. The negotiations started in 2013; the European Commission submitted a list of activities opened up for liberalisation and declared that they will not include publicly funded health services and social insurance, since in the EU it is the right of each EU country to decide the public or private nature of each service.[6] The TiSA agreement would also lead to additional protection for private foreign investments, limiting the scope for national and European policy and regulation.

Free trade agreements: CETA, TTIP and EPA

Major policy developments have emerged since 2013 in Europe with the talks for the Transatlantic Trade and Investment Partnership (TTIP) with the United States, followed by those with Canada (CETA) and Japan (EPA). CETA has been signed and is now close to approval by EU national parliaments. TTIP talks have been suspended after the election of Donald Trump as US President. EPA talks accelerated in 2017. All treaties would move Europe further along the road to trade liberalisation and would offer strong protection for private foreign investment, with an arbitration procedure that may challenge government power, outside the judicial system. They would scale back the scope for public policy and regulation in major fields, including environmental rules, GMOs, utilities and other public services.[7] With such Treaties, the scope for industrial policy and, more generally, for public action in the economy would be drastically reduced.

The possibility of developing an industrial policy in Europe will crucially depend on the ability to stop or slow down the above initiatives and introduce a clear principle that all the activities falling under the industrial policy mandate be temporarily exempted (say, for a period of five years) from current EU competition rules, from State aid restrictions, from Single Market regulations, as well as from the provisions of TiSA and free trade agreements if they are introduced.

A re-discovery of industrial policy?

The continuing liberalisation drive of the EU coexists with policy objectives that move in the opposite direction. The Europe 2020 strategy and other major policy documents emphasise the goals of developing high-knowledge economic activities, expanding industry, reaching environmental sustainability and achieving greater convergence, but such objectives generally lack effective policy tools. In recent years, however, new policies have "re-discovered" the importance of industrial policy, including the "Industrial Compact", the *flagship initiative* "An integrated industrial policy for the globalisation era", the activities supporting "Smart specialisations" of regions, the European Fund for Strategic Investment, and measures for Industry 4.0 initiatives (a detailed analysis is in Pianta et al., 2016). At the same time, little space for industrial policy is envisaged by the *Five Presidents' Report* "Completing Europe's Economic and Monetary Union", published in 2015 (European Commission, 2015b), emphasising the need for "flexible" economies able to quickly adjust to "shocks" and for a "new convergence process".

The Juncker plan and EFSI

The failure of private investment to recover after the crisis, and the growing realisation that Europe needed some sort of answer to industrial decline, led the European Commission President in late 2014 to launch the "Juncker Investment Plan", with the aim of supporting public and private investment. In 2015, the European Fund for Strategic Investments (EFSI) was created and located in the European Investment Bank (EIB). EFSI is expected to fund new investment projects of up to EUR315 billion. EU funds are providing EUR8 billion; the EU guarantee on the projects is expected to bring in an additional EUR8 billion, and EUR5 billion have come from funds of the EIB. This total of EUR21 billion is expected to mobilise private funds of an amount 15 times greater, relying on a huge leverage effect in financial markets expecting high returns on investment.

EFSI is expected to fund investments in infrastructure and innovation; it also provides finance for small and medium-sized enterprises (SMEs) – with the role of the EIB's European Investment Fund (EIF). Interestingly enough, by spring 2015, member states had proposed 1,300 projects costing a total of EUR2,000 billion. This shows the great need for public investment in EU countries and the huge mismatch with current policies and available resources.

Since its inception, several criticisms have been made of the Juncker Plan and EFSI. First, EU resources available are limited and consist of a repackaging of resources from previous EU programmes, relying on a huge leverage effect in financial markets. Second, there is an imbalance between private and public interests; private investors have guaranteed returns in low risk activities, while public-interest projects may have to generate greater income (paid by users) than in the case of traditional public investment. In fact, projects funded exclusively by public agencies are excluded from the plan. Third, it envisages a collection of disparate investment projects with no public authority providing a framework strategy and coordinating the projects; this may allow large oligopolistic firms to expand their market power and their involvement in public interest activities (De Masi et al., 2015, GUE/NGL, 2015).

However, the creation of EFSI and the role assumed by the EIB in managing it – including the EIF for investing in SMEs – open an important policy space for the possibility of a European industrial policy. For the first time, there is an EU-level programme that can obtain resources to be invested for improving countries' infrastructures and production systems. For the first time, there is a modest investment plan driven by public policy that expands demand and tries to fill – to a very limited extent – the gap left open by the collapse of private investment since the 2008 crisis. For the first time, there is an EU policy action that recognises that markets cannot be considered perfectly capable of identifying appropriate investment opportunities. For the first time, a public policy initiative drives and attracts private financial resources that have been left idle. All these aspects are important starting points for the possible evolution of an industrial and investment policy in Europe.

Industry 4.0

The most recent international trend in business and policy concerning the future of industry and manufacturing is the Industry 4.0 framework on the digital transformation of production (Roland Berger, 2014). The idea was launched by international consulting companies and the German government, and has now made inroads into national and EU policies. In most countries, national programmes have been developed supporting the diffusion of new technologies such as cloud computing, Big Data, sensors, 3D-printers, expanding current policy tools and proposing a new governance system including business and policy makers.

The impact that such policies may have on industry's evolution is problematic. The emphasis is usually on automation and robotisation of production, systematically reducing human labour in service activities as well. A close interaction is expected between technological development, forms of organisation and actual production, where human labour and skills play a secondary role. There is a risk that Industry 4.0 may fill the gap left open by the lack of an industrial policy, while directing public policy and private investment in a direction that would benefit large corporations and the "core" countries of Europe only.

These developments point towards a broadening of the debate on the need for a new industrial policy emerging from a wide range of voices – institutions, experts, social and political forces (reviewed in detail in Pianta et al., 2016). How should Europe act in this respect with its current treaties and regulations?

2. The policy space

2.1 The policy space for investment in European fiscal rules

European fiscal rules, from the Maastricht Treaty to the Stability and Growth Pact, to the Fiscal Compact, have been a cornerstone of the neoliberal trajectory of European integration for 25 years. Their rigidity has been at the root of the fall in public expenditure and in public investment in particular. The European inability to change such rules, even after the 2008 crisis, is a major cause of the long depression and stagnation that has hit European economies.

In recent years, very modest openings have emerged in this regard. The first one is the "investment clause", concerning the opportunity to exclude investments for co-financed public investments from the deficit/GDP ratio. The "investment clause" was introduced in 2012, allowing temporary deviations from the structural deficit path linked to the realisation of "projects co-funded by the EU under the Structural and Cohesion policy, Trans-European Networks or Connecting Europe Facility with a positive, direct and verifiable long-term budgetary effect" (European Commission, 2012). However, its use was associated with restrictive conditions, and its implementation for member countries has been strongly limited (Truger, 2015). Although the European Parliament had supported the idea to push for a more ambitious plan (Prota and Viesti, 2013), the European Commission has put forward no new concrete proposals. Recently, the European Commission slightly revised conditions for using the "investment clause" to take better account of country-specific situations: "The Commission will apply the 'investment clause' irrespective of the economic condition of the euro area or EU as a whole, in order to link it only to the cyclical conditions faced by individual Member States". This interpretation "will permit a broader application of the clause than in the past, and one which better reflects country-specific conditions" (European Commission, 2015a).

The second measure is the opportunity to obtain a temporary deviation from the path of consolidation of public deficit for countries involved in structural reforms. This, however, has no specific association with investment activities. These two measures have provided some degree of flexibility in managing public resources, but they do not allow significant counter-cyclical expenditure; neither do they appear able to foster additional investments.

An important debate has emerged on the introduction of a "golden rule" that excludes public investment from the restrictions on public deficits. The argument is that public investment will mainly benefit future generations and it is therefore reasonable to fund it not through tax receipts, but through public debt. Moreover, current cuts in public investment can be detrimental to future economic growth, with negative effects on future wellbeing and fiscal budgets (Feigl and Truger, 2015).

A specific proposal for a "golden rule" that excludes (some) public investment from deficit calculations has been developed by Truger (2015). The specific components of public investment that could be included in such an exemption are discussed in detail, but the study argues that by itself the rule would be unable to trigger significant new expenditure and has therefore to be complemented by a large investment plan. Such a "golden rule" could be introduced without a change in treaties. The inclusion of the public financing of intangible investments (innovation, patents, software and education) among the exempted expenditure lines could stimulate sectors and activities that are more related to a sustainable path of growth for Europe (Truger, 2015). However, the range of activities that could be exempted from deficit restrictions requires a broad agreement. They should include investments that are growth-enhancing: a stricter definition could consider infrastructural projects alone, while a wider definition could include investments in education and training, R&D and human capital. In order to avoid the accumulation of excessive debt, an upper limit to the investment exempted from deficit restrictions could be established, taking into consideration the parallel evolution of GDP (Feigl and Truger, 2015).

A parallel proposal concerns the extension of the built-in flexibility of the current fiscal pact with a "silver rule" for investments. When structural reforms are undertaken, member countries could be allowed to spend more than by the Fiscal Pact allotted for two years for debt-financed investments that are highly relevant for long-term growth and for slowing down climate change (Aiginger, 2014; Aiginger and Janger, 2015).

The adoption of a "golden rule" would allow a significant reduction of austerity in public budgets and would tackle the issue of demand shortage. In the short term, a significant extension of flexibility in the calculation of allowed budget deficits for EU countries could represent the most immediate and easiest possibility for counter-cyclical fiscal policy supporting domestic demand. This is what several EU governments have demanded, opening up occasional confrontations with the European Commission. An informal, ad hoc relaxation of fiscal rules could indeed be the most feasible way for moving out of current austerity policies. Giving a new priority to investment expenditure associated with industrial policy and public infrastructure could be a reasonable and effective way to implement such a policy change in a "soft" and legitimate way. The concrete possibility to use such an opportunity, however, depends on the balance of power within European institutions and among national governments and political forces.

2.2 Actions at the national level

In addition to Europe-wide programmes, several tools for industrial policy have been maintained at the national and regional levels. The report of the European Parliament (2015, table 4, p.61) summarises some common policies and approaches present in major countries. On the policies concerning R&D and innovation, the EU has produced annual "RIO reports" for all countries, assessing national funding, horizontal actions, targeted innovation initiatives and other forms of public action that are generally relevant from an industrial policy perspective (see Nascia and Pianta, 2017 for the RIO report on Italy). A summary of the main policy areas present in most countries is provided here.

R&D tax credits and incentives. One of the main tools for "horizontal" industrial and innovation policy is the R&D tax credit, introduced by many EU countries in past decades with a wide variety of programmes. This represents the largest public financing of private activity associated with industrial policy currently available.

The patent box. The emphasis in recent decades put on the greater role and protection of intellectual property rights (IPRs) has brought to some countries the "patent box", a specific tax benefit for firms' earnings coming from patents, trademarks, licences and software. A deduction from the firm's tax base is provided for a share of the income from patents, trademarks, licences and software. Patent boxes are indirect, semiautomatic incentives common in OECD countries. Their objective is to stimulate the production of patents and IPRs, but no empirical evidence on such an impact is available, as argued by Mazzucato (2013).

In fact, the patent box plays a key role in the strategies of large firms to reduce taxation on their technology-related earnings. In particular, the global tax planning strategies of multinational companies often "hide" profits in royalty payments for patents and IPRs, moving them to "fiscal havens". Often, the location of subsidiaries owning patents and earning royalties is chosen with consideration of the tax reductions offered – such as the patent box. For the patent box, as for R&D tax credits, serious evidence is lacking on the real additionality effect of such measures, especially when the international dimension is considered, including the potential shift of the same activities from one country to another.

Loan guarantees for SMEs. A growing emphasis has been put on improving access to financial markets for SMEs. The main tool in this regard is a system of loan guarantees. National programmes differ widely in this respect, and a variety of good practices in order to stimulate investment, reduce risk and support change have been developed.

Support for start-up firms. In many countries, legislation has been introduced supporting the emergence of innovative "start-up firms". They were defined as new small firms focusing on technological innovation, located in an EU country with some additional characteristics. Start-up firms are generally offered indirect incentives (tax holidays, lower administrative costs, some exceptions to labour laws and tax bonuses for investors), access to loan guarantees and support for their internationalisation efforts. Some results have been obtained in this regard, but it is too early to make a proper assessment of such policies. More generally, previous policy analysis on the impact of support for new firm creation has shown that the main problem is not the creation of new small firms *per se*, but rather their ability to survive in the medium term in less favourable market conditions.

2.3 Actions at the regional level

Most countries and regions have programmes and tools for supporting local development, often using resources from EU Structural Funds. While national policies have scaled down their attention to industrial policy, a range of experiences have emerged in regions and large cities characterised by rapid economic change, deindustrialisation and the emergence of new dynamic activities. In some regions and cities with progressive local governments, a new policy space has been developed with novel actions that have brought industrial policy within the reach of their responsibilities.

The specific production structure of regions has led to tailor-made measures that could support current specialisations (including actions in the context of the EU "smart specialisation" initiatives; Foray et al., 2015) or the emergence of novel economic activities building on existing competences and resources. The quality of employment, learning processes and environmental issues has generally been paramount in shaping such new local policies.

Such policies tend to focus on the key strengths of local economies, considering the presence of different models of local activities, in particular:

- "Industrial districts" – a geographical concentration of a large number of small firms closely integrated in a highly specialised production system, often with a coordinating role played by a larger firm. They are typical of traditional industries in Southern Europe and have been deeply affected and transformed by the crisis (see Bianchi and Labory, 2011a, 2016).
- "Anchor" organisations – large firms, major infrastructure or public institutions with large economic footprints. They are important nodes of broader business networks, favouring local development through learning processes, procurement from suppliers, creation of employment, etc. They can include a large firm, universities, R&D centres, high technology hubs, advanced business services, etc. In France, they have centred on the "pole de competitivité" initiatives. In these contexts, policies have aimed at specific actions supporting high-impact firms whose dynamics could be assessed at the level of the local production system as a whole, rather than at the level of an individual firm.

Some of these policies have been developed by progressive local and regional governments and provide important lessons on how a generalisation of good local practices could integrate and support a broader European industrial policy.

Policy experiences in these cases have been reviewed, for example, by Bailey, Cowling and Tomlinson (2015) in the case of the UK, and by Bianchi and Labory (2011b, 2016) in the case of the Emilia-Romagna region in Italy. In addition, the transition to the environmental sustainability of local production systems has been addressed by Coffey and Thornley (2015).

The range of tools that have been used in progressive local and regional policies include:

- Public financial guarantees for the loans that small firms can obtain from local banks.
- Low-cost provision of business services to industrial district firms, ranging from technical aspects to design, internationalisation and marketing.
- Funding of research or design consortia among firms and with public research organisations.
- Support for the creation of local "filières" with vertically integrated production systems.
- Support for diversification efforts in expanding activities.
- Local demand policies using public procurement.
- Support for diffusion of know-how, training, learning processes, business creation.
- Provision of appropriate local infrastructures in disadvantaged areas.
- Employment creation programmes in public, environmental and socially relevant activities.
- Promotion of local agricultural and food production through locally sourced, coordinated buying.
- Specific programmes – in urban mobility, resource use, energy, waste reduction and recycling, etc. that can increase environmental sustainability.

The potential of local and regional policies for supporting economic development has also been at the centre of a growing number of US initiatives, which are analysed in detail by Rogers and Rhodes-Conway (2014). US experiences of progressive local and city governments have focused on the identification of critical industries and firms, the assessment of the value flows in the local economy, and the consideration of infrastructure, human resources and competences that are present. Specific policy actions have used urban planning tools, procurement contracts and local subsidies in order to obtain some improvements in the quality of local activities, higher wages and employment protection from key firms. Infrastructure investment and environmental improvements have also been financed by funding programmes involving firms and non-profit organisations. In some cities, a local land bank has been created to fund the transformation of abandoned properties into affordable housing, local businesses and parks.

Many of these regional approaches fall into the "place-based policy" advocated in Barca (2009) in the context of the debate of the reform of EU cohesion policy. A discussion on such an approach has also been developed in the UK context (Bailey, Hildreth and De Propis, 2015). However, large resources available from EU Structural Funds have not been really used as tools for advancing such local production systems, diversifying activities and upgrading their competences. With the crisis, the result in most areas has been a weakening of local systems and a widening of regional disparities in Europe (Meliciani, 2015).

The need for the involvement of social actors, public participation and consensus building has long been an element in progressive regional policy experiences. Based on the Emilia-Romagna case, Bianchi and Labory (2011b) argued that "a long-term and sustainable vision of industrial development can be effectively defined and implemented if this is done in a process involving local stakeholders and ensuring consensus". Along the same lines, the Eurofound (2013) report stressed the importance of social dialogue in the development of industrial policies.

2.4 Policies for IPRs, open source and digital activities

A specific field of industrial and innovation policy is that of Intellectual Property Rights (IPR). The rapid scientific and technical advances in information and communication technologies has given new importance to traditional IPRs, leading to a "commodification" of knowledge and technology under the legal protection of more stringent IPR regulations.

In the US, the Bayh-Dole Act (1980) triggered a patent rush by research institutions. In 1998, the Digital Millenium Copyright Act extended copyright to a broad range of digital services, strengthening the process of privatisation of digital goods. US IPR legislation has been extended to also include technical information and business methods formerly in the public domain.

In the analysis of Paul David, this policy has helped incumbent firms "to stabilize traditional business models by blocking incursions by new entrants' pursuit of disruptive business strategies" (David, 2014). Although the mainstream policy approach justified increased IPR protection as a greater incentive to innovation, IPRs have not been a factor in triggering ICT growth or innovation. In fact, many innovations have emerged and continue to spread in an "open" framework.

The scientific community has reacted to such a privatisation process with the development of a new group of digital procedures and new modalities of "open" research: open science, open data and open repositories. The analysis of Paul David (2014) has pointed out several experiences of "bottom-up", cooperative, "opened" responses by the scientific community, including the Neurocommons project (a collaboration between Science Commons and the Teranode Corporation), the Human Genome Project and the Haplotide Mapping Project. All are major international programmes that adopted open commons licences to prevent the patenting of their output.

Also in the digital industry, a similar "open" approach found major success with the development of open source software communities such as Linux or Wikipedia, the worldwide collaborative free encyclopaedia developed by the collaboration of users. The portal SourceForge.net, a major open source community, provided tools for developers to create software in over 430,000 projects with a daily average of 4.8 million downloads.

The open source approach led to innovative typologies of licensing, such as copyleft, with a huge international adoption. Online creation communities (OCCs) have emerged, bringing together individuals that mainly interact via a platform of online participation, with the goal of building and sharing common resources (Fuster Morell, 2013).

There is a lack of wide-ranging EU policies for supporting the expansion of open source activities. The EU Commission does not look at open source as a competitive factor for the economy; collaborative projects are left to specific cooperation agreements between interested actors and software communities. The only exception is copyleft licensing and open source software for public administrations. A major interest has recently emerged on organisation and access to open data. This includes data released by governments and is associated with the emergence of Big Data, very large databases that could be used as inputs for digital industries and new services. In fact, Greenwald and Stiglitz (2013) argue that greater attention to open source and lower protection of IP would boost innovation by expanding collaborative behaviour between scientists, researchers and firms that is currently discouraged by the strict protection of IPR.

An appropriate, imaginative industrial policy for digital activities could therefore expand the space for "open activities" – open source, open data, open collaboration – both in the market and in non-market, socially relevant activities. This would favour the emergence of new forms of producing, sharing and using knowledge, and in new forms of work (see the analysis of Rushkoff, 2016 on the alternative to "digital industrialism" and experiences such as the videogame company Valve Inc., where workers have introduced self-management practices).

2.5 An overview of current EU policies

Figure 11.4 presents a summary of the main policy actions by the EU so far described, documenting the limited policy space for building industrial capacity and supporting investment. EU policy has continued to disregard the seriousness of industrial decline and continues to rely on a policy frame wherein priority is given to market liberalisation. Even after the dramatic effects of the crisis, "horizontal" actions remain the main forms of permitted public intervention, and no significant EU-wide resources have been made available to member states. Moreover, even the very mild tools of present EU industrial policies have lacked an adequate governance mechanism; industry lobbies exert major influence and there is a lack of democratic processes and broad participation in decision making – a weakness that, unfortunately, is found in all fields of the present model of European integration.

Moreover, while there is some opening for industrial policy in recent policies and debates, a set of other EU policies is likely to further reduce the space for such action. They include competition and State aid rules, the prospects for integration proposed by the Five Presidents' Report, TTIP negotiations and Industry 4.0 strategies.

3. A proposal for a European industrial and investment policy

The specific proposal that is advanced in this section builds on conceptual arguments and on the existing policy space provided by European institutional arrangements and policy actions discussed earlier. The main components of an industrial policy are addressed in this section, proposing a "preferable" model of progressive industrial and investment policy that takes into account

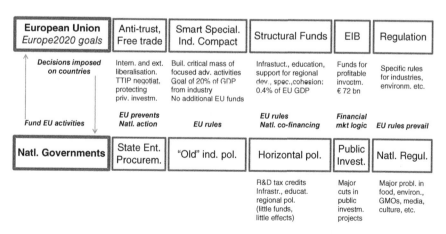

Figure 11.4 A summary of current industrial policy actions in the EU.
Source: Pianta (2014b).

the constraints for short-term action and the obstacles to political change. In addition, a longer-term course of action and a variety of policy options that could be pursued in particular contexts are also proposed. Figure 11.5 summarises the new framework for European institutions, funding and policy making that could be associated with the new European industrial policy.

3.1 A European policy, not just national ones

The earlier analysis has shown that a fully integrated European industrial and investment policy is needed. The new industrial policy has to be firmly set within the EU and – if required – within the institutions of the Eurozone. This is needed in order to coordinate industrial policy with macroeconomic, monetary, fiscal, trade, competition, regulatory and other EU-wide policies, providing full legitimation to public action at the European level for influencing what is being produced (and how). Changes in some rules and interpretations are required in current EU regulations, in particular those on competition, State aid and trade which prevent public action from "distorting" the operation of markets. As this policy is likely to meet with opposition by some EU countries, a "variable geometry" EU policy could be envisaged, excluding the countries that do not wish to participate.

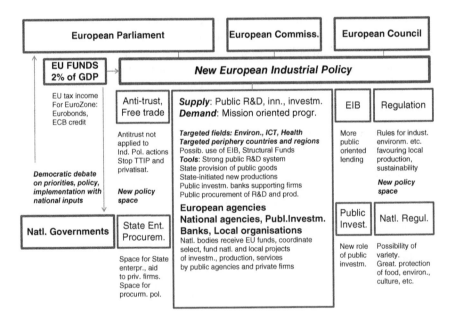

Figure 11.5 A summary of the new European industrial policy proposed.

Source: Pianta (2014b).

Close integration has to be developed between the European dimension (providing policy coherence, overall priorities and funding), the national dimension (where public agencies have to operate and an implementation strategy has to be defined), and the local dimension (where specific public and private actors have to be involved in the complex tasks associated with the development of new economic activities).

3.2 A policy mobilising 2% of Europe's GDP

This policy has to be significant in terms of the size of new resources that are mobilised, which should be about 2% of Europe's GDP for ten years, about EUR 260 billion per year. This is the order of magnitude of most proposals that have emerged so far, and such an amount would make an impact in all the aspects, from macroeconomic to technological considerations. As a term of reference, we can note that the EFSI envisages an investment plan of EUR 315 billion over several years. In the period December 2011–March 2012 the European Central Bank alone provided EUR 1,000 billion in special funds to private banks at a 1% interest rate, with no success in turning them into real investment. EU Structural Funds in the period 2007–2013 reached EUR 347 billion and lending by the EIB was EUR 72 billion in 2013. An investment effort of about 2% of EU GDP appears to be feasible, considering the size and power of European institutions, and would be big enough to compensate (at the macroeconomic level) for the lack of private investment and low exports, effectively ending Europe's stagnation. This integrated European industrial policy has to go well beyond the specific, modest, disparate actions on investment, innovation, environmental protection, etc. that are currently carried out in Europe. Industrial policy has to include an important investment programme but cannot be reduced to the setting up of an investment fund such as EFSI (see later on funding sources).

3.3 Greater national policy space and a "golden rule" for public investment

At the same time, national governments should be provided with a much greater policy space, relaxing the constraints on public investment through some form of "golden rule" (Truger, 2015). Such a policy change could spur countries to invest annually the equivalent of at least 1% of Europe's GDP for the next ten years, also taking advantage of the current extremely low interest rates. The mobilisation of national resources in addition to the ones made available by European industrial policy could have a major impact on Europe's recovery.

3.4 Reducing the divergence between Europe's centre and periphery

A fundamental objective of industrial policy in the present European context is the reduction of the divergence in economic activities among European countries and regions that brings with it the danger of a disintegration of Europe. Industrial policy will have to focus on the reconstruction of production capacities in the regions and countries that have been most affected by the current crisis. A practical way of assuring this is to pre-determine a criteria for regional and national distribution of resources. For instance, 75% of industrial policy funds could go to activities located in "periphery" countries (Eastern and Southern Europe, plus Ireland). At least 50% of the funds should be devoted to the poorer regions of such countries and 25% could go to the poorer regions of the countries of the "centre". This approach would ensure that industrial policy has a positive impact on the reduction of disparities among regions within countries and Europe as a whole.

3.5 Public investment, public enterprises, support of private firms and other policy tools

An investment programme is at the core of the proposed European industrial policy, but other policy tools should be used with an integrated approach. In particular, the policy tools to be adopted by European industrial policy should include the following:

- A public investment programme providing public infrastructure and public goods.
- Support for existing public enterprises and creation of new ones for the provision of public services and public interest activities.
- Participation with capital shares in the creation of new private firms in key areas.
- New public-private partnerships.
- Public procurement programmes for the goals of industrial policy.
- "Mission-oriented" innovation programmes guiding R&D and technological change.

Within the available resources assigned to each country, national governments should be able to decide the most appropriate combination of these policy actions.

3.6 A policy targeted to sustainability, ICTs and public services

Industrial policy should favour the evolution of knowledge, technologies and economic activities in directions that improve economic performance, social conditions and environmental sustainability. It should favour activities and industries characterised by learning processes for individuals and in organisations, rapid technological change, scale and scope economies, and strong growth in demand and productivity.

This requires a set of targeted actions that have to replace the horizontal approach of the past decades, which treated all activities and firms in the same way to avoid "interfering" with the market. Clear choices must be made on which activities are desirable and are to be supported. Three sets of economic activities are proposed here as targets for industrial policy: activities centred on the environment and energy; knowledge and information and communication technologies (ICTs); and health and welfare.

Environment and energy. The current industrial model has to be deeply transformed in the direction of environmental sustainability. The technological paradigm of the future could be based on "green" products, processes and social organisations that use much less energy, resources and land, have a much lighter effect on climate and eco-systems, move to renewable energy sources, organise transport systems beyond the dominance of cars with integrated mobility systems, rely on the repair and maintenance of existing goods and infrastructures, and protect nature and the Earth. Such a perspective raises enormous opportunities for research, innovation and new economic and social activities that may develop either in markets or in the sphere of public, non-market activities. A new set of coherent policies should address these complex, long-term challenges.

Knowledge and ICTs. Current change is dominated by the diffusion throughout the economy of the paradigm based on ICTs. Its potential for wider applications, higher productivity and lower prices, and new goods and social benefits should be supported, including their use in traditional industries. Moreover, ICTs and web-based activities are reshaping the boundaries between the economic and social spheres. On the positive side, we have seen the success of open source software that copyleft, Wikipedia and peer-to-peer clearly show. Much more problematic is the rise of platforms that use people's social activities to obtain a market advantage, as in the case of Airbnb and Uber, where a lack of policy and regulation is having serious consequences on existing economic activities in the same field. More generally, policies should encourage the practice of innovation as a social, cooperative and open process, easing rules on access to and sharing of knowledge, rather than enforcing and restricting it based on intellectual property rules designed for a previous technological era.

Health and welfare. Europe is an aging continent with the best health systems in the world, rooted in their nature as a public service outside the market. Advances in care systems, instrumentation, biotechnologies, genetics and drug research have to be supported and regulated, considering their ethical and social consequences (as in the cases of GMOs, cloning, access to drugs in developing countries, etc.). Social innovation may spread in welfare services with a greater role of citizens, users and non-profit organisations, renewed public provision and new forms of self-organisation of communities.

All these fields are characterised by labour-intensive production processes and by a requirement of medium and high skills, with the potential to provide "good" jobs.

3.7 The EIB first, a Public Investment Bank second

Existing institutions could be renewed and integrated in such a new industrial policy, including – at the EU level – Structural Funds and the EIB. However, their mode of operation should be adapted to the different requirements of the role proposed here. While, in the short term adapting existing institutions is the most effective way to proceed, in the longer term, there is a need for a dedicated institution – possibly a European Public Investment Bank – coherent with the mandate of reshaping economic activities in Europe.

3.8 European policy, national and regional implementation

A system could be envisaged where the EU Council and the European Parliament agree on the objectives, tools, guidelines and funding of industrial policy, calling the European Commission to implement appropriate policy tools and spending mechanisms. In each country, a specific institution – either an existing or a new one, possibly a National Public Investment Bank – could assume the role of coordinating the implementation of industrial policies at the national level, interacting with the existing national innovation system, policy actors, the financial sector, etc. More specific agencies, consortia or enterprises, with flexible institutional arrangements but with a strong public orientation, could be created (or adapted, if already in place) for action at the local and regional level and for initiatives in particular fields. The institutions at the national and local level would take responsibility for the selection of the new public activities that are required, of the appropriate policy tools, of spending decisions and projects to be developed. They would be subject to the strict monitoring described later. National initiatives would be able to use assigned resources from European industrial policy and be encouraged to combine them with additional national public funds and private capital that could be attracted to invest in key areas identified by industrial policy.

3.9 Democratic processes, not just technocracy

Europe's industrial policy cannot be reduced to financially based investment decisions as currently done by the EIB. It has to be rooted and legitimised by a broad democratic process centred in the European Parliament, where key decisions on objectives, tools, guidelines and funding of industrial policy will have to be made. Rebuilding and re-orienting Europe's economies requires technical skills but is not a job that can be left to technocrats. The political process and democratic participation have to take centre stage in the shaping of Europe's industrial policy. A key role has to be played by the European Parliament in debating and deliberating the objectives, tools and guidelines of industrial policy. The European institutions of industrial policy should be accountable to the European Parliament, who appoints its board, where representatives from business, research organisations, trade unions, environmental groups, civil society organisations should be included. No "revolving door" between industrial policy institutions and private firms and banks would be allowed. European institutions should engage in consultation with EU political, economic and social actors for developing the proposed industrial policy.

3.10 An integrated policy programme, not just budget lines

Current EU policies are often split between strategies without budget and budget lines without strategies. An industrial policy has to integrate objectives, policy programmes and the resources available. It has also to integrate the use of different, complementary policy tools and spending programmes.

3.11 European public funds, no national funds

Funds for a Europe-wide industrial policy should come from Europe-wide resources. It is essential that troubled national public budgets are not burdened with the need to provide additional resources and that national public debt is not increased. For the group of Eurozone countries, financing through EMU mechanisms could be considered. Eurobonds could be created to fund industrial policy; the EIB or a new European Public Investment Bank could borrow funds directly from the ECB; the ECB could directly provide industrial policy funds to the spending agencies concerned.

An alternative may come from a deeper European fiscal reform, introducing an EU-wide tax on corporations, thus effectively eliminating fiscal competition between EU countries. A share of proceeds – perhaps 15% – could go to fund industrial policy, public investment, knowledge generation and diffusion at the EU level; the rest could be transferred to the countries' treasuries. Other sources of EU funds could include an extended Financial Transaction Tax or a Europe-wide wealth tax such as the one proposed by Thomas Piketty (2013). All these measures, however, are more difficult to design and implement.

3.12 Long-term, high-risk public capital first, private capital second

The public nature of many activities that industrial policy is called to support means that public funds have to play a crucial role in financing such initiatives. The economic activities targeted by industrial policy tend to be characterised by high uncertainty, high-risk, low short-term private returns and potentially high long-term public benefits. Some investment, however, may also involve private capital. In fact, funding arrangements could differ according the relevance of the "public" dimension:

a)   The priority of public funds should go to public investment in non-market activities, such as public goods provision, infrastructures, knowledge, education and health.

b) Public funds and long-term private investment should be combined in funding new "strategic" market activities, such as the provision of capital for new firms in emerging sectors.

c) Public support could stimulate financial markets and private actors to invest in firms and non-profit organisations developing "desirable" market activities that could more easily repay the investment.

In all cases, the rationale for financing industrial policy cannot be reduced to the financial logic of the "return on investment". The benefits in terms of environmental quality, social welfare, greater territorial cohesion and more diffused growth at the European level have to be considered, and the costs have to be shared accordingly.

3.13 Reinventing the governance of public interest economic activities

A major challenge for the effective functioning and legitimation of a European industrial policy is the development of a new governance system that overcomes the problems of lack of efficiency, collusion between political and economic power and corruption that have emerged in the past. A practical arrangement could be that monitoring and evaluation procedures similar to those required by EU Structural Funds would be introduced in the case of industrial policy activities. More generally, the public interest activities that will be supported in various ways by industrial policy will have to be managed in a way that assures inclusive and participatory decision making, takes into account the diversity of social interests involved, is accountable to democratic processes, assures transparency in all steps, using also the tools now made available by open data systems.

3.14 Bottom-up competences and projects first

The targeting of selected areas for European industrial policy has to be implemented, as much as possible, with a bottom-up approach that is able to allow the potential for new production capacities to emerge at the local level. The approach developed by the EU "smart specialisations" strategy could be extended in this context to identify effective initiatives with a critical mass and a significant local impact

3.15 Suspending European competition and State aid rules for these activities

The specific objectives and targeted activities of Europe's industrial policy should be temporarily exempted from the norms on competition, restrictions on State aid and EU Single Market rules for a period of five years. The very objective of industrial policy, in fact, is to develop activities that markets are unable to carry out and expand. This includes the possibility that targeted firms – with either private or public ownership – could be supported in various ways, including public procurement, in order to restructure economic activities and reshape market competition. The emergence of new forms of organisation for the new activities could also be supported.

3.16 Favouring coordination and pervasive effects in the economy

The transformation envisaged by Europe's industrial policy requires coordination at the European, national and regional levels among the different aspects of economic and social activities. For example, moves towards a sustainable economy have to coordinate changes in production and in consumption patterns, favouring more sober and responsible lifestyles. Institutions will have to evolve alongside economic activities. Education, welfare, distribution and many other policies will have to interact with the changes emerging in production systems. The activities targeted by industrial policy tend to have pervasive effects throughout the economy and society; this process has to be favoured in order to obtain all the potential benefits from industrial policy.

3.17 A political and social consensus on rebuilding European economies

Finally, a new major European policy requires a wide consensus from European citizens, social forces and political parties. The concrete benefits of ending Europe's stagnation, providing jobs and wages, and improving environmental sustainability and social justice could make the challenge of mobilising broad support around the proposal of a European industrial policy easier.

4. An appropriate policy context

4.1 A fair distribution of the benefits of industrial policy

Industrial policy aims, among other things, at increasing innovation and productivity growth. When new products and industries do emerge as a result of these efforts, however, the new markets are dominated by firms, often with monopoly power, that are in the position to appropriate huge "Schumpeterian" profits. Such development has often had a strong financial dimension, with high-risk investments involved and booming stock values for high technology firms. The gains from this have been highly concentrated in top incomes, while the funding of the research that made such innovations possible has largely come from public sources, and the public sector has often had to cover the losses when new projects fail (Mazzucato, 2013). A more balanced distribution of the benefits of technology between public and private interests has been proposed through changes that would assign a greater share of the gains to the public organisations that have shaped the emergence of new technologies and to the workers involved. Tools that have been proposed include granting State institutions shares in the high technology firms benefitting from public R&D; creating and expanding public investment banks that could fund risky projects and obtain the benefits of success; and modifying intellectual property rights rules to emphasise the public dimension of knowledge created through public R&D. Greater resources flowing to public organisations would limit the rise in top incomes and, moreover, provide greater resources for underfunded basic R&D and public education that are essential for the innovation process itself (Lazonick and Mazzucato, 2015; Lazonick, 2015).

A second way technological change has affected income distribution is through the direction taken by innovations. Considering the functional distribution of income, profits have increased much more than wages as a result both of new products that offer temporary monopoly power and as a result of new processes that replace labour. The latter often have the effect of reducing the quantity (and sometimes also the quality) of employment used, weakening labour in its relationship with capital. Technology and industrial policies could be introduced and expanded in order to orient innovation in a direction that could have less inegalitarian effects, as argued by Atkinson (2015), and expand (rather than replace and reduce) the quality of labour used, especially in services where human activity remains important. Public organisations could directly introduce labour-enhancing innovations; tax incentives and R&D support could primarily go to firms that give priority to new products, rather than new processes; and labour-intensive activities where labour skills and wages are higher than average could be encouraged. As pointed out earlier, the fields and missions where resources should go could include environmental sustainability, appropriate ICT applications, health and welfare services.

Technological change is a major driver of productivity growth in firms, which draws from a variety of other factors – increased education, organisational change, better work practices, etc. Considering the wide gap that has opened in recent decades between productivity and wage growth, it is important to design better institutional arrangements that may allow productivity increases to be equally shared between capital and labour, and among all workers (see ILO, 2014; Franzini and Pianta, 2016). It is important that a discussion on the distribution of the envisaged benefits of industrial policy defines from the start the conditions for a distribution between profits, rents and wages (and within wages) capable of reducing inequalities and increase social justice.

4.2 Policies in other fields that are supportive of industrial policy goals

Several policies in other fields – from education to public infrastructure – have an indirect effect on the ability to carry out industrial policies and on the possibility of success. We concentrate here on only a few aspects that have a direct impact on the strategies and governance of firms that could be involved in industrial policy actions; other chapters in this book address complementary issues.

Labour rights, wages, social insurance. Providing more jobs with high skills, security and wages is a major objective of industrial policy. This is in direct contrast with current "structural reforms" pushed by the EU in most countries, which aim to reduce workers' protection and increase flexibility in labour markets. Labour market and social policies that stop the current rise of "non-standard" employment, especially among youth, and that assure higher wages through a greater role of national collective contracts and minimum wage rules could be complementary to industrial policy in improving employment and wages. EU-wide unemployment benefits and new norms on the full portability of social rights, social insurance and pensions all over the EU would also play an important role. The connection between Europe's industrial policy and improved labour rights could also be made in a more direct way. As industrial policy envisages an expansion of high-skill, high-wage labour, specific guidelines – stricter than national legislation – on limits to non-standard employment, on the types of contracts used, on labour protection, wage levels, etc. could be defined as part of industrial policy for the activities and firms that are funded by EU industrial policy. These guidelines should be mandatory within the public sector. Private firms could be required to adopt such guidelines in order to receive industrial policy funds, access public procurement and other forms of support, on the grounds that improved labour conditions and a fair distribution of the benefits are key goals of industrial policy.

Tax harmonisation. Tax harmonisation within the EU – especially taxation on corporations, capital income and wealth – is a crucial complement to industrial policy. The current lack of tax harmonisation creates incentives to firms' location, investment and production that are worsening the problems of divergence within the EU and make the notion of "fair" competition among European firms meaningless. The 2007 Treaty on the Functioning of the European Union (TFEU) does not specifically cover tax harmonisation, though Articles 110–113 under the unanimity of the Council makes the harmonisation of indirect tax possible. This has resulted in the lack of harmonisation of taxation policy in Europe, but action has become urgent in this regard. This would make the implementation of industrial policy easier and reduce the extent of divergence across EU countries. The notion of State aid has to consider the tax treatment of economic activities, since taxation is a factor of bias in the competition among countries. However, a fully harmonised corporation tax is still far from the agenda of the EU Commission, especially for capital income taxation. Tax competition has been a major tool used to attract foreign investments and has led to a reduction of tax rates. In the period 1996–2015, top statutory corporate income tax rates recorded a general fall across EU28 member states. In 1996 the average corporate income tax rate was 35%, as opposed to 22.8% in 2015. In the same period, top statutory personal income tax rates also recorded a general downturn, from 47% to 39.3%.

Regulating finance. The regulation of finance is an issue at the heart of Europe's problems that can deeply influence the behaviour of firms and therefore the success of an industrial policy for reconstructing economic activities. The specific measures in this field – proposed by a very large pool of literature – include a return to a division between commercial and investment banking; a generalised tax on all financial transactions to limit speculative trading; and strong limitations on financial derivatives. In more radical versions, some regulations on capital movement are proposed. Such a downsizing of finance would put less pressure on profit maximisation in firms and leave more room for real investment and higher wages.

Controlling top managers' compensation. In the top 350 US firms, the ratio of the compensation of managers to that of average employees rose tenfold, from 30 to 1 in 1978 to 296 to 1 in 2013 (Mishel and Davis, 2014). This creates obvious problems of inequality, social justice, legitimation and efficiency. A reduction of top managers' incomes in private firms cannot be legislated and enforced, but several actions can be taken that would make the current behaviour socially unacceptable. A European, national or regional policy for reducing income disparities within firms and organisations could define guidelines on acceptable ratios between the best-paid, average-paid and worst-paid workers. These guidelines could be enforced within the public sector. They could then state that private firms violating such guidelines will be penalised in access to public procurement, incentives and tax relief, on the grounds that extreme disparities burden society with unacceptable social costs, which eventually have to be met by public expenditure. This would create incentives within firms among responsible managers, shareholders, employees and stakeholders to change the current model of corporate governance that has led to such disparities, also introducing (when possible) greater accountability and democracy in corporate governance.

5. Conclusions

This chapter has shown how urgent (and at the same time) complex the task is to develop a progressive European industrial and investment policy. The goal is to develop new economic activities that are socially desirable and environmentally sustainable, as well as economically efficient, filling the investment gaps left by the operation of markets. These activities should be located in the poorer countries and regions of the EU, so that the worst effects of the crisis started in 2008 and the current divergence within the EU can be reversed. The industrial policy of the EU should target relevant areas of new economic activities and provide funds for a variety of policy tools: public investment, public enterprises, support to private firms, procurement programmes, mission-oriented innovation programmes, etc. Such initiatives could set in motion a new trajectory of European development, orienting R&D and technological change, attracting private investment, and reshaping business organisations and the use of labour. A European industrial policy could create and organise markets that the short-sighted, risk-averse decisions of private firms and banks are unable to develop. In order to allow major expansion of environmentally sustainable activities, appropriate ICT applications and public health and welfare services, important new public resources at the European scale, have to be directed towards such activities. A public investment bank has to fill the gap currently left by the finance-driven allocation of investment; thus the current EU regulations on competition, State aid and the Single Market have to be temporarily suspended. Industrial policy could become a major force supporting cohesion objectives within the EU, driving a new process of convergence that could lead to a rethinking of the use of Structural Funds.

A progressive European industrial policy would introduce a major change of direction in the process of European integration. Since the late 1980s, neoliberal views on the ability of markets to operate efficiently and regulate themselves and on the liberalisation of finance have dominated the process of European integration. The 2008 crisis showed that finance and markets do fail, and they have proven to be unable to pull Europe out of a long stagnation. In this context, the introduction of a European industrial policy would be a concrete step towards introducing much needed corrections in the way markets and finance operate, re-orienting their activities towards a new trajectory of sustainable and equitable development for Europe.

This new policy would require an important political change in the views of Europe's political élites and public opinion. The failure of austerity policies to end Europe's stagnation and the risks of disintegration to Europe are important factors that may encourage a change of views in governments, parliaments, political parties and European institutions. Investment plans that expand the quantity and quality of employment, raise wages, reduce inequality and make Europe's development more sustainable could encourage a change of views among European citizens, workers, trade unions and civil society organisations.

The fact that all this could only be possible in a European context, and cannot be reached by national policy alone, would provide a new legitimation for an EU based on the principles of solidarity, social justice and sustainability. Moreover, the launch of a European industrial policy could be the opportunity for extensive public consultations and a democratic debate about what and how we produce, building consensus for such an EU-wide action.

Opening up such a debate on industrial policy in Europe is indeed an urgent task. A wide range of ideas and proposals have to be shared and discussed. Major changes would be required in order to implement it. But the results of such efforts could be very important: ending stagnation, creating new high-wage jobs where they are most needed, greater EU cohesion and public action, progress towards an ecological transformation of Europe, and greater democracy in economic decision making.

Notes

1 This chapter is based on the final part of the report "What is to be produced? The making of a new industrial policy in Europe" prepared for the Rosa-Luxemburg–Stiftung, Brussels Office, in 2016. We thank Roland Kulke and Martin Schirdewan for their support and suggestions. These proposals were first presented at the EuroMemorandum conference in London in September 2013 and further presentations have taken place

at the 2013 EAEPE conference in Paris, at seminars at WIIW in Vienna (2014, 2016), at Sapienza University of Rome (2014, 2015), at Rosa-Luxemburg–Stiftung conferences in Berlin, Madrid and Brussels. We thank the participants in such events for lively discussions and criticisms. Articles where such issues are developed include Pianta (2014b, 2015) and Lucchese et al. (2016). The text does not necessarily reflect the views of the affiliating institutions of the authors.

2 The divergence in technological activities is documented in Chapter 10 of this volume. Analyses of the recent evolution of European industries and production networks include Stöllinger et al. (2013), Simonazzi et al. (2013), Reinstaller et al. (2013), Amador et al. (2013), Aiginger (2014), Pianta (2014b), Cirillo and Guarascio (2015), Celi et al. (2018).

3 State Aid expenditure is defined on the basis of four requirements. State aid must come from a public source and must give an advantage to specific firms with an alteration of business competition and of the flow of exchanges between states. It refers to manufacturing industries, services, agriculture and fisheries, and includes resources devoted to "horizontal" objectives of common interest or granted to particular sectors of the economy and for specific objectives (such as the rescue of firms and restructuring aid). Aid granted to the financial sector as a response to the financial crisis is excluded from non-crisis State aid.

4 EC (2012) Guidance Paper on state aid-compliant financing, restructuring and privatisation of State-owned enterprises, Staff working paper, Brussels.

5 Subsidies of scarce amount compliant with the current EU limitations.

6 http://trade.ec.europa.eu/doclib/press/index.cfm?id=1254.

7 On TTIP and the expected economic benefits, see CEPR (2013); a critical review is in EuroMemo Group (2014, ch. 7). On global activism against liberalisation of trade and investment, see Utting et al. (2012) and Pianta (2014a).

References

Aiginger, K. (2014). *Industrial Policy for a Sustainable Growth Path*, WIFO Working Papers No. 469.

Aiginger, K. and Janger, J. (2015). Intangibles and green investments for restarting growth, in *Investing in Europe's future*, BMWFW, Federal Ministry of Science, Research and Economy. Available at: www.bmwfw.gv.at/Wirtschaftspolitik/Documents/InvestingInEurope.pdf.

Amador, J., Cappariello, R. and Stehrer, R. (2013). *Global Value Chains: A View from the Euro Area*, paper presented at the ECB/CompNet, PIIE and World Bank Conference, Washington DC.

Atkinson, A. (2015). *Inequality. What Can Be Done?* Cambridge, UK: Cambridge University Press.

Bailey, D., Cowling, K. and Tomlinson, P. (eds.) (2015). An industrial strategy for UK cities, in *New Perspectives on Industrial Policy for a Modern Britain*, Oxford, UK: Oxford University Press.

Bailey, D., Hildreth, P. and De Propis, L. (2015). Mind the gap! What might a place-based industrial and regional policy look like? in Bailey, D., Cowling, K. and Tomlinson, P. (eds) *New Perspectives on Industrial Policy for a Modern Britain*, Oxford, UK: Oxford University Press.

Barca, F. (2009). *An Agenda for a Reformed Cohesion Policy*, Independent Report. Available at: www.europarl.europa.eu/meetdocs/2009_2014/documents/regi/dv/barca_report_/barca_report_en.pdf.

Bianchi, P. and Labory, S. (eds). (2011a). *Industrial Policy after the Crisis: Seizing the Future*, Cheltenham, UK: Edward Elgar.

Bianchi, P. and Labory, S. (2011b). Industrial policy after the crisis: The case of the Emilia-Romagna region in Italy, *Policy Studies, Special Issue: Industrial Policy after the Crisis*, 32, 4.

Bianchi, P. and Labory, S. (2016). *Towards a New Industrial Policy*, Milano, Italy: McGraw-Hill.

Celi, G., Ginzburg, A., Guarascio, D. and Simonazzi, A. (2018). *Crisis in the European Monetary Union: A Core-Periphery Perspective*, Oxford, UK: Routledge.

CEPR. (2013). *Reducing Transatlantic Barriers to Trade and Investment: An Economic Assessment*, Brussels.

Cirillo, V. and Guarascio, D. (2015). Jobs and competitiveness in a polarised Europe, *Intereconomics*, 50(3), 156–160.

Coffey, D. and Thornley, C. (2015). Industrial policy: A green agenda, in Bailey, D., Cowling, K. and Tomlinson, P. (eds) *New Perspectives on Industrial Policy for a Modern Britain*, Oxford, UK: Oxford University Press.

David, P.A. (2014). *The Republic of Open Science The Institution's Historical Origins and Prospects for Continued Vitality*, SIEPR Discussion Paper No. 13–037, Stanford, CA.

De Masi, F., Lopez, P. and Viegas, M. (2015). *Juncker-Voodoo: Why the "Investment Plan for Europe" Will Not Revive the Economy*, Brussels. Available at: www.fabio-de-masi. de/kontext/controllers/document.php/15.d/4/de7f7b.pdf.

Eurofound (European Foundation for the Improvement of Living and Working Conditions). (2013). *Role of Social Dialogue in Industrial Policies*, Dublin. Available at: www.eurofound.europa.eu/sites/default/files/ef_files/docs/eiro/tn1311011s/tn 1311011s.pdf.

EuroMemorandum. (2014). *The Deepening Divisions in Europe and the Need for a Radical Alternative to EU Policies*, EuroMemo Group. Available at: www.euromemo.eu/ euromemorandum/euromemorandum_2014/index.html.

European Commission. (1990). *Industrial Policy in an Open and Competitive Environment. Guidelines for a Community Approach*, Communication of the Commission to the Council and to the European Parliament. COM (90) 556 final.

European Commission. (2012). *Blueprint for Deep and Genuine Economic and Monetary Union*, COM (2012) 777 final/2.

European Commission. (2014). *State Aid Scoreboard*, DG Competition.

European Commission. (2015a). *Communication from the Commission to the European Parliament, the Council, the European Central Bank, the Economic and Social Committee, the Committee of the Regions and the European Investment Bank; Making the Best Use of the Flexibility Within the Existing Rules of the Stability and Growth Pact*, COM (2015) 12 final.

European Commission. (2015b). *Completing Europe's Economic and Monetary Union*.

European Parliament. (2015). *EU Industrial Policy: Assessment of Recent Developments and Recommendations for Future Policies*, on Behalf of DG for Internal Policies, Policy Department A: Economic and Scientific Policy, Study for the ITRE Committee.

Feigl, G. and Truger, A. (2015). *The Golden Rule of Public Investment: Protecting Fiscal Leeway and Public Infrastructure in the EU*, ETUI Policy Brief NO. 12.

Foray, D., David, P. and Hall, B. (2015). Smart specialisation: The concept, in *Knowledge for Growth: Prospects for Science*, Technology and Innovation Report EUR 24047, European Union.

Franzini, M. and Pianta, M. (2016). *Explaining Inequality*, Oxford, UK: Routledge.

Fuster Morell, M. (2013). Governance of online creation communities for the building of digital commons: Viewed through the framework of the institutional analysis and development, in Brett, M., Frischmann, Madison, M.J. and Strandburg, K.J. (eds) *Governing Knowledge Commons*, Oxford Scholarship Online.

Greenwald, B. and Stiglitz, J. (2013). Industrial policies, the creation of a learning society and economic development, in Stiglitz, J. and Lin Yifu, J. (eds) *The Industrial Policy Revolution I: The Role of Government Beyond Ideology*, IEA Conference Volume. Basingstoke, UK: Palgrave Macmillan.

GUE/NGL. (2015). *What Europe Needs: A True Public Investment Plan. An Alternative to the Juncker Plan/EFSI*, GUE/NGL Discussion Paper, Brussels, European Parliament. Available at www.fabio-de-masi.de/kontext/controllers/document.php/54.7/d/ecf701.pdf.

ILO International Labour Office. (2014). *Global Wage Report 2014/15. Wages and Income Inequalities*. Geneva: ILO.

Lazonick, W. (2015). *Labor in the Twenty-First Century: The Top 0.1% and the Disappearing Middle Class*, Institute for New Economic Thinking, Working Paper No. 4.

Lazonick, W. and Mazzucato, M. (2015). The risk-reward nexus in the innovation-inequality relationship: Who takes the risks? Who gets the rewards? *Industrial and Corporate Change*, 22(4), 1093–1128.

Lucchese, M., Nascia, L. and Pianta, M. (2016). Industrial policy and technology in Italy, *Economia e Politica Industriale – Journal of Industrial and Business Economics*, 43(3), 233–260.

Mazzucato, M. (2013). *The Entrepreneurial State*, London: Anthem Press.

Meliciani, V. (2015). *Regional Disparities in the Enlarged EU*, Oxford, UK: Routledge.

Mishel, L. and Davis, A. (2014). *CEO Pay Continues to Rise as Typical Workers Are Paid Less*, Issue brief, Economic Policy Institute, Washington DC.

Nascia, L. and Pianta, M. (2017). *RIO Country Report, Italy 2016*, JRC Science and Policy Report, European Commission, Joint Research Centre, Institute for Prospective Technological Studies.

Pianta, M. (2014a). Slowing trade: Global activism against trade liberalization, *Global Policy*, 5(2), 214–221.

Pianta, M. (2014b). An industrial policy for Europe, *Seoul Journal of Economics*, 27(3), article 3.

Pianta, M. (2015). What is to be produced? The case for industrial policy, *Intereconomics: Review of European Economic Policy*, 50(3), 140–146.

Pianta, M., Lucchese, M. and Nascia, L. (2016). *What Is To Be Produced? The Making of a New Industrial Policy in Europe*, Brussels: Rosa-Luxembourg-Stiftung.

Piketty, T. (2013). *Capital in the Twenty-First Century*, Cambridge, MA: Harvard University Press.

Prota, F. and Viesti, G. (2013). *Which European Investment Clause?* SocialEurope.eu. Available at: www.socialeurope.eu/2013/10/which-european-investment-clause/.

Reinstaller, A., Hölzl, W., Kutsam, J. and Schmid, C. (2013). *The Development of Productive Structures of EU Member States and Their International Competitiveness*, WIFO Research Study.

Rogers, J. and Rhodes-Conway, S. (2014). *Cities at Work: Progressive Local Policies to Rebuild the Middle Class*, COWS, Center on Wisconsin Strategy. www.cows.org/_data/documents/1585.pdf.

Roland Berger. (2014). *Industry 4.0 The New Industrial Revolution: How Europe Will Succeed*, Roland Berger Strategic Consultant GMBH.

Rushkoff, D. (2016). *Throwing Rocks at the Google Bus: How Growth Became the Enemy of Prosperity*, New York: Penguin.

Simonazzi, A., Ginzburg, A. and Nocella, G. (2013). Economic relations between Germany and southern Europe, *Cambridge Journal of Economics*, 37(3), 653–675.

Stöllinger, R., Foster-McGregor, N., Holzner, M., Landesmann, M., Pöschl, J. and Stehrer, R. (2013). *European Competitiveness Report. A 'Manufacturing imperative' in the EU: Europe's Position in Global Manufacturing and the Role of Industrial Policy*, Vienna: WIIW.

Truger, A. (2015). *Implementing the Golden Rule for Public Investment in Europe Safeguarding Public Investment and Supporting the Recovery*, Working Paper-Reihe Der ak Wien.

Utting, P., Ellersiek, A. and Pianta, M. (eds). (2012). *Global Justice Activism and Policy Reform in Europe. Understanding How Change Happens*, Oxford, UK: Routledge.

Index

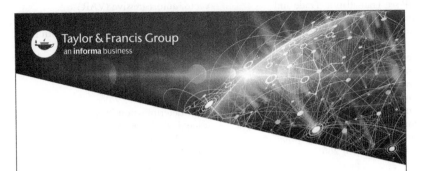

For Product Safety Concerns and Information please contact our EU representative GPSR@taylorandfrancis.com Taylor & Francis Verlag GmbH, Kaufingerstraße 24, 80331 München, Germany

Printed and bound by CPI Group (UK) Ltd, Croydon, CR0 4YY

01/05/2025

01858414-0007